FORMULA 1 YEARBOOK
2004-05

Photos
ZeroBorder
Mario Renzi
WRI

(ZeroBorder: Paul-Henri Cahier, Steve Domenjoz, Thierry Gromik, Filippo di Mario, Masakazu Miyata, Boris & Rainer Schlegelmilch.
WRI: Jean-François Galeron, Jad Sherif & Laurent Charniaux)

Conception and Grands Prix reports
Luc Domenjoz

Page layout
Sabrina Favre, Cyril Davillerd

Results and statistics
Solange Amara, Cyril Davillerd

Drawings 2004
Pierre Ménard

Gaps charts and Lap charts
Michele Merlino

Technical summary
Giorgio Piola

CHRONOSPORTS
EDITEUR

LAUSANNE – PARIS

Contents

Foreword

"*It gives me great pleasure to write the preface to the 15th Formula 1 Yearbook. 2004 has been a very positive season for us and we achieved the objectives we set ourselves, namely, to finish the F1 Constructors' Championship ahead of both Williams and McLaren. We ended the year just behind BAR which, at the start, we did not expect to be such a serious rival. Like everybody else I'm a bit disappointed we did not finish second in the championship but what is important is that Renault is progressing quickly.*

Overall, it was a better season than 2003. Ferrari's domination was difficult to stomach for the other teams and there were few occasions when the first two places were up for grabs. However, we showed what we were capable of and reaped the fruit of our effort. The team did a great job with the new car and new engine and we improved our performance compared to last year. We will build on this to make further progress in 2005.

Personally I am satisfied with my season, which, I feel, has been better and more studied than in 2003. I finished on the rostrum on four occasions and set pole once. What is missing is a win, which probably slipped through our fingers in Canada or in Belgium. Last year we had only one occasion. I came fourth in the Drivers' Championship, a very encouraging result.

Luckily the passion for racing binds us together and gives us the strength and motivation to carry on both from a technical and sporting point of view and our aim is to beat Ferrari in a straight fight. I am sure that next year's championship will be much more closely fought and that the best is yet to come for Renault. We will work flat out to make sure that happens."

Fernando Alonso,
November 15, 2004

SEASONAL ANALYSIS

Ferrari kissed perfection and Michael Schumacher was in a class of his own. Nobody could get near the world champion.

So how did this happen? On the one hand Ferrari have created a formidable war machine, which has virtually no flaws, and on the other, its rivals failed to achieve their aims either through a lack of preparation or of competitiveness. The longest season in F1's history did not lack interest, however, and the spectacular form of the BAR-Hondas and Renault as well the problems met by Williams and McLaren lent a certain flavour to a year that was placed under the sign of the Prancing Horse.

An almost perfect season

Analysis

In the history of F1 rarely has a team flirted with perfection to such a degree, and above all never over such a long period. The Scuderia Ferrari has dominated the last six seasons with six Constructors' titles on the trot. As for Michael Schumacher he won his seventh world championship title in 2004 – another outright record – and also his fifth consecutive one. Hats off! Lotus, McLaren and Williams, Clark, Prost, Senna and Mansell all had their moments of glory but not with the same consistency or the same unrelenting success.

It took the arrival of Michael Schumacher at Ferrari for team and driver to maintain such excellence. It also required Jean Todt's rigour, exigencies and his spirit blowing through the corridors of Maranello for the mythic Scuderia to recover its former glory after twenty years' in the wilderness. Today its rivals wilt under the pressure and complain:" nothing's more boring than perfection," groused the boss of a big English team jealous because he was unable to match it. "They're going to kill F1," hit out another crushed by Ferrari's success. At the end of the 2003 championship there were some who thought that it would all be different in 2004 as the battle for the titles had been a hotly disputed one that had gone down to the wire. McLaren, Williams and Ferrari had fought it out for the Constructors'

> All year, Rubens Barrichello tried to match Michael Schumacher's performances. He eventually won two Grands Prix.

Championship and for the Drivers' one it was touch and go as to whether it would go to Schumacher, Montoya or Raïkkönen. So there was a valid reason for optimism and the hungry challengers thought that they were capable of taking the fight to Ferrari. During the 2003/04 winter Pat Symonds, the Renault team's head of engineering, forecast that, "Ferrari won't have an easy task as its comfort margin has shrunk. We've all made a lot of progress."

This, however, was without counting on Ferrari's capacity to react and hit back helped by Bridgestone, its tyre manufacturer which made a lot of progress in relation to 2003.

The Scuderia's supremacy had been hotly contested and its pride wounded so it reacted. Quickly. When Michael Schumacher drove the F2004 for the first time his comments should have alerted his rivals. "It's the best Ferrari I've ever sat in", he said right from the start and this is an area where he rarely attempts to wind up his rivals. He sounded a warning to his opponents that was loud and clear; all the more so as in the past when he made such statements he won the world championship.

His rivals gave the impression of not taking the danger seriously so what happened in Melbourne on 7th March was all the harder to stomach. Michael left the others shell-shocked, pole, win

and fastest lap! Two weeks later in Malaysia it was a repeat performance apart from the fact that Juan Pablo Montoya set the fastest lap, a poor consolation. Then came the Bahrain Grand Prix and there again Michael swept the board. The pre-season

optimism of certain teams was starting to look a bit threadbare. What if the red cars really were unbeatable?

In contrast to his poor start to the 2003 season Michael could not have got off to a better one in 2004 racking up five consecutive victories until Jarno Trulli's Renault broke his run in Monaco. It was a mere hiccup as Michael took up where he had left off at the European Grand Prix and went on to score another seven wins on the trot, a record in a single season. Bernie Ecclestone, the F1 financial supremo started to regret that one driver so dominated his rivals, and in a friendly fashion pointed the finger at Jean Todt, the man responsible for created the Ferrari winning machine. "As much as I tried to push Jean on Ferrari in 1993, as he was the only one who could redress the situation, I now ask myself if it isn't the right moment to get rid of him," joked Bernie one day.

McLaren-Mercedes and Williams-BMW who, in 2003, were on the same level as Ferrari both made a dog's breakfast of their 2004 season. The main reasons were poor reliability plus a lack of performance in the case of McLaren while Williams suffered from an aerodynamic innovation the work of ex-Ferrari engineer, Antonia Terzi, which never really worked. Williams wanted above all to get the most out of its unusual nose and lost half-a-season. When the FW26 appeared at Silverstone with a normal appendage the car was suddenly a lot more competitive but still not quick enough to threaten the Ferrari steamroller. In the McLaren camp the engineers got down to designing a new car when the faults of the 2004 model quickly became apparent. The new vehicle came out at the French Grand Prix and allowed Kimi Raïkkönen, up to then the man with the most retirements, to mix it with the men up front on an episodic basis. He scored his one and only win of the season in the Belgian Grand Prix at the end of August.

The teams that really made their mark were BAR-Honda and Renault. The former created in 1999 had been expected to perform for several years while the latter set up in 2001 had already announced its aim for 2004, third place in the Constructors' Championship. Mission accomplished even if, at one moment, it looked like it could do even better.

Bernie Ecclestone, the F1 financial supremo started to regret that one driver so dominated his rivals

---

The BAR 006 designed under the guidance of Geoff Willis, ex-Williams, was quick out of the box. Several engine failures early of which Takuma Sato was the main victim lost precious points but once this problem was solved the BARs were always among the front-runners. Jenson Button scored ten rostrum finishes usually alongside the two Ferrari drivers.

While the 006 seemed to become increasingly efficient as the car was developed the Renault R24 engineers had problems correcting its defects. It was quick but difficult to drive and set up and not very inclined to pardon the slightest error. It distinguished itself by its early season reliability and enabled Renault to hold onto second place in the Constructors' Championship for most of the year – from Bahrain to Monza - some five months.

However, the more the BAR progressed the more the Renault team's balloon deflated. It was really all over after the Italian Grand Prix. Flavio Briatore, the team boss, tried to shock the French outfit into action by replacing Jarno Trulli with Jacques Villeneuve who had not found a seat for 2004.

His gamble failed even if it was a success from a media point of view. There was nothing at stake in the championship after Belgium when Michael clinched the Drivers' one so it gave the men of the pen something to write home about and filled a lot of airtime.

The other piece of news – a much sadder one – was Ford's decision to pull the plug on the Jaguar and Cosworth outfits for 2005.

So at the end of a season, which had been totally dominated by Michael Schumacher, all his rivals greeted the arrival of winter with a sigh of relief. Would four months be enough to digest such a defeat and then prepare a comeback for 2005?

The paddock new star, Fernando Alonso, nd his fan-club.
v

Drivers

1.	**M. Schumacher**	**148**
2.	R. Barrichello	114
3.	J. Button	85
4.	F. Alonso	59
5.	J. Montoya	58
6.	J. Trulli	46
7.	K. Räikkönen	45
8.	T. Sato	34
9.	R. Schumacher	24
10.	D. Coulthard	24
11.	G. Fisichella	22
12.	F. Massa	12
13.	M. Webber	7
14.	O. Panis	6
15.	A. Pizzonia	6
16.	C. Klien	3
17.	C. Da Matta	3
18.	N. Heidfeld	3
19.	T. Glock	2
20.	Z. Baumgartner	1
21.	J. Villeneuve	0
22.	R. Zonta	0
23.	M. Gené	0
24.	G. Pantano	0
25.	G. Bruni	0

Constructors

1.	**Scuderia Ferrari Marlboro**	**262**
2.	Lucky Strike B.A.R Honda	119
3.	Mild Seven Renault F1 Team	105
4.	BMW WilliamsF1 Team	88
5.	West McLaren Mercedes	69
6.	Sauber Petronas	34
7.	Jaguar Racing	10
8.	Panasonic Toyota Racing	9
9.	Jordan Ford	5
10.	Minardi Cosworth	1

Renault: a satisfying season

Bob Bell, the Renault F1 Team's chassis technical director reviews the hard-fought season which saw the team meet its objectives and prepare for the future.

- Bob, do you remember your impressions when the R24 completed its first laps last January?
Bob Bell: As always, we had planned for the new car to be a step forward in performance over its predecessor. That's always the goal you have – to design a stiffer, lighter car with optimised weight distribution... Those things were all confirmed on the track. It was a significant step forward and our drivers noted that immediately.
The strengths of the R24 chassis were the aerodynamics, its traction and the way it used its tyres.
The engine was also impressive, especially considering we were working with a new architecture. And finally, I think we were perhaps the strongest team when it came to exploiting our electronic systems.

- So, there were no bad surprises with this car?
Bob Bell: I must admit that we did not expect it to be more difficult to drive, because we did not make any decisions during the design process that were likely to affect this area. According to the drivers, though, the car was less predictable on the limit and a little more nervous in fast corners. We therefore immediately began working to correct this: first isolating the problem, understanding it and then resolving it.

- Did you succeed in this?
Bob Bell: To a certain extent, yes. We worked hard in this area and made significant progress. However, to completely eradicate the defect would have required the modification of fundamental parts of the car, such as the monocoque, and we chose not to pursue this route.

- Why?
Bob Bell: Firstly, the changes for 2005 meant we had to mobilise material and human resources very early in order to begin assessing their implications. And it should not be forgotten that the R24 was fast enough to allow us to fight at the front of the field without undertaking these fundamental modifications. Given that next year's regulations include significant changes, was it difficult to balance the development of the R24 with the design of the 2005 car?
Bob Bell: In actual fact, we were working on three fronts. We pursued a normal development programme on the R24, worked on resolving its high-speed instability... and began designing the 2005 car last July. There are no miracles in F1 – everything is a question of rigour, organisation, resource management and good planning. In that perspective, I do not think Enstone suffered from this three-fold programme.

- Did you extract all the possible performance from the R24?
Bob Bell: We might have unlocked more by diverting resources from the 2005 programme late in the season, but that would have been the wrong decision.

- In reliability terms, are you happy with how the car performed?
Bob Bell: Yes. We retired three times with failures on the chassis – both cars in Canada, and one in Silverstone. These incidents apart, the car was reliable from day one.

- Can you talk about next year already?
Bob Bell: The aerodynamic losses generated by the new regulations are significant, and we are working very hard in the wind tunnel. We already know that our next car will be a good one. It will have new electronics and a heavily-modified engine. On the mechanical side, Chief Designer Tim Densham and his team are focusing on reliability as well as making the car easy to use and work on.

- Are you in favour of performance reductions?
Bob Bell: Yes. I think we had reached a situation that could have become problematic had we not responded to it. The cars were incredibly fast this year and we had to react. Otherwise, F1 would have become unacceptably dangerous.

- Finally, do you agree that Formula 1 nowadays is primarily a question of design offices, virtual simulations, tyres and data analysis?
Bob Bell: No, and that's why I love this job. The car is simply a tool – you also need to know how to make proper use of it. And on that level, it is still the human factor that makes a difference in this sport. Winning races is not just about optimum lap times, but effective teamwork: choosing the right strategy, making good pit-stops, managing the weekend properly, the drivers' performance... F1 may be full of high technology, but it still comes down to a group of individuals, united by their passion for racing, who achieve the end result. Personally, I always find that exciting.

Pierre Dupasquier: "We fulfilled many key objectives"

"There are two ways of judging the Formula One season just past: you can look at it in terms of hard results, where we didn't achieve all the goals we set ourselves, or you can gauge our technical progress – and here we fulfilled many key objectives.

We produced a range of tyres that gave our six partner teams strong, consistent and reliable performance in a wide range of climatic conditions. It was clear that Michelin had a tyre advantage in 2003 and I don't believe the situation was any different this year.

You have to remember, though, that our main rival Michael Schumacher gave a very public indication of the aerodynamic progress Ferrari had made when he completed a back-to-back pre-season test with his team's 2003 and 2004 chassis at Imola and immediately went a full second quicker with the latest car. A second! That's a huge margin and I knew then that we would be in for a very tough campaign.

Despite that, there were some very encouraging performances. We scored victories with three different teams, ended the season with a resounding one-two and made considerable progress with our wet-weather tyres. We were aware that we had ground to make up in this domain and I think Kimi Räikkönen's performance during the opening stages of the Brazilian Grand Prix, when he streaked into the lead during the brief period when conditions were tailor-made for intermediates, proved that we have succeeded. We didn't have many opportunities during the season to gauge our wet tyres' potential, but when we did – at Spa and Monza, for instance – they were very competitive.

We are proud of the excellent working relationship we have all our partner teams and I was pleased to monitor the progress B·A·R-Honda made in its first year on Michelins. The team had its best F1 season to date, with its first pole position, 11 podium finishes and second place in the world championship for constructors.

Next year we will welcome Sauber as a partner team and I look forward to developing another of the productive relationships that typify our approach to motorsport in all its forms. Peter Sauber is convinced that Michelin will give his team an advantage – and that speaks volumes for the reputation we have built up during the past four seasons.

What else might 2005 hold in store? It is too soon to discuss things in detail because we don't know exactly how the latest rule changes will affect tyre manufacturers. Will there be limited testing or no testing at all, other than during the Friday of a race weekend? Either way, we will be well prepared. The combined efforts of our engineers – at Michelin's Clermont-Ferrand base, as well as at the track – and our partners have enabled us to build up a valuable database. That experience will stand us in good stead and we are looking to the future with great confidence."

The details make the difference

Drawings: Giorgio Piola

In Formula One everything is in the details. Here are some of the most interesting ones:

The Ferrari F2004, probably the best Ferrari ever, according to Michael Schumacher. The winglets (arrows) were introduced specifically for high-downforce circuits.

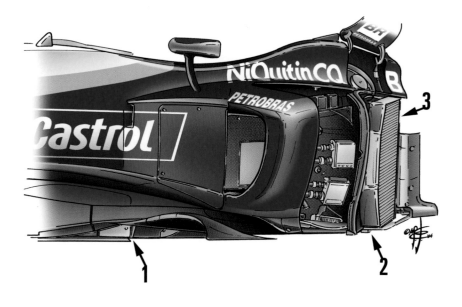

Williams: the "walrus" nose is definitely the most distinctive element on the English designed car. It was born out of the need to deal in the best way possible with the twin-keel front of the chassis, which is higher off the ground. This strange nose was the work of Antonia Terzi and was dropped in favour of a conventional design as from the Hungarian GP. At Williams, a virtually new car appeared for the French GP, with a heavily modified chassis. Inspiration taken from the Renault is evident, starting from the opening in the lower part of the side pods (1,) the sculpted radiators (2) although still mounted in the vertical position (3.)

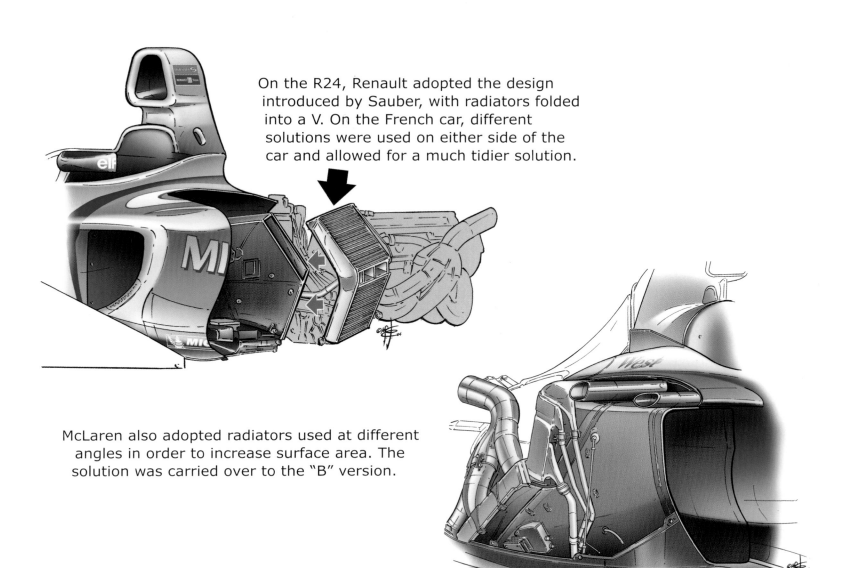

On the R24, Renault adopted the design introduced by Sauber, with radiators folded into a V. On the French car, different solutions were used on either side of the car and allowed for a much tidier solution.

McLaren also adopted radiators used at different angles in order to increase surface area. The solution was carried over to the "B" version.

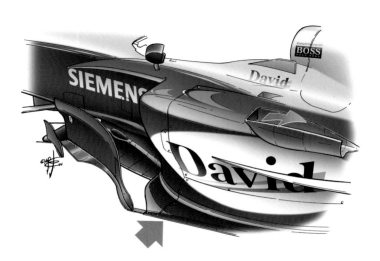

McLaren MP4-19B
Two new cars for McLaren. The most obvious difference are the Ferrari and Renault-style cut-outs at the beginning of the side pods, but with a more accentuated solution. The hot air vents in the side pods are bigger and higher, while the radiator layout remains unchanged.

Ferrari introduced chimney inclined at a greater angle towards the outside compared to those on the Renault. It improved cooling, but above all they genuinely deflect air flow, improving the efficiency of air flow at the back end. The small sized side deflectors on the side pods are bigger. The rear wing end plates are inclined towards the outside in the upper part.

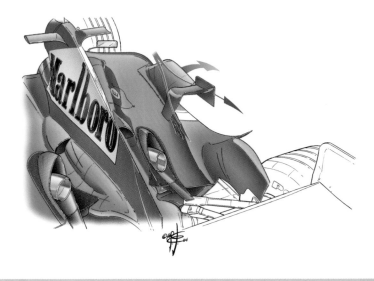

The most obvious development on the new Sauber are the right hand side radiators which are completely different to those on the Ferrari F2003 GA and introduced a new technology, as had already been expected. It is almost folded in two, thus increasing the surface cooling area by around 20%.

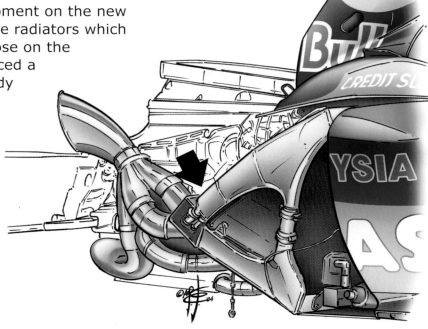

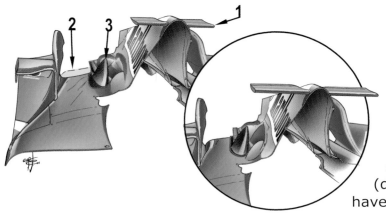

A new engine cover, easily recognisable because of the winglet behind the roll-over bar (1) that is narrower than the original. The new cover is narrower and lower (2) in the end part (difference shown in yellow.) The "chimney pots" have a different base.

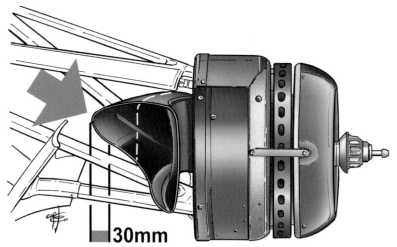

30mm

Discussions continued over interpretation of the intermediate rear wing flaps introduced by BAR right from the Australian GP. These are not allowed to deflect more than (a) than 30% from a straight line drawn between the two ends of the same profile. BAR therefore later reduced the size of the deflection, which had already been cut at Imola (the difference between the two versions shown in red.)

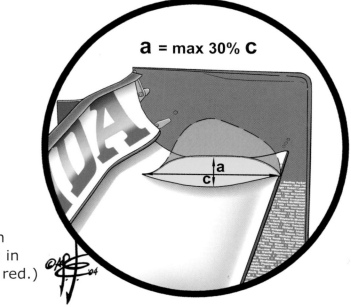

a = max 30% c

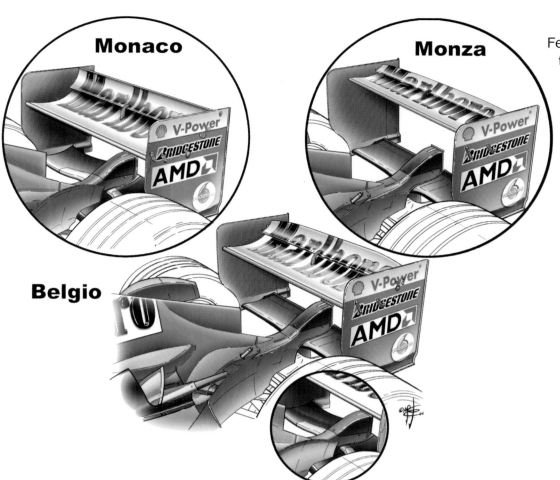

Monaco

Monza

Ferrari changed several
times the rear wing.
Here are a few
examples according to
the various
aerodynamical loads
suited to the race
tracks.

Belgio

McLaren changed the shape of its
nose with the MP4-19B, having it
much lower than in the initial
version of the car.

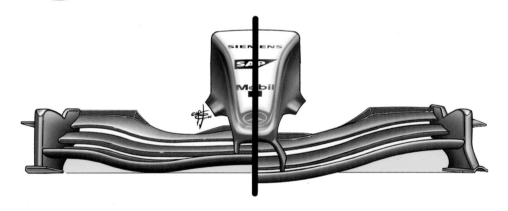

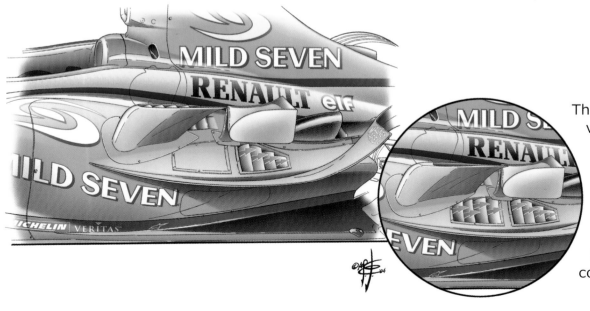

The shape of the R24 was
very appealing. The side
seems to almost
disappear into the rear
area. The car retained
the original rear wing
with a separate flap. It
could have either one or
two openings for better
cooling.

THE PLAYERS

Ten teams represent twenty cars but above all thousands of employees, tens of thousands of kilometres covered during the year and unceasing effort to put the cars on the grid each Grand Prix Sunday.

Ferrari

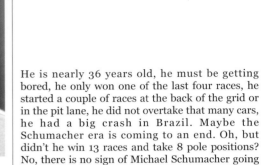

1. Michael SCHUMACHER

DRIVER PROFILE

- Name — *SCHUMACHER*
- First name — *Michael*
- Nationality — *German*
- Date of birth — *January 3, 1969*
- Place of birth — *Hürth-Hermühlheim (D)*
- Lives in — *Vufflens-le-Château (CH)*
- Marital status — *married to Corinna*
- Kids — *daughter and son (Gina-Maria & Mick)*
- Hobbies — *karting, football, cycling, skiing*
- Favorite music — *rock*
- Favorite meal — *italian food, sushis*
- Favorite drink — *apple juice with mineral water*
- Height — *174 cm*
- Weight — *73 kg*
- Web — *www.michael-schumacher.de*

STATISTICS | PRIOR TO F1

STATISTICS		PRIOR TO F1
Nber of Grand Prix	213	1984-85 *Karting*
Starts	211	*Junior Champion (D)*
Victories	83	1986 *Karting 3rd (D & EUR)*
Pole positions	63	1987 *Karting*
Fastest lap	66	*Champion (D & EUR)*
Podiums	137	1988 *F. Koenig Champion,*
Accidents/offs	24	*F. Ford 1600 (EUR) (2nd),*
Not qualified	0	*F. Ford 1600 (D) (6th)*
GP in the lead	126	1989 *F3 (D) (3rd)*
Laps in the lead	4,657	1990 *F3 Champion (D)*
Kms in the lead	21,954	1990-91 *Sport-prototypes*
Points scored	1186	*Mercedes (5th & 9th)*

F1 CAREER

1991	*Jordan-Ford, Benetton-Ford. 4 pts. 12th of Championship.*
1992	*Benetton-Ford. 53 pts. 3rd of Championship.*
1993	*Benetton-Ford. 52 pts. 4th of Championship.*
1994	*Benetton-Ford. 92 pts.* **World Champion.**
1995	*Benetton-Renault. 102 pts.* **World Champion.**
1996	*Ferrari. 49 pts. 3rd of Championship.*
1997	*Ferrari. 78 pts. Exclude of the Championship (2nd).*
1998	*Ferrari. 86 pts. 2nd of Championship.*
1999	*Ferrari. 44 pts. 5th of Championship.*
2000	*Ferrari. 108 pts.* **World Champion.**
2001	*Ferrari. 123 pts.* **World Champion.**
2002	*Ferrari. 144 pts.* **World Champion.**
2003	*Ferrari. 93 pts.* **World Champion.**
2004	*Ferrari. 148 pts.* **World Champion.**

2. Rubens BARRICHELLO

DRIVER PROFILE

- Name — *BARRICHELLO*
- First name — *Rubens Gonçalves*
- Nationality — *Brazilian*
- Date of birth — *May 23, 1972*
- Lieu de naissance — *São Paulo (BR)*
- Lives in — *Monaco (MC)*
- Marital status — *married to Silvana*
- Kids — *a son (Eduardo)*
- Hobbies — *karting, bowling*
- Favorite music — *pop, rock, Biagio Antonacci*
- Favorite meal — *pasta*
- Favorite drink — *Red Bull*
- Height — *172 cm*
- Weight — *71 kg*
- Web — *www.barrichello.com.br*

STATISTICS | PRIOR TO F1

STATISTICS		PRIOR TO F1
Nber of Grand Prix	198	1981-88 *Karting (5 times*
Starts	195	*Brazilian Champion)*
Victories	9	1989 *F. Ford 1600 (3rd)*
Pole positions	13	1990 *Opel Champion*
Fastest lap	15	*Lotus Euroseries,*
Podiums	57	*F. Vauxhall (11th)*
Accidents/offs	28	1991 *F3 Champion (GB)*
Not qualified	0	1992 *F3000 (3rd)*
GP in the lead	42	
Laps in the lead	699	
Kms in the lead	3,389	
Points scored	451	

F1 CAREER

1993	*Jordan-Hart. 2 pts. 17th of Championship.*
1994	*Jordan-Hart. 19 pts. 6th of Championship.*
1995	*Jordan-Peugeot. 11 pts. 11th of Championship.*
1996	*Jordan-Peugeot. 14 pts. 8th of Championship.*
1997	*Stewart-Ford. 6 pts. 13th of Championship.*
1998	*Stewart-Ford. 4 pts. 12th of Championship.*
1999	*Stewart-Ford. 21 pts. 7th of Championship.*
2000	*Ferrari. 62 pts. 4th of Championship.*
2001	*Ferrari. 56 pts. 3rd of Championship.*
2002	*Ferrari. 77 pts. 2nd of Championship.*
2003	*Ferrari. 65 pts. 4th of Championship.*
2004	*Ferrari. 114 pts. 2nd of Championship.*

He is nearly 36 years old, he must be getting bored, he only won one of the last four races, he started a couple of races at the back of the grid or in the pit lane, he did not overtake that many cars, he had a big crash in Brazil. Maybe the Schumacher era is coming to an end. Oh, but didn't he win 13 races and take 8 pole positions? No, there is no sign of Michael Schumacher going off the boil. He has always said that he will hang up his helmet when he realises that he is no longer on the pace, but at the moment it seems that he looks set to try for an eighth title in 2005. Can you honestly say there is another man on the grid who is as complete a racer as Schumi?

It is difficult to assess a driver who has been Michael Schumacher's team-mate for five years, a job which previous incumbent, Eddie Irvine described as being hit over the head with a baseball bat every day of your life. It is hard to say whether the Brazilian, who finished second in the Drivers' championship and won twice, is the second best driver in the world or the best Number 2 in the world. Whatever Ferrari says, the team is built around Schumacher and any other driver is simply a guest. Rubens took a bit too long adapting to the F2004, possibly because he got less pre-season testing in it than his illustrious team-mate, but when he got into his stride, he was often a match for Schumacher in terms of speed. The cruellest blow was being robbed of victory in Brazil by his Bridgestone tyres.

Jean Todt

Ross Brawn

Nigel Stepney

Luca Badoer

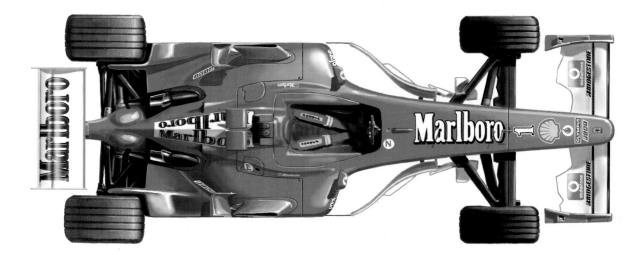

**FERRARI F2004
MICHAEL SCHUMACHER
GERMAN GRAND PRIX**

P. MÉNARD

Ferrari F2004

SPECIFICATIONS

- Chassis — Ferrari F2004
- Type — Carbon-fibre and honeycomb composite structure
- Suspensions — Independent suspension, push-rod activated torsion springs (F./R.)
- Engine — V10 Ferrari Type 053 (90°)
- Displacement — 2,997 cm³
- Distribution — 40, pneumatic distribution
- Electronic ignition — Magneti Marelli
- Transmission — Ferrari 7 speed + reverse longitudinal gearbox, operated by semiautomatic sequential electronically controlled gearchange
- Clutch — Sachs - AP
- Radiators — Secan
- Fuel / oil — Shell
- Brakes (discs) — Brembo (ventilated carbon)
- Brakes (calipers) — Brembo
- Spark plugs — NGK
- Shock absorbers — not revealed
- Tyres — Bridgestone Potenza
- Wheels diameter — 13"
- Rims — BBS
- Weight — 605 kg, driver, on board camera, ballast
- Wheel base — 3,050 mm
- Total length — 4,545 mm
- Total width — 1,796 mm
- Total height — 959 mm
- Front track — 1,470 mm
- Rear track — 1,405 mm

TEAM PROFILE

- Address — Ferrari SpA
  Via A. Ascari 55-57
  41053 Maranello (MO)
  Italia
- Phone number — + 39.536.949111
- Fax number — + 39.536.946488
- Web — www.ferrariworld.com
- Founded in — 1929
- First Grand Prix — Monaco 1950
- Official name — Scuderia Ferrari Marlboro
- General Director — Jean Todt
- Technical Director — Ross Brawn,
  Paolo Martinelli (engine)
- Director of F1 racing activities — Stefano Domenicali
- Chief Designer — Rory Byrne
- Race Technical Manager — Nigel Stepney
- Race Engineer (M.S.) — Chris Dyer
- Race Engineer (R.B.) — Gabrielle Delli Colli
- Number of employees — 700
- Sponsors — Philip Morris (Marlboro), Vodafone, Shell, Bridgestone, Fiat, AMD, Olympus
- Official Suppliers — Acer, Brembo, Magneti Marelli, Mahle, OMR, SKF, Beta, Europcar, Finmeccanica, Fila, Infineon, Iveco, Momo, NGK, ZF Sachs
- Suppliers — BBS, Cima, Mecanica, Mecel, Poggipolini, PTC, Sabelt, VeCa, TRW

TEST DRIVER 2004

- Luca BADOER (I)

STATISTICS

- Number of Grand Prix — 704
- Number of victories — 182
- Number of pole positions — 178
- Number of fastest laps — 181
- Number of podiums — 553
- Number of drivers Championship — 14
- Number of constructors Championship — 14
- Number of points scored — 3,299.5 (3.346.5)

POSITION IN WORLD CHAMPIONSHIP

1958	2ⁿᵈ – 40 ⁽⁵⁷⁾ pts	1970	2ⁿᵈ – 52 ⁽⁵⁵⁾ pts	1982	1ˢᵗ – 74 pts	1994	3ʳᵈ – 71 pts
1959	2ⁿᵈ – 32 ⁽³⁸⁾ pts	1971	4ᵗʰ – 33 pts	1983	1ˢᵗ – 89 pts	1995	3ʳᵈ – 73 pts
1960	3ʳᵈ – 26 ⁽²⁷⁾ pts	1972	4ᵗʰ – 33 pts	1984	2ⁿᵈ – 57.5 pts	1996	2ⁿᵈ – 70 pts
1961	1ˢᵗ – 40 ⁽⁵²⁾ pts	1973	6ᵗʰ – 12 pts	1985	2ⁿᵈ – 82 pts	1997	2ⁿᵈ – 102 pts
1962	5ᵗʰ – 18 pts	1974	2ⁿᵈ – 65 pts	1986	4ᵗʰ – 37 pts	1998	2ⁿᵈ – 133 pts
1963	4ᵗʰ – 26 pts	1975	1ˢᵗ – 72.5 pts	1987	4ᵗʰ – 53 pts	1999	1ˢᵗ – 128 pts
1964	1ˢᵗ – 45 ⁽⁴⁹⁾ pts	1976	1ˢᵗ – 83 pts	1988	2ⁿᵈ – 65 pts	2000	1ˢᵗ – 170 pts
1965	4ᵗʰ – 26 ⁽²⁷⁾ pts	1977	1ˢᵗ – 95 ⁽⁹⁷⁾ pts	1989	3ʳᵈ – 59 pts	2001	1ˢᵗ – 179 pts
1966	2ⁿᵈ – 31 ⁽³²⁾ pts	1978	2ⁿᵈ – 58 pts	1990	2ᵗʰ – 110 pts	2002	1ˢᵗ – 221 pts
1967	4ᵗʰ – 20 pts	1979	1ˢᵗ – 113 pts	1991	3ʳᵈ – 55.5 pts	2003	1ˢᵗ – 158 pts
1968	4ᵗʰ – 32 pts	1980	10ᵗʰ – 8 pts	1992	4ᵗʰ – 21 pts	2004	1ˢᵗ - 262 pts
1969	5ᵗʰ – 7 pts	1981	5ᵗʰ – 34 pts	1993	4ᵗʰ – 28 pts		

SUCCESSION OF DRIVERS 2004

- Michael SCHUMACHER — all 18 Grands Prix
- Rubens BARRICHELLO — all 18 Grands Prix

Approaching perfection

Scuderia Ferrari completed more laps (2196) and therefore more kilometres (10745) than any other team during the 2004 season, the longest in the history of Formula 1. The Italians re-wrote the record books with an extraordinary set of results – fifteen wins, twelve pole positions, fourteen fastest race laps, eight one-two finishes and 262 points scored out of a possible total of 324. Of course, this being F1, instead of being congratulated, the team was portrayed as the destroyer of the sport. In Brazil things got particularly heated as Jean Todt was held personally responsible for not signing up to rule changes agreed by the other nine teams and somehow, the fate of the British and French GPs was also laid at his door. Obviously, there is no such thing as a good loser in F1. Having let the championship go down to the final race in 2003, the Scuderia got a big wake-up call and responded in style. The key to its unparalleled success is continuity of staff, a big budget, the relationship with Bridgestone – although the F2004 and Japanese tyres don't work in the damp, as we saw in Brazil – and a lot of hard work. Having the best driver in the world probably helps a bit too.

Williams BMW

3. Juan Pablo MONTOYA

DRIVER PROFILE

- Name — MONTOYA ROLDÁN
- First name — Juan Pablo
- Nationality — Colombian
- Date of birth — September 20, 1975
- Place of birth — Bogota (COL)
- Lives in — Monaco (MC), Oxford (GB), Miami (USA) and Madrid (E)
- Marital status — married to Connie
- Kids — -
- Hobbies — water ski, computers and video games
- Favorite music — rock
- Favorite meal — pasta
- Favorite drink — orange juice
- Height — 168 cm
- Weight — 72 kg
- Web — www.jpmontoya.com

STATISTICS

		PRIOR TO F1
Nber of Grand Prix	68	1981-91 Karting (2 times Jr. Wold Champion)
Starts	68	
Victories	4	1992 F. Renault (COL)
Pole positions	11	1993 Swift GTI (COL)
Fastest lap	11	1994 Karting-Sudam 125
Podiums	23	Champ. Barber Saab (3rd)
Accidents/offs	6	1995 F. Vauxhall (GB)
Not qualified	0	1996 F3 (GB)
GP in the lead	24	1997 F3000 (2nd)
Laps in the lead	382	1998 F3000 Champion
Kms in the lead	1,792	1999 CART Champion
Points scored	221	2000 CART (9th)

F1 CAREER

1997 Williams- Renault. Test driver
2001 Williams- BMW. 31 pts. 6th of Championship.
2002 Williams- BMW. 50 pts. 3rd of Championship.
2003 Williams- BMW. 82 pts. 3rd of Championship.
2004 Williams- BMW. 58 pts. 5th of Championship.

Sir Frank Williams

Sam Michael

Patrick Head,
Frank Dernie

When "JPM" came into F1, he was billed as the next big thing, the man who would knock Herr Schumacher off his perch. It never happened and it is now fashionable to criticise the Colombian for being lazy, fat, lacking motivation and the knowledge necessary to set up the car. True or not, and you can add the defect of a fiery Latin temperament to the list of faults, Montoya has the one virtue of being a true racer who relies on his talent. Unfortunately, during his four years with Williams, the team has not been at its best and therefore there have been times when Montoya has appeared to have lost commitment during the 2004 season. But winning the final race of the season was a great leaving gift to the team and given that McLaren are far better at "taming" their drivers than Williams, 2005 might finally give us a glimpse of what Monty can do.

4. Ralf SCHUMACHER

DRIVER PROFILE

- Name — SCHUMACHER
- First name — Ralf
- Nationality — German
- Date of birth — June 30, 1975
- Place of birth — Hürth-Hermühlheim (D)
- Lives in — Hallwang (Salzburg) (A)
- Marital status — married to Cora
- Kids — a son (David)
- Hobbies — karting, tennis, cycling, backgammon
- Favorite music — soft rock
- Favorite meal — pasta
- Favorite drink — apple juice with mineral water
- Height — 178 cm
- Weight — 73 kg
- Web — www.ralf-schumacher.de

STATISTICS

		PRIOR TO F1
Nber of Grand Prix	128	1978-92 Karting
Starts	127	1993 F3 ADAC Jr. (2nd)
Victories	6	1994 F3 (D) (3rd)
Pole positions	5	1995 F3 (D) (2nd),
Fastest lap	7	Winner F3 Macau
Podiums	24	1996 F3000 Champion (J)
Accidents/offs	26	
Not qualified	0	
GP in the lead	19	
Laps in the lead	387	
Kms in the lead	1,858	
Points scored	259	

F1 CAREER

1997 Jordan-Peugeot. 13 pts. 11th of Championship.
1998 Jordan-Mugen-Honda. 14 pts. 10th of Championship.
1999 Williams-Supertec. 35 pts. 6th of Championship.
2000 Williams-BMW. 24 pts. 5th of Championship.
2001 Williams-BMW. 49 pts. 4th of Championship.
2002 Williams-BMW. 42 pts. 4th of Championship.
2003 Williams-BMW. 58 pts. 5th of Championship.
2004 Williams-BMW. 24 pts. 9th of Championship.

Like team-mate Montoya, Ralf Schumacher's commitment to Williams was probably affected by the fact he knew he would be leaving the team, although it was hard to tell, given that Michael's little brother has always blown hot and cold in performance terms. He certainly has the speed, but he, like many of his peers, has a habit of falling asleep in the middle of a race. When everything is going fine, Ralf will deliver, but when technical problems interrupt his flow, he goes off the boil. His engineers know that if Schumacher encounters a problem in Friday practice, the rest of his race weekend is compromised. Perhaps a change of scene at Toyota and the odd kick or two from Mike Gascoyne, will bring out the best in the German on a more regular basis.

4. Marc GENÉ

DRIVER PROFILE

- Name — GENÉ GUERRERO
- First name — Marc
- Nationality — Spanish
- Date of birth — March 29, 1974
- Place of birth — Sabadell (E)
- Lives in — St Quirze del Valles (E)
- Marital status — single
- Kids — -
- Hobbies — reading, Movie films and sports
- Favorite music — Dire Straits, rock and techno
- Favorite meal — pasta and paella
- Favorite drink — milk
- Height — 173 cm
- Weight — 69 kg
- Web — www.marcgene.com

STATISTICS

		PRIOR TO F1
		1990 Kart Sr. Champion (E)
		1991 Kart Sr. Champion (CAT.)
Nber of Grand Prix	36	Karting World Champ. FA (13rd)
Best result	1 x 5th	1992 F. Ford (E) (5th)
Best qualification	1 x 5th	1993 F. Ford Festival (2nd)
Accidents/offs	4	F. Ford (EUR) (2nd)
Points scored	5	1994 F3 (GB)
		1995 F3 (GB) (10th)

PRIOR TO F1

	1996 II Golden Cup FISA
1987 Karting (2nd)	Superformula Champion
1988 Kart Champion (E)	1997 F3000
1989 Karting Jr. (EUR) (10th)	1998 Open Fortuna
Karting World Champ. (19th)	Nissan Champion

F1 CAREER

1999 Minardi-Ford. 1 pt. 17th of Championship.
2000 Minardi-Fondmetal. 0 pt. 19th of Championship.
2001-02 Williams- BMW. Test driver
2003 Williams- BMW. 4 pts. 17th of Championship.
2004 Williams- BMW. 0 pt. 23rd of Championship.

The likeable test driver who could win an Olympic gold for talking was promoted to the race team for the French and British GPs after Ralf Schumacher's Indianapolis accident. He finished both races, but only in 10th and 12th places, so he was replaced by....

4. Antonio PIZZONIA

DRIVER PROFILE

- Name — PIZZONIA Júnior
- First name — António Reginaldo
- Nationality — Brazilian
- Date of birth — September 11, 1980
- Place of birth — Manaus (BR)
- Lives in — Monaco (MC) and Manaus (BR)
- Marital status — single
- Kids — -
- Hobbies — football, tennis, surf, protection of nature
- Favorite music — everything, from opera to rock
- Favorite meal — barbecue, churrascaria, chicken, pasta
- Favorite drink — tropical fruit juice
- Height — 173 cm
- Weight — 68 kg
- Web — www.antoniopizzonia.net

STATISTICS

		PRIOR TO F1
Nber of Grand Prix	15	1991-96 Karting,
Best result	3 x 7th	Champion (BR)
Best qualification	1 x 6th	1996 F. Barber Dodge (USA) (2nd)
Accidents/offs	3	1997 F. Vauxhall (GB) (2nd)
GP in the lead	1	1998 F. Vauxhall Champion (GB)
Laps in the lead	1	1999 F. Renault Champion
Kms in the lead	7	(GB), F. Renault (EUR) (2nd)
Points scored	6	2000 F3 Champion (GB)
		2001 F3000 (6th)
		2002 F3000 (8th)

F1 CAREER

2001-02 Williams-BMW. Test driver.
2003 Jaguar. 0 pt. 21th of Championship.
2004 Williams-BMW. 6 pts. 15th of Championship.

Pizzonia returned to testing duties with Williams, after destroying his reputation the previous season, racing for Jaguar. Then, he was called in to race in Germany, Hungary and Belgium. He finished just outside the points in the first two and was cruelly robbed of a podium finishing third place in Spa. He is now favourite to get a permanent Williams drive next year, although he is not Mark Webber's choice!

**WILLIAMS FW26-BMW
JUAN PABLO MONTOYA
MALAYSIAN GRAND PRIX**

Williams FW26-BMW

SPECIFICATIONS

- Chassis — *Williams FW26*
- Type — *Carbone/epoxy composite*
- Suspensions — *WilliamsF1 independant roll bar / pushrods (Front / Rear)*
- Direction — *WilliamsF1*
- Engine — *V10 BMW P84 (90°)*
- Displacement — *2,998 cm³*
- Distribution — *4 valves per cylinder*
- Electronic ignition — *BMW*
- Transmission — *WilliamsF1 semi-automatic 7 gears + reverse RE*
- Clutch — *Automotive Products*
- Radiators — *Secan / IMI Marston*
- Fuel / oil — *Petrobras / Castrol*
- Brakes (discs) — *Carbone Industrie*
- Brakes (calipers) — *AP Racing*
- Spark plugs — *Champion*
- Shock absorbers — *Williams / Penske*
- Tyres — *Michelin Pilot*
- Wheels diameter — *13 x 12 (FR) / 13 x 13,7 (RE)*
- Rims — *O.Z. Racing*
- Weight — *605 kg, driver, on board camera, ballast*
- Wheel base — *3,140 mm*
- Total length — *4,540 mm*
- Total width — *not revealed*
- Total height — *not revealed*
- Front track — *Maximum allowance*
- Rear track — *Maximum allowance*

TEAM PROFILE

- Address — *Williams F1 Grove, Wantage, Oxfordshire, OX12 0DQ - Great Britain*
- Phone number — *+44 (0) 1235 7777 00*
- Fax number — *+44 (0) 1235 7777 39*
- Web — *www.bmw.williamsf1.com*
- Founded in — *1969*
- First Grand Prix — *Argentina 1975 (ARG 1973, under ISO)*
- Official name — *BMW WilliamsF1 Team*
- Team Principal — *Sir Frank Williams*
- Technical Director — *Patrick Head*
- Director BMW Motorsport — *Dr Mario Theissen*
- Head of Engine Development — *Heinz Paschen*
- Chief Operations Engineer — *Sam Michael*
- Chief Designer — *Gavin Fisher*
- Team Manager — *Dickie Stanford*
- Chief Aerodynamicist — *Dr Antonia Terzi*
- Race Engineer (J.P.M.) — *Tony Ross*
- Race Engineer (4) — *Gordon Day*
- Number of employees — *500 (Williams) / 250 (BMW)*
- Partners — *HP, Allianz, Budweiser, FedEx, NiQuitin CQ, Accenture, Castrol, Michelin, Petrobras, Reuters, Hamleys, O.Z. Racing, MAN, Puma, O2, PPG, ORIS, W.L. Gore, Boysen, Intelsat, Würth*

STATISTICS

- Number of Grand Prix — *496*
- Number of victories — *113*
- Number of pole positions — *124*
- Number of fastest laps — *127*
- Number of podiums — *290*
- Number of drivers Championship — *7*
- Number of constructors Championship — *9*
- Number of points scored — *2,429.5*

BMW.WilliamsF1 Team

POSITION IN WORLD CHAMPIONSHIP

1975	9th – 6 pts	1983	4th – 38 pts	1991	2nd – 125 pts	1999	5th – 35 pts
1976	not classified	1984	6th – 25,5 pts	1992	1st – 164 pts	2000	3rd – 36 pts
1977	not classified	1985	3rd – 71 pts	1993	1st – 168 pts	2001	3rd – 80 pts
1978	9th – 11 pts	1986	1st – 141 pts	1994	1st – 118 pts	2002	2nd – 92 pts
1979	2nd – 75 pts	1987	1st – 137 pts	1995	2nd – 112 pts	2003	2nd – 144 pts
1980	1st – 120 pts	1988	7th – 20 pts	1996	1st – 175 pts	2004	4th – 88 pts
1981	1st – 95 pts	1989	2nd – 77 pts	1997	1st – 123 pts		
1982	4th – 58 pts	1990	4th – 57 pts	1998	3rd – 38 pts		

TEST DRIVERS 2004

- Marc GENÉ (E)
- Antonio PIZZONIA (BR)

SUCCESSION OF DRIVERS 2004

- Juan Pablo MONTOYA — *all 18 Grands Prix*
- Ralf SCHUMACHER — *12 Grands Prix (Australia > USA, China > Brazil)*
- Marc GENÉ — *2 Grands Prix (France, Great Britain)*
- Antonio PIZZONIA — *4 Grands Prix (Germany, Hungary, Belgium, Italy)*

Treading water

It was another disappointing year for the "Frank 'n Patrick" show, which at least ended on a high note, when Montoya won the final race of the year in Brazil. In fact, it wasn't the "Frank 'n Patrick" show for much of the year as Patrick Head was so upset with himself for failing to spot several technical shortcomings – the gearbox and that ugly "Walrus" nose for example, that he handed technical control to the young Sam Michael. The Australian's new job did not get off to the best start in Canada and Indianapolis with both cars disqualified for illegal brake ducts in Montreal, followed seven days later by Ralf Schumacher's big smash into the wall at Indianapolis. Quite why English teams insist on working with German engine manufacturers is a mystery as, on a political and personal front, they never get on. The Williams-BMW marriage was tolerated while the men from Munich provided a big power advantage as they had done in the past, but this year, the BMW lost its sparkle. Chaos on the driver front did not help matters, with Gene and Pizzonia drafted in to replace the injured Ralf, while Montoya continued to annoy his mechanics and engineers who could not wait to see him pack his bags and his "Bogota Coffee Club" friends and head off to cause chaos at McLaren!

McLaren Mercedes

5. David COULTHARD

DRIVER PROFILE

- Name — *COULTHARD*
- First name — *David*
- Nationality — *Scottish*
- Date of birth — *March 27, 1971*
- Place of birth — *Twynholm (Scotland, GB)*
- Lives in — *Monaco (MC)*
- Marital status — *single*
- Kids — *-*
- Hobbies — *Golf, swimming, Movie films*
- Favorite music — *The Cranberries, Oasis, The Corrs*
- Favorite meal — *pasta*
- Favorite drink — *tea and mineral water*
- Height — *182 cm*
- Weight — *72,5 kg*
- Web — *www.davidcoulthard-f1.com*

STATISTICS | PRIOR TO F1

STATISTICS		PRIOR TO F1
Nber of Grand Prix	175	1983-88 *Karting (3 times Jr.*
Starts	175	*and Open Kart Champion (Ecos.), 2*
Victories	13	*times Super Kart1 Champion (GB))*
Pole positions	12	1989 *F. Ford 1600 Champion (GB)*
Fastest lap	18	1990 *F. Vauxhall-Lotus (4th),*
Podiums	60	*GM Lotus Euroseries (5th)*
Accidents/offs	19	1991 *F3 (GB) (2nd), F3 Macau*
Not qualified	0	*and Marlboro Masters Winner*
GP in the lead	58	1992 *F3000 (9th)*
Laps in the lead	894	1993 *F3000 (3rd)*
Kms in the lead	4,195	1994 *F3000 (9th)*
Points scored	475	

F1 CAREER

1994	*Williams-Renault. 14 pts. 8th of Championship.*
1995	*Williams-Renault. 49 pts. 3rd of Championship.*
1996	*McLaren-Mercedes. 18 pts. 7th of Championship.*
1997	*McLaren-Mercedes. 36 pts. 3rd of Championship.*
1998	*McLaren-Mercedes. 56 pts. 3rd of Championship.*
1999	*McLaren-Mercedes. 48 pts. 4th of Championship.*
2000	*McLaren-Mercedes. 73 pts. 3rd of Championship.*
2001	*McLaren-Mercedes. 65 pts. 2nd of Championship.*
2002	*McLaren-Mercedes. 41 pts. 5th of Championship.*
2003	*McLaren-Mercedes. 51 pts. 7th of Championship.*
2004	*McLaren-Mercedes. 24 pts. 10th of Championship.*

6. Kimi RÄIKKÖNEN

DRIVER PROFILE

- Name — *RÄIKKÖNEN*
- First name — *Kimi Matias*
- Nationality — *Finnish*
- Date of birth — *October 17, 1979*
- Place of birth — *Espoo (SF)*
- Lives in — *Wollerau (CH), Espoo (SF), Chigwell (GB)*
- Marital status — *married to Jenni*
- Kids — *-*
- Hobbies — *snowboard, skateboard, jogging*
- Favorite music — *U2, Darude, Bomfunk Mc, Eminem*
- Favorite meal — *pasta, chicken, finnish dish with reindeer*
- Favorite drink — *ananas juice, water and milk*
- Height — *175 cm*
- Weight — *63 kg*
- Web — *www.kimiraikkonen.com*

STATISTICS | PRIOR TO F1

STATISTICS		PRIOR TO F1
Nber of Grand Prix	68	1988-99 *Karting*
Starts	67	1998 *Champion karting*
Victories	2	*Formula A (SF & Nordic)*
Pole positions	3	1999 *Karting*
Fastest lap	6	*Formule A (SF) (2nd),*
Podiums	18	*Formula Super A World*
Accidents/offs	8	*Championship (10°)*
Not qualified	0	2000 *F. Renault*
GP in the lead	16	*Champion (GB)*
Laps in the lead	209	
Kms in the lead	1,071	
Points scored	169	

F1 CAREER

2001	*Sauber-Petronas. 9 pts. 9th of Championship.*
2002	*McLaren-Mercedes. 24 pts. 6th of Championship.*
2003	*McLaren-Mercedes. 91 pts. 2nd of Championship.*
2004	*McLaren-Mercedes. 45 pts. 7th of Championship.*

Being cruel, one could say that for a hotel owner - he owns the Colombus in Monaco, David Coulthard is a pretty good grand prix driver. However, his day has passed at what should be the end of a very lucky career. Why lucky? Because since his 1994 debut, he has only driven for Williams and McLaren. Not for him the years in the lower ranks. David is quick, he can bring a car home, he can set it up and he is a sponsor's dream as the personification of the gentleman driver. But the Scotsman has had the misfortune to share his office with the likes of Mika Hakkinen, a double world champion and Kimi Rakkonen a future champion. Undoubtedly, his Achilles Heel over the past two seasons has been the one lap qualifying format. Coulthard has tried but failed to get to grips with it and you cannot win races starting three rows further back than you should do.

He speaks! After taking a well deserved victory in the Belgian Grand Prix on the type of circuit where a driver counts for more than his equipment, the Ice Man almost melted in the press conference and answered questions in whole sentences, rather than single words. Was the McLaren PR machine finally having an effect? Possibly not, as in Brazil, where he had a great drive to second place, when asked about the team's new deal with Nescafe, he made the mistake of admitting he did not drink coffee. As for his driving, well that was the same as ever: quick, committed, brave and stylish. He is possibly the only man who can really trouble Michael Schumacher on a regular basis, so please Mr. Dennis, please give Kimi a car worthy of his talent in 2005.

Ron Dennis

Adrian Newey

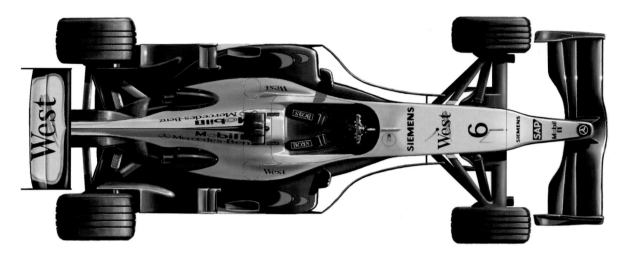

MCLAREN MP4/19B-MERCEDES
KIMI RÄIKKÖNEN
BELGIAN GRAND PRIX

McLaren MP4/19B-Mercedes

SPECIFICATIONS

- Chassis — McLaren MP4-19 & McLaren MP4-19B
- Type — Moulded carbon fibre / aluminium honeycomb composite
- Suspensions — inboard torsion bar/damped system operated by pushrod and bell crank with a double wishbone arrangement (F./R.)
- Engine — V10 Mercedes-Benz FO 110Q (72°)
- Displacement — 2,997 cm³
- Distribution — 4 valves per cylinder
- Electronic ignition — TAG Electronic Systems
- Transmission — McLaren semi-automatic 7 gears + reverse
- Clutch — AP Racing
- Radiators — McLaren / Calsonic / Marston
- Fuel / oil — Mobil Unleaded / Mobil 1
- Brakes (discs) — Hitco
- Brakes (calipers) — AP Racing
- Spark plugs / battery — NGK / GS Battery
- Shock absorbers — Penske/McLaren
- Tyres — Michelin
- Wheels diameter — 13"
- Rims — Enkei
- Weight — 605 kg, driver, on board camera, ballast
- Wheel base — not revealed
- Total length — not revealed
- Total width — not revealed
- Total height — not revealed
- Front track — not revealed
- Rear track — not revealed

TEAM PROFILE

- Address — McLaren Technology Centre Chertsey Road, Woking, Surrey GU21 5JY Great Britain
- Phone number — +44 (0) 1483 711 117
- Fax number — +44 (0) 1483 711 119
- Web — www.mclaren.com
- Founded in — 1963
- First Grand Prix — Monaco 1966
- Official name — West McLaren Mercedes
- Principal TAG McLaren Group — Ron Dennis
- CEO F1 — Martin Whitmarsh
- Managing Director — Jonathan Neale
- Vice President Mercedes-Benz Motorsport — Norbert Haug
- Technical Director — Adrian Newey Mario Illien (Mercedes-Ilmor)
- Executive Director of Engineering — Neil Oatley
- Chief Designer — Mike Coughlan
- Chief Mechanic — Stephen Giles
- Race Engineer (D.C.) — Phil Prew
- Race Engineer (K.R.) — Mark Slade
- Number of employees — 520
- Corporate Partners — Reemtsma (West), SAP, Warsteiner, Hugo Boss, Schüco, TAGHeuer • (Technology) Mobil 1, Siemens, Michelin, BAE Systems, Computer Associates, Sun microsystems • (Associate) T-Mobile • (Official Suppliers) Advanced Composites, Canon, Henkel, Nescafé XPress, Charmilles, Gs-Yuasa, Mazak, Targetti Lighting, Enkei, Sonax, Eisenmann, Sports Marketing Surveys, Kenwood, 3D Systems, Sparco.

STATISTICS

- Number of Grand Prix — 577
- Number of victories — 138
- Number of pole positions — 115
- Number of fastest laps — 114
- Number of podiums — 367
- Number of drivers Championship — 11
- Number of constructors Championship — 8
- Number of points scored — 2,856.5 (2,862.5)

POSITION IN WORLD CHAMPIONSHIP

1966	7th – 2·¹ pts	1976	2nd – 74 pts	1986	2nd – 96 pts	1996	4th – 49 pts
1967	8th – 3 pts	1977	3rd – 60 pts	1987	2nd – 76 pts	1997	4th – 63 pts
1968	2nd – 49·³ pts	1978	8th – 15 pts	1988	1st – 199 pts	1998	1st – 156 pts
1969	4th – 38 (40) pts	1979	7th – 15 pts	1989	1st – 141 pts	1999	2nd – 124 pts
1970	4th – 35 pts	1980	7th – 11 pts	1990	1st – 121 pts	2000	2nd – 152 pts
1971	6th – 10 pts	1981	6th – 28 pts	1991	1st – 139 pts	2001	2nd – 102 pts
1972	3rd – 47 pts	1982	2nd – 69 pts	1992	2nd – 99 pts	2002	3rd – 65 pts
1973	3rd – 58 pts	1983	5th – 34 pts	1993	2nd – 84 pts	2003	3rd – 142 pts
1974	1st – 73 pts	1984	1st – 143.5 pts	1994	4th – 42 pts	2004	5th – 69 pts
1975	3rd – 53 pts	1985	1st – 90 pts	1995	4th – 30 pts		

TEST DRIVERS 2004

- Alexander WURZ (A)
- Pedro DE LA ROSA (E)

SUCCESSION OF DRIVERS 2004

- David COULTHARD — all 18 Grands Prix
- Kimi RÄIKKÖNEN — all 18 Grands Prix

De la Rosa, Räikkönen,
Coulthard, Wurz

A record low

If Mercedes engineers were Japanese, they would have been falling on their swords in the pit lane. The team's year was wrecked by a dreadful start, as the German engine supplier delivered a power plant that did not have enough power and, to make matters worse, was dreadfully unreliable. It meant that using full power in qualifying was always a risk. The chassis had some faults of its own to compound the problem. Ron Dennis was left to pull out what is left of his hair, while Norbert Haug became even more bad tempered than usual. It looked as though the Dennis Palace, the new factory opened by the Queen in the middle of the year, would be a Taj Mahal-style mausoleum to the team's F1 ambitions. However, plenty of hard work turned the situation round in time for Raikkonen to serve up a well-deserved win in Spa and a strong second place in Brazil. It points to a more encouraging future in 2005, but, come the first race in Europe, F1 onlookers will be interested to see how the team's huge (non) Communication Centre fits into the fifth placed slot, as the teams line up in championship order in the paddock.

Renault

7. Jarno TRULLI

DRIVER PROFILE

- Name — *TRULLI*
- First name — *Jarno*
- Nationality — *Italian*
- Date of birth — *July 13, 1974*
- Place of birth — *Pescara (I)*
- Lives in — *Wokingham (GB)*
- Marital status — *married to Barbara*
- Kids — *-*
- Hobbies — *music, Movie films, karting, computers*
- Favorite music — *pop, rock, jazz, blues*
- Favorite meal — *pizza*
- Favorite drink — *Coca-Cola*
- Height — *173 cm*
- Weight — *60 kg*
- Web — *www.jarnotrulli.com*

STATISTICS

- Nber of Grand Prix — 130
- Starts — 128
- Victories — 1
- Pole positions — 2
- Fastest lap — 0
- Podiums — 4
- Accidents/offs — 17
- Not qualified — 0
- GP in the lead — 7
- Laps in the lead — 141
- Kms in the lead — 574
- Points scored — 117

PRIOR TO F1

- 1983-86 *Karting*
- 1988-90 *Champion Kart 100 (I)*
- 1991 *World Champion Kart 100 FK*
- 1992 *Kart 125 FC (2ⁿᵈ)*
- 1993 *Kart 100 SA (2ⁿᵈ)*
- 1994 *World Champion Kart 125 FC and Champion Kart 100 FSA (EUR & Nord USA)*
- 1995 *Kart 100 FA Champion (I)*
- 1996 *Champion F3 (D)*

F1 CAREER

1997 *Minardi-Hart, Prost-Mugen Honda. 3 pts. 15ᵗʰ of Championship.*
1998 *Prost-Peugeot. 1 pt. 15ᵗʰ of Championship.*
1999 *Prost-Peugeot. 7 pts. 11ᵗʰ of Championship.*
2000 *Jordan-Mugen-Honda. 6 pts. 10ᵗʰ of Championship.*
2001 *Jordan-Honda. 12 pts. 9ᵗʰ of Championship.*
2002 *Renault. 9 pts. 8ᵗʰ of Championship.*
2003 *Renault. 33 pts. 8ᵗʰ of Championship.*
2004 *Renault, Toyota. 46 pts. 6ᵗʰ of Championship.*

There is no better example of the fickle nature of Formula 1 than Jarno Trulli's season. When team-mate Alonso won in Hungary in 2003, the Italian got a big wake-up call and realised he had to up his game. He did it with such success that he was the dominant force at Renault early in the season. Taking pole position and the win in Monaco boosted him into orbit and the usually morose Italian was all smiles in the paddock. But then, at the French GP, he was heading for the podium and third place, when he let Barrichello steal it off him at the final corner. Team boss Flavio Briatore reached meltdown and went mad. From then on, the writing was on the wall and Briatore, to whom drivers have always been a commodity to buy and sell, decided it was time to put Trulli in the "Bargain Bin." Jarno's fragile psyche took a knock and it was downhill from there. Fortunately, Toyota were on a shopping trip at the time and Jarno will be the acceptable face of their team, alongside Ralf Schumacher.

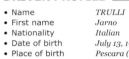
Flavio Briatore

Bob Bell

Denis Chevrier

Bernard Dudot

8. Fernando ALONSO

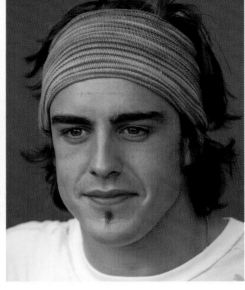

DRIVER PROFILE

- NOM — *ALONSO DÍAZ*
- First name — *Fernando*
- Nationality — *Spanish*
- Date of birth — *July 29, 1981*
- Place of birth — *Oviedo (E)*
- Lives in — *Oviedo (E) and Oxford (GB)*
- Marital status — *single*
- Kids — *-*
- Hobbies — *sports on TV, Movie films, computers*
- Favorite music — *spanish groups*
- Favorite meal — *pasta*
- Favorite drink — *mineral water*
- Height — *171 cm*
- Weight — *68 kg*
- Web — *www.fernandoalonso.com*

STATISTICS

- Nber of Grand Prix — 51
- Starts — 50
- Victories — 1
- Pole positions — 3
- Fastest lap — 1
- Podiums — 8
- Accidents/offs — 5
- Not qualified — 0
- GP in the lead — 13
- Laps in the lead — 157
- Kms in the lead — 718
- Points scored — 114

PRIOR TO F1

- 1984-98 *Karting, Champion Jr. (E) (93-94-95-96)*
- *Jr. World Champion (96)*
- *Inter-A Champion (E & I) (97)*
- *Inter-A Champion (E) (98)*
- 1999 *Champion Euro-Open Movistar Nissan*
- 2000 *F3000 (4ᵗʰ)*

F1 CAREER

2001 *Minardi-European. 0 pt. 23ᵗʰ of Championship.*
2002 *Renault. Test driver.*
2003 *Renault. 55 pts. 6ᵗʰ of Championship.*
2004 *Renault. 59 pts. 4ᵗʰ of Championship.*

In 2003, Alonso had been the rising star of the sport, but twelve months on, the Spaniard did not look so good. It was as though his new found fame and status had gone to his head and, for the first part of the year, he was put in the shade by Trulli. Alonso also seemed to struggle with the one-lap qualifying format, making a couple of costly mistakes and towards the end of the year, it seemed that all the fuss about Trulli's departure also affected his concentration. However, he always gave his all in the races, in a car that was not the easiest to deal with over a race distance. But the man from Oviedo is still very young and an undoubted talent. Going up against Fisichella next season will definitely sharpen him up and show his true worth.

7. Jacques VILLENEUVE

DRIVER PROFILE

- Name — *VILLENEUVE*
- First name — *Jacques*
- Nationality — *Canadian*
- Date of birth — *April 9, 1971*
- Place of birth — *St-Jean-sur-Richelieu, Québec, (CDN)*
- Lives in — *Monaco (MC)*
- Marital status — *engaged with Ellen*
- Kids — *-*
- Hobbies — *ski, guitar playing, music, electronics*
- Favorite music — *unplugged pop/rock*
- Favorite meal — *pasta*
- Favorite drink — *milk and "Root beer"*
- Height — *171 cm*
- Weight — *63 kg*
- Web — *www.jv-world.com*

STATISTICS

- Nber of Grand Prix — 134
- Starts — 133
- Victories — 11
- Pole positions — 13
- Fastest lap — 9
- Podiums — 23
- Accidents/offs — 14
- Not qualified — 0
- GP in the lead — 20
- Laps in the lead — 633
- Kms in the lead — 2,965
- Points scored — 219

PRIOR TO F1

- 1986 *Jim Russel School*
- 1987 *Spenard-David driving school*
- 1988 *F. Alfa (I)*
- 1989-91 *F3 (I) (-, 14ᵗʰ, 6ᵗʰ)*
- 1992 *F3 (J) (2ⁿᵈ)*
- 1993 *F. Atlantic (3ʳᵈ)*
- 1994 *IndyCar (6ᵗʰ)*
- 1995 *Champion IndyCar*

F1 CAREER

1996 *Williams-Renault. 78 pts. 2ⁿᵈ of Championship.*
1997 *Williams-Renault. 81 pts. **World Champion.***
1998 *Williams-Mecachrome. 21 pts. 5ᵗʰ of Championship.*
1999 *B·A·R-Supertec. 0 point. 21ᵗʰ of Championship.*
2000 *B·A·R-Honda. 17 pts. 7ᵗʰ of Championship.*
2001 *B·A·R-Honda. 12 pts. 7ᵗʰ of Championship.*
2002 *B·A·R-Honda. 4 pts. 12ᵗʰ of Championship.*
2003 *B·A·R-Honda. 6 pts. 16ᵗʰ of Championship.*
2004 *Renault. 0 pt. 21ᵗʰ of Championship.*

Putting Jacques Villeneuve in Trulli's car for the last three races was a great Briatore publicity coup, but it served no useful purpose. The Canadian was about as useless as he had been in the B.A.R the previous year, proving yet again that a monkey could have won the world title in the 1997 Williams. And wearing a race suit that looks like a baby's romper suit should be classified as a crime by the style police. One can only feel sorry for Peter Sauber who will have the pleasure of JV in 2005.

**RENAULT R24
JARNO TRULLI
MONACO GRAND PRIX**

Renault R24

SPECIFICATIONS

- Chassis — Renault R24
- Type — Moulded carbon fibre / aluminium honeycomb composite monocoque
- Suspensions — Carbon fibre top and bottom wishbones, pushrod system / torsion bar and damper (Front / Rear)
- Engine — V10 Renault RS24 (72°)
- Displacement — 3,000 cm³
- Distribution — 4 valves per cylinder
- Electronic ignition — Magneti Marelli
- Transmission — Renault F1 semi-automatic 6 gears + reverse
- Clutch — not revealed
- Radiators — Secan / Marston
- Fuel / oil — Elf
- Brakes (discs) — Hitco (carbon fibre)
- Brakes (calipers) — AP Racing
- Spark plugs / battery — Champion
- Shock absorbers — Dynamics
- Tyres — Michelin
- Wheels diameter — 13"
- Rims — BBS
- Weight — 605 kg, driver, on board camera, ballast
- Wheel base — 3,100 mm
- Total length — 4,600 mm
- Total width — 1,800 mm
- Total height — 950 mm
- Front track — 1,450 mm
- Rear track — 1,400 mm

TEAM PROFILE

- Address — Renault F1 UK, Whiteways Technical Centre, Enstone, Chipping Norton, Oxon OX7 4EE, Great Britain | Renault F1 France, 1-15, avenue du Président Kennedy, 91177 Viry-Châtillon, France
- Phone number — +44 (0) 1608 678 000 | +33 (0) 1 69 12 58 00
- Fax number — +44 (0) 1608 678 609 | +33 (0) 1 69 12 58 17
- Web — www.renaultf1.com
- Founded in — 1973
- First Grand Prix — Great Britain 1977
- Official name — Mild Seven Renault F1 Team
- Chairman and CEO — Patrick Faure
- Managing Director — Flavio Briatore
- Deputy Managing, Director, France — Bernard Dudot
- Technical Director — Bob Bell (Chassis), Rob White (Engine)
- Executive Director of Engineering — Pat Symonds
- Engine Operations Manager — Denis Chevrier
- Chief Designers — Mark Smith, Tim Densham
- Race Engineer (7) — A. Permane, N. Chester, F. Lom
- Race Engineer (8) — P. Monaghan, R. Nelson, R. Taffin
- Number of employees — 390 (GB) / 280 (F)
- Team Partners — Mild Seven, Elf, Michelin, Hanjin, i-mode, Telefonica, Guru
- Official Suppliers — 3D Systems, Alpinestars, Altran, Charmilles, Clearswift, DMG, Elysium, Eutelsat, Jobs, Lancel, Magneti Marelli, Network Appliance, O.Z. Racing, Puma, Veritas, Vistagy
- Associate Suppliers — CD Adapco Group, Fluent, Lectra, Tetco, Schroth Racing

STATISTICS

- Number of Grand Prix — 174
- Number of victories — 17
- Number of pole positions — 36
- Number of fastest laps — 19
- Number of podiums — 47
- Number of drivers Championship — 0
- Number of constructors Championship — 0
- Number of points scored — 528

RENAULT [F1] Team

POSITION IN WORLD CHAMPIONSHIP

1977	not classified	1983	2nd – 79 pts
1978	12th – 3 pts	1984	5th – 34 pts
1979	6th – 26 pts	1985	7th – 16 pts
1980	4th – 38 pts	2002	4th – 23 pts
1981	3rd – 54 pts	2003	4th – 88 pts
1982	3rd – 62 pts	2004	3rd – 105 pts

TEST DRIVER 2004

- Franck MONTAGNY (F)

SUCCESSION OF DRIVERS 2004

- Jarno TRULLI — 13 Grands Prix (Australia > Italy)
- Jacques VILLENEUVE — 3 Grands Prix (China, Japan, Brazil)
- Fernando ALONSO — all 18 Grands Prix

Franck Montagny

Progress but not enough

Having finished fourth in 2003, the Anglo-French team's stated aim was to finish third this year. They achieved their aim, but there were no smiling faces in the camp, as they effectively let second place behind Ferrari slip through their grasp. Both its drivers scored points in the first five races and then it got even better, as Trulli won from pole in Monaco. But then, a disastrous double retirement in Canada signalled the start of a downward turn for the team and its drivers. The French V10 engine made excellent progress, but the R24, despite its rearward weight bias which guaranteed brilliant traction off the start line, allowing its drivers to make up several places, was a difficult car to drive. Then, as usual, with any Briatore-run team, driver politics unsettled the team, as Trulli was shown the door. At a time when every point was needed in its battle with B.A.R-Honda for second place, bringing the over-rated Jacques Villeneuve into the team may have been good for publicity, but it did absolutely nothing on the track or in the points table. However, Renault's real stumbling block, in what was still a positive season, was the amazing progress made at B.A.R.

B·A·R Honda

9. Jenson BUTTON

DRIVER PROFILE

- Name — *BUTTON*
- First name — *Jenson*
- Nationality — *British*
- Date of birth — *January 19, 1980*
- Place of birth — *Frome, Somerset (GB)*
- Lives in — *Monaco (MC)*
- Marital status — *engaged to Louise*
- Kids — -
- Hobbies — *web surfing, video game, shopping*
- Favorite music — *Jamiroquaï, Kool And The Gang, les 70'*
- Favorite meal — *pasta*
- Favorite drink — *orange juice*
- Height — *182 cm*
- Weight — *68,5 kg*
- Web — *www.racecar.co.uk/jensonbutton/*

STATISTICS

		PRIOR TO F1
• Nber of Grand Prix	85	1989-95 *Karting, Champion*
• Starts	84	*Cadet (GB) (90-91) / Open (GB)*
• Best result	4 x 2ⁿᵈ	*(91-92-93) / Jr. TKM (GB)*
• Pole positions	1	*(91-92) / Senior ICA (I) (95)*
• Fastest lap	0	1996 *Karting (3ʳᵈ in World Cup*
• Podiums	10	*and championship (USA))*
• Accidents/offs	14	1997 *Karting Super A*
• Not qualified	0	*Champion (EUR) and*
• GP in the lead	7	*A. Senna Cup Winner*
• Laps in the lead	70	1998 *F. Ford Champion and*
• Kms in the lead	358	*F. Ford Festival (GB)*
• Points scored	130	1999 *F3 (GB) (3ʳᵈ)*

F1 CAREER

2000 *Williams-BMW. 12 pts. 8ᵗʰ of Championship.*
2001 *Benetton-Renault. 2 pts. 17ᵗʰ of Championship.*
2002 *Renault. 14 pts. 7ᵗʰ of Championship.*
2003 *B·A·R-Honda. 17 pts. 9ᵗʰ of Championship.*
2004 *B·A·R-Honda. 85 pts. 3ʳᵈ of Championship.*

10. Takuma SATO

DRIVER PROFILE

- Name — *SATO*
- First name — *Takuma*
- Nationality — *Japanese*
- Date of birth — *January 28, 1977*
- Place of birth — *Tokyo (J)*
- Lives in — *Marlow (GB)*
- Marital status — *single*
- Kids — -
- Hobbies — *cycling, being with friends*
- Favorite music — *pop, some japanese groups*
- Favorite meal — *Japanese meal*
- Favorite drink — *fresh fruit juice, beer from time to time*
- Height — *163 cm*
- Weight — *58 kg*
- Web — *www.takumasato.com*

STATISTICS

		PRIOR TO F1
• Nber of Grand Prix	36	1996 *Karting Champion (J)*
• Starts	36	1997 *Karting Champion (J),*
• Best result	1 x 3ʳᵈ	*Honda driving school*
• Best qualification	1 x 2ⁿᵈ	1998 *F. Vauxhall Jr. (GB)*
• Fastest lap	0	1999 *F. Opel Euroseries (GB)*
• Podiums	1	*(6ᵗʰ), F3 (GB)*
• Accidents/offs	5	2000 *F3 (GB) (3ʳᵈ)*
• Not qualified	0	2001 *F3 Champion (GB)*
• GP in the lead	1	
• Laps in the lead	2	
• Kms in the lead	10	
• Points scored	39	

F1 CAREER

2001 *B·A·R-Honda. Test driver.*
2002 *Jordan-Honda. 2 pts. 15ᵗʰ of Championship.*
2003 *B·A·R-Honda. 3 pts. 18ᵗʰ of Championship.*
2004 *B·A·R-Honda. 34 pts. 8ᵗʰ of Championship.*

This year, we saw the promise that Frank Williams had spotted back in 2000 come to fruition. The Englishman was the only man to mount a consistent challenge to the Ferrari pair. Free of the all-pervading influence of Jacques Villeneuve within B.A.R, Jenson took on the mantle of team leader and finished on the podium ten times. There is no reason to think he will not be even stronger in 2005. His only weakness was in listening to his mad management in the stupid "Button to Williams" saga. He showed the two key signs of a great driver in the making, by putting up strong performances on tracks where driver input counts for more than the car package and by instantly getting on the pace at new tracks.

The little man is the very first Japanese driver who deserves his place on the F1 grid, purely in terms of merit, rather than just because some Japanese engine supplier wants him there. He is undoubtedly the bravest man on the track, showing total commitment in the quickest corners. He is not afraid of any of his rivals either, willingly going wheel to wheel with more established stars. He has the speed, skill and intelligence to go much further and his only weakness is an underdeveloped sense of race craft and experience, but this will come. Obviously, his relationship with Honda is a boost, not just for his own performance but that of the B.A.R team as a whole. Could he be the first Japanese to win a grand prix in 2005?

David Richards

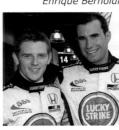

Geoffrey Willis

*Anthony Davidson,
Enrique Bernoldi*

B·A·R 006-HONDA
JENSON BUTTON
SAN MARINO GRAND PRIX

B·A·R 006-Honda

SPECIFICATIONS

- Chassis — B·A·R 006
- Type — Moulded carbon fibre / aluminium honeycomb composite monocoque
- Suspensions — Wishbone & pushrod-activated torsion springs and rockers, mechanical anti-roll bar (Front / Rear)
- Engine — V10 Honda RA004E (90°)
- Displacement — 3,000 cm³
- Distribution — 4 valves per cylinder
- Electronic ignition — Honda PGM-IG
- Transmission — B·A·R Xtrac longitudinal, semi-automatic, hydraulic 7 gears + reverse
- Clutch — AP Racing
- Radiators — Calsonic
- Fuel / oil — Elf / Nisseki
- Brakes (discs) — Alkon (carbon)
- Brakes (calipers) — AP Racing
- Spark plugs / battery — NGK / 3Ah
- Shock absorbers — Koni
- Tyres — Michelin
- Wheels dimensions — Width 312 mm (FR) / 360 mm (RE)
- Rims — BBS
- Weight — 605 kg, driver, on board camera, ballast
- Wheel base — 3,140 mm
- Total length — 4,465 mm
- Total width — 1,800 mm
- Total height — 950 mm
- Front track — 1,460 mm
- Rear track — 1,420 mm

STATISTICS

- Number of Grand Prix — 101
- Best result in race — 4 x 2ⁿᵈ
- Number of pole positions — 1
- Number of fastest laps — 0
- Number of podiums — 13
- Number of drivers Championship — 0
- Number of constructors Championship — 0
- Number of points scored — 189

POSITION IN WORLD CHAMPIONSHIP

1999	not classified	2002	8ᵗʰ – 7 pts
2000	5ᵗʰ – 20 pts	2003	5ᵗʰ – 26 pts
2001	6ᵗʰ – 17 pts	2004	2ⁿᵈ – 119 pts

TEST DRIVERS 2004

- Anthony DAVIDSON (GB)   • Enrique BERNOLDI (BR)

SUCCESSION OF DRIVERS 2004

- Jenson BUTTON — all 18 Grands Prix
- Takuma SATO — all 18 Grands Prix

TEAM PROFILE

- Address — British American Racing Operations Centre, Brackley, Northants NN13 7BD Great Britain
- Phone number — +44 (0) 1280 84 40 00
- Fax number — +44 (0) 1280 84 40 01
- Web — www.barf1.com
- Founded in — 1997
- First Grand Prix — Australia 1999
- Official name — Lucky Strike B·A·R Honda
- Team Principal — David Richards
- Technical Director — Geoffrey Willis
- Group Managing Director — Nick Fry
- Group Marketing Director — Hugh Chambers
- Senior Aerodynamicist — Willem Toet, Mariano Alperin-Bruvera & Simon Lacey
- Team Manager — Ron Meadows
- Chief Mechanic — Alistair Gibson
- Chief Race Engineer — Craig Wilson
- Race Engineer (J.B.) — Andrew Shovlin
- Race Engineer (T.S.) — Jock Clear
- Number of employees — 300
- Team Partners — British American Tabacco, Honda, Intercond, Brunotti, Michelin, Mac Tools, Ray-Ban
- Technical Partners — Alcon, SAP, UGS PLM Solutions
- Team Suppliers — Alpine Stars, Ascent Technology, Autoglym, BBS, BlueArc, Cablefree Solutions Ltd, Creative Print Group, CYTEC, Endless Advance Ltd, Glasurit Automotive Refinish, Haas Automation, JOBS, Koni, Lincoln Electric, Matrix Network Solutions, Sandvik Coromant, STL Communications Ltd

A "real" team now

"They used to be a joke team, but now they are a real team," said an F1 insider when asked about B.A.R. B.A.R's incredible pace over the winter was dismissed as showboating by cynics, but they had to eat their words, as the Brackley based squad soon became the only true challenger to Ferrari's dominance. It became the first team in history to finish second in the Constructors' championship without winning a single grand prix. It got there thanks to reliability and consistency in terms of producing a package that worked well at nearly every track. David Richards' laborious re-structuring of what was a top-heavy organisation finally paid off, while Geoff Willis and his team delivered the goods on the technical front: items like its all-carbon gearbox and its interesting front axle, first banned and then approved by FIA, all

point to a squad that was confident in its abilities. Honda did its share, producing plenty of horsepower, as it overhauled its marketing driven operation, reintroducing many of the old faces from the glory days of Senna and Prost at McLaren. Even the wranglings over Button's future did not upset B.A.R's equilibrium as they made the more experienced McLaren and Williams teams look like rookies. The big question is whether or not they can sustain that momentum in 2005 and finally win a grand prix.

Sauber Petronas

11. Giancarlo FISICHELLA

DRIVER PROFILE

- Name — *FISICHELLA*
- First name — *Giancarlo*
- Nationality — *Italian*
- Date of birth — *January 14, 1973*
- Place of birth — *Roma (I)*
- Lives in — *Roma (I) and Monaco (MC)*
- Marital status — *married to Luna*
- Kids — *daughter (Carlotta) and son (Christopher)*
- Hobbies — *football, tennis, stream fishing, pool*
- Favorite music — *Elton John, Madonna, Robbie Williams*
- Favorite meal — *pasta "bucatini alla matriciana"*
- Favorite drinks — *Coca-Cola and orange juice*
- Height — *172 cm*
- Weight — *66 kg*
- Web — *www.giancarlofisichella.com*

STATISTICS

		PRIOR TO F1
Nber of Grand Prix	142	1984-88 *Karting*
Starts	141	1989 *Karting cat. 100,*
Victories	1	*World Championship (4th)*
Pole-positions	1	1990 *Karting ,*
Fastest lap	1	*Intercontinental*
Podiums	10	*Championship (3rd)*
Accidents/offs	19	1991 *Karting (EUR) (2nd),*
Not qualified	0	*F. Alfa Boxer*
GP in the lead	4	1992 *F3 (I) (8th)*
Laps in the lead	36	1993 *F3 (I) (2nd)*
Kms in the lead	176	1994 *F3 Champion (I)*
Points scored	116	1995 *DTM/ITC Alfa Romeo*

F1 CAREER

- 1995 *Minardi-Ford. Test driver.*
- 1996 *Minardi-Ford. 0 pt. 19th of Championship.*
- 1997 *Jordan-Peugeot. 20 pts. 8th of Championship.*
- 1998 *Benetton-Playlife. 16 pts. 9th of Championship.*
- 1999 *Benetton-Playlife. 13 pts. 9th of Championship.*
- 2000 *Benetton-Playlife. 18 pts. 6th of Championship.*
- 2001 *Benetton-Renault. 8 pts. 11th of Championship.*
- 2002 *Jordan-Honda. 7 pts. 11th of Championship.*
- 2003 *Jordan-Ford. 12 pts. 12th of Championship.*
- 2004 *Sauber-Petronas. 22 pts. 11th of Championship.*

12. Felipe MASSA

DRIVER PROFILE

- Name — *MASSA*
- First name — *Felipe*
- Nationality — *Brazilian*
- Date of birth — *April 25, 1981*
- Place of birth — *São Paulo (BR)*
- Lives in — *Hinwill (CH)*
- Marital status — *single*
- Kids — *-*
- Hobbies — *water ski, football, Movie films, music*
- Favorite music — *all, from hip hop to techno*
- Favorite meal — *pasta, meat and Brazilian cooking*
- Favorite drinks — *Rostrum Champagne*
- Height — *166 cm*
- Weight — *59 kg*
- Web — *www.felipemassa.com*

STATISTICS

		PRIOR TO F1
Nber of Grand Prix	34	1990-97 *Karting*
Starts	34	1998 *F. Chevrolet (BR) (5th)*
Best result	1 x 4th	1999 *F. Chevrolet*
Best qualification	2 x 4th	*Champion (BR)*
Fastest lap	0	2000 *F. Renault Champion*
Podiums	0	*(EUR & I)*
Accidents/offs	7	2001 *F3000 Champion*
Not qualified	0	*Euroseries (I)*
GP in the lead	1	
Laps in the lead	2	
Kms in the lead	9	
Points scored	16	

F1 CAREER

- 2002 *Sauber-Petronas. 4 points. 13th of Championship.*
- 2003 *Ferrari. Test driver.*
- 2004 *Sauber-Petronas. 12 points. 12th of Championship.*

The Italian is going back to a top team in the shape of Renault next year and he really deserves it. He was undoubtedly one of the stars of the season, working wonders in the Sauber. His qualifying performances were excellent and he was if anything even better in the races. Forced to start from the back of the grid in the British GP, he charged round Silverstone to go from 20th at the start to 6th at the flag. "Fisi" is not your typical Italian and does not appear to suffer from mood swings and tantrums, preferring to get on with the job. It would often be hard to remember what he did in a race, but a glance at the results sheet showed he had somehow worked his way up to sixth or fourth. He will be much missed according to team insiders, especially when you consider they are now going to have to deal with Villeneuve.

Every day is "Groundhog Day" for the Brazilian, with the same erratic driving style, more suited to rallying than racing, repeated race after race. For a man who spent a year in the "Ferrari finishing school" as a Scuderia test driver, he appears to have a limited capacity to learn, although Sauber engineers reckoned he had made progress since his earlier stint with the Swiss team. There is no doubting that the Brazilian has the necessary speed, but it seems that more homework and more diligence are required

Peter Sauber

Willy Rampf

SAUBER C23-PETRONAS
GIANCARLO FISICHELLA
BELGIAN GRAND PRIX

Sauber C23-Petronas

SPECIFICATIONS

- Chassis — *Sauber C23*
- Type — *Moulded carbon-fibre / aluminium honeycomb composite*
- Suspensions — *Upper and lower wishbones, inboard springs and dampers, actuated by pushrods (Front / Rear)*
- Engine — *V10 Petronas 04A (90°) (Ferrari 053)*
- Displacement — *2,997 cm³*
- Distribution — *4 valves per cylinder*
- Electronic ignition — *Magneti Marelli*
- Transmission — *Sauber longitudinal semi-automatic 7 gears + reverse*
- Clutch — *AP*
- Radiators — *Calsonic*
- Fuel / oil — *Petronas*
- Brakes (discs) — *Brembo*
- Brakes (calipers) — *Brembo*
- Spark plugs / batterie — *Champion / SPE*
- Shock absorbers — *Sachs Race Engineering*
- Tyres — *Bridgestone Potenza*
- Wheels dimensions — *265/55R13 (AV) - 325/45R13 (AR)*
- Rims — *O.Z. Racing > 12"-13 (AV) / 13.7"-13 (AR)*
- Weight — *605 kg, driver, on board camera, ballast*
- Wheel base — *3,120 mm*
- Total length — *4,600 mm*
- Total width — *1,800 mm*
- Total height — *1,000 mm*
- Front track — *1,470 mm*
- Rear track — *1,410 mm*

TEAM PROFILE

- Address — *Sauber Motorsport AG*
  Wildbachstrasse 9
  CH - 8340 Hinwil
  Switzerland
- Phone number — *+ 41 19 37 90 00*
- Fax number — *+ 41 19 37 90 01*
- Web — *www.sauber-petronas.com*
- Founded in — *1970*
- First Grand Prix — *South of America 1993*
- Official name — *Sauber Petronas*
- Team Principal and CEO — *Peter Sauber*
- Technical Director — *Willy Rampf*
  Osamu Goto (engine)
- Team Manager — *Beat Zehnder*
- Head of vehicle engineering — *Jacky Eeckelaert*
- Race Engineer (G.F.) — *Giampaolo Dall'Ara*
- Race Engineer (F.M.) — *Mike Krack*
- Chief mechanic — *Urs Kuratle*
- Number of employees — *270*
- Team Partners — *Petronas, Credit Suisse, Red Bull*
- Partners — *Adelholzener Alpenquellen, Adnovum Informatik, AMD, AS Lifts, Balzers, Bridgestone, Brütsch/Rüegger, Catia, Cisco Systems, DaimlerChrysler, Dalco, Druckerei Flawil, Egro AG Kaffeemaschinen, Elektro Frauchiger, Emil Frey, Ericsson, Fluent Deutschland, Gamatech Bottarlini, Italdesign / Giugiaro, Jacques Germanier, Kaeser Kompressoren, Klauke Industries, Lista Group, Magneti Marelli, Microsoft, Mobile TeleSystems, MSC.Software, MTS Systems, Ozalid, Paninfo, Philips, Pilatus, Plenexis, Puma, Sokhna Port, Stoll Giroflex, Sun World, Supag Spichtig and Partners, Swisscom Mobile, Taikang Life, Vescal, Walter Meier, Winkler Veranstaltungstechnik*

STATISTICS

- Number of Grand Prix — 197
- Best result in race — 6 x 3rd
- Best qualification — 2 x 2nd
- Number of fastest laps — 0
- Number of podiums — 6
- Number of drivers Championship — 0
- Number of constructors Championship — 0
- Number of points scored — 141

POSITION IN WORLD CHAMPIONSHIP

Year	Result		Year	Result
1993	6th – 12 pts		1999	8th – 5 pts
1994	8th – 12 pts		2000	8th – 6 pts
1995	7th – 18 pts		2001	4th – 21 pts
1996	7th – 11 pts		2002	5th – 11 pts
1997	7th – 16 pts		2003	6th – 19 pts
1998	6th – 10 pts		2004	6th – 34 pts

TEST DRIVER 2004

- Neel JANI (CH)

SUCCESSION OF DRIVERS 2004

- Giancarlo FISICHELLA — *all 18 Grands Prix*
- Felipe MASSA — *all 18 Grands Prix*

Neel Jani

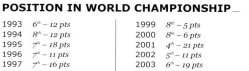

The wind (tunnel) of change

For much of the season, it looked as though the least extrovert team in the pit lane would end up fifth, but in the end, they were overtaken by McLaren and had to settle for sixth again. But that is a great achievement, making the Swiss crew the top privateer team, ahead of the might of Toyota, Jaguar and the other two private teams. Peter Sauber has to be congratulated on running a very efficient operation and his cars became more efficient aerodynamically during the year, as the new Hinwil wind tunnel came on stream. This year, Sauber had the huge benefit of running the current year Ferrari V10, (as well as the ultra-compact Italian gearbox) so there was no shortage of power on tap. Sauber was the only team entitled to run a Friday driver that did not bother with this luxury, but it did not seem to count against them. Sauber encountered more engine problems than Ferrari, but on the positive side, the car evolved consistently throughout the year, which had not always been the case in the past. Never a team to follow the herd, Sauber tacticians frequently put their drivers on different strategies to the rest of the pack, often making one less stop than the norm and this tactic was generally rewarded with a points finish. The biggest problem Sauber faces for 2005 is the loss of Giancarlo Fisichella. In his choice of Jacques Villeneuve, the usually level-headed Peter Sauber has either made a big mistake or knows something the rest of the paddock has ignored.

Jaguar

14. Mark WEBBER

DRIVER PROFILE

- Nom — *WEBBER*
- First name — *Mark Alan*
- Nationality — *Australian*
- Date of birth — *August 27, 1976*
- Place of birth — *Queanbeyan, NSW, AUS)*
- Lives in — *Buckinghamshire (GB)*
- Marital status — *single*
- Enfant — *-*
- Hobbies — *VTT, guided planes, Playstation2*
- Favorite music — *INXS, U2, relaxing music*
- Favorite meal — *pasta, pizza, chocolate, ice cream and desserts*
- Favorite drinks — *apple juice, lemonade and mineral water*
- Height — *184 cm*
- Weight — *74 kg*
- Web — *www.markwebber.com*

STATISTICS | PRIOR TO F1

• Nber of Grand Prix	51	1991-93 *Karting, NSW*
• Starts	50	*and ACT Champion (92)*
• Best result	1 x 5th	1994 *F. Ford (AUS) (14th)*
• Best qualification	1 x 2nd	1995 *F. Ford (AUS) (4th)*
• Fastest lap	0	1996 *F. Ford (GB) (2nd),*
• Podiums	0	*F. Ford Festival Winner*
• Accidents/offs	7	1997 *F3 (GB) (4th)*
• Not qualified	0	1998 *FIA-GT Series (2nd)*
• GP in the lead	1	2000 *F3000 (3rd)*
• Laps in the lead	2	2001 *F3000 (2nd)*
• Kms in the lead	8	
• Points scored	26	

F1 CAREER

1999 *Arrows-Supertec. Test driver.*
2000 *Benetton-Playlife. Test driver.*
2001 *Benetton-Renault. Test driver.*
2002 *Minardi-Asiatech. 2 pts. 16th of Championship.*
2003 *Jaguar. 17 pts. 10th of Championship.*
2004 *Jaguar. 7 pts. 13th of Championship.*

15. Christian KLIEN

DRIVER PROFILE

- Nom — *KLIEN*
- First nom — *Christian*
- Nationality — *Austrian*
- Date of birth — *February 7, 1983*
- Place of birth — *Hohenems, Vorarlberg (A)*
- Lives in — *Hohenems (A)*
- Marital status — *single*
- Kids — *-*
- Hobbies — *Web, VTT, skiing*
- Favorite music — *everything*
- Favorite meal — *Italian cooking*
- Favorite drinks — *apple juice with mineral water*
- Height — *168 cm*
- Weight — *64 kg*
- Web — *www.christian-klien.com*

STATISTICS | PRIOR TO F1

• Nber of Grand Prix	18	1996-98 *Karting,*
• Starts	18	*Champion (96) (CH)*
• Best result	1 x 6th	1999 *F. BMW Jr. Cup (D) (4th)*
• Best qualification	1 x 10th	2000 *F. BMW (D) (10th)*
• Fastest lap	0	2001 *F. BMW (D) (3rd)*
• Podiums	0	2002 *F. Renault Champion (D),*
• Accidents/offs	3	*F. Renault (EUR) (5th)*
• Not qualified	0	2003 *F3 Euro Series (2nd),*
• GP in the lead	0	*F3 Marlboro Masters*
• Laps in the lead	0	*Zandvoort Winner*
• Kms in the lead	0	
• Points scored	3	

F1 CAREER

2004 *Jaguar. 3 pts. 16th of Championship.*

Webber is one Jaguar employee who knows where he is going in 2005, as the likeable Australian landed a plum drive with BMW-Williams. Apart from a bad day at Spa, when he collided with Barrichello at the first corner and later with Sato, he was consistent, quick and got the very most out of the R5. His class as a driver was particularly noticeable in a brilliantly committed lap in qualifying at Suzuka. Yet again, Webber proved he is a real team player, contributing in all areas of the development of the technical package and his articulate, easy going nature make him a natural choice for Williams, who no doubt hope he will help them recreate their early glory days with that other charismatic Australian champion, Alan Jones. The move to Sir Frank's team will show whether or not he really is a top class driver, because one should not forget that his best F1 result to date is only a fifth place in his home race with Minardi!

There is nothing essentially wrong with being a "pay driver" in Formula 1; after all, a certain Niki Lauda bought his way into the sport and he didn't do too badly. However, Jaguar's claims that they chose Klien to partner Webber, based on his ability behind the wheel, were a trifle hard to swallow. Especially, as the young Austrian brought with him a very big cheque from the Red Bull energy drink company. Aggressive and confident, the youngster did not disgrace himself, however he faced a very steep learning curve and it was not until the championship got to Belgium that he began to show signs of some potential. By then, it was much too late of course.

Tony Purnell

David Pitchforth

Malcolm Oastler

Björn Wirdheim

JAGUAR R5
MARK WEBBER
GERMAN GRAND PRIX

Jaguar R5

SPECIFICATIONS

- Chassis — *Jaguar R5*
- Type — *Carbon-fibre and honeycomb composite structure*
- Suspensions — *Double wishbone, push rods / roll bar (FR/RE)*
- Engine — *V10 Cosworth Racing CR-6 (90°)*
- Displacement — *2,998 cm³*
- Distribution — *40 valves*
- Electronic ignition — *Pi Research, Pi 'VCS' System*
- Transmission — *Jaguar longitudinal, hydraulic pressure system, 7 gears + reverse*
- Clutch — *AP Racing*
- Radiators — *IMI*
- Fuel / oil — *Castrol Racing / Castrol Fluid Technology*
- Brakes (discs) — *Carbone Industrie or Brembo (carbon)*
- Brakes (calipers) — *AP Racing*
- Spark plugs / batterie — *Champion / JRL*
- Shock absorbers — *Koni*
- Tyres — *Michelin*
- Wheels dimensions — *12.7"-13 (AV) / 13.4"-13 (AR)*
- Rims — *O.Z. Racing*
- Weight — *605 kg, driver, on board camera, ballast*
- Wheel base — *not revealed*
- Total length — *not revealed*
- Total width — *not revealed*
- Total height — *not revealed*
- Front track — *not revealed*
- Rear track — *not revealed*

STATISTICS

- Number of Grand Prix — 85
- Best result in race — 2 x 3rd
- Best qualification — 1 x 2nd
- Number of fastest laps — 0
- Number of podiums — 2
- Number of drivers Championship — 0
- Number of constructors Championship — 0
- Number of points scored — 49

POSITION IN WORLD CHAMPIONSHIP

2000	9th – 4 pts	2003	7th – 18 pts
2001	8th – 9 pts	2004	7th – 10 pts
2002	7th – 8 pts		

TEST DRIVER 2004

- Björn WIRDHEIM (S)

SUCCESSION OF DRIVERS 2004

- Mark WEBBER — *all 18 Grands Prix*
- Christian KLIEN — *all 18 Grands Prix*

TEAM PROFILE

- Address — *Jaguar Racing Ltd Bradbourne Drive, Tilbrook, Milton Keynes, MK7 8BJ Great Britain*
- Phone number — *+44 (0) 1908 27 97 00*
- Fax number — *+44 (0) 1908 27 97 11*
- Web — *www.jaguar-racing.com*
- Founded in — *2000*
- First Grand Prix — *Australia 2000*
- Official name — *Jaguar Racing*
- Group Vice President & Head of F1 — *Richard Parry-Jones*
- CEO, Premier Performance division — *Tony Purnell*
- Managing Director — *David Pitchforth (Jaguar) Nick Hayes (Cosworth Racing)*
- Director of engineering — *Dr. Ian Pocock*
- Chief engineer — *Malcolm Oastler*
- Head of Aerodynamics — *Ben Agathangelou*
- Head of vehicle Perfomance — *Dr. Mark Gillan*
- Head of vehicle Designer — *Robert Taylor*
- Race Engineer (M.W.) — *Peter Harrison*
- Race Engineer (C.K.) — *Stefano Sordo*
- Number of employees — *270*
- Major Partners — *HSBC, RedBull, UGS, DuPont, AT&T, Pioneer, Michelin, Beck's, Amik Italia Spa*
- Technical Partners — *Castrol, Lear*
- Official Suppliers — *Tom Tailor, Rolex, Puma, 3D Systems, Jaguar Shoes, Mumm*

Put out of its misery

So it's farewell then to one of the most famous names in the motor industry and one with a glorious past in sports car racing. Jaguar's F1 history will always be seen as a sad one, with too many bosses, but not enough money. Parent company, Ford's behaviour and poor management was scandalously inept and Detroit has now pulled the plug. It's a shame, as this year, the green cars were beginning to show some potential and generally ran reliably, if not quickly, although the gearbox and hydraulics were a weak point. Over the winter, the team focussed on the one engine per weekend rule and apart from some silly accidents, generally got to the finish with a reliable car, but only saw points on five occasions. Having been one of the heaviest users of Michelin tyres in the past, this was another area where the team made big progress. There were the occasional flashes of hope, such as Mark Webber's front row qualifying in Malaysia, but the car was simply not quick enough and, inevitably, once news came through the team was pulling out, development pretty much came to a complete halt.

Toyota

16. Cristiano DA MATTA

DRIVER PROFILE

- Nom — DA MATTA
- First name — *Cristiano Monteiro*
- Nationality — *Brazilian*
- Date of birth — *September 19, 1973*
- Place of birth — *Belo Horizonte (BR)*
- Lives in — *Monaco (MC)*
- Marital status — *single*
- Kids — -
- Hobbies — *play and listen music, cycling*
- Favorite music — *rock, blues, jazz*
- Favorite meal — *Brazilian cooking*
- Favorite drinks — *ice tea*
- Height — *165 cm*
- Weight — *59 kg*
- Web — *www.damatta.com*

STATISTICS | PRIOR TO F1

STATISTICS		PRIOR TO F1
Nber of Grand Prix	28	1990-92 *Karting, Minas*
Starts	28	*Champion (90-91), (BR) (91)*
Best result	*3 x 6th*	1993 *F. Ford Champion (BR)*
Best qualification	*1 x 3rd*	1994 *F3 Champion (BR)*
Fastest lap	0	1995 *F3 (GB) (8th)*
Podiums	0	1996 *F3000 (8th)*
Accidents/offs	4	1997 *Indy Lights (3rd)*
Not qualified	0	1998 *Indy Lights Champion*
GP in the lead	1	1999 *CART (18th)*
Laps in the lead	17	2000 *CART (10th)*
Kms in the lead	87	2001 *CART (5th)*
Points scored	13	2002 *CART Champion*

F1 CAREER

2003   *Toyota. 10 pts. 13th of Championship.*
2004   *Toyota. 3 pts. 17th of Championship.*

He didn't look like a grand prix star, he didn't act like one, he didn't drive like one... next.

16/17. Ricardo ZONTA

DRIVER PROFILE

- Nom — *ZONTA*
- First name — *Ricardo*
- Nationality — *Brazilian*
- Date of birth — *March 23rd 1976*
- Place of birth — *Curitiba (BR)*
- Lives in — *Monaco (MC)*
- Marital status — *single*
- Kids — -
- Hobbies — *surfing, water ski, Motocross*
- Favorite music — *The Corrs, Paralamas do Sucesso*
- Favorite meal — *pasta with chicken*
- Favorite drinks — *fresh oranges*
- Height — *172 cm*
- Weight — *64 kg*
- Web — *www.ricardozonta.com.br*

STATISTICS | PRIOR TO F1

STATISTICS		PRIOR TO F1
Nber of Grand Prix	36	1987-92 *Karting, Curitiba*
Starts	36	*Champion(91)*
Best result	*3 x 6th*	1993 *F. Chevrolet (BR) (6th)*
Best qualification	*1 x 6th*	1994 *F3 (BR) (5th)*
Fastest lap	0	1995 *F3 Champion (BR &*
Podiums	0	*South America)*
Accidents/offs	6	1996 *F3000 (4th)*
Not qualified	0	1997 *F3000 Champion*
GP in the lead	0	
Laps in the lead	0	
Kms in the lead	0	
Points scored	3	

F1 CAREER

1997   *Jordan-Peugeot. Test driver.*
1998   *McLaren-Mercedes. Test driver.*
1999   *B·A·R-Supertec. 0 pt. 22th of Championship.*
2000   *B·A·R-Honda. 3 pts. 14th of Championship.*
2001   *Jordan-Honda. 0 pt. 19th of Championship.*
2003   *Toyota. Test driver.*
2004   *Toyota. 0 pt. 22th of Championship.*

The Brazilian did his job as a Friday driver for the team, using his considerable experience to move the programme along. Given four chances to race, while Toyota played Musical Chairs, he did nothing to make any team bosses sit up and take notice.

16. Jarno TRULLI

SEE RENAULT, PAGES 28-29

17. Olivier PANIS

DRIVER PROFILE

- Nom — *PANIS*
- First name — *Olivier Denis*
- Nationality — *French*
- Date of birth — *September 2nd 1966*
- Place of birth — *Lyon (F)*
- Lives in — *Varses près de Grenoble (F)*
- Marital status — *married to Anne*
- Kids — *2 daughters and son (Caroline, Lauren & Aurélien)*
- Hobbies — *family, skiing, cycling, tennis, boating, karting*
- Favorite music — *Florent Pagny, Barry White, Garou*
- Favorite meal — *Olive oil pasta, parmesan*
- Favorite drinks — *water and Coca-Cola*
- Height — *173 cm*
- Weight — *72 kg*
- Web — *www.olivier-panis.com*

STATISTICS | PRIOR TO F1

STATISTICS		PRIOR TO F1
Nber of Grand Prix	158	1981-87 *Karting*
Starts	157	1987 *Volant Elf Winfield*
Victories	1	*Paul Ricard Winner*
Best qualification	*3 x 3rd*	1988 *F. Renault (F) (4th)*
Fastest lap	0	1989 *F. Renault Champion (F)*
Podiums	5	1990 *F3 (F) (4th)*
Accidents/offs	20	1991 *F3 (F) (2nd)*
Not qualified	0	1992 *F3000 (10th)*
GP in the lead	1	1993 *F3000 Champion*
Laps in the lead	16	
Kms in the lead	53	
Points scored	76	

F1 CAREER

1994   *Ligier-Renault. 9 points. 11th of Championship.*
1995   *Ligier-Mugen-Honda. 16 pts. 8th of Championship.*
1996   *Ligier- Mugen-Honda. 13 pts. 9th of Championship.*
1997   *Prost-Mugen-Honda. 16 pts. 9th of Championship.*
1998   *Prost-Peugeot. 0 point. 18th of Championship.*
1999   *Prost-Peugeot. 2 pts. 15th of Championship.*
2000   *McLaren-Mercedes. Test driver.*
2001   *B·A·R-Honda. 5 pts. 14th of Championship.*
2002   *B·A·R-Honda. 3 pts. 14th of Championship.*
2003   *Toyota. 6 pts. 15th of Championship.*
2004   *Toyota. 6 pts. 14th of Championship.*

Olivier Panis left Formula 1 the way he lived his life in the sport – quietly. Sunday in Japan was a sad day, because not only did Panis' retirement from the sport mean there would be no French drivers on the grid next year, it also meant that F1 had to say goodbye to one of the nice guys, a hard worker, a gentleman and pretty good racer who rarely had the machinery to show what he could really do. But at least he will be able to tell his grandchildren that he won the Monaco GP.

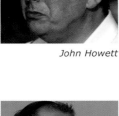

Tsutomu Tomita

John Howett

Mike Gascoyne

Ryan Briscoe

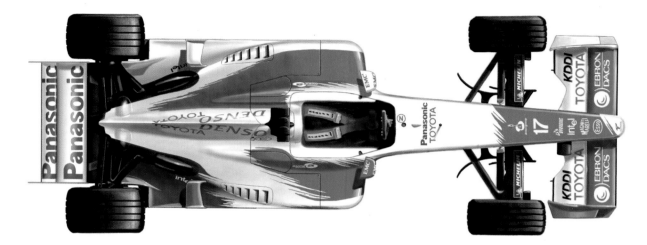

**TOYOTA TF104
OLIVIER PANIS
USA GRAND PRIX**

Toyota TF104

SPECIFICATIONS

- Chassis — Toyota TF104 & TF104B
- Type — Carbon-fibre and honeycomb composite structure
- Suspensions — Double wishbone, push rod with Torsion bar (Front / Rear)
- Engine — V10 Toyota RVX-04 (90°)
- Displacement — 3,000 cm³
- Distribution — 4 valves per cylinder
- Electronic ignition — Magneti Marelli
- Transmission — Toyota sequential longitudinal hydraulic semi-automatic 7 gears + reverse
- Clutch — Sachs
- Radiators — Denzo
- Fuel / oil — Esso / Esso
- Brakes (discs) — Brembo
- Brakes (calipers) — Brembo
- Spark plugs / battery — Denso / Panasonic
- Shock absorbers — Sachs/Toyota
- Tyres — Michelin Pilot
- Wheels dimensions — 13" x 13" (FR) / 12.5" x 13.7" (RE)
- Rims — BBS Magnesium
- Weight — 605 kg, driver, on board camera, ballast
- Wheel base — 3,090 mm
- Total length — 4,547 mm
- Total width — not revealed
- Total height — not revealed
- Front track — 1,425 mm
- Rear track — 1,411 mm

STATISTICS

- Number of Grand Prix — 51
- Best result in race — 2 x 5ᵗʰ
- Best qualification — 2 x 3ʳᵈ
- Number of fastest laps — 0
- Number of podiums — 0
- Number of drivers Championship — 0
- Number of constructors Championship — 0
- Number of points scored — 27

POSITION IN WORLD CHAMPIONSHIP

- 2002 — 10ᵗʰ – 2 pts
- 2003 — 8ᵗʰ – 16 pts
- 2004 — 8ᵗʰ – 9 pts

TEST DRIVERS 2004

- Ricardo ZONTA (BR)
- Ryan BRISCOE (AUS)

SUCCESSION OF DRIVERS 2004

- Olivier PANIS — 17 Grands Prix (Australia > Japan)
- Cristiano DA MATTA — 12 Grands Prix (Australia > Germany)
- Ricardo ZONTA — 5 Grands Prix (Hungary > China & Brazil)
- Jarno TRULLI — 2 Grands Prix (Japan & Brazil)

TEAM PROFILE

- Address — Toyota Motorsport GmbH Toyota-Allee 7 50858 Köln Deutschland
- Phone number — +49 (0) 223 418 23 444
- Fax number — +49 (0) 223 418 23 37
- Web — www.toyota-f1.com
- Founded in — 1999
- First Grand Prix — Australia 2002
- Official name — Panasonic Toyota Racing
- Chairman and Team Principal — Tsutomu Tomita
- President — John Howett
- Advisor — Ove Andersson
- Vice President — Toshiro Kurusu
- General Manager, F1 op. — Richard Cregan
- Chief Race Engineer — Dieter Gass
- Technical Director — Mike Gascoyne (chassis) Luca Marmorini (engine)
- Dir. Technical Coordination — Keizo Takahashi
- Chief Designer — Gustav Brunner
- Team manager — Ange Pasquali
- Race Engineer (16) — Ossi Oikarinen
- Race Engineer (17) — Humphrey Corbett
- Number of employees — 580
- Title Partner — Panasonic
- Technical Partners — BMC Software, Dassault Systèmes, EMC-Information strage, EOS, Exxon Mobile Corporation (Esso), KTC, MAN, Michelin, Toyoda
- Corporate Partners — AVEX Inc., DENSO, Ebbon-Dacs, ESPN STAR Sports, Intel Corporation, Kärcher Cleaning Systems, KDDI, Time Inc.
- Official Suppliers — BBS, DEA, Future Sports, Magneti Marelli, M.B.A. Production, Nolan, Pertinence - Software Solutions, Sika, Sparco, St.Georges, Technogym, Vuarnet, Yamaha

The powerless giant

People point at Ferrari's budget as a reason for their success, but the same argument certainly does not work in the case of Toyota. Yes, they are the youngest team in the sport, but given their huge resources and the targets they have set themselves, they should have done better than eighth in the Constructors,' just four points ahead of the cash-strapped Jordan crew. It is bad enough trying to run a team outside England – just ask Peter Sauber, but when your F1 effort is based in Cologne and the big decisions are made in Tokyo, you have a recipe for disaster. There is nothing wrong with the team's engine, but the chassis didn't work aerodynamically and even worse, the squad lacked

direction and leadership. The arrival of Mike Gascoyne will certainly help to get rid of the dead wood, as the Englishman's true skill lies, not with his engineering ability, but with his organisational chutzpah. However, a 2005 driver line up of Jarno Trulli and Ralf Schumacher does not look promising. Did the naïve Japanese not realise there are two Schumacher brothers in F1? Did they think they were buying the other one?

Jordan Ford

18. Nick HEIDFELD

DRIVER PROFILE

- Nom — *HEIDFELD*
- First name — *Nick*
- Nationality — *German*
- Date of birth — *May 10, 1977*
- Place of birth — *Mönchengladbach (D)*
- Lives in — *Stäfa (CH)*
- Marital status — *engaged with Patricia*
- Kids — *-*
- Hobbies — *tennis, golf, moto, music, Movie films*
- Favorite music — *big hits*
- Favorite meal — *pasta, appetizers*
- Favorite drinks — *orange juice with mineral water*
- Height — *164 cm*
- Weight — *59 kg*
- Web — *www.nickheidfeld.com*

STATISTICS | PRIOR TO F1

STATISTICS		PRIOR TO F1
Nber of Grand Prix	85	1986-92 *Karting*
Starts	84	1993 *Formula A Laval (F)*
Best result	*1 x 3ʳᵈ*	1994 *F. Ford 1600*
Best qualification	*1 x 4ᵗʰ*	*Champion (D)*
Fastest lap	0	1995 *F. Ford Champion*
Podiums	1	*1800 (D), F. Ford (D) (2ⁿᵈ)*
Accidents/offs	9	1996 *F3 (D) (3ʳᵈ)*
Not qualified	0	1997 *F3 Champion (D)*
GP in the lead	0	1998 *F3000 (2ⁿᵈ)*
Laps in the lead	0	1999 *F3000 Champion*
Kms in the lead	0	
Points scored	28	

F1 CAREER

1997 *McLaren-Mercedes. Test driver*
1998 *McLaren-Mercedes. Test driver*
1999 *McLaren-Mercedes. Test driver*
2000 *Prost-Peugeot. 0 pt. 20ᵗʰ of Championship.*
2001 *Sauber-Petronas. 12 pts. 8ᵗʰ of Championship.*
2002 *Sauber-Petronas. 7 pts. 10ᵗʰ of Championship.*
2003 *Sauber-Petronas. 6 pts. 14ᵗʰ of Championship.*
2004 *Jordan-Ford. 3 pts. 18ᵗʰ of Championship.*

19. Giorgio PANTANO

DRIVER PROFILE

- Nom — *PANTANO*
- First name — *Giorgio*
- Nationality — *Italian*
- Date of birth — *February 4, 1979*
- Place of birth — *Conselve (I)*
- Lives in — *Padova (I) & London (GB)*
- Marital status — *single*
- Kids — *-*
- Hobbies — *computers, Movie films*
- Favorite music — *Simon and Garfunkel*
- Favorite meal — *fish, raw shrimps*
- Favorite drinks — *mineral water with red wine*
- Height — *166 cm*
- Weight — *67 kg*
- Web — *www.giorgiopantano.com*

STATISTICS | PRIOR TO F1

STATISTICS		PRIOR TO F1
Nber of Grand Prix	14	1988-99 *Karting,*
Starts	14	*Jr. Champion (I) (93-94),*
Best result	*2 x 13ʳᵈ*	*(EUR) (93), (World) (93-94),*
Best qualification	*1 x 14ᵗʰ*	*FA Champion (EUR) (95-96),*
Fastest lap	0	*F. Super A (97 & 99) (3ʳᵈ),*
Podiums	0	*Paris-Bercy Cup (98) (3ʳᵈ)*
Accidents/offs	4	1999 *F. Palmer Audi (3ʳᵈ)*
Not qualified	0	2000 *F3 Champion (D & CH)*
GP in the lead	0	2001 *F3000 (3ʳᵈ)*
Laps in the lead	0	2002 *F3000 (2ⁿᵈ)*
Kms in the lead	0	2003 *F3000 (3ʳᵈ)*
Points scored	0	

F1 CAREER

2004 *Jordan-Ford. 0 pt. 24ᵗʰ of Championship.*

Nick Heidfeld seems to be one of those drivers who has the knack of being in the wrong place at the wrong time. Given that his career was supported by Mercedes, that he was Raikkonen's team-mate when they were both at Sauber and that he was tipped for stardom, how come he ended up driving (unpaid) for the financially and technically bankrupt Jordan team? No one said life had to be fair, but it did not stop Little Nick bringing all his talent to bear on the job of driving the uncompetitive yellow car to the best of his ability. There is plenty of talk of commitment in F1, but if you want to see what it means, go and stand at the side of the track and watch Heidfeld at work. His skill certainly flattered the performance of the EJ14. His reward may come late in life as, at the time of writing, he is due to be tested by Williams with a view to a 2005 drive.

He joined the team with all the right credentials, but he was far too wild in the cockpit as he realised he had plenty to learn about Formula 1. Although Pantano began to get to grips with the job, when the results did not come, he started to overdrive and financial and contractual problems provided the team with a good reason to sack him and replace him with Timo Glock, who had already stood in for the Italian in Canada, for the last three races

19. Timo GLOCK

DRIVER PROFILE

- Nom — *GLOCK*
- First name — *Timo*
- Nationality — *German*
- Date of birth — *March 10ᵗʰ 1982*
- Place of birth — *Lindenfels (D)*
- Lives in — *Lohne (D)*
- Marital status — *single*
- Kids — *-*
- Hobbies — *Go-Kart, tennis, bowling, skiing*
- Favorite music — *pop, rock*
- Favorite meal — *pasta*
- Favorite drinks — *mineral water*
- Height — *169 cm*
- Weight — *65 kg*
- Web — *www.timoglock.com*

STATISTICS | PRIOR TO F1

STATISTICS		PRIOR TO F1
Nber of Grand Prix	4	1998-99 *Karting*
Best result	*1 x 7ᵗʰ*	2000 *F. BMW ADAC Jr. Champion*
Best qualification	*2 x 16ᵗʰ*	2001 *F. BMW ADAC Champion*
Accidents/offs	0	2002 *F3 (D) (3ʳᵈ)*
Points scored	2	2003 *F3 Euro series (5ᵗʰ)*

F1 CAREER

2004 *Jordan-Ford. 2 pts. 19ᵗʰ of Championship.*

The joke goes that he got the job because Eddie Jordan thought he was a fellow Irishman called Tim O'Glock! But in all seriousness, winter testing had shown that here was a young man with a good technical understanding and a cool head, who could bring some useful data home as a Friday tester. He got his first race break in Canada and having messed up qualifying, he drove a sensible race to score points in his F1 debut. A job well done.

Eddie Jordan

James Robinson

Tim Edwards

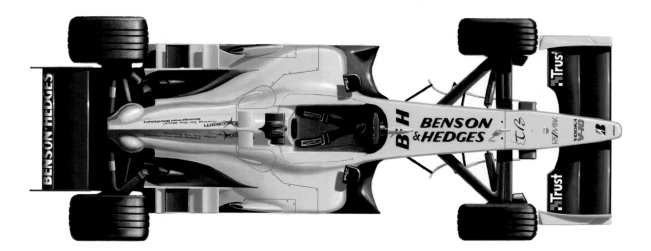

JORDAN EJ14-FORD
NICK HEIDFELD
MONACO GRAND PRIX

R. MENARD

Jordan EJ14-Ford

SPECIFICATIONS

- Chassis — Jordan EJ14
- Type — Full carbon fibre and honeycomb composite monocoque
- Suspensions — Composite pushrods activating chassis (F.) / gearbox (R.) mounted dampers and torsion bars, unequal length composite aerodynamic wishbones, anti-roll bar and cast uprights
- Engine — V10 Ford Cosworth RS2 (90°)
- Displacement — 2,998 cm³
- Distribution — 4 valves per cylinder
- Electronic ignition — Pi Research
- Transmission — Jordan longitudinal with sequential electrohydraulic gear changes, 7 gears + reverse
- Clutch — Jordan / AP Racing
- Radiators — Secan / IMI Marston
- Fuel / oil — Elf / Elf
- Brakes (discs) — Carbone Industrie
- Brakes (calipers) — Brembo
- Spark plugs/battery — Champion / not reveald
- Shock absorbers — Jordan Penske
- Tyres — Bridgestone Potenza
- Wheels dimensions — 13"
- Rims — BBS
- Weight — 605 kg, driver, on board camera, ballast
- Wheel base — + 3,000 mm
- Total length — 4,600 mm
- Total width — 1,800 mm
- Total height — 950 mm
- Front track — 1,480 mm
- Rear track — 1,418 mm

TEAM PROFILE

- Address — Jordan Grand Prix Ltd., Buckingham Road, Silverstone, Northants, NN12 8TJ Great Britain
- Phone number — +44 (0) 1327 850 800
- Fax number — +44 (0) 1327 857 993
- Web — www.f1jordan.com
- Founded in — 1981
- First Grand Prix — USA 1991
- Official name — Jordan Ford
- Chief Executive and Team Principal — Eddie Jordan
- Chief Operating Officer & Chief Financial Officer — Richard O'Driscoll
- Head of Race and Test Engineering — James Robinson
- Head of Design — John McQuilliam
- Head of Aerodynamics — Nicolo' Petrucci
- Head of electronic — Mike Wroe
- Head of Operations — David Williams
- Team Manager — Tim Edwards
- Head of race and test engineering — James Robinson
- Race Engineer — Dominic Harlow, Gerry Hughes
- Chief mechanic — Andrew Stevenson
- Number-one mechanic (N.H.) — Nick Burrows
- Number-one mechanic (G.P.) — Matt Deane
- Number of employees — 200
- Official Sponsors — Benson and Hedges, Puma, RE/MAX Europe, Phard, TB, Trust
- Official Suppliers — Vielife, Powermarque, Laurent-Perrier, TMA, NHK Spring Co. Ltd, Principal Colour, Quicksilver, Liqui Moly, ATI
- Technical Partners — Bridgestone, Celerant Consulting, Sabelt, Touchpaper, Scientio

STATISTICS

- Number of Grand Prix — 231
- Number of victories — 4
- Number of pole positions — 2
- Number of fastest laps — 2
- Number of podiums — 18
- Number of drivers Championship — 0
- Number of constructors Championship — 0
- Number of points scored — 279

POSITION IN WORLD CHAMPIONSHIP

1991	5th – 13 pts	1998	4th – 34 pts
1992	11th – 1 pt	1999	3rd – 61 pts
1993	10th – 3 pts	2000	6th – 17 pts
1994	5th – 28 pts	2001	5th – 19 pts
1995	6th – 21 pts	2002	6th – 9 pts
1996	5th – 22 pts	2003	9th – 13 pts
1997	5th – 33 pts	2004	9th – 5 pts

Robert Doornbos

TEST DRIVERS 2004

- Timo GLOCK (D)
- Robert DOORNBOS (MC)

SUCCESSION OF DRIVERS 2004

- Nick HEIDFELD — all 18 Grands Prix
- Giorgio PANTANO — 14 Grands Prix (except CDN, CHN, J, BR)
- Timo GLOCK — 4 Grands Prix (CDN, CHN, J, BR)

Show me the money!

The colourful Irish team's fourteenth F1 season looked like being its last. The glory days of wins and being third in the championship were long gone and the yellow trucks were parked with Minardi next to the paddock dustbins. The loss of Gary Anderson as technical director meant that, although Jordan had some competent designers and engineers, it had no technical leadership. Money was short, so there was no pre-season testing – the EJ14 was only signed off very late in November 2003 - and therefore no understanding of their Bridgestone tyres. The Cosworth engine was at least 70 horsepower down on the one used by Jaguar. The need to survive meant no money was spent on development and, having occasionally given Jaguar, Toyota and Sauber a hard time in the early races, by the end of the year, Jordan struggled to beat Minardi. But you cannot write off Eddie Jordan and it seems the team has secured a last gasp deal to secure Toyota engines and there are a couple of buyers for the team waiting in the wings. The biggest obstacle to getting its cars on the grid for 2005 will be EJ's willingness to take a back seat in running the operation, as this is a condition of purchase for the buyers. "The team is like a mistress to Eddie," said an insider. "He can't bear the idea of anyone else getting their hands on her."

Minardi Cosworth

20. Gianmaria BRUNI

DRIVER PROFILE

- Nom — *BRUNI*
- First name — *Gianmaria*
- Nationality — *Italian*
- Date of birth — *May 30, 1981*
- Place of birth — *Roma (I)*
- Lives in — *Roma (I)*
- Marital status — *single*
- Kids — *-*
- Hobbies — *giving himself a workout, karting*
- Favorite music — *everything except opera*
- Favorite meal — *chicken salad and white pasta*
- Favorite drinks — *Coca-Cola light, orange juice*
- Height — *182 cm*
- Weight — *70 kg*
- Web — *www.gianmariabruni.it*

STATISTICS

Nber of Grand Prix	18
Starts	18
Best result	3 x 14th
Best qualification	1 x 16th
Fastest lap	0
Podiums	0
Accidents/offs	2
Not qualified	0
GP in the lead	0
Laps in the lead	0
Kms in the lead	0
Points scored	0

PRIOR TO F1

- 1991-94 *Karting*
- 1995 *Karting (EUR) (3rd)*
- 1997 *F. Renault Campus (I)*
- 1998 *F. Renault Campus Champion (I)*
- 1999 *F. Renault Champion (EUR)*
- 2000 *F3 (GB) (5th)*
- 2001 *F3 (GB) (4th), Zandvoort Marlboro Masters (4th)*
- 2002 *F3000 Euro series (12th)*
- 2003 *F3000 Euro series (3rd)*

F1 CAREER

2004 *Minardi-Cosworth. 0 pt. 25th of Championship.*

21. Zsolt BAUMGARTNER

DRIVER PROFILE

- Nom — *BAUMGARTNER*
- First name — *Zsolt*
- Nationality — *Hungarian*
- Date of birth — *January 1, 1981*
- Place of birth — *Budapest (H)*
- Lives in — *Budapest (H)*
- Marital status — *single*
- Kids — *-*
- Hobbies — *Airborne acrobatics, web, football*
- Favorite music — *hits, music of the 80s*
- Favorite meal — *pasta, salads*
- Favorite drinks — *tap water*
- Height — *178 cm*
- Weight — *74 kg*
- Web — *www.zsolt.baumgartner.hu*

STATISTICS

Nber of Grand Prix	20
Starts	20
Best result	1 x 8th
Best qualification	3 x 17th
Fastest lap	0
Podiums	0
Accidents/offs	4
Not qualified	0
GP in the lead	0
Laps in the lead	0
Kms in the lead	0
Points scored	1

PRIOR TO F1

- 1994-95 *Karting Jr. A (H) (2nd)*
- 1996 *Go-kart*
- 1997 *F. Renault (D) (2nd)*
- 1998 *F. Renault ("La Filière" School)*
- 1999 *F. Renault 2000 (D & EUR) (3rd)*
- 2000 *F3 (D) (9th)*
- 2001 *F3 (D)(17th), F3000*
- 2002 *F3000 (15th)*
- 2003 *F3000 (14th)*

F1 CAREER

2003 *Jordan-Ford. 0 pt. 24th of Championship.*
2004 *Minardi-Cosworth. 1 pt. 20th of Championship.*

After a handful of races with Jordan in 2003, the Hungarian pay-driver made the inevitable switch to Minardi. It was all too easy to write Baumgartner off as a dilettante son of a rich father, but laughter in the paddock turned to respect by the end of the year. Zsolt actually worked at his job and improved, gaining the respect of the team. He proved to be very reliable and would usually bring the car home, if it allowed him to do so. And finishing races is vitally important for a little team like Minardi. Finishing eighth and scoring a point in Indianapolis of all places was the icing on the cake.

The Italian arrived at Minardi with a more impressive cv than his team-mate. His season started well and he showed the speed the team had hoped for. However, he then went through a mid-season dip, clashing with members of the team on a variety of issues, before producing some good drives at the tail end of the season. As usual, when you are behind the wheel of a Minardi, it is hard to show what you can do.

Paul Stoddart

Gabriele Tredozi

**MINARDI PS04B-COSWORTH
ZSOLT BAUMGARTNER
JAPANESE GRAND PRIX**

Minardi PS04B-Cosworth

SPECIFICATIONS

- Chassis — Minardi PS04B
- Type — Carbon fibre, honeycomb composite monocoque
- Suspensions — Double wishbone, push rods / roll bar (FR / RE)
- Engine — V10 Cosworth Racing CR-3L (72°)
- Displacement — 2,998 cm³
- Distribution — 4 valves per cylinder
- Electronic ignition — Magneti Marelli Step 10
- Transmission — Minardi sequential longitudinal hydraulic semi-automatic 6 gears + reverse
- Clutch — AP Racing
- Radiators — Secan Minardi
- Fuel / oil — Elf / Elf
- Brakes (discs) — Hitco / Brembo
- Brakes (calipers) — Hitco / Brembo
- Spark plugs / battery — Champion / not revealed
- Shock absorbers — Sachs
- Tyres — Bridgestone Potenza
- Wheels dimensions — 13" x 12" (AV) / 13" x 13.7" (AR)
- Rims — O.Z. Racing
- Weight — 605 kg, driver, on board camera, ballast
- Wheel base — 3,097 mm
- Total length — 4,548 mm
- Total width — 1,800 mm
- Total height — 950 mm
- Front track — 1,480 mm
- Rear track — 1,410 mm

TEAM PROFILE

- Address — Minardi Team SpA
  Via Spallanzani, 21
  48018 Faenza (RA) - Italy
- Phone number — +39 0 546 696 111
- Fax number — +39 0 546 620 998
- Web — www.minardi.it
- Founded in — 1974
- First Grand Prix — Brazil 1985
- Official name — Minardi Cosworth
- Team Principal — Paul Stoddart
- Director in charge of young driver development — Gian Carlo Minardi
- Technical Director — Gabriele Tredozi
- Chief Aerodynamicist — Loïc Bigois
- Sporting Director — John Walton
- Chief Mechanic — Paolo Pincastelli
- Race Engineer (G.B.) — Greg Wheeler
- Race Engineer (Z.B.) — Alex Varnava
- Number of employees — 113
- Sponsors — (Wilux), Superfund, Tosinvest, CIB Lizing, Uniqa, Standox, Santogal, Fondmetal, Golden Palace, Allegrini, X-Drinks
- Technical Sponsors — Cosworth, Bridgestone, Magneti Marelli, Brevi, Puma, 3D Systems, Cimatron, Aurora Engineering, Fedem, Beta, CD adapco Group, IT Unlimited, Netscalibur, Feedback
- Official Suppliers — LeasePlan, X-Drinks, Global Group, Calligaris, Caravell, Poderi Morini, Acqua Fabia, Rustichella, Ursini, Rekico

STATISTICS

- Number of Grand Prix — 321
- Best result in race — 2 x 4th
- Best qualification — 1 x 2nd
- Number of fastest laps — 0
- Number of podiums — 0
- Number of drivers Championship — 0
- Number of constructors Championship — 0
- Number of points scored — 31

POSITION IN WORLD CHAMPIONSHIP

1985	no class.	1992	11th – 1 pt	1999	10th – 1 pt
1986	no class.	1993	8th – 7 pts	2000	no class.
1987	no class.	1994	10th – 5 pts	2001	11th – 0 pt
1988	10th – 1 pt	1995	10th – 1 pt	2002	9th – 2 pts
1989	10th – 6 pts	1996	no class.	2003	10th – 0 pt
1990	no class.	1997	no class.	2004	10th – 1 pt
1991	7th – 6 pts	1998	no class.		

TEST DRIVERS 2004

- Bas LEINDERS (B)
- Tiago MONTEIRO (P)

SUCCESSION OF DRIVERS 2004

- Gianmaria BRUNI — all 18 Grands Prix
- Zsolt BAUMGARTNER — all 18 Grands Prix

Bas Leinders

Hanging on as usual

How much longer can Minardi stay in Formula 1 and what purpose does it serve? The tiny Faenza-based squad, the fourth oldest in the sport, has a colourful and honourable past and without them, the grid would be poorer in spirit. But in racing terms, Paul Stoddart's squad achieved little more than survival, coming away with just one little point. With only one day of testing before the start of the season, virtually no wind tunnel work over the winter and the same Cosworth CR3 engine as in 2003, you have to give the team an "A" for effort and they did actually score one point. Reliability was not too bad, given the lack of development and Minardi could virtually ignore the one engine per weekend rule, as the penalty for an engine change – dropping ten places on the grid, could hardly affect a team that had a season ticket booking for the back row. However, given the rate at which the top teams pressed on with development, Minardi did well to prevent the performance gap from growing too much during the year and, occasionally, it embarrassed its nearest rival, Jordan. Stoddart's greatest contribution to the season was galvanising the other teams (except Ferrari) into trying to come up with a workable solution to reduce costs and improve the show.

SPOTLIGHTS

As in the past the F1 Yearbook
provides an analysis of the season
from the pen of five of the best
journalists of different nationalities in
F1. This gives the reader an insight
into the state of mind of the
Japanese, German, English, Canadian
and French actors in the Formula 1
drama.

2004: a British point of view

Flavio Briatore, the good friend

Bernie Ecclestone once described himself as, "A very good friend, and a very bad enemy",
and in the F1 paddock there are those who say the same of Flavio Briatore, the team principal
to whom Bernie is closest.

Nigel Roebuck - Autosport, London

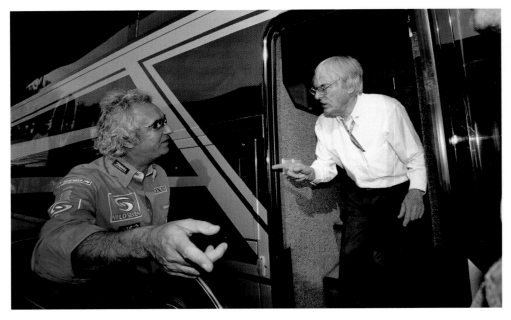

They hit it off from the moment Flavio came into F1 in the early '90s, taking command of Benetton's F1 team. By 1994 it was making history, Michael Schumacher winning his first World Championship.

"*Flavio,*" said Ecclestone, "*knew nothing about racing before he came into the business. He never served an apprenticeship - so he can maybe have a different approach from the other team principals.*"

Indeed, Briatore does have a different approach, not least in the way he sometimes speaks about his drivers. At the US Grand Prix in 2000 Giancarlo Fisichella qualified a poor 15th, and Flav was furious. "*Why? Because Fisichella is f****** lazy!*"

Not the sort of quote you get from Jean Todt or Ron Dennis.

"*I was angry that day,*" Briatore said, "*because Indy was a new track, and I sent the engineers in early. And Fisichella? He arrives two days late, because he was in Hawaii, and the weather was good! I don't accept that. When we have fun, we have fun, but when we're working, we need rules, and if someone does something like that - or like Jenson did in Monte Carlo - I think there's something wrong.*"

What did Button do in Monte Carlo?
"*Well, he was very young. He'd had some success with Williams in his first year, and now he had all the*

British press around him like he was the new Senna. Suddenly he had some money, so he had this big boat moored alongside the motorhome, and I didn't like that at all! He was like Giancarlo: very talented, but lazy. Now he's a driver. Eventually I had a good relationship with him, and also with Fisichella.*"

For 2002 Briatore replaced Fisichella with Trulli, and now for '05 he replaces Jarno with...Giancarlo. "*Actually, Fisichella did a good job in 2001, but then his manager asked for an amount of money that made no sense to me. We didn't have the car to win, and I really didn't need heavy expenses in the driver budget. The paddock is full of managers, but 90% of them don't understand the business.*"

One of those managers, of course, is Briatore himself, and he seems to understand the business pretty well. As team principal of Renault, he is also the manager of number one driver Fernando Alonso.

"*I want to win with Renault, OK? Everybody says I employ only 'my' drivers, but I only care about the team. I was the manager of Trulli, and our contract expired this year - and people assume that's why I didn't keep him for '05. Then they said I fired him because he didn't keep the third place in Magny-Cours, and, sure, I was very upset by that, but it was not one issue which made me change.*"

When Trulli won superbly in Monaco, his future looked assured, not least because it seemed unlikely a French-owned team could drop the winner of the most prestigious race in F1. Asked to confirm that Jarno would be staying, however, Briatore refused.

"*Yes, because everyone was over-emotional. This is business, OK? You never make a decision on emotion - if you do that, you're not the manager any more. Jarno can be a great driver - his qualifying lap in Monte Carlo was a masterpiece, for example. But*

Nigel Roebuck
56 years old, decided to quit his industrial job and enter journalism at the age of 24. In 1971, he starts writing for the American magazine «Car & Driver», before joining the British weekly motor racing magazine «Autosport» in 1976. He is covering Formula One since 1977, while working for the «Sunday Tmes», for the «Auto Week» and the Japanese magazine «Racing On».

you have to keep your feet on the ground. Yes, it's great if you win a race - but in the meantime you lose 200, and I have to pay you for 201! Maybe his motivation will come back with Toyota..."

In the meantime, Fisichella returns to Renault, a development which surprised many, given past difficulties with Briatore.

"You see a lot of drivers," said Flav, "with fantastic talent - Jean Alesi was like that - but they never develop it. I think Fisichella still has the chance to do that, and he knows he must, because it's the last chance for him, isn't it? If he misses this train, in three years nobody will remember him - because he's done nothing. Absolutely nothing."

While not even Briatore would claim his financial interest in drivers to be altruistic, several, including Mark Webber, might not be in F1 without him. "Some guys," said Mark, "have moaned, 'Jesus, I've signed my life away to Flav', but I had no choice. I did my first year with Minardi, and said to Flavio, 'Look, I've got some baggage', meaning that Paul Stoddart had bankrolled me to that point, and he was going to have a slice of my earnings for the future. So Flavio helped out, and without him I wouldn't be in F1. He's been very fair with me."

"Sure," Briatore said. "I don't think any team or driver has had any problems with me in the last 15 years. I'm very hard, but if I give my word, it's my word. In F1 some people change opinions between morning and afternoon. I'm not like that."

Of all the drivers on his books, however, the most valuable is Alonso, and it mystifies Flavio still that he didn't need to fight to get him. "When I bought Fernando from Minardi - for a number less than a million dollars - I was the only one there with a cheque. OK, a lot of people are happy to pay $25m - later! Talk is easy, but I'm doing business. And if I buy a driver, maybe in the end I'm repaid for what I spent, simple as that."

"Alonso for sure is special: if he can develop his talent 100%, he'll be as good as anyone in the last 20 years. In the races he tries very, very, hard, and his consistency is fantastic."

"A driver is an employee of the company, and a lot depends on him, but you have hundreds of people working very hard to make things good for him, and they don't vacation in Hawaii. So sometimes, yes, I've had problems with a driver like Alesi, or Fisichella, or Button. You don't keep saying, 'Oh, you're the star,

you're so wonderful'. No. When you're wonderful, you're wonderful, and when you're bad, you're bad. If you damage a car, I don't care, really. But if I see you doing something not correct when it comes to the people working for you, then I get really furious."

'Hedonist' is the word that comes to mind when you think of Flavio Briatore. In the papers you won't normally find too many pictures of F1 team principals, and only then in the sports pages, but Flav is frequently to be seen elsewhere, invariably with a supermodel on his arm. As he said earlier, "When we have fun, we have fun," andundoubtedly there is more in his life than motor racing. "I'm different from a lot of people, in that I have other means. For example, I have a restaurant and night club - the Cipriani - in London. And when you're dealing with something like this, you're not talking about millions here, millions there. That keeps my feet on the ground. I have other businesses, and they're all successful." He is optimistic about Renault's prospects for 2005. "For the first time we should be competitive on engines. In 2003 I said we should forget the wide-angle engine, and nobody at Renault was happy, but if we hadn't changed the engine, the team was going nowhere. Now we're going in the right direction. Maybe we won't be at the level of the very top - Ferrari, BMW, Honda - but it won't be a difference of 80 or 100 horsepower, like in '03. One per cent here or there is no big deal for us - we're used to 20%..."

In 1997 Briatore left Benetton, and - apparently - F1. Then, he said, he spotted a commercial opportunity. "It seemed to me like nobody had an engine, so I put together a deal with Renault, and took the risk of creating Supertec. Commercially it worked very well."
It certainly did. There were deals with Williams, Benetton, Arrows and BAR, and all the time Flav was working closely with the Renault people - who decided ultimately on a return to F1, and with a very ambitious project. "We decided the only way was to take over another team. We discussed it briefly with Jordan, and then did a deal with Benetton."

As and when his time at Renault ends, what comes next for Briatore? Some believe he will be involved in another engine project, supplying the forthcoming 2.4-litre V8 motors to teams perhaps left high and dry by departing manufacturers.

"It's true," he allowed, "that I want relatively simple engine rules, so that somebody like Meccachrome can have the possibility to make engines, and not be 80 horsepower behind the manufacturers. That way, if Frank lost BMW, or Ron lost Mercedes, or whatever, they could make a commercial deal with Meccachrome, at the right price, and they could carry on racing. Right now nobody seems to be thinking about that, but what would Williams and BAR have done without Supertec?"

"I worry about the state of F1, because I think we treat our customers so badly. For the event we are putting on, we spend way too much money, on too much stupid, unnecessary, technology and people don't understand why we do. They don't like it - they want to see the driver really driving the car, and they're right! The fact is, we are in the entertainment business - and where is the money coming from? No one ever came in my office with a cheque, saying, 'I want to buy your technology'!"

"So I worry, but I think there are others who should worry more, because I don't have one cent in the business now. But people who have millions and millions invested...these are the people I don't understand that they don't see things have to change. Because of the Concorde Agreement, we have a situation in F1 where you need agreement from everybody if anything is to change. I never saw a company run with 100% of the vote - Jesus, you don't manage a condominium with 100% agreement! "
"So now I have the boat on charter, OK? So if the sea's bad, f*** it, I give it back to the owner. But somebody who owns their own boat, and maybe the boat sinks...oh my god! Not for me, no way. I charter..."
A different approach from the rest. Bernie, as usual, had it right.

<
Jarno Trulli wins the Monaco Grand Prix. Flavio is happy, but he keeps his feet on the ground. "Yes, it's great if you win a race - but in the meantime you lose 200, and I have to pay you for 201!"

<
(opposite)
Bernie and Flavio: a solid trust in each other.

2004 aus deutscher Sicht

Mercedes-Benz nearly bought McLaren and BMW almost threw in the towel.

The Scuderia Ferrari's domination of the 2004 season left almost nothing for its rivals, not even crumbs! The Mercedes-Benz and BMW Boards of Directors hesitated about making a radical change of direction. Italian domination was hard to swallow on the other side of the Rhine.

Anno Hecker – Frankfurter Allgemeine Zeitung

Towards mid-season when it looked like nothing could stop Michael Schumacher's triumphal march towards the title he refused to accept any congratulations. "*What if McLaren or Williams were to turn the situation around?*" he asked. "*It could happen next week.*"
Michael was very reluctant to talk about his rivals. He preferred to praise the "fantastic performance" of his Ferrari. In fact, his reticence did not fool anybody. The traditional top teams were far too weak to threaten the Scuderia and previous mid-field runners like Renault and BAR were not yet quick enough to carry the fight to the Italians.
In the DaimlerChrysler headquarters in Stuttgart Schumacher's comment soon spread around. But how to answer it? Wasn't the Anglo-German team already working flat out? During the summer it had brought out a 'B'version of the MP4-19 to try and compensate for the flaws of the basic version. "B" is for better," quipped an optimistic Norbert Haug, the boss of the Mercedes competitions department after its first race. Kimi Raïkkönen's win in Belgium added weight to his words; "*It's all going in the right direction,*" he said. However, the frequent changes of cars over the past couple of seasons combined with the large number of defeats by Ferrari and BMW left their mark. And just a short time before the last grand prix a rumour that nobody would dare confirm at either DaimlerChrysler or McLaren started doing the rounds, namely, that the team would be completely restructured, DaimlerChrysler would take over McLaren and Ron Dennis and Norbert Haug would both go.

"*Ask Stuttgart what's happening!*" said Norbert Haug when he was questioned about these rumours in November 2004. "*You'll be told that I'm still the competitions boss.*" He was right. Haug is solidly installed in his job, maybe more so than ever. He does a good job but one wrong step and he'll be out. Immediately. In fact behind all this there was a big battle going on. On 1st October Eckhard Cordes took the place of Jürgen Hubbert as Mercedes-Benz managing director responsible to Daimler-Chrysler. Cordes thus inherited the responsibility for motor sport and he is someone who holds the company's image in high esteem so he was very dissatisfied with the McLaren-Mercedes team, which he wanted to transform into a 100% Mercedes-Mercedes entity.
DaimlerChrysler already owns 40% of McLaren and by the end of 2005 the engine manufacturer Ilmor will belong to it completely as was planned a long time ago by Haug and Hubbert. They both want to integrate McLaren into the Mercedes-Benz family as they did in the past with AGM. The year 2005 will see the fiftieth anniversary of the 'Silver Arrows' era when Mercedes withdrew from racing, following the Le Mans accident which cost the lives of some seventy people, and the company wants to celebrate it in style. Norbert Haug is one tough customer. Every year doubts are cast on his role so he is ready for anything. He has been in charge of his department for fifteen years but they way Cordes saw it he would not be there when Mercedes achieved its aim of a 100% in-house team. It was not that his competence

was questioned but Cordes wanted to start with a clean sheet. He had no objection to a two-handed management system: one contact for the complex political games in F1and another for the technical side. It was similar to the BMW system where Gerhard Berger was in one role and Mario Theissen in the other. It then became obvious that Mercedes had approached the former Austrian driver about this role. Berger after a couple of year rest was aching to get back into F1 in a position that BMW had refused him. Gerhard left the Munich Company as his proposal for the firm to separate from Williams and do everything itself had been rejected at the last minute. Thus, he would find exactly what he wanted at Mercedes.
However, this enticing prospect ran into a snag: Ron Dennis! His demands upset the applecart at the last minute. He wanted 750 million euros for his factory, which he reduced a little in the spring. In May Jürgen Hubbert, the DaimlerChrysler director, suggested that both parties get round a table to discuss it. But the sum of 500 million euros that Ron wanted was

Anno Hecker
39 years old, worked first as a physical education instructor befor turning to journalism in 1986. After working as a political correspondent for a Bonn news agency, he joined "Frankfurter Allgemeine Zeitung" in 1991 to cover motor sports. He specialised in stories combinig politics and sport.

still too high for the German company caught in fact between the hammer and the anvil. On the one hand how could it ask its employees to make a bigger effort because of the poor economic situation and on the other, spend half-a-million euros on a race team? The factory that Ron Dennis had built was designed by the famous architect Sir Norman Foster and it had cost - if the English papers were to be believed - some 300 million pounds (around 500 million euros) instead of the 200 million originally foreseen.

«On the one hand how could it ask its employees to make a bigger effort because of the poor economic situation and on the other, spend half-a-million euros on a race team?»

So Mercedes quickly realised that buying the team was no longer a real option. Either Ron Dennis was prepared to concede a big reduction or Cordes had to change his mind. In fact, what materialised was that he had other more urgent problems to solve and he decided to wait for the 2005 season. His sound bite, "*we can start from scratch too,*" gave a lot of room for interpretation. Could DaimlerChrysler envisage stopping purely and simply? "*No,*" said Jürgen Hubbert during his farewell speech at the beginning of November in Stuttgart. "*This team has many more successful years ahead of it.*" In the BMW camp the F1 enthusiasts are not quite so sure. The win scored in the last round of the 2004 championship ahead of their national 'enemy' helped to reconcile the company and F1. However, the Sao Paolo winner did not hesitate to remind the Munich Company that he was leaving. Juan Pablo Montoya, a genius behind the wheel, is off to McLaren-Mercedes. Ralf Schumacher is joining Toyota perhaps given a 'friendly' push by Frank Williams. So what was "*the best pair in the pit lane*" as Gerhard Berger said in 2001 had split up and there was no happy end. The make's discontent with all these political problems was never mentioned in public. Only Berger said what people thought in private, "*Williams only wants drivers still in the waiting room,*" by which he meant that the team would only hire what remained. Mark Webber is certainly very good and Frank Williams made the right decision in taking

him on. But is he a potential grand prix winner and world champion?
The search for the second driver is a management disaster. The sad story of Jenson Button, who was already under contract for 2005 while Williams was trying to get his signature on a piece of paper, shows to what extent BMW is dependent on the English team. It is just another bone of contention to add to a well stocked cupboard. Since the start of the partnership between the two companies the former has complained of constant weaknesses. "*It's the same thing each year. The car's aerodynamics are not good enough and when the problem is solved, it's too late,*" said Berger in the spring. And how right he was. To coin a phrase: Williams's new nose was a broken nose for the team!
Under pressure from BMW the Williams engineers are now obliged to collaborate more closely with their BMW counterparts. In the spring Patrick Head finally left his seat as technical director and was replaced by the young Sam Michel. "*That'll do the team good,*" commented Ralf Schumacher. Yes provided that peace is restored in the department. The dismissal of Aontonia Terzi in the autumn is not really a step in this direction. She has been replaced by Loic Bigeois ex-Prost and Minardi but he is

not generally reckoned to be an ace in the wind tunnel. The rumour that Adrian Newey was about to leave McLaren to return to Williams was soon quashed. The era of individualism seems to be over in F1. Both Munich and Grove seem to consider 2005 as a transition year. But will BMW still be present?
The era where a hyper-powerful engine in an average chassis was an excellent publicity vehicle is over. BMW's rivals have closed the gap in terms of sheer grunt and the V10 from Bavaria was no longer the reference in 2004. Towards the end of the season it looked like Honda had seized the advantage.
It would have been a good basis on which to build. To be able to stop everything at the height of success is the golden rule of German company directors. Other wise the image that stays in everybody's mind is that of failure.
The on-going battle concerning the 2006 engine may have dealt a deathblow to BMW's ambitions. The make has no wish to develop a 2.4 litre V8, which resembles a series production model. This rule changed decided by Max Mosley could serve as an excellent pretext to pull out. Thus, BMW could quit without a world title and whose fault?
Why other people's, of course!

∧
Kimi Raïkkönen will go for it whatever the circumstances, even on two wheels. The Finn never gave up trying but not until the appearance of the 'B' spec version of the MP4-19 did he begin to obtain some results including his Belgian Grand Prix victory.

<
(Page opposite)
Above:
Mario Theissen and Norbert Haug caught in deep conversation. What are they discussing? The Future?

"And you find it funny, this Formula 1 lark?" "Not really, but at least we're well paid!" Jürgen Hubbert and Norbert Haug cast a jaundiced eye over the track. The 2004 season failed to live up to their expectations.
∨

In Italy, when one says Ferrari one means Fiat...

... and cars in general mean Turin, the capital of the Italian auto industry. While one might see badges proclaiming Fiat, Alfa Romeo, Lancia, Autobianchi, Ferrari and Maserati, they are all part of the one Fiat family.

Paolo Ciccarone - Radio Monte Carlo

Paolo Ciccarone, was born in Lucera, in the Italian province of Foggia on 29th May 1958. His Formula 1 career began as a freelance photographer for Autosprint, before he switched to journalism, working for motor sport magazine Rombo. Since April 2000 he has headed up Radio Monte Carlo's racing coverage. He follows the grands prix, digging out all the secrets Formula 1 has to hide. He has also worked for the digital TV station, Tele+. Over the past few seasons, he has written for daily papers like Avvenire and Gazzetta de Mezzogiorno, writing profiles of the heroes of Formula 1.

It is a double edged sword that, on the one hand, solidly ties the Italian car industry to the Turin company and on the other, it represents the hopes and aspirations of the entire nation. Italy is not like Germany, where the market is unaffected by problems for BMW, or how Mercedes is doing or if VW and Porsche are expanding or contracting. Italy has nothing in common with France either, where the state supported Renault firm is in competition with Citroen and Peugeot. In Italy,

everything goes through Turin: for better or for worse, everything depends on the one group that includes the most prestigious marques such as Ferrari and Maserati. The links and agreements are too complicated to explain unless one can see all the contracts. Michael Schumacher's successes in Formula 1 have helped relaunch Italian style in the car world. But to say Ferrari in this instance does not mean Fiat. Ever since Luca di Montezemolo agreed to take over the presidency

of the Turin group, he has pushed hard to sell the "made in Italy" brand that, strangely enough, passes through Germany. It is not just Schumacher and F1, but a philosophy and a strategy that Montezemolo pursues within the group. Turin is a cosmopolitan city and at Fiat, they talk in several tongues. In November 2003, after the arrival at Fiat of Austrian, Herbert Demel, it was the turn of Spain's Jose Maria Alapont to take the reins at Iveco, while just two months later, Stefen Ketter (ex Audi and BMW) took over quality control. Then, Johann Wohlfarter (ex Volkswagen) was put in charge of development and communications for the sales network and Englishman Martin Leach took charge at Maserati. Since the 1st November 2004, Harald Wester, another refugee from Audi, heads up engineering and design. Other new arrivals in Turin include Karl-Heinz Kalbfell, the former president of BMW-owned Rolls Royce, who is now the top man at Alfa Romeo, replacing Daniele Bandiera. And let's not forget Wolfgang Egger, in charge of "Centro Stile."

This so called "normalisation" process, instigated by Sergio Marchionne, the CEO of the Holding company, is taking place on all fronts and has made those at managerial level rather nervous, as they hang on in the face of savage power struggles. In Turin, those worries continue, because of the delay in ratifying Kalbfell's appointment at Alfa Romeo, given that it had been considered a done deal for quite a while. The managers had hoped to halt this Italian blood bath thanks to various personal ties to members of the Agnelli clan. That was not the case and Fiat is finding itself more and more in the hands of "foreigners." Despite this, Luca di Montezemolo, president of Fiat, of

Confidustria (the Italian industrial association,) of Ferrari and various other companies, continues to talk about made in Italy, about style and strength, much of it based on victories that have come courtesy of yet another German, Michael Schumacher, who took his 7th world title in 2004, his 5th in a row with Ferrari. And yet, for the first time in ages, the usually positive Ferrari accounts have shown signs of a slight shudder. Investment in Maserati was held to blame. However, not one Italian newspaper pointed out that the deficit of 18.2 million Euros, accumulated by Ferrari in 2003 was exactly the sum paid out as an exceptional bonus that the shareholders had given president Montezemolo a year earlier, in recognition of the good results obtained in terms of sport and sales, with record sales and profits on the up. After 12 months, what had seemed to be the goose that laid the golden eggs for Fiat, began to run out of steam, like someone who grows weary of balancing the books. The Fiat accounts continue to be negative and balancing the budget has been delayed for a further two years. The lack of new models, the reduction in market share at home (in 2004, 2.2 million cars were sold, pretty much the same as in 2003) to the benefit of foreign brands such as Toyota, Nissan, Citroen, Ford and Renault, to name but a few) had no influence on F1.

An irony of sorts! When, in 1969, Gianni Agnelli signed an agreement with Enzo Ferrari, worth around 250,000 Euros to save the team and stop it being sold to Ford, no one could have known that 30 years later, Ferrari would have settled a large part of Fiat's debt. The capitalisation and subsequent flotation on the stock market, produced enough profit to get rid of much of Fiat's debt. That is why one should not say today that Turin's problems will create problems for Ferrari. On the contrary, the world championship titles have brought a financial surplus that Fiat has welcomed with relief as it plugs some holes in the books. All of it is down to Schumacher's wins and the man is now an idol in Italy, for creating an aura of invincibility around Ferrari. The sponsors, ever more generous despite a general economic crisis in the world, are banging on the gates of Maranello. The F1 team runs on a budget of around 800 million Euros, most of it covered by the sponsors, the F1 prize fund, the TV rights money and merchandising. It means Ferrari can concentrate on F1, without the problems faced by other teams. However, Maserati also needs to be relaunched and there is never enough money. This is why, for some time now, Luca di Montezemolo has been at war with Bernie Ecclestone, fighting for a bigger slice of the F1 cake.

With a shrinking market and despite endless wins for Schumacher and Ferrari, the balance sheets are beginning to creak. What will happen if one day, another team and another manufacturer started to win as much? Currently, this a dream time for Ferrari, which is why the time has arrived to tighten the belt and ask for a better cut from the money controlled by Ecclestone. It is a financial war, which has nothing to do with sport or F1. In fact, the fans have no interest in the money side, nor in the prospect of a rival series. All they want is to see a Ferrari win. Michael Schumacher is now regarded as a god of speed and the fact that he now "feels obliged" to speak Italian during press conferences on home turf, has even warmed the hearts of the Italian fans as he creates an aura around him that never existed in the past. While he might be more popular and there is even a Schumacher signature edition of the Fiat Stilo, it has not been enough to help the Fiat group sell more cars. If there are no attractive models in the range, then it does not matter how many cars Schumacher signs. Because when it comes to putting his hand in his pocket, the Italian buyer looks at the small amount of money in his wallet and goes for the best mix of quality and price, which today does not necessarily mean chosing a Fiat. It is not by chance that the biggest selling models in Italy are the Punto and the new Panda, followed by the Lancia Y. As for the rest, apart from the Alfa Romeo 147 and 156 (leaders in the Italian "D" category,) it is an absolute desert. Lancia has not one car in the competitive mid-sized category, while the Thesis has been a total disaster and has failed to live up to expectations. Maserati is not selling enough either. Even if the new Quattroporte is a beautiful car, it is beaten in the sales charts by BMW and Mercedes. Investment in the shape of money is needed and that is why Fiat's problems can affect the competitive development of other makes. While Ferrari's racing books are in order, thanks to its F1-generated revenue, Maserati is struggling in the FIA GT championship, not because of its car, the magnificent MC12, but to get the right budget. Alfa Romeo was due to enter the DTM, through its premier team, Autodelta. However, so far there is no news of a project that should have been up and running in February 2004 and for which Giuseppe d'Agostino left his job running the F1 engines at the track for Ferrari. As for rallying, don't even ask, as neither Fiat nor Alfa Romeo has a car they can bank on.

A lack of resources and the need to balance the books means that the bosses in Turin have made cuts where they can. Their decisions have sparked off an internal battle which could break the solidarity of the group. Someone is waging war on the Maserati programme and putting a stick in its spokes at every opportunity, which has even given rise to rumours of a clean break between Ferrari and Maserati. At the moment, that would be like removing a runner's leg just before he starts racing.

Against this backdrop, Schumacher's wins with Ferrari, are a calling card to the industrial world, especially in the case of China, which has enormous potential but still needs time to develop. Unfortunately, time and money are two attributes lacking within Fiat. Even the Schumacher miracle and the efforts of the Scuderia cannot solve them in the next few years. Because these problems started a long time ago in Turin, when it was still the undisputed leader of the Italian automobile industry and when German was a language spoken in Germany and not in the top floor offices of the Italian firm, as was the case in 2004.

<
Rubens Barrichello, the winner of the first ever Chinese Grand Prix.

<<
Rubens Barrichello, Luca di Montezemolo, Jean Todt, Michael Schumacher and Luca Badoer: no need to change a winning team!

The new Fiat Panda 4x4 is launched at the Monza circuit in the presence of the Ferrari team.
∨

Black or white, what do you think?

Stéphanie Morin – La Presse, Montréal

2004 vu du Canada

It took time and some zealous effort for Jacques Villeneuve to extricate himself from his forced retirement. It was a tale of resurrection and symptomatic of the sport's lack of characters. Another season, but the same dominant force. Out on track, the 2004 season was being painted red and exasperatingly boring as a result. But on the rumour and speculation side, the paddock held its breath with not much else to talk about. Lies and half truths, exclusive revelations later officially denied and the usual game of driver musical chairs all created quite a stir.

Rumours concerning the return of the Canadian probably topped the list in terms of column inches. In fact, it was the driver's manager, Craig Pollock who got the ball rolling when he told the English newspaper "The Sun," at the end of April: "I have already begun talks with some top teams. Jacques had some offers to race this year, but he only wants to drive for a team that will give him the necessary equipment to fight against Michael Schumacher for the title. Williams looks like a good option."

At the Spanish Grand Prix, some so-called well informed sources swore that that the Canadian had been spotted spending an entire day at the Grove headquarters of his old team, Williams. Later, it transpired that Villeneuve had never even set foot there, but that he had met Sir Frank Williams, Patrick Head and Sam Michael in London to try and persuade them to give him a drive.

It did not need much to send people jumping to conclusions: Villeneuve was back with the team that took him to the title in 1997. Some were already dreaming of epic battles between Jacques in a Williams and Michael Schumacher in a Ferrari. As far as his most fervent fans were concerned, Villeneuve's return was akin to the second coming, with the future of the sport in his hands no less!

The problem was that the rumour seemed to be taking a long time to come true. Frank Williams admitted in May that Villeneuve's name was in the frame as a replacement for Juan Pablo Montoya or Ralf Schumacher. But he refused to go further. With nothing else to go on, the rumour mill fired up again, having the former champion testing at Monza one week and Silverstone the next, with a further session at Jerez. Journalists went off in all directions like headless chickens! And the Villeneuve entourage did nothing to calm the situation, under the assumption that it was always an advantage to have its driver talked about.

The fact that this business caused such a stir is proof of the malaise that grips the sport. Formula 1 is crying out for some charismatic characters and racing on the tracks and the nostalgic notion of getting Villeneuve back again was seen as the promise of better days ahead. When one man wins 13 out of 18 races and the press conferences are as dull as a damp day, it is hardly surprising that people turn to thoughts of a return for Villeneuve and even Hakkinen while we are at it. The Finn's name also came up in the course of the year. Bernie Ecclestone himself admitted that the current driver line-up was lacking in personality and that the return of two former champions would be a great boost. If one is expecting miracles from men of 33 and 36 years old, it's a sign that all is not well. Indeed, the current crop of young lions did not seem to appreciate all this talk of the oldies coming back. "Is Villeneuve in the right frame of mind to make a

Stéphanie Morin quit a career in teaching to switch to journalism five years ago. A journalist with "La Presse" a Montreal daily, she covers several sports, including tennis, hockey and boxing, as well as Formula 1. Aged 32, this is her third year in the paddock.

comeback?" asked Mark Webber, adding that there were plenty of good drivers coming up through the ranks who deserved to be given a chance. "Villeneuve wants to come back? Well, good for him," was Juan Pablo Montoya's typically disinterested response. Surprisingly, one of the few positive comments came from none other than Michael Schumacher. "Honestly, I don't have anything against Villeneuve coming back to F1," claimed the German at the European Grand Prix. "I would even be quite happy about it. We met up at the party after the Monaco race and we had a laugh. There was a good atmosphere between us."

Desperately seeks drive

Flirting with Williams was one thing, but Villeneuve went much further when it came to hoping for a drive. He even wanted to mend the broken fences between him and his former boss, David Richards.
Putting past events well and truly behind him, he went on a charm offensive as soon as the "Button Affair" burst on the scene. He was convinced he was the best candidate to replace Button at BAR, if the Englishman did indeed go to Williams. He kept calling in the hope of rejoining the team that had forced him into retirement ten months earlier. He contacted the people at Honda, British American Tobacco and, unthinkable just a short time earlier, he even got in touch with David Richards.
In any other sport, the driver's comeback would have been a foregone conclusion. After all, Villeneuve had worked with the team for five years and understood how it worked. But would it be so easy to wipe out all those bitter quarrels from the past? "If people put the politics to one side and if egos don't get in the way, it could work," reckoned the Canadian. But in Formula 1, asking people to put aside politics and ego is an impossibility.

Despite the Canadian's veteran status in the sport, with eight seasons under his belt, the big circus had managed to disappoint him more than he had expected. He was particularly fed up with the attitude of the folk at Williams. "I met Frank, Patrick and Sam Michael in April. It all seemed serious and positive, but I never heard from them again," he said. They did not get in touch when they thought they had Button under contract either. "They said they would keep in touch and that they would be straight with me. I'm disappointed, but it's not surprising. This is Formula 1 we are talking about!" If he hoped his 1997 performance would swing it for him at Grove, he had a rude awakening.
In the middle of all this brouhaha, Villeneuve made his first public appearance since the 2003 United States Grand Prix. He drove at the Goodwood Festival of Speed in the Ferrari 312 T3 raced by his father Gilles when he took his first F1 win, at Montreal in 1978.
Up until now, Villeneuve had always been reticent when it came to talking about his father and many saw this new openness as nothing more than a great PR scam to get himself back in the cockpit. "It's something I would never have done while I was racing," he admitted. "When you are racing, you have a career and it makes you a bit more like a robot. You block your emotions. But now, I've been at home for seven or eight months and there's a feeling of release. The page had never been turned. I never put a barrier between our two careers. Not because I had a problem with my father or did not like him, but because I wanted to make my own way and not necessarily continue down the same path that he had taken. But I'm not racing now and I wanted to pay tribute to him. It was both a thank you and a farewell to my father."

Twenty four busy hours

Having repeated ad nauseam that he wanted to come back to a top team that would allow him to fight at the front of the field, Villeneuve then switched tack. He realised that the big teams would not be opening their doors to him, so he turned to the Sauber squad, taking the initiative in contacting Peter Sauber. In mid-August, he visited the Hinwil factory and the story goes that the two men hit it off immediately. The news broke on 15th September 2004 that Villeneuve had signed a two year contract with Sauber. He was well aware that the little team would not turn him into the next world champion, but he said he was ready to roll his sleeves up, with the sole aim of helping the team progress. "I spoke a lot with Peter Sauber and I was impressed by the man and his organisation. It's a team with no politics and everything is very clean and tidy. It is also the only team that treated me with respect and spoke to me seriously. I really felt that Peter Sauber and his crew have a genuine wish that I should join them. That made the difference."
That same day, 15th September, Villeneuve made his official comeback to F1, wearing the colours of the Renault team. The Anglo-French team had decided to ditch Jarno Trulli and to take a gamble on the former world champion helping them to close the gap to BAR in the fight for second place in the Constructors' championship. In the space of 24 hours, Villeneuve had come out of retirement to become the man in demand in F1.
However, his time with Renault did not reap the results that had been hoped for as he failed to shine in the final three races of the season. In Canada, there is disagreement among the pundits as to how to interpret these races. Some pilloried the driver after just one race, saying that his performance was

"lamentable, inexcusable and saddening." Others saluted his courage in taking on such a risky challenge. It took nerve to return to racing after a ten month break, with just two days to get used to a new car, a new team, new tyres and, as if that wasn't enough, on a new circuit. Depending on your point of view, his return was either all black or all white. One thing is certain; his intensive training regime during his absence was not enough. The driver was exhausted at the end of each race. In ten months, Formula 1 had moved on and the drivers now face greater G forces, as the cars are three tenths of a second quicker per lap and the tyres offer more grip than ever. It seems that Villeneuve was not ready for this new reality.
So, those three races with Renault did nothing to revive his reputation. Peter Sauber is still confident of having made the right decision, but there has to be some doubt regarding Villeneuve's ability to return to the top. The nightmare years at BAR may have left a deeper scar than the driver realises.

We will find out soon enough in 2005.

∧
A truly emotional moment at the 2004 Goodwood Festival of Speed, as Jacques Villeneuve gets behind the wheel of the Ferrari 312 T3, in memory of his father, Gilles.

Jacques Villeneuve and Peter Sauber have high hopes for their partnership in 2005.
∨

Making the difference

The BAR-Honda team was the revelation of 2004. After four years hard graft they have finally moved to the sharp end of the leader board. Takuma Sato's excellent performances were also unexpected. On the other hand Toyota was a big disappointment. So why such a big difference?

Kunio Shibata – Autosport, Tokyo

Sato, what flair!

The Japanese driver really made his mark at the Nürburgring in May. He proved he was as quick as his team-mate Jenson Button by qualifying on the front row for the first time even though he had a heavier fuel load than Michael Schumacher pole. In the race he was in second place between the two Ferraris and on lap 44 after his final stop he rejoined just behind Barrichello so his first rostrum finish was almost assured. Sato, though, had other ideas and on the run down to the first corner he braked very late and tried to go past the Brazilian on the inside. Rubens did not see him and they collided. However, Takuma does not deserve to be blamed for the incident. On the straight before the corner there were at least twenty metres between the two drivers and nobody, except Sato, would have dared attack in such a situation. In the incident he lost his front wing and had to pit. He was finally eliminated by a blown engine; something that happened to him seven times in 2004.

After the race Barrichello said that his move was that of an amateur and slagged off the Japanese journalists (me included) for saying that he deliberately deprived Sato of a rostrum finish.

The 'culprit' himself had no regrets. *"I'd do exactly the sama thing again,"* he insisted. *"Even if there's only the slightest chance you have to go for it. That's the way I drive and that's what's got me into F1."* His style did not vary for the rest of the year. In Montreal, he spun when really pushing and then at Indianapolis in free practice he hit Massa's Sauber but the Brazilian was not paying attention. Sato did not really need to go flat out as it was neither in qualifying nor in the race. When I looked at his damaged car I said that he had missed his place on the rostrum. But I was wrong. In the race the two Safety Car appearances completely negated the two-stop strategy that BAR has decided for Takuma who fell back to tenth. But Sato was not giving up without a fight and went for it. He passed Fisichella, Coulthard and Panis and with just twelve laps to go he attacked Trulli in the first corner. A lap before one of the Jaguar engines had spread oil on the track, which was very slippery. Jarno slowed when he saw the oil flag but not Takuma. So he saw the flag in third place the first rostrum finish by a Japanese driver since 1990.

"It's true that our cars went really well here, probably better than the Ferraris," commented Shuhei Nakamoto, the Honda engineering director. *"But Sato really earned his third place as it wasn't just the engine or the strategy."*

When he made his debut in F1 I heard people in Japan say that Sato was not considered as a talented driver and that there were others who were quicker and more consistent. Maybe they forgot to analyse the reasons why he is in F1. His strong points are his professionalism (if you listen to his English you would never believe that he learned it in only two years as he did not know a word of the language when he arrived in the country in 1999), plus his knowledge of mechanics and vehicle dynamics. Nakamoto says that he probably knows more than some of the engineers who have two or three years' experience. And do not forget his will to win. Since he met Ayrton Senna at Suzuka in 1988 Takuma always wanted to be a racing driver. But he had to be content with a bicycle up to the age of twenty so he began his career with ten years less experience than guys like Button or Raïkkönen. It is both his strength and his weakness. This year Takuma reminded us that overtaking is still possible in F1. With an extra year's experience under his belt he will surprise us again in 2005.

Honda: "Sat on a stone for four years!"

In Japan there is a proverb that says, "Sitting on a stone for three years." It means that if you can put up with misfortune for three years, you will overcome it. I heard it several time last year from the Honda

Kunio Shibata
45 years old, he left Japan, giving up his jov in journalism in 1982 to move to Paris and study Politocal Science. He became a freelance producer for Japanese television and havinf always been interested in motor racing, he began covering the Grand Prix for a press agency in 1987 when Satoru Nakajima arrived on the scene. He has written for the specialist Japanese magazine «Grand Prix Xpress» since 1991.

people. They began their adventure in 2000 and three years later they were still waiting for the results. And suddenly this year it has all come together.

BAR-Honda has done better than Williams or McLaren and finished second in the Constructors' Championship behind Ferrari.

"It hasn't been an overnight success or a lucky one," insisted Takeo Kuichi, the F1 project leader. *"The first two years with BAR were a disaster. It was because we didn't know how to cooperate with the team. One of our goals for the third year was to develop a complete car, but in fact we concentrated on the engine and they concentrated on the chassis. However, the situation has changed radically over the last two years."*

The two men responsible for this are Geoff Willis, ex-Williams and now the BAR technical director and Shuhei Nakato. He has been a racing engineer for over twenty years but with motorbikes. He is a chassis specialist and has become the director of the factory team. Honda in motorbike racing is almost the equivalent of Ferrari in F1. So he knows exactly what to do to get the winning machine up and running. Willis and Nakato are a pair of accomplices who have managed to get things done while putting aside their individual interests and in two years they have changed the mentality in the BAR-Honda team. BAR and Honda now listen to each other. The fruits of this cooperation are the ultra-light gearbox, the very sophisticated electronic management system and some aerodynamic elements, which have all made a big contribution to this season's success. Honda also has its say about grand prix strategy. For the moment the Japanese firm has no wish to buy BAR or set up its own team as the present system functions very well. This does not mean that the Honda people are completely satisfied with their relations with the BAR team. On the contrary they are very unhappy that the team has not won a grand prix this year.

BAR, though, is delighted with its second place in the Constructors' Championship, an attitude that sticks in Honda's craw. "If we can win just one grand prix then we don't give a damn about the rest, even if we retire in them all, stated Kuichi. Honda is condemned to win; BAR too, is after the elusive victory it has been searching for since its creation in 1999. But not at any price. This difference in attitude could have a negative effect but the immediate future looks rosy for the BAR-Honda partnership.

Toyota, a real tortoise!

This is not the case with Toyota. In the 17th edition last year I described the two

Japanese giants as the tortoise and the hare as I was convinced that Toyota would progress slowly but surely and eventually overtake its rival. This year progress has been slow but certainly not effective. The main innovation in 2004 was the single engine per weekend and Toyota went for reliability rather than speed. They believed that at the start of the season the former would play a primordial role and that their rivals would have problems finishing races. This was not at all the case, as apart from a few exceptions like McLaren, the majority of cars had no difficulty in covering twice the distance and lapping over two seconds quicker than in 2003. Toyota did not blow any engines but how slow they were. They rarely finished the race on the same lap as the winner and scored only nine points; about 1/30th of Ferrari's total and 1/13th of BAR-Honda's. Toyota's problem is not only revealed by the figures: it is also one of policy, which seems very confused. To quote one example; the drivers were changed once again in mid-season. Just after the German Grand Prix Zonta replaced da Matta *"because Ricardo showed how quick he was as the third driver, and we wanted to test him in race conditions to compare him with da Matta and Panis. We kept the latter as he scores more points."*

Just as one feared Zonta finished with poor results and it was evident that the Toyota's lack of performance was not down to the drivers but to the design of the car and its exploitation. In a nutshell it is the management that is responsible. The engineers and the mechanics are all professionals but they are badly directed. Mike Gascoyne's arrival looks like it may change things but this will take time in that the management think that he is some kind of superman who can do everything with a wave of his magic wand.

Concerning the management I would like to mention the doubtful choice of drivers for next year but there is not enough space.

To finish I'd just like to quote one of the directors. *"For the moment Ferrari dominates. In the near future it will be ourselves and Honda who will battle for the title!"*

Who can possibly agree with that?

^
Takuma Sato has every reason to smile. His 2004 season showed that he is made of the right stuff and he is probably the best driver to come out of Japan.

<
(opposite)
A happy trio on the Indianapolis rostrum. Takuma finished third and shared the glory with the two Ferrari drivers.

Sato and David Richards get on like a house on fire.
∨

The 1964 World Championship: Surtees and Ferrari by a whisker

by Jacques Vassal
«Automobile historique»

Silverstone, 11th July 1964: a superb shot of John Surtees, flat out in the Ferrari 158 at the British Grand Prix in which he finished 3rd, behind Clark and Hill. It's the start of the comeback.
>

Jacques Vassal,
Journalist, writer and translator, as well as being an expert in singing and popular music, Jacques Vassal has worked for "Auto Passion" magazine for over eleven years. Since 2000, he has worked as a freelance for various specialist magazines, especially the monthly magazine "Automobile Historique", writing tests, portraits, interviews, retrospectives and articles on cars and motor sport of today and yesteryear. Along with Pierre Menard, he is also the co-author of "Legendes de la Formule 1", a new Chronosports publication.

Forty years ago, Scuderia Ferrari raced in several categories at the same time: endurance, European hillclimb championship with prototype and GT cars, as well as Formula 1 of course. The 1964 season was to be a memorable one, as John Surtees fought hard to take the Drivers' title, ably supported by Lorenzo Bandini, while Ferrari took the Constructors' Cup.

In early 1963, Ferrari announced it was building a new Formula 1 156, with a semi-monocoque, which would be ready at some point during the season. On 4th March at Monza, the Maranello marque unveiled its other new cars, including prototypes of the 2 litre Dino V6 and the 3 litre P V12 with a centrally mounted engine for endurance racing. They also produced an experimental front engined 4 litre coupe, the 330 LM/B, that would race several times, including at Le Mans. In the Grand Touring class, the front engined 3 litre V12 250 GTO would continue a brilliant career that began in 1962. As for drivers, the big news centred on the arrival of Englishman, John Surtees, the former motorcycle world champion (seven titles, 350 and 500 cc from 1956 to 1960.) He made his debut with a Lotus 18 and had just enjoyed a great 1962 season in a Lola-Climax, with which he took fourth place in the world championship, with 19 points. Surtees brought plenty of technical know-how with him, making him the ideal candidate to work with the engineers and mechanics. He would be partnered in Formula 1, prototypes and

sometimes in the GT races by Belgium's Willy Mairess and the two most promising Italians of the day, Lorenzo Bandini and Lodovico Scarfiotti. Since 1962, Scuderia Ferrari was run by Sporting Director, Eugenio Dragoni, a Milanese businessman, who through the Scuderia Sant'Ambroeus ran a sort of nursery school for talented young Italians. It was Dragoni who, in 1961, convinced Enzo Ferrari to supply his private team with a Formula 1 car and it was with this squad that a young Giancarlo Baghetti won on his Formula 1 debut in a non-championship race at Syracuse. Even more surprising, Baghetti went on to win the ACF Grand Prix at Reims, thus saving the Scuderia's honour, when its official drivers – Phil Hill, Richie Ginther and Wolfgang Von Trips – were all out of the running. From then on, Baghetti continued his career in prototype and GT racing, without ever confirming his talent in Formula 1. However, Bandini and to a lesser extent, Scarfiotti, who won the European Hillclimb championship in 1962, in a 2 litre Dino, showed their potential in F1, with Bandini being favoured by Dragoni.

Chasing the championships

Unlike the current era of F1 specialisation, back then the Maranello constructor had an eclectic approach to racing, competing in Endurance racing, winning the Le Mans 24 Hours in 1963 with the Scarfiotti-Bandini 250 P and the following year with the Guichet-Vacarella 330 P. Sports cars were a priority, to such an extent that, up until June, the development and build of the Formula 1 cars was put on the back burner. The 1963 world championship was dominated head and shoulders by Team Lotus and its type 25, with a monocoque chassis and a V8 Coventry-Climax engine. Its success was down to the brilliance of Colin Chapman and its number 1 driver, the extraordinary Jim Clark. Winners in 1962, BRM were treading water, with just the odd flash of brilliance, including another win at his favourite Monaco circuit for Graham Hill. Cooper was inexorably in decline, but its former driver and double world champion, Jack Brabham, also using a V8 Coventry-Climax, but in a conventional tubular chassis, was making a name for himself. He was driving well and had put his second car in the hands of a first rate American, Dan Gurney. Ferrari began the season with an intermediate 156, which had been worked on by the engineer, Mauro Forghieri. The engine was still the 120 degree V6, with direct injection, developing 200 horsepower at 10,000 rpm. The tubular chassis had been tweaked, while the team waited for the new car. Surtees used it to good effect, coming 4th in Monaco, while taking the lap record and 3rd in Holland, where Scarfiotti replaced Mairesse and secured his first point in his first grand prix. After that, the Scuderia failed twice. Surtees and Mairesse both suffered engine failures in Belgium. At Reims, Bandini was back in F1, at the wheel of a BRM 56, belonging to the privateer Milanese Centro-Sud team and Surtees was the only Ferrari driver in the ACF Grand Prix, as team-mate Willy Mairesse was badly burnt at le Mans when his 250 P caught fire. Lodovico Scarfiotti was due to stand in for the Belgian in a 156, but he was injured in practice. After an excellent start, John had to retire with a faulty fuel pump. Then, at Silverstone, on 20th July, the fruits of all their efforts came good, as the Scuderia was no longer working on its Le Mans project, having easily won the Endurance Constructors' World Championship, with wins at Le Mans, the Sebring 12 Hours and the Nurburgring 1000 Km.

The Scuderia is back

At the British GP, Surtees was still the only Ferrari driver. It was a long race (385 km) and he had an extra fuel tank fitted to his car. He finished second, 25" behind Clark's Lotus and 12" ahead of Hill's BRM. On the way, he beat the lap record three times. Hill had been second, but ran out of fuel on the final lap, which promoted the Ferrari up a place, while proving Surtees had been right about the fuel tank. Ferrari did not take part in the non-championship race at the Solitude circuit, near Stuttgart, spending the time working with Bosch on improving the workings of its injection system at low revs and it was to prove crucial in the German Grand Prix. The Nurburgring on 4th August was the backdrop for a great battle between Ferrari, Lotus and BRM, with Surtees, Clark and Hill as the respective protagonists. On the tortuous 22.810 km track with its 172 corners which "Big John" liked so much and where he had recently won the 1000 Kilometres with Willy Mairesse, he put on a bravura demonstration. He shadowed Clark and when the Scotsman's Climax V8 began to misfire, he went into the lead and stayed there to the flag. After the race, Clark admitted that, even without his problems, he would not have been able to beat the Ferrari and its driver who was

Monaco, 26th May 1963: In his first official grand prix for Ferrari, Surtees got the most out of a 156 which he knew was already past it. His efforts were rewarded with a modest 4th place, but his best race lap, in 1'34"5, at an average of 119.809 km/h speaks volumes about the driver's ability.

v

<
In the same Monaco Grand Prix, Surtees drifts the 156 out of the Station Hairpin (yet to be renamed Loews) ahead of Tony Maggs in the Cooper.

on scintillating form that day. For Clark to say that means it must be true. A fortnight later, in Sicily, Surtees won a non-championship race at Enna Pergusa. It meant Ferrari was in great shape for the Italian GP at Monza on 8th September. The new Aero version, with its semi-monocoque construction was finally ready, although not the Angelo Bellei designed V8, so Surtees raced with an interim V6 engine, while Bandini used the tubular chassis. Lorenzo was back in the Scuderia following Mairesse's Nurburgring accident, which claimed the life of a marshal, leaving the driver seriously injured. Surtees took a brilliant pole ahead of Graham Hill and led for a few laps but retired on lap 17 with a broken valve. The final three grands prix, in the States at Watkins Glen, in Mexico (Mexico City) and in South Africa (East London) saw further

retirements for Surtees who therefore finished fourth in the championship on 22 points, behind Clark's Lotus (54) and the two BRM drivers, Hill and Ginther (29.) Bandini finished fifth in the States and South Africa. Ferrari finished fourth of six in the Constructors' Cup.

Surtees the Ring Master

For 1964, Forghieri produced a 180 degree 12 cylinder engine, the 1512, but it was not ready in time and Surtees and Bandini, the Scuderia's lead drivers, had to make do with the 158. The V8, designed by Angelo Bellei, Forghieri's assistant, put out 210 horsepower in its twin plug version. On 12th April, Surtees and Bandini scored a one-two at Syracuse, in a non-championship race. In the international Trophy at

Silverstone, Surtees retired with fuel pump failure and the injection system would remain a weak point in the early part of the championship. Surtees was second in Holland, but only scored 6 points from four races, while Bandini had none. Clark (Lotus) and Hill (BRM) once again ran away in the Drivers' championship and Constructors' cup. Once again, with Le Mans out of the way, the Scuderia began winning as it concentrated on improving its Formula 1 cars. Forghieri added a fuel cooler to the front of the engine, which could be seen behind the driver's left shoulder and it allowed them to use all their power over the full race distance. Ferrari had to get its act together, because apart from Lotus and BRM, another challenger appeared on the horizon. Dan Gurney won at Rouen-Les-Essarts in the ACF GP. Surtees, using the new cooler

Despite the fact that Clark and the Lotus were dominant in the early part of the year, John Surtees and the Ferrari 158 would leave their mark on the 1964 season.
<

managed to qualify on the front row, alongside Clark and Gurney. But he retired from the race with a faulty pump. Unhappy with the V8's lack of power and reliability, he wanted the Scuderia to make an immediate switch to the V12. Nevertheless, at Brands Hatch for the British GP, Clark won again, ahead of Hill, with Surtees third and Bandini fifth. In Germany, the Italian team and its English lead driver would get back on track for the title fight. At Solitude, Surtees finished second after a close fight with Clark's Lotus. Bosch had developed a new injection system, controlled by the driver, which made the difference at low and medium revs. In qualifying for the German GP, which saw the debut of the Honda with its tranverse V12 and a new driver in the shape of America's Ronnie Bucknum, Surtees was in a class of his own at his much loved Nurburgring. He took pole in 8'38"4, beating Clark and Gurney by 4 and 9 tenths respectively, which on a track measuring 22.810 km shows how close these three were. Bandini completed the front row in 8'42"6 as the width of the track allowed for a 4-3-4-3 grid formation, with Graham Hill relegated to the second row. Lorenzo made a demon start and took the lead for a short while, but Clark led by the end of the opening lap. Next time round, Surtees attacked and took the lead with Gurney making the most of Clark's gearchange problems to take up the challenge. The American and the Englishman duelled for several laps, before Gurney was forced to slow with cooling problems. This left Hill to have a go at Surtees, but the Ferrari man gave it his all, setting the fastest race lap to take his second consecutive German GP win. The Scuderia's work had paid off, as Bandini charged through to third. Just three weeks later at the Zeltweg airfield for the first Austrian GP, the Italian took an unexpected win, while Surtees, Clark, Hill and Gurney all retired. The bumpy track had taken its toll on suspension and transmission and Lorenzo was rewarded for nursing his car. Surtees could console himself with the fact that his title rivals had failed to score.
On 6th September, Surtees and Ferrari hammered in another nail with a win in the Italian GP, much to the delight of the tifosi packed into the Monza park, who began to believe their team could take

the title. Bandini had tested the 1512, but raced the 158 at Monza and finished third. Second place had gone to Bruce McLaren; an unexpected performance given the poor form of the Cooper-Climax. Once again, Hill, Clark and Gurney all retired. Surtees, nicknamed "Big John" by the tifosi, really enjoyed this win, coming a week after he had a big crash in the Goodwood Tourist Trophy at the wheel of a NART 250 GT, when he was hit by another competitor. His neck was still hurting when he got to Monza, but the win washed away the pain!

Suspense in the final

The championship would therefore be decided at the last two races on the other side of the Atlantic. In the meantime, Enzo Ferrari took a theatrical and angry

stance against the Italian Automobile Club, which had refused to persuade the Commission Sportive Internationale to homologate the 250 LM as a GT car. 100 cars had to be produced, or at least, be in production, whereas there were only around 30 of them built. With no apparent logic, Ferrari threatened to withdraw all his cars from competition, including F1! However, so as not to lose his chances, the Commendatore entered his cars in the blue and white colours of his friend and US importer, Luigi Chinetti under the North American Racing Team banner, which raced regularly in endurance, but never in Formula 1. The move fooled no one. So, in this new livery, Bandini gave the 1512 its debut at Watkins Glen, while Surtees finished second, with Hill and BRM taking the win. Clark (injection) and Gurney (oil pressure) retired yet again,

Monza, 6th September 1964: after Germany, Italy brought further proof that Ferrari was back on form. Here on the grid, (from left to right) Graham Hill (BRM,) Dan Gurney (Brabham-Climax) and John Surtees (Ferrari 158.)
v

SPOTLIGHTS — **HISTORY: JOHN SURTEES**

having been part of the lead group, along with the Ferrari and the BRM. Coming up to the final round in Mexico, three drivers were in with a chance of taking the title: Hill, Surtees and Clark. Surtees was 5 points down on Hill, with Clark a further 4 behind, which made it difficult for the Scotsman, but not impossible, although he would have to win, with Surtees finishing no higher than third and Hill failing to score. But if John was second and Jim won in Mexico, the title would go to the Ferrari man. The race was a memorable one. Clark led from pole and built up a lead ahead of Gurney, Spence in the second Lotus and Bandini. Hill made a bad start, fumbling with his goggles and Surtees, fourth on the grid with an off-song V8, lost time as his engine

misfired and stalled coming up to the first corner and John saw several cars shoot past before getting going again. Bandini, in the 1512 was ahead of him. On lap 20 of 65, Clark led Gurney by 7 seconds, followed by Hill who had staged an energetic climb back up the order. Then came Bandini and Surtees. On lap 31, braking for the hairpin, the Italian's Ferrari ran into the back of Hill's BRM, forcing the Englishman to pit. He left pit lane after a long delay for repairs, his title chances gone. All the flegmatic and moustachioed Londoner would say later was that, "Bandini really deserves his Ferrari salary!" But the two men still shook hands later. According to Surtees, who had been following them for several laps, it was a simple racing incident. Hill had been warned

from the pits that his other rival, apart from Clark, was coming back at him and he was doing all in his power to stay ahead of Bandini. In his memoirs, Surtees wrote: "it had almost happened several times before and then the inevitable occurred. The BRM and Ferrari both locked their wheels and skidded and I was able to go past to take third place."

Bandini was accused of doing it deliberately to help Surtees, but the Englishman is adamant this was not the case. "The anti-Bandini crowd had failed to realise that, if Clark had gone on to win the race, he would have been World Champion anyway. But things worked out so that the title dropped in my lap on the very last lap!" Clark seemed to have the race wrapped up and the world title with it. But on the penultimate lap, he was passed by Gurney who went on to win. The Lotus engine had lost all its oil and the Scotsman crawled home in fifth place. Ferrari saw Hill and Clark in trouble and worked out that if Bandini, now second, let Surtees go by, "Big John" would be world champion, even with Gurney winning the race. At the time, only the best 6 of 10 results were counted. So did Bandini indeed slow to let Surtees pass? John recalls in his memoirs that Bandini was slowed by an injection problem on the final lap, adding that, "I'm not sure that he would have let me pass." It seems unbelievable, but of course there was no radio contact between pit and car in those days and in the heat of battle of the final lap, a driver would be concentrating on the finish. Whatever the answer, Surtees finished second in Mexico to become 1964 world champion with 40 points – just one more than Graham Hill. He deserved it, but so did his rivals!

Results

Mexican Grand Prix, 25th October 1964, cMagdalena Mixhuca, circuit, Mexico

1. Dan Gurney (USA, Brabham-Climax), 325 km in 2 h 09'50"32/100, average 150, 186 km/h ;
2. John Surtees (G.-B., Ferrari),1'08"94 ;
3. Lorenzo Bandini (I, Ferrari), 1'09"63 ;
4. Mike Spence (G.-B., Lotus-Climax, 1'21"40) ;
5. Jim Clark (G.-B., Lotus-Climax), 1 lap ;
6. Pedro Rodriguez (MEX, Ferrari), 1 lap ;
7. Bruce McLarin (N.-Z., Cooper-Climax), 1 lap ;
8. Richie Ginther (USA, BRM) , 1 lap ;
9. Phil Hill (USA, Cooper-Climax), 2 laps ;
10. Moise Solana (MEX, Lotus-Climax), 2 laps ;
11. Graham Hill (G.-B., BRM), 2 laps ;
12. Innes Ireland (G.-B., BRP-BRM), 4 laps ;
13. Hap Sharp (USA, Brabham-BRM), 5 laps ;
14. Jack Brabham (AUS, Brabham-Climax, 21 laps).

Fastest lap: Jim Clark (G.-B., Lotus-Climax), 1'58"37, 152,15 km/h

1964 Drivers' World Championship

(10 GRANDS PRIX RUN - 6 BEST RESULTS TO COUNT - Points for first 6 : (9-6-4-3-2-1)

1. John Surtees (G.-B.), 40 points ;
2. Graham Hill (G.-B.), 39 ;
3. Jim Clark (G.-B.), 32 ;
4. Lorenzo Bandini (I) and Richie Ginther (USA), 23
6. Dan Gurney (USA), 19 ;
7. Bruce McLarin (N.-Z.), 13 ;
8. Jack Brabham (AUS) and Peter Arundell (G.-B.), 11
10. Joseph Siffert (CH), 7 ;
11. Bob Anderson (G.-B.), 5 ;
12. Tony Maggs (SA), Mike Spence (G.-B.) and Innes Ireland (G.-B.), 44 ;
15. Joachim Bonnier (S), 3 ;
16. Chris Amon (N.-Z.), Walt Hansgin (USA) and Maurice Trintignant (F), 2 ;
19. Trevor Taylor (G.-B.), Phil Hill (USA), Mike Hailwood (G.-B.) and Pedro Rodriguez (MEX), 1

1964 Constructors' Cup

1. Ferrari, 45 points (49);
2. BRM, 42 points (51);
3. Lotus, 37 points (40);
4. Brabham, 33 points (37);
5. Cooper, 16 points.

John Surtees

John Surtees was born on 11th February 1934, in Tatsfield, Surrey. He was the son of a bus driver turned racing motorcycle builder. John was an average student, interested in sport, particularly boxing and athletics. He was interested in things mechanical and, inevitably, began racing on two wheels at the age of 15, competing in grass track events on an Excelsior-JAP. Then aged 17, he switched to track racing on a 500 Vincent-HRD, moving up to a 1000cc machine. On 3rd June 1951, at Brands Hatch, he was the man of the meeting, taking his first three wins, in the 500, 1000 and handicap classes! In 1952, he switched from the Vincent to a Manx-Norton and took part in the Ulster GP on 16th August, his first world championship event. He won many races in the '53 and '54 British championships with 350 and 500 Nortons. In 1955, he also raced a 250 NSU and won the Ulster GP at Dundrod, his first world championship win, as well as several races in the UK. He was recruited by MV Agusta in 1956, racing in the 350 and 500 World Championships. He won 37 grands prix and seven world titles (three in 350 and four in 500, between 1956 and 1960.

In 1958, he tried his hand on four wheels, testing the Vanwall F1 and the Aston Martin DBR 1. He made the switch to car racing in 1960, while completing his final year in bikes. That year, Rob Walker entered him in Formula Junior at the wheel of a Cooper-BMC and a Lotus Ford and in Formula 2 with a Cooper and Lotus-Climax (2nd at Oulton Park.) He even raced in Formula 1 with a Lotus 18 (Monaco, Portugal and the United States.) In 1961, with a Cooper Climax T53, he scored his first world championship points: 5th in Belgium and Germany at Spa and the Nurburgring, the two toughest tracks on the calendar. His performance brought him to Ferrari's attention, but he turned down their offer, or at least, put it on hold, as he did not feel he was ready for it! It was a wise move, as Ferrari hit rock bottom in 1962, while Surtees and his Lotus-Climax Mk IV had a good season, scoring 19 points in the world championship, the highpoint being a superb second place in Germany. He made a brilliant debut with Ferrari in a 250 GTO, coming second in the Paris 1000 kms with Mike Parkes. He then signed with Ferrari for 1963. In Formula 1, he won the German GP to record the first of his six world championship wins from 111 starts and scored 22 points. In endurance racing, he took convincing wins with the 250 P in the Sebring 12 Hours and the Nurburgring 1000 kms. In 1964, still with Ferrari, he became world champion with two wins

in Germany and Italy and a total of 40 points scored in the Ferrari 156 then the 158, after an action packed Mexican GP. He is still the only man to have taken the world championship on both two and four wheels. In prototype cars, he finished 3rd at Sebring and Le Mans, 2nd at Reims, still with Ferrari and partnered with Lorenzo Bandini. The two men got on well and held one another in high regard. But behind the scenes at Ferrari, the mood was tense between Surtees and Dragoni. In 1965, Surtees switched from the 158 Ferrari to the 1512, which he was less keen on and which let him down on several occasions. He came fifth in the championship with only 17 points. In sports cars, he was 2nd in the Monza 1000 km, winning the Nurburgring race yet again, this time with Scarfiotti and a Ferrari 330 P2. But his life at Ferrari was complicated by his collaboration with Eric Broadley and Lola, for whom he developed the Chevrolet powered T70, winning at Mosport, Brands Hatch and Sainte Jovite. Life with Dragoni got tense. In September, he suffered a serious accident at Mosport in Canada, at the wheel of the Lola. He returned from the incident at the start of 1966, still with Ferrari and scored two sparkling victories in the Monza 1000 Km with Parkes and the 330 P3 and in the Belgian GP, driving a 312 F1, both wins coming in the pouring rain. Things went from bad to worse with Dragoni and the equally fiery Surtees packed his bags just before the Le Mans 24 Hours. He continued in F1 with a Cooper-Maserati, recording two podium finishes and one win (Mexico) with this heavy and outdated car. Despite switching teams halfway through the season, he still finished runner up in the

championship, behind Jack Brabham. He also won the first CANAM series in a Lola Chevrolet. In 1967, he joined Honda's F1 effort, developing the RA273 V12 and also fine tuned the Lola RA 300, known as the "Hondola." He took this car to an incredible win in the Italian GP. He finished fourth in the world championship, equal with Chris Amon. He stayed with Honda for '68, driving the RA 301, finishing second in France and third in the States. Unfortunately, Honda pulled out of the sport at the end of the year. Surtees then signed with BRM, when the Bourne team was a mere shadow of its former self, enduring a mediocre season in the P138. He drove for Chaparral in CANAM, where he also struggled with the fragile 2H. In 1970, Big John raced for McLaren in F1 and was called back by Ferrari for a few endurance races in the 512 S. (3rd at Monza and the Nurburgring, 4th at Spa.) In 1971, he followed the example of his mates, Brabham and Gurney (Eagle) and McLaren, setting up his own team. The Surtees-Cosworth TS 7 and TS 9 had varying fortunes in the world championship, while in Formula 2, the Hart powered TS10 brought John his last two victories as a driver, in Japan and Imola in 1972. He also entered a car in F5000, driven by his friend and former motorcycle racer, Mike Hailwood.

Surtees still loves to compete in historic events, using his exceptional collection of racing motorbikes as well as cars. Despite the fact that he seemed to fall out with all his employers, not to mention his drivers and was often controversial, misunderstood and very obstinate, he remains an immense talent.

<
Ferrari 156 «Aero»

<
Ferrari 158 «Aero»

ATMOSPHERE

If it's a truism to say that a photo is worth a thousand words what do the hundreds of photos in this book represent if one follows that kind of logic! Anyway hereafter the reader can catch just a brief glimpse of the riches of the 2004 season.

Paddock beauties

What would F1 be without a touch of femininity? Groupies, grid girls, journalists, top models or press attaches, the prettiest girls on planet earth haunt the circuits. And it's possible that the most beautiful of them all is not to be found on these pages.

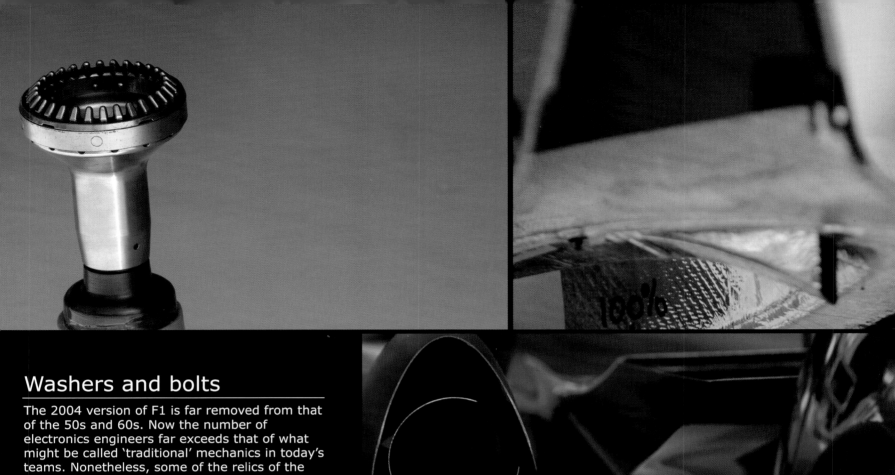

Washers and bolts

The 2004 version of F1 is far removed from that of the 50s and 60s. Now the number of electronics engineers far exceeds that of what might be called 'traditional' mechanics in today's teams. Nonetheless, some of the relics of the good old days like bolts; screws and washers tightened or loosened by real 'wrenches' can still be found under the Kevlar bonnets

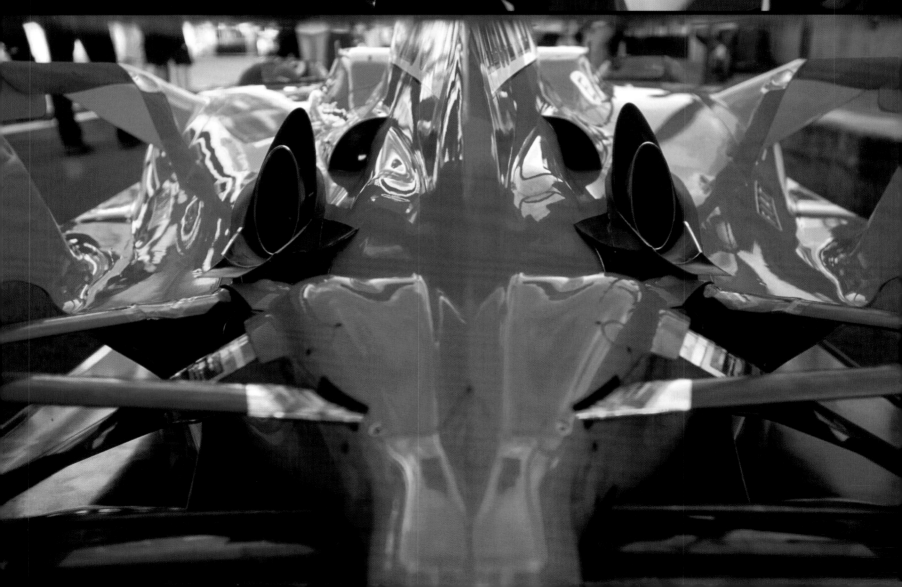

Yellow: colour of hope?

Jordan's 2004 season was more or less what the little Irish team expected. The Silverstone-based outfit battled with its usual courage and scored five points, an honourable achievement. What, though, can it do against the huge budgets of some of its rivals?

Studies in concentration

Helmeted, belted in, ready to do battle, the F1 drivers
in full concentration before the off. Can you recognise
them behind their protective facemasks?

From left to right: Takuma Sato, Jarno Trulli,
Giancarlo Fisichella, Marc Gené, Michael Schumacher,
Kimi Räikkönen, Nick Heidfeld, Juan Pablo Montoya

THE 18 GRANDS PRIX

Australia, Brazil, Japan, Bahrain and China: the never-ending 2004 championship was particularly rich in action and each race had its own special atmosphere. With the season over at last this review of the Grands Prix evokes both good and bad memories.

IT'S THAT MAN AGAIN !

At the end of the first grand prix of the season the question on everybody's lips in the Melbourne paddock was, *"Who can beat Michael Schumacher?"*

The German took pole by a wide margin and dominated the race leading from start to finish despite three refuelling stops.

Rubens Barrichello was second quickest in practice and that is where he finished giving Ferrari a double. Fernando Alonzo came home third showing that Renault would be a force to be reckoned with throughout the year.

Michael starts the ball rolling with pole

On Friday morning Michael Schumacher came out of the pits in his new Ferrari F2004. After an exploratory lap in 1m 52s he got round in the mind-blowing time of 1m 25.127s, and then pitted.
This incredible lap blitzed his rivals, as none would get anywhere near it during the session.

At midday there were a lot of glum faces in the paddock. In the Michelin tent Pierre Dupasquier, the competitions boss did not know what to think. *"It's bloody unbelievable. It's not that there are bad engineers at Williams and McLaren,"* he thundered,

"the laws of physics are the same for everybody. I don't understand how Ferrari could've gained such an advantage." In the Bridgestone camp, however, it was a different story. The Ferrari tyre supplier was delighted. After its poor performance the previous year it looked like all the work done during the winter was paying dividends. What about Sauber? The car had the same engine/gearbox as the Ferrari, the same Bridgestone tyres and a chassis that bore a strikingly close resemblance to that of the Scuderia's 2003 car so theoretically Giancarlo Fisichella and Felipe Massa should have been hot on the Ferraris' heels.

Far from it as the Saubers finished the day almost two seconds behind Schumacher. *"We weren't expecting such a gap,"* Peter Sauber admitted. *"I don't know how Ferrari has done it but the Scuderia has left everybody stunned today."* So did it look like the 2004 season was going to be a Schumacher walkover? According to a Williams engineer who wished to remain anonymous, it was very possible. *"The Ferraris have got off to such a good start that I think it'll be very difficult for us to close the gap this season. In my opinion they'll win all the races."*

There were no surprises on Saturday. The F2004s filled the first two places on the grid and were separated by only 74/1000s while third man Juan Pablo Montoya was a good half-second behind. The only consolation for the Scuderia's rivals was that the gap was less than the day before. *"The car was great as soon as we went out on Friday morning,"* said Michael Schumacher. *"The whole team's done a fantastic job."*

Colour the 2004 season red

Michael Schumacher is usually fairly non-committal at the start of a new season. In previous years when he arrived in Melbourne he always came out with a few ordinary comments reminding people that he didn't know what the opposition was like, or underlining the fact that it was going to be a tough season: a form of understatement that seemed a bit over the top as he has won the last four championships.

In a politically correct climate Schumacher surprised his entourage by affirming that he was *"very confident"* about the coming season. *"I think we'll be right on the ball,"* he commented. *"I love this new car and I feel completely at home behind the wheel. I really think we're going to have a good year."*

His words did not reassure his rivals. The new Williams FW26 had been quick out of the box while the McLaren MP4-19 was still an unknown quantity but Michael did not seem to fear these two teams as much as in the past. *"I'm maybe a bit wrong about the McLarens,"* he stated. *"Given the times they set this winter I don't think they'll be much of a threat: not at the start anyway. You can't discount the Williams either but I think that my most dangerous rival will be my team-mate, Rubens Barrichello; he's got the same car as me!"* It is a well-known fact that the Brazilian has never really posed a threat to the German and it was enough to give cold shivers down the spine of

lovers of closely fought grands prix. If Michael's predictions proved true, the colour red was going to dominate the 2004 season.

Sixth quickest in practice, Mark Webber shines in front of his home crowd.

Mark Webber is just too good to be true. His matinee idol looks earn him the envy of both men and women some of whom cannot stomach his Teflon character.

He does lay it on a bit thick from time to time. He is always happy, always smiling, never criticises which gets on the nerves of some people in the little world of F1. In addition to driving he looks after the GPDA, the Grand Prix Drivers' Association, whose aim is to improve circuit safety and he also wants to allow the public to get closer to the drivers. On the track he rarely makes a mistake. He is quick, a good test driver and never puts a foot wrong in front of the journalists. Mr Perfect, in fact!

He has had an easy ride so far. Now people want to see if he is made of the right stuff. He made his F1 debut in a Minardi in the 2002 Australian Grand Prix and finished in a remarkable fifth place sending his home crowd into spasms of ecstasy. He was even carried up onto the rostrum. His performances caught the eye of Jaguar and he joined the team in 2003 scoring 17 points and putting in a few remarkable qualifying performances. He stayed with the Cat for 2004 so the onus was on him to do better than the previous year. It all depended on his new car, the R5. *"It's not going to be easy,"* he admitted. *"This year I'd like to score a rostrum finish for the first time, but if it doesn't happen, no worries. We're going to have to fight against very powerful teams on our level, BAR, Toyota and Sauber for example."* In fact, the Australian's 2004 best was sixth in Germany.

He got off to a good start by qualifying sixth. *"It's really fantastic,"* he smiled. *"The car behaves well but we're going to have to work on our race performance which is still not up to scratch."* Today Mark Webber is one of the stars of F1. But it's a cruel world and to make his mark (to coin a phrase) Mr Clean as some call him is going to have to deliver. *"Going from Minardi to Jaguar was a marvellous opportunity for me,"* he confided. *"I know that the toughest is still to come."*

^
Kimi Raïkkönen could do no better than tenth on the grid. The MP4-19s failed to fulfil the hopes placed in them.

<<
It was impossible to escape from F1 in the Melbourne pedestrian zones. Anybody who was a Michael Schumacher fan was in for a hard time.

<
Mark Webber was on home territory and must have had writer's cramp by the time he finished signing autographs!

Starting grid

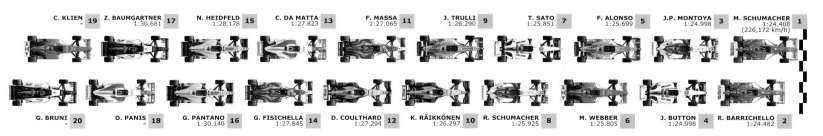

Driver	No.	Time
C. KLIEN	19	-
Z. BAUMGARTNER	17	1:30.681
N. HEIDFELD	15	1:28.178
C. DA MATTA	13	1:27.823
F. MASSA	11	1:27.065
J. TRULLI	9	1:26.290
T. SATO	7	1:25.851
F. ALONSO	5	1:25.699
J.P. MONTOYA	3	1:24.998
M. SCHUMACHER	1	1:24.408 (226,172 km/h)
G. BRUNI	20	-
O. PANIS	18	-
G. PANTANO	16	1:30.140
G. FISICHELLA	14	1:27.845
D. COULTHARD	12	1:27.294
K. RÄIKKÖNEN	10	1:26.297
R. SCHUMACHER	8	1:25.925
M. WEBBER	6	1:25.805
J. BUTTON	4	1:24.998
R. BARRICHELLO	2	1:24.482

First corner shenanigans!

While the Ferraris strolled off into the sunset, there was a bit of racing going on behind. The F2004s made a perfect start which could not be said for the volatile Colombian. Montoya missed his braking for the first corner and Fernando Alonso fifth on the grid promptly slipped through to take third behind the red cars. And there he stayed for the rest of the afternoon. *"I made a good start,"* said the Spaniard," even if Juan forced me to put a couple of wheels on the grass.

Then I realised that I was not quick enough to catch the leaders and I ended up feeling a bit lonely like I was in the middle of nowhere! I had no problems and this rostrum finish is a whole lot better than what we were expecting here. We know we have a good car and our main objective is to score points during the first three grands prix before the arrival of a major engine evolution."

Jarno Trulli in the second Renault finished seventh a lap down and scored two points. The two Williams in the hands of Ralf Schumacher and Montoya in fourth and fifth were never in the hunt. Although the Colombian qualified much higher than his team-mate the latter passed him during the refuelling stops, which numbered three like all the other drivers. Into sixth came Jenson Button in his Lucky Strike BAR-Honda after being in fourth for a good part of the race while Takuma Sato in the other BAR was ninth.

Mark Webber's excellent qualifying performance was reduced to nothing by a gearbox problem, which led to his retirement: a bit of a disappointment for the masses of Aussies come to cheer him on.

Total domination

Sunday 13h30: Pascal Vasselon, the man in charge of the Michelin F1 programme was walking up and down the grid gazing at the sky with a worried look in his eye. The temperature in Melbourne was only 18° and there was no sign of the hot weather that had been forecast. This meant that the French tyres did not have the hoped for advantage.

Would it have made any difference? Unlikely given Ferrari's incredible domination of the grand prix.

It was not a race: it was a master class. In Melbourne the Prancing Horse cars dashed their rivals' hopes and won the first round of the championship in a canter. *"I thought we'd be competitive but not to that extent. You could say it was a perfect race but a tough one as well. At the start Rubens was very quick and I had to really push to keep in front of him. It wasn't until the end when Alonso slowed that we were able to lift off. As it was the first race with the new regulations, which allow only one engine per weekend, we preferred not to take any risks and nurse it as much as possible. I really slowed down at the end of the grand prix."* Even Michael Schumacher was surprised afterwards.

In the Williams camp Mario Theissen, the BMW competitions manger did not hide his disappointment. *"We didn't expect that,"* he groaned, *"especially the fact that Ferrari would be able to open up such a huge gap. We've going to have to work very hard."*

Many people in the paddock after the Australian Grand Prix were asking themselves where Michael Schumacher drew his motivation from. *"I drive for a great team,"* he replied. *"The atmosphere is fantastic. I love this sport. I love driving; it's what I do best. I'll continue as long as it pleases me even if I've nothing left to prove. It's far too early to state that I'm going to dominate the whole season in this fashion. We'll have to see what happens on other circuits and in other weather conditions to get a clearer picture of the situation. Last year we had a difficult season. If the race here had gone normally we'd have scored a double. So it's a bit early to draw any conclusions."*

< First rostrum ceremony and first double of the year for the Scuderia.

Michael Schumacher finished 13 seconds ahead of his team-mate and over 30 ahead of Fernando Alonso. He was never under threat throughout the race.
<

Juan Pablo blows it in public!

Was Juan Pablo Montoya already losing his cool before the season had really begun? On the Thursday before the race Allianz one of the Williams team's main sponsors, organised a press conference. A couple of actors slipped in among the journalists and began to pose ridiculous questions. One of them answered his mobile while he was asking Juan Pablo a question and speaking loudly made it clear he was talking to his mother. He then asked the Colombian if he could come and play golf with her! It was all too much for the Williams driver who got up and stalked out of the conference. So no luck for the Allianz guests who were supposed to have done a few laps of the track with Montoya in a BMW. When he arrived at the circuit he made a few digs at Williams. *"The Williams team, it's a little like certain girl friends. There comes a moment when you get fed up and it's time to dump them,"* he quipped concerning his transfer to McLaren in 2005. If the rest of the season was to continue in the same vein a confrontation with his employers seemed inevitable.

"Good luck!" Pierre Dupasquier went to say hello to Jean Todt on the grid. He worked with the Scuderia boss when the latter looked after Peugeot in the World Rally Championship. Since then Todt has become a redoubtable rival.
V

Go for it!

David Coulthard in maximum attack mode with a couple of wheels on the grass. The Scot was having a difficult start to the season after winning on this same circuit in 2003. He qualified twelfth and finished in a humble eighth position.

paddock

Weekend gossip

> 00.00s was the gap separating Montoya and Jenson Button after qualifying practice. They both set exactly the same time and normally speaking the driver who set it first has pride of place on the grid. This time the new regulations stipulated that the driver who was quickest in the first part of the qualifying session would start in front. As it had been Montoya he was ahead of Button on the grid.

> Contrary to Ferrari the Saubers did not exactly set the track on fire during qualifying. Fisichella could probably have been in the top ten had he not made a big mistake in the first sector. *"I managed to get the car back but I lost concentration and made a number of small errors afterwards,"* Fisico commented. *"It's a pity as the car was handling really well."*

> The new qualifying format which gave each driver two bites at the cherry on the same day did not really convince many people in Melbourne. There was not much point to the first run as all it did was decide the order of the second one. Immediately rumours began to go round that the format would be changed but in fact, the teams were stuck with it for the rest of the season. Only the Minardi squad really suffered in Melbourne as it had just two minutes to change the car in qualifying trim (with virtually no fuel) to race set up. In the light of this the regs were changed slightly to create a bigger gap between the two sessions and final qualifying was started at the scheduled time rather than straight after the end of the first run.

> The Bahrain Grand Prix, which was going to be held for the first time on 4th April, was threatened with terrorist attacks. The organisers claimed that all the necessary safety measures had been taken and to demonstrate their faith and cool things down sponsored the Jordan team. Throughout the season the flanks of the yellow cars were decorated with a sign of peace.

> The new regulations specified that apart from the four teams in the first four places in the 2003 Constructors' Championship all the others could enter a third car for the Friday practice session. Which they all did at Melbourne except Minardi and Sauber. Paul Stoddart's outfit was supposed to have Belgian Bas Linders as third driver but he was refused his super licence, while Peter Sauber said he did not have enough money to enter three cars. *"Even if we had the cash for a third car we wouldn't do so with Neel Jani, the official test driver. It'd be stupid. What we really need is someone with experience."*

> A record crowd turned up for Friday's practice, some 81500, the highest ever figure since the grand prix came to Melbourne in 1996. It showed a fresh burst of enthusiasm for F1 after years of steady decline.

> On Friday Bernie Ecclestone made a rare appearance in the press room to say that he had detested the first day's practice. *"I don't like what I saw"*, he said. *"The cars didn't do a lot of laps today and it's not good for the spectators."*

> The drivers did in fact limit their track time because of the new single engine rule, which stated that the same block had to last the whole weekend. Bernie should have known that it would be like that. He began to fight for the suppression pure and simple of the Friday session so that he could add another couple of races to the calendar making a total of 20 grands prix in all. It was an old chestnut that would re-emerge throughout the whole season back stage when the future of F1 was being discussed.

Practice

All the time trials

N°	Driver	N° Chassis - Engine	Practice 1 Friday	Pos.	Practice 2 Friday	Pos.	Practice 3 Saturday	Pos.	Practice 4 Saturday	Pos.	Pre-qual. Saturday	Pos.	Qualif. Saturday	Pos.
1.	Michael Schumacher	Ferrari F2004 234	1:25.127	1	1:24.718	1	1:25.786	1	1:25.093	1	1:25.301	2	1:24.408	1
2.	Rubens Barrichello	Ferrari F2004 236	1:25.361	2	1:24.826	2	1:26.159	2	1:25.649	4	1:25.992	8	1:24.482	2
3.	Juan Pablo Montoya	Williams FW26 05 - BMW	1:27.462	6	1:26.206	7	1:26.195	3	1:25.255	2	1:25.226	1	1:24.998	3
4.	Ralf Schumacher	Williams FW26 03 - BMW	1:27.675	7	1:25.882	6	1:26.390	4	1:25.628	3	1:25.445	3	1:25.925	8
5.	David Coulthard	McLaren MP4-19 03 - Mercedes	1:27.264	4	1:26.215	8	1:26.428	5	1:26.133	10	1:25.652	5	1:27.294	12
6.	Kimi Räikkönen	McLaren MP4-19 04 - Mercedes	1:28.233	12	1:26.579	10	1:26.725	7	1:26.127	9	1:25.592	4	1:26.297	10
7.	Jarno Trulli	Renault R24-03	1:27.025	3	1:25.757	3	1:26.817	9	1:25.927	7	1:27.357	15	1:26.290	9
8.	Fernando Alonso	Renault R24-02	1:27.359	5	1:25.853	5	1:26.610	6	1:25.908	5	1.25.928	7	1:25.699	5
9.	Jenson Button	B.A.R 006-02 - Honda	1:27.867	8	1:25.786	4	1:26.995	10	1:26.403	11	1:25.898	6	1:24.998	4
10.	Takuma Sato	B.A.R 006-01 - Honda	1:28.874	13	1:26.967	12	1:28.438	15	1:27.592	16	1:26.737	11	1:25.851	7
11.	Giancarlo Fisichella	Sauber C23-02 - Petronas	1:29.120	15	1:26.601	11	1:27.744	13	1:27.195	15	1:26.286	10	1:27.845	14
12.	Felipe Massa	Sauber C23-03 - Petronas		24	1:26.969	13	1:28.341	14	1:27.172	14	1:26.833	12	1:27.065	11
14.	Mark Webber	Jaguar R5-03	1:28.089	10	1:26.312	9	1:26.804	8	1:26.066	8	1:26.232	9	1:25.805	6
15.	Christian Klien	Jaguar R5-01	1:30.046	19	1:27.724	17	1:28.572	16	1:27.088	13	1:27.258	14		19
16.	Cristiano da Matta	Toyota TF104/02	1:28.955	14	1:27.710	16	1:27.717	16	1:26.597	12	1:28.274	17	1:27.823	13
17.	Olivier Panis	Toyota TF104/03	1:29.169	16	1:27.807	18	1:27.107	11	1:25.916	6	1:27.253	13		18
18.	Nick Heidfeld	Jordan EJ14/03 - Ford	1:29.826	17	1:27.826	19	1:30.233	18	1:27.755	17	1:27.469	16	1:28.178	15
19.	Giorgio Pantano	Jordan EJ14/02 - Ford	1:30.100	20	1:30.061	23	1:30.057	17	1:28.825	18	1:29.156	18	1:30.140	16
20.	Gianmaria Bruni	Minardi PS04B/02 - Cosworth	1:33.236	23	1:28.991	21	1:31.310	19	1:30.496	19	1:30.912	19		20
21.	Zsolt Baumgartner	Minardi PS04B/01 - Cosworth	1:32.886	22	1:29.708	22	1:32.295	20	1:31.763	20	1:32.606	20	1:30.681	17
35.	Anthony Davidson	B.A.R 006-03 - Honda	1:27.921	9	1:27.516	15								
37.	Björn Wirdheim	Jaguar R5-02	1:30.033	18	1:28.781	20								
38.	Ricardo Zonta	Toyota TF104/04	1:28.118	11	1:27.165	14								
39.	Timo Glock	Jordan EJ14/02 - Ford	1:30.618	21	1:30.291	24								

Maximum speed

N°	Driver	P1 Qualifs	Pos.	P1 Race	Pos.	P2 Qualifs	Pos.	P2 Race	Pos.	Finish Qualifs	Pos.	Finish Race	Pos.	Trap Qualifs	Pos.	Trap Race	Pos.
1.	M. Schumacher	291,8	2	294,5	2	302,0	1	311,5	3	304,0	2	308,3	3	317,0	3	323,4	3
2.	R. Barrichello	291,8	3	296,3	1	301,0	3	308,6	5	305,2	1	309,0	1	317,9	2	323,9	2
3.	J.P. Montoya	291,9	1	294,4	3	301,5	2	311,9	2	303,5	3	308,3	4	316,2	5	320,1	6
4.	R. Schumacher	286,1	9	293,1	5	299,6	7	310,8	4	303,4	4	307,4	5	316,7	4	321,8	5
5.	D. Coulthard	285,4	10	289,5	9	295,6	12	306,4	9	298,6	9	302,3	9	312,8	9	318,2	12
6.	K. Räikkönen	285,0	11	287,8	11	296,5	11	306,9	7	298,2	10	302,8	8	311,2	10	318,7	11
7.	J. Trulli	283,0	14	287,3	12	294,3	14	304,0	14	294,8	14	300,6	14	309,7	14	311,6	17
8.	F. Alonso	287,3	7	289,6	8	294,2	15	303,2	16	296,7	13	300,5	15	310,7	12	312,3	16
9.	J. Button	289,7	5	293,2	4	299,6	6	305,0	11	300,0	7	301,6	10	306,7	10	319,3	8
10.	T. Sato	290,0	4	285,7	16	299,0	8	306,4	10	299,2	8	301,0	12	314,6	7	318,8	10
11.	G. Fisichella	288,5	6	292,7	6	300,4	4	311,9	1	302,7	5	308,5	2	318,7	1	323,0	4
12.	F. Massa	284,1	12	289,0	10	299,8	5	306,7	8	300,8	6	305,5	6	315,3	6	323,9	1
14.	M. Webber	286,9	8	289,8	7	296,9	9	304,3	13	298,1	11	301,2	11	310,9	11	319,9	7
15.	C. Klien	269,8	18	285,7	14	296,5	10	307,9	6			304,6	7	207,5	18	318,9	9
16.	C. Da Matta	283,1	13	287,2	13	295,4	13	303,8	15	296,7	12	300,0	16	309,8	13	315,4	13
17.	O. Panis			280,5	18			304,5	12			300,8	13			313,1	14
18.	N. Heidfeld	281,6	15	285,7	15	289,3	18	298,5	18	293,9	15	296,4	17	306,9	16	311,5	18
19.	G. Pantano	274,9	17	280,7	17	289,4	17	296,9	20	291,1	17	294,7	20	302,9	17	310,4	20
20.	G. Bruni			277,0	20			302,1	17			295,6	18			311,2	19
21.	Z. Baumgartner	276,0	16	278,4	19	291,8	16	297,7	19	292,6	16	295,6	19	307,7	15	312,4	15

Race

Classification & Retirements

Pos.	Driver	Team	Lap	Time	Average
1.	M. Schumacher	Ferrari	58	1:24:15.757	219,010 km/h
2.	R. Barrichello	Ferrari	58	+ 13.605	218,423 km/h
3.	F. Alonso	Renault	58	+ 34.673	217,519 km/h
4.	R. Schumacher	Williams BMW	58	+ 1:00.423	216,424 km/h
5.	J.P. Montoya	Williams BMW	58	+ 1:08.536	216,081 km/h
6.	J. Button	B.A.R Honda	58	+ 1:10.598	215,994 km/h
7.	J. Trulli	Renault	57	1 lap	215,191 km/h
8.	D. Coulthard	McLaren Mercedes	57	1 lap	215,004 km/h
9.	T. Sato	B.A.R Honda	57	1 lap	213,998 km/h
10.	G. Fisichella	Sauber Petronas	57	1 lap	212,448 km/h
11.	C. Klien	Jaguar	56	2 laps	210,693 km/h
12.	C. Da Matta	Toyota	56	2 laps	210,376 km/h
13.	O. Panis	Toyota	56	2 laps	208,686 km/h
14.	G. Pantano	Jordan Ford	55	3 laps	207,645 km/h

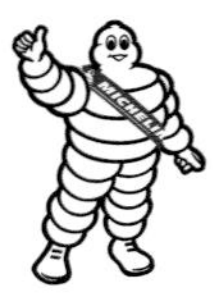

Driver	Team		Reason
F. Massa	Sauber Petronas	45	Engine problem
N. Heidfeld	Jordan Ford	44	Clutch problem, gearbox stuck in 1st
G. Bruni	Minardi Cosworth	44	15 laps 160,473 km/h Not classified
M. Webber	Jaguar	30	Loss of 6th and 7th gears
Z. Baumgartner	Minardi Cosworth	14	Electronic engine management
K. Räikkönen	McLaren Mercedes	10	Blown engine because of loss of water pressure

Fastest laps

	Driver	Time	Lap	Average
1.	M. Schumacher	1:24.125	29	226,933 km/h
2.	R. Barrichello	1:24.179	8	226,788 km/h
3.	F. Alonso	1:25.088	10	224,365 km/h
4.	J.P. Montoya	1:25.286	42	223,844 km/h
5.	R. Schumacher	1:25.824	11	222,441 km/h
6.	M. Webber	1:25.952	15	222,110 km/h
7.	J. Button	1:25.982	24	222,032 km/h
8.	T. Sato	1:26.077	43	221,787 km/h
9.	J. Trulli	1:26.275	9	221,278 km/h
10.	G. Fisichella	1:26.282	39	221,260 km/h
11.	D. Coulthard	1:26.328	13	221,142 km/h
12.	F. Massa	1:26.846	11	219,823 km/h
13.	N. Heidfeld	1:27.503	27	218,173 km/h
14.	O. Panis	1:27.807	35	217,417 km/h
15.	C. Da Matta	1:27.820	41	217,385 km/h
16.	C. Klien	1:27.840	6	217,336 km/h
17.	K. Räikkönen	1:27.936	7	217,098 km/h
18.	G. Pantano	1:28.523	15	215,659 km/h
19.	G. Bruni	1:30.161	10	211,741 km/h
20.	Z. Baumgartner	1:30.621	8	210,666 km/h

Pit stops

	Driver	Time	Lap	Stop n°
1.	G. Fisichella	22.147	8	1
2.	J.P. Montoya	23.044	10	1
3.	R. Barrichello	21.737	11	1
4.	F. Alonso	20.294	11	1
5.	J. Button	21.787	11	1
6.	G. Bruni	23.909	11	1
7.	M. Schumacher	22.930	12	1
8.	Z. Baumgartner	1:09.349	11	1
9.	J. Trulli	22.598	12	1
10.	R. Schumacher	20.509	12	1
11.	T. Sato	21.746	12	1
12.	C. Da Matta	34.030	12	1
13.	M. Webber	23.993	13	1
14.	D. Couthard	24.708	14	1
15.	F. Massa	24.060	14	1
16.	N. Heidfeld	21.737	14	1
17.	O. Panis	23.099	14	1
18.	C. Klien	28.144	16	1
19.	G. Pantano	23.213	18	1
20.	F. Alonso	21.994	24	2
21.	C. Da Matta	21.459	24	2
22.	J. Button	23.459	26	2
23.	J.P. Montoya	22.595	26	2
24.	G. Bruni	25.646	25	2
25.	M. Webber	21.548	27	2
26.	T. Sato	26.120	27	2
27.	R. Schumacher	22.061	28	2
28.	J. Trulli	22.799	28	2
29.	R. Barrichello	20.889	29	2
30.	N. Heidfeld	21.477	28	2
31.	G. Fisichella	22.079	28	2
32.	M. Schumacher	20.919	30	2
33.	D. Coulthard	23.562	36	2
34.	F. Massa	24.053	36	2
35.	G. Bruni	17:36.035	35	3
36.	C. Klien	26.732	37	2
37.	G. Pantano	24.199	37	2
38.	O. Panis	22.972	37	2
39.	F. Alonso	22.194	40	3
40.	J. Trulli	20.426	41	3
41.	J. Button	22.224	42	3
42.	C. Da Matta	21.959	42	3
43.	R. Barrichello	20.958	44	3
44.	J.P. Montoya	24.331	44	3
45.	M. Schumacher	21.321	45	3
46.	N. Heidfeld	1:19.542	43	3
47.	G. Fisichella	21.342	44	3
48.	R. Schumacher	21.729	45	3
49.	T. Sato	21.338	45	3

Race leader

Driver	Laps in the lead	Nber of Laps
M. Schumacher	1 > 58	58

Driver	Nber of Laps	Kilometers
M. Schumacher	58	307,574 km

Gaps on the leader board

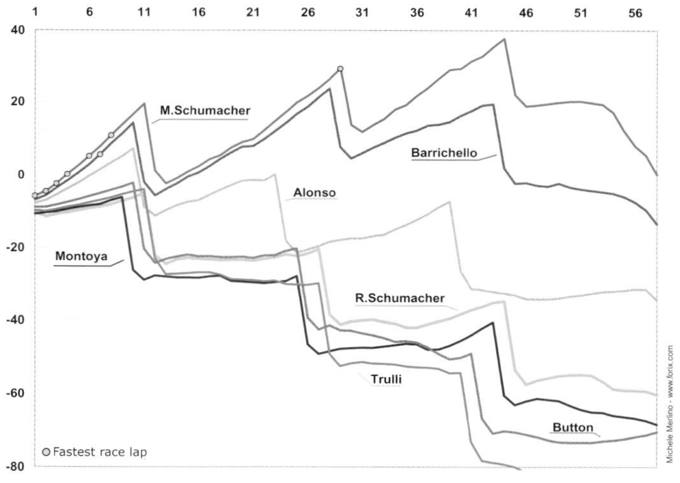

The table of „ Leading Gaps „ is based on the lap by lap information, but only for some selected drivers (for ease of understanding). It adds-in the gaps between these drivers. The line marked „0" represents the winner's average speed. In general, this starts at a slower speed than its eventual average speed, because of the weight of fuel carried on board the car. Then, it goes above the average, before dropping again during the refueling pit stops. This graph therefore allows one to see at any given time the number of seconds (vertically) seperating the drivers on every lap (horizontally)

Tour par tour

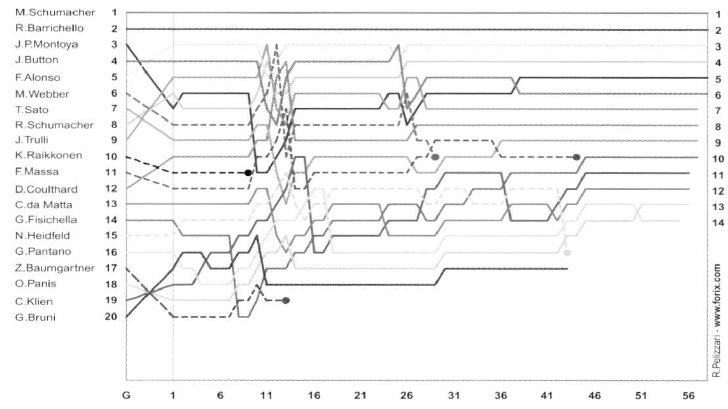

Championship after one round

Drivers

1. M. Schumacher ....(1 win) 10
2. R. Barrichello...8
3. F. Alonso..6
4. R. Schumacher 5
5. J.P. Montoya 4
6. J. Button..3
7. J. Trulli 2
8. D. Coulthard 1
9. T. Sato...0
10. G. Fisichella..0
11. C. Klien 0
12. C. Da Matta...0
13. O. Panis..0
14. G. Pantano..0

F. Massa ....-
N. Heidffeld ....-
G. Bruni ....-
M. Webber..-
Z. Baumgartner...-
K. Räikkönen ....-

Constructors

1. Scuderia Ferrari Marlboro ......(1 win).........18
2. BMW WilliamsF1 Team..............................9
3. Mild Seven Renault F1 Team.......................8
4. Lucky Strike B.A.R Honda 3
5. West McLaren Mercedes.............................1
6. Sauber Petronas 0
7. Jaguar Racing..0
8. Panasonic Toyota Racing 0
9. Jordan Ford...0

Minardi Cosworth ....-

The circuit

Name	Albert Park, Melbourne
Length	5303 meters
Distance	58 laps, 307.574 km
Date	March 7, 2004
Weather	cloudy, 19-18°c
Track temperature	24-23°c

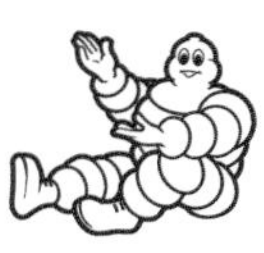

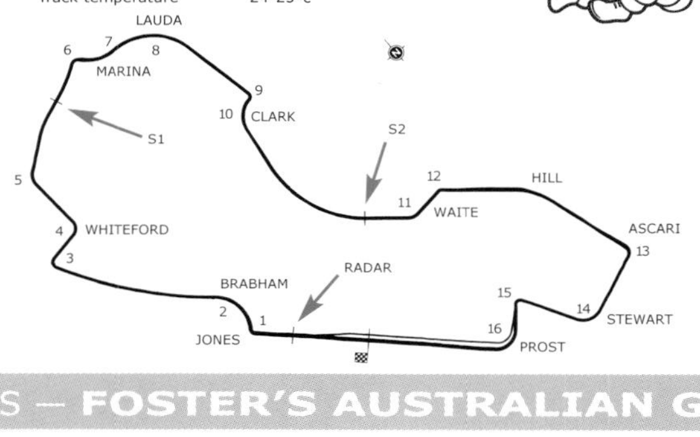

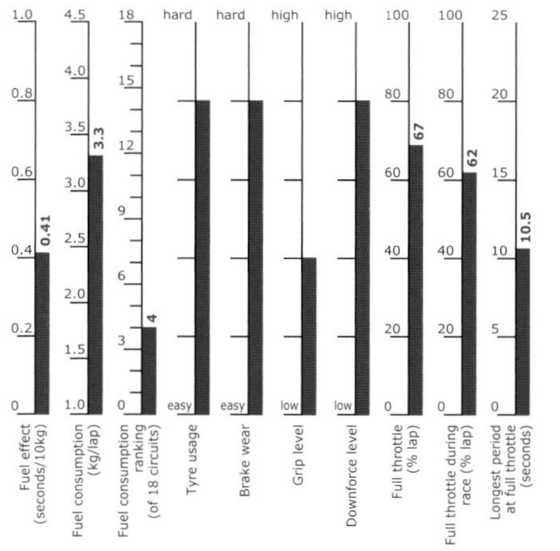

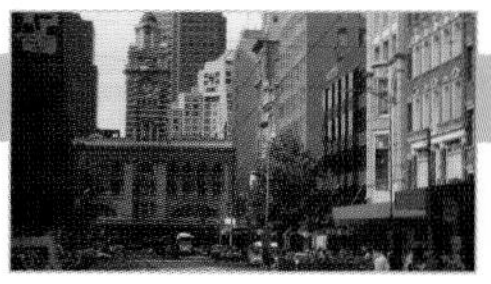

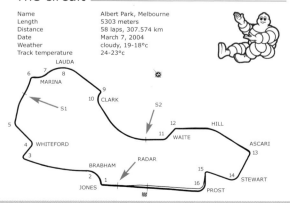

THE MOMENT OF TRUTH

Ferrari's second consecutive win in conditions that were completely different from those in Melbourne showed that the F2004 was at home everywhere whatever the circuit or the weather. With only two races gone Michael Schumacher looked odds-on favourite for the title.
At last Jenson Button scored a rostrum finish after 68 grands prix. He was delighted: *"It's not the high point of my career but it's a great way to kick off the year,"* he smiled. *"At the start I had a slight coming together with Jarno Trulli and I was afraid that my car was damaged. Finally, it ran perfectly."*

The outcome of the season decided at Sepang?

When the teams present their new cars during the winter optimism is generally de rigueur! The Williams squad in particular was oozing confidence. Had they not almost won the 2003 Constructors' Championship being pipped by Ferrari in the very last race?

The ambience at McLaren was the same and 2004 looked all roses and sunshine! However, after only one race the rose was already losing its petals as the Ferraris had blitzed their rivals in Australia.

The only cause for optimism was the fact that the weather had been cool in Melbourne and as it looked like the remaining races would take place in higher temperatures it seemed possible that the Bridgestones which were not as quick in such conditions, would prevent Ferrari from exercising total domination.

This was the main subject of discussion doing the rounds in the Sepang paddock. The Japanese manufacturer had been working on this heat problem during the winter but had it done enough? In the answer to this question lay the key to the rest of the year. And the Malaysian race was the ideal yardstick as it is generally the hottest of the whole championship.

Saturday was another body blow to the Ferrari's rivals. In conditions where the temperature hovered around 50° the red cars met no problems. Michael was on pole and Rubens in third place. Both drivers were surprised as well.

"We didn't think we'd be so far behind the Ferraris," said Ralf Schumacher, *"above all not behind the Renaults. We're not where we expected to be and I hope the engineers can turn the situation round."*

In the Michelin camp the highest-placed car was Mark Webber's Jaguar on the front row! Behind came the Williams and McLarens, not a very promising sign. Only the endurance of the French tyres could make a difference. So if Ferrari won again it would be because Bridgestone had closed the gap to its rival in hot weather conditions; and the probability was that the red cars would dominate the rest of the season.

> A lightly clothed Michael Schumacher arrived the Sepang Paddock. Like most of the members of the F1 circus he had just spent a quiet week's holiday after the Australian Grand Prix.

It was bloody hot. Watching practice in such conditions required a large dose of courage. The Malaysians are used to the scorching heat and did their best to protect themselves from the sun. >

The Minardis qualified in 16 and 17th places on the grid. Not bad for a team with such little funding. v

The grid

Fernando Alonso set the quickest time in the prequalifying session and looked like he would bag a place on the front row. In fact, the young Spaniard found himself down in nineteenth spot after he aborted his qualifying lap. *"It's my fault,"* he stated. *"The rear of the car broke away in corner 14. But I'm confident. Even though I'm starting from the last row I know I can fight for points."*

The fact that Mark Webber was on the front row was a big surprise. He did not expect it himself. *"Frankly we're very surprised to be there,"* smiled the Australian. *"Yesterday the car was working well. So we didn't change anything. Just waited for qualifying."*

> It was Mark Webber's first and last front row of the season. He did not take advantage of it and made a dreadful start.

In Brief

> After a couple of grands prix, it seemed a bit premature to talk about transfers. At Sepang, however, Ralf Schumacher's future was one of the main topics of conversation. Some said that he was leaving the Williams squad on Sunday evening! It was possible that he would join Toyota in 2005, which was confirmed by a member of the Japanese outfit. *"I've spoken to Frank Williams. I'd like to stay with his team next year but I can't say anything else for the moment,"* commented the German.

> Both Renault drivers were on holiday in the Maldives between the Australian and Malaysian events and Fernando Alonso only learned of the terrorist attack in Madrid when he spoke to his parents on the phone. *"We're really going through hard times which doesn't spare ordinary people like you and me,"* said the Spanish driver. *"I'm devastated by what's happened and I'd like to present my deepest sympathies to all the families of the victims."*

> After the mix-up in Australia where the new qualifying formula was unanimously lambasted Bernie Ecclestone asked for it to be split into two distinct halves with the first part starting at13h00 and the second at 14h00. This move was to enable the TV channels to show only the second half of the qualifying session.

Starting grid

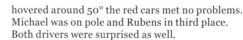

* G. PANTANO — Starts from pit lane		

Top row:
F. ALONSO 19 — Z. BAUMGARTNER 17 1:39.272 — N. HEIDFELD 15 1:36.569 — C. KLIEN 13 1:35.158 — F. MASSA 11 1:35.039 — D. COULTHARD 9 1:34.602 — R. SCHUMACHER 7 1:34.235 — K. RÄIKKÖNEN 5 1:34.164 — R. BARRICHELLO 3 1:33.756 — M. SCHUMACHER 1 1:33.074 (214,397 km/h)

Bottom row:
T. SATO 20 — G. PANTANO* 18 1:39.902 — G. BRUNI 16 1:38.577 — O. PANIS 14 1:35.617 — G. FISICHELLA 12 1:35.061 — C. DA MATTA 10 1:34.917 — J. TRULLI 8 1:34.413 — J. BUTTON 6 1:34.221 — J.P. MONTOYA 4 1:34.054 — M. WEBBER 2 1:33.715

A few drops, three stops and a win

As the cars lined up on the grid in Malaysia little did the protagonists realise that Michael Schumacher's win in Australia was a pointer of what was to come. Few, however, even in their wildest dreams would have imagined that the sextuple world champion would rack up another twelve victories in the remaining seventeen grands prix.

Hopes for a closely contested race were dashed as soon as the lights went out. Mark Webber made a dog's breakfast of his start and the two Ferraris opened up a gap with Michael in front of Rubens. The Brazilian however, was caught out on the section of the circuit made greasy by a few drops of rain, went wide and Juan Pablo Montoya and Kimi Raïkkönen slipped past. The Williams driver spent the rest of the race trying to catch the Ferrari and as refuelling stops intervened the gap got as low as 3.3s. *"In the last part of the race I thought that I could put pressure on Michael but I was held up by Rubens Barrichello so I decided to settle for eight points; it was the best I could do for myself and for my team. My car was much better than in Australia."* As proof the Colombian set the fastest lap of the race twenty-eighth time round in 1m 34.223s.

On the same lap Ralf Schumacher in the second FW 26 retired when his engine blew. He was fourth at the time.

Jenson Button finished third finally climbing up onto the rostrum for the first time in his F1

"Take that!" Michael Schumacher ensures Jenson Button enjoys his first visit to the podium.

All the BAR team clustered under the rostrum to celebrate Button's fantastic result. It was not his last either, as he was to finish in the top three another nine times during the season.

career. He was obviously very pleased to achieve this feat on a circuit where he had been so close to it in 2002. His team-mate Takuma Sato had a pretty eventful race that included an off and a blown engine on lap 53 – a foretaste of what was to come for the little Japanese. Finally, he finished in fifteenth place as he had covered the minimum distance to be classified. This grand prix, which is generally reckoned to be the toughest of the season, saw a remarkably small number of retirements as 16 out of the 20 starters finished.

Michael in seventh heaven

Michael was one happy bunny after his victory scored in totally different conditions to his first of the season in Australia. It opened up new perspectives for the rest of the year, comforting ones. *"After the way things went in practice, I was hoping for a win here,"* he declared. It's great! The start of the race was tricky, as the rain had fallen on two places on the circuit. As I was in front I had to be especially careful. After that the car was very quick at the crucial moments, just before and after the tyre changes.

His success was perhaps all the more unexpected, as the Sepang circuit is not one that favours the red cars. *"True,"* replied the victor. *"This year we haven't run into the same problems as before on this track. Bridgestone have done a great job and solved their problems in hot weather conditions. So if we're good here then it shouldn't be any different on the other circuits where there are high temperatures. I prefer having a couple of wins in my pocket rather than zero like last year. This being said there are another sixteen grands prix to go and we know that our rivals can react very swiftly.*

Honestly, I think it's going to be a difficult season and the race coming up in Bahrain is a completely unknown quantity for everybody so we don't know which cars will be the quickest."

Each driver had his own way of coping with the heat. Rubens Barrichello douses himself one last time before climbing into his Ferrari's sweltering cockpit.

Fill'er up!

Michael Schumacher at the pump. In Malaysia the German stopped three times on his way to notching up his second victory of the year. The best was yet to come.

Disaster for Jaguar

> Juan Pablo Montoya with his father Juan Montoya and his wife Connie who all travelled to Malaysia. He was the only drive to remotely threaten Schumacher during the race. He finished second and set the fastest lap.

Mark Webber, qualified on the front row, soon had his illusions shattered and his race finished on the grass on lap 24. *"It's been a very disappointing day,"* said a shattered Aussie. *"I made a bad start and lost seven places. Then I passed Ralf Schumacher who nudged me from behind which caused a puncture. I had to stop and I was penalised for exceeding the speed limit in the pit lane. After that I went off several times before finally spinning out under braking."*

Fernando's exploit

Fernando Alonso made a fighting comeback. He was second last on the grid and by the end of lap 1 he was in an amazing tenth place! He then ran up against David Coulthard and came home seventh. *"I'm happy to have scored two points after yesterday's incident,"* he concluded. *"I don't think that our strategy really paid off and I'm sure I could have been even higher up."*

> Kimi Raïkkönen qualified fifth but transmission problems ended his gallop. It was the 2003 runner-up's second retirement in two races.

No rest for the Williams engineers

> Olivier Panis in his Toyota came home in a lowly twelfth place in the grand prix after his thirteenth place in Melbourne. He stopped at his pit five times which did not exactly help matters. The season had got off to a rotten start for the Japanese team.
> ∨

This was the moment of truth for the boys from Williams. Before the race the opinion of numerous engineers and Michael Schumacher himself was that the result of the Malaysian Grand Prix would be a strong pointer to the outcome of the 2004 world championship. Another win by the Ferrari-Bridgestone duo and it was time for the bookies to pack up and go home. If Ferrari tripped up then everything was possible. As things turned out Schumacher and the Scuderia scored their second win on the trot.

The first was on a city circuit in cool weather and no.2 on a fast track in high temperatures. *"They seem to have a car that's adapted to all kinds of conditions,"* sighed a realistic Frank Dernie, one of the designers of the Williams FW 26. *"There's not much we can do about them this year."* Jean Todt, the Scuderia's boss,

was not on exactly the same wavelength. *"Today we've shown that the Ferraris are competitive even in a set-up that is the exact opposite of the one in Melbourne. We can't leave anything to chance. The championship is going to be very close,"* the Frenchman declared.

It was maybe a tongue in cheek statement as after only two races Schumacher was already eight points ahead of his closest challenger Montoya.

In Malaysia the Williams driver managed to close the gap to almost 3 seconds after his first refuelling stop. After that the leading Ferrari was able to pull away at will. In such conditions there was no way the Colombian could threaten him. *"It's early days yet,"* said Juan Pablo. *"Our car has to be in front, everywhere all the time like the Ferrari. We're close but we're going to have to work hard to beat it."*

In the race he was held up by Barrichello and also by Felipe Massa whom he was lapping. *"That bloody blue Ferrari's behaviour was disgraceful,"* he complained after the finish. The blue Ferrari was an allusion to the fact that the Swiss team receives a lot of help from Maranello such as engines, gearboxes, electronic aids etc.

The year had got off to a disappointing start for Williams. The FW 26's aerodynamics were not yet the focal point of contention. Only much later in the season were they revised leading to the firing of their designer, Antonia Terzi.

She, together with the other Williams' engineers, was not going to get much sleep in the weeks that followed the Malaysian Grand Prix. There was a lot of work to be done.

results

Practice

All the time trials

N°	Driver	N° Chassis - Engine	Practice 1 Friday	Pos.	Practice 2 Friday	Pos.	Practice 3 Saturday	Pos.	Practice 4 Saturday	Pos.	Pre-qual. Saturday	Pos.	Qualif. Saturday	Pos.
1.	Michael Schumacher	Ferrari F2004 234	1:34.437	1	1:35.094	4	1:33.391	1	1:33.526	1	1:33.865	4	1:33.074	1
2.	Rubens Barrichello	Ferrari F2004 236	1:35.380	2	1:35.373	10	1:34.362	4	1:34.061	5	1:34.132	6	1:33.756	3
3.	Juan Pablo Montoya	Williams FW26 05 - BMW	1:36.606	8	1:35.100	5	1:34.547	7	1:33.563	2	1:34.941	11	1:34.054	4
4.	Ralf Schumacher	Williams FW26 03 - BMW	1:36.229	5	1:34.693	2	1:34.239	3	1:33.973	3	1:34.777	9	1:34.235	7
5.	David Coulthard	McLaren MP4-19 03 - Mercedes	1:37.438	11	1:35.301	9	1:34.415	5	1:34.181	8	1:34.321	7	1:34.602	9
6.	Kimi Räikkönen	McLaren MP4-19 04 - Mercedes	1:36.314	6	1:34.395	1		20	1:34.163	7	1:33.452	3	1:34.164	5
7.	Jarno Trulli	Renault R24-03	1:37.816	13	1:35.115	6	1:34.482	6	1:34.041	4	1:33.264	2	1:34.413	8
8.	Fernando Alonso	Renault R24-02	1:37.119	10	1:35.300	8	1:34.175	2	1:34.194	9	1.33.193	1		19
9.	Jenson Button	B.A.R 006-03 - Honda	1:37.018	9	1:35.407	11	1:34.839	9	1:34.128	6	1:34.528	8	1:34.221	6
10.	Takuma Sato	B.A.R 006-01 - Honda	1:38.023	15	1:36.292	15	1:35.697	12	1:35.144	15	1:34.971	12		20
11.	Giancarlo Fisichella	Sauber C23-02 - Petronas	1:37.995	14	1:36.353	16	1:35.516	10	1:35.036	14	1:34.877	10	1:35.061	12
12.	Felipe Massa	Sauber C23-03 - Petronas	1:42.718	24	1:35.288	7	1:35.813	14	1:34.943	12	1:35.132	13	1:35.039	11
14.	Mark Webber	Jaguar R5-03	1:36.478	7	1:35.054	3	1:34.770	8	1:34.381	10	1:34.016	5	1:33.715	2
15.	Christian Klien	Jaguar R5-01	1:38.554	17	1:35.996	14	1:36.106	15	1:34.953	13	1:35.618	15	1:35.158	13
16.	Cristiano da Matta	Toyota TF104/02	1:38.734	18	1:36.907	19	1:35.678	11	1:35.441	16	1:35.684	16	1:34.917	10
17.	Olivier Panis	Toyota TF104/03	1:37.590	12	1:35.524	12	1:35.697	13	1:34.929	11	1:35.247	14	1:35.617	14
18.	Nick Heidfeld	Jordan EJ14/03 - Ford	1:38.831	20	1:37.725	20	1:37.194	16	1:36.607	17	1:36.769	17	1:36.569	15
19.	Giorgio Pantano	Jordan EJ14/02 - Ford	1:39.860	21	1:39.324	24	1:38.302	17	1:38.059	18		20	1:39.902	18
20.	Gianmaria Bruni	Minardi PS04B/02 - Cosworth	1:41.149	22	1:37.818	21	1:39.209	19	1:38.554	19	1:38.729	18	1:38.557	16
21.	Zsolt Baumgartner	Minardi PS04B/01 - Cosworth	1:42.556	23	1:38.588	22	1:39.013	18	1:39.893	20	1:34.321	19	1:39.272	17
35.	Anthony Davidson	B.A.R 006-02 - Honda	1:35.970	3	1:36.708	17								
37.	Björn Wirdheim	Jaguar R5-02	1:38.086	16	1:36.883	18								
38.	Ricardo Zonta	Toyota TF104/04	1:36.147	4	1:35.850	13								
39.	Timo Glock	Jordan EJ14/01 - Ford	1:38.788	19	1:38.796	23								
40.	Bas Leinders	Minardi PS04B/04 - Cosworth	1:43.424	25	1:41.485	25								

Maximum speed

N°	Driver	P1 Qualifs	Pos.	P1 Race	Pos.	P2 Qualifs	Pos.	P2 Race	Pos.	Finish Qualifs	Pos.	Finish Race	Pos.	Trap Qualifs	Pos.	Trap Race	Pos.
1.	M. Schumacher	302,6	2	308,3	2	154,6	7	155,1	5	276,2	1	276,4	6	309,9	1	315,7	5
2.	R. Barrichello	301,2	3	308,3	3	154,5	8	154,2	10	276,1	2	276,8	4	309,8	2	317,8	3
3.	J.P. Montoya	301,1	4	306,2	4	155,8	5	256,2	2	276,0	3	277,0	2	308,1	4	319,1	2
4.	R. Schumacher	300,9	6	309,1	1	152,5	11	153,5	11	275,9	4	277,2	1	309,1	3	320,9	1
5.	D. Coulthard	298,5	10	304,8	5	153,0	9	153,4	12	271,4	6	273,0	9	305,2	9	312,5	13
6.	K. Räikkönen	299,0	8	301,9	10	157,4	1	154,7	9	271,2	10	272,1	10	304,4	11	313,4	11
7.	J. Trulli	296,2	15	303,7	7	156,4	2	155,9	3	269,8	13	271,4	15	303,8	12	309,9	15
8.	F. Alonso	295,8	16	301,6	14	156,4	3	157,0	1	268,2	16	276,9	3	294,8	20	309,7	16
9.	J. Button	297,4	12	301,7	13	152,7	10	154,9	7	270,3	12	271,1	17	303,6	15	312,6	12
10.	T. Sato	299,1	7	303,2	8	155,1	6	155,6	4	269,0	15	271,9	12	300,2	19	314,3	9
11.	G. Fisichella	301,0	5	301,9	11	156,0	4	154,8	8	271,3	8	275,5	7	304,7	10	315,4	6
12.	F. Massa	303,3	1	303,7	6	150,1	14	154,9	6	272,6	5	276,5	5	307,5	5	317,3	4
14.	M. Webber	298,9	9	301,5	15	150,1	13	149,9	16	271,3	9	273,4	8	305,8	8	314,5	7
15.	C. Klien	297,2	13	300,0	17	151,8	12	150,9	15	271,3	7	271,1	16	306,6	6	312,2	14
16.	C. Da Matta	297,8	11	301,7	12	146,2	18	151,6	14	271,0	11	271,9	13	306,2	7	313,7	10
17.	O. Panis	297,1	14	302,9	9	149,6	16	149,7	17	269,3	14	271,5	14	303,7	13	314,4	8
18.	N. Heidfeld	292,3	19	299,2	18	149,7	15	149,4	18	267,5	17	271,9	11	300,2	18	309,3	17
19.	G. Pantano	291,2	20	300,1	16	144,2	19	148,5	20	264,6	20	268,1	18	300,6	17	308,0	18
20.	G. Bruni	293,7	18	297,6	19	148,2	17	151,7	13	267,2	19	267,3	20	301,2	16	307,2	20
21.	Z. Baumgartner	293,8	17	295,2	20	142,6	20	148,7	19	267,2	18	267,7	19	303,6	14	307,6	19

Race

Classification & Retirements

Pos.	Driver	Team	Lap	Time	Average	
1.	M. Schumacher	Ferrari	56	1:31:07.490	204,384 km/h	
2.	J.P. Montoya	Williams BMW	56	+ 5.022	204,196 km/h	
3.	J. Button	B.A.R Honda	56	+ 11.568	203,952 km/h	
4.	R. Barrichello	Ferrari	56	+ 13.616	203,876 km/h	
5.	J. Trulli	Renault	56	+ 37.360	202,997 km/h	
6.	D. Coulthard	McLaren Mercedes	56	+ 53.098	202,418 km/h	
7.	F. Alonso	Renault	56	+ 1:07.877	201,877 km/h	
8.	F. Massa	Sauber Petronas	55	1 lap	200,013 km/h	
9.	C. Da Matta	Toyota	55	1 lap	199,780 km/h	
10.	C. Klien	Jaguar	55	1 lap	198,572 km/h	
11.	G. Fisichella	Sauber Petronas	55	1 lap	197,941 km/h	
12.	O. Panis	Toyota	55	1 lap	197,464 km/h	
13.	G. Pantano	Jordan Ford	54	2 laps	194,395 km/h	
14.	G. Bruni	Minardi Cosworth	53	3 laps	192,656 km/h	
15.	T. Sato	B.A.R Honda	52	4 laps	201,319 km/h	Broken engine
16.	Z. Baumgartner	Minardi Cosworth	52	4 laps	189,658 km/h	

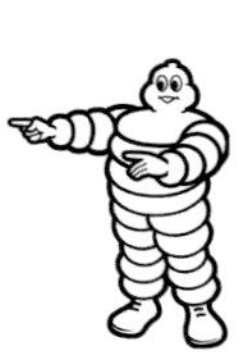

Driver	Team		Reason
K. Räikkönen	McLaren Mercedes	41	Transmission problem/blown engine
N. Heidfeld	Jordan Ford	35	Gearbox stuck in 5th gear
R. Schumacher	Williams BMW	28	Broken engine
M. Webber	Jaguar	24	Spin

Fastest laps

	Driver	Time	Lap	Average
1.	J.P. Montoya	1:34.223	28	211,782 km/h
2.	M. Schumacher	1:34.819	6	210,451 km/h
3.	J. Button	1:34.967	28	210,123 km/h
4.	J. Trulli	1:35.039	12	209,964 km/h
5.	K. Räikkönen	1:35.156	12	209,706 km/h
6.	R. Barrichello	1:35.350	7	209,279 km/h
7.	R. Schumacher	1:35.607	10	208,716 km/h
8.	T. Sato	1:35.679	13	208,559 km/h
9.	D. Coulthard	1:35.852	26	208,183 km/h
10.	F. Alonso	1:35.888	7	208,105 km/h
11.	O. Panis	1:35.951	23	207,968 km/h
12.	C. Da Matta	1:36.544	22	206,691 km/h
13.	F. Massa	1:36.570	7	206,635 km/h
14.	G. Fisichella	1:36.675	54	206,411 km/h
15.	M. Webber	1:36.922	9	205,885 km/h
16.	C. Klien	1:37.031	12	205,653 km/h
17.	N. Heidfeld	1:37.433	15	204,805 km/h
18.	G. Pantano	1:39.527	41	200,496 km/h
19.	G. Bruni	1:39.911	11	199,725 km/h
20.	Z. Baumgartner	1:40.123	12	199,302 km/h

Pit stops

	Driver	Time	Lap	Stop n°
1.	M. Webber	30.778	5	1
2.	G. Fisichella	26.795	8	1
3.	M. Schumacher	26.339	9	1
4.	D. Coulthard	25.062	9	1
5.	F. Alonso	25.760	9	1
6.	F. Massa	27.579	9	1
7.	C. Klien	26.585	9	1
8.	G. Bruni	27.415	9	1
9.	K. Räikkönen	25.956	10	1
10.	R. Barrichello	28.085	10	1
11.	J. Trulli	24.763	10	1
12.	C. Da Matta	26.836	10	1
13.	Z. Baumgartner	27.598	10	1
14.	M. Webber	15.220	10	2
15.	R. Schumacher	26.445	11	1
16.	O. Panis	25.555	11	1
17.	J.P. Montoya	24.883	12	1
18.	J. Button	25.899	12	1
19.	N. Heidfeld	29.045	12	1
20.	N. Heidfeld	27.307	13	2
21.	T. Sato	29.002	14	1
22.	J. Trulli	26.344	20	2
23.	C. Da Matta	26.140	20	2
24.	O. Panis	25.498	21	2
25.	G. Pantano	27.937	22	1
26.	C. Klien	27.292	23	2
27.	F. Alonso	31.468	24	2
28.	D. Coulthard	25.447	24	2
29.	K. Räikkönen	27.709	25	2
30.	G. Bruni	28.013	24	2
31.	F. Massa	27.847	25	2
32.	M. Schumacher	26.214	26	2
33.	J.P. Montoya	25.619	26	2
34.	J. Button	25.882	26	2
35.	G. Fisichella	49.145	26	2
36.	Z. Baumgartner	27.678	26	2
37.	R. Barrichello	26.011	28	2
38.	N. Heidfeld	26.709	27	3
39.	T. Sato	29.320	35	2
40.	C. Da Matta	26.053	36	3
41.	C. Klien	45.845	36	3
42.	D. Coulthard	27.120	38	3
43.	Z. Baumgartner	31.839	36	3
44.	O. Panis	25.946	38	3
45.	J.P. Montoya	26.062	39	3
46.	M. Schumacher	25.532	40	3
47.	J. Button	26.338	40	3
48.	K. Räikkönen	28.470	40	3
49.	G. Bruni	27.715	38	3
50.	J. Trulli	25.777	40	3
51.	F. Massa	30.300	40	3
52.	G. Pantano	26.639	39	2
53.	G. Fisichella	1:03.895	41	3
54.	R. Barrichello	24.921	44	3
55.	O. Panis	15.893	45	4
56.	O. Panis	15.372	48	5

Race leaders

Driver	Laps in the lead	Nber of Laps
M. Schumacher	1 > 9	9
J.P. Montoya	10 > 12	3
M. Schumacher	13 > 26	14
R. Barrichello	27	1
M. Schumacher	28 > 56	29

Driver	Nber of Laps	Kilometers
M. Schumacher	52	288,236 km
J.P. Montoya	3	16,629 km
R. Barrichello	1	5,543 km

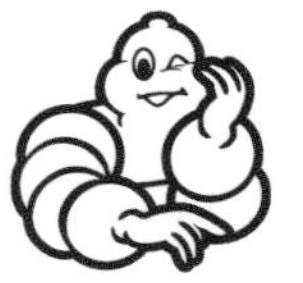

Lap chart

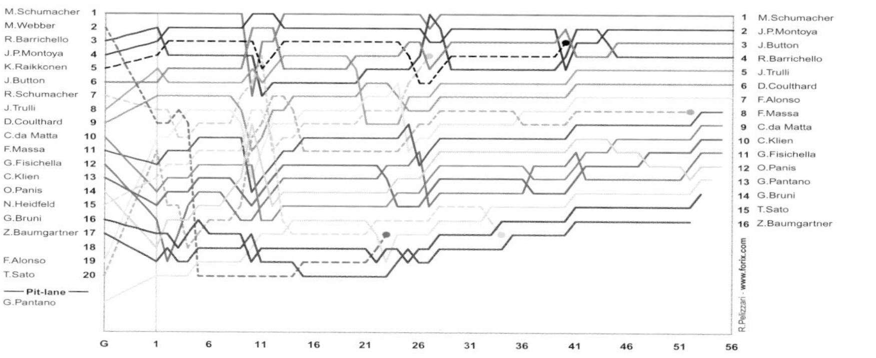

Gaps on the leader board

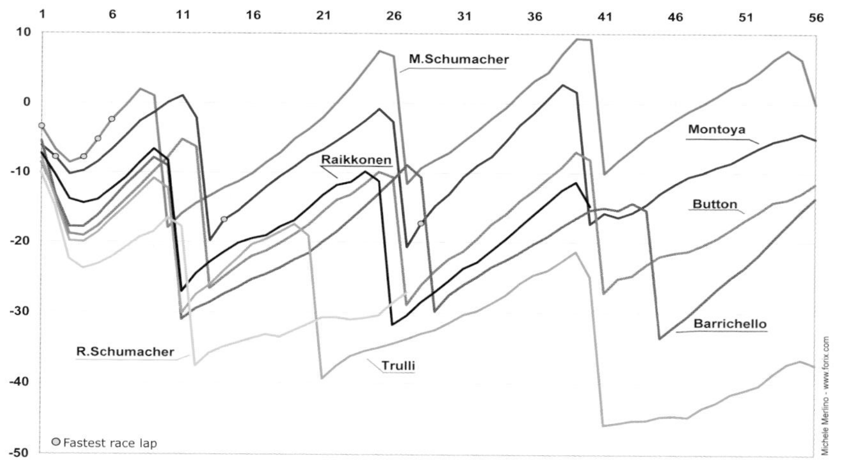

Championship after two rounds

Drivers

1. M. Schumacher ....(2 wins)................20
2. R. Barrichello..13
3. J.P. Montoya 12
4. J. Button...9
5. F. Alonso...8
6. J. Trulli 6
7. R. Schumacher 5
8. D. Coulthard 4
9. F. Massa 1
10. C. Da Matta..0
11. T. Sato...0
12. G. Fisichella...0
13. C. Klien 0
14. O. Panis...0
15. G. Pantano...0
16. G. Bruni...0
17. Z. Baumgartner 0

N. Heidffeld ....-
M. Webber..-
K. Räikkönen ....-

Constructors

1. Scuderia Ferrari Marlboro ......(2 wins) 33
2. BMW WilliamsF1 Team 17
3. Mild Seven Renault F1 Team 14
4. Lucky Strike B.A.R Honda 9
5. West McLaren Mercedes............................4
6. Sauber Petronas 1
7. Panasonic Toyota Racing 0
8. Jaguar Racing...0
9. Jordan Ford..0
10. Minardi Cosworth.....................................0

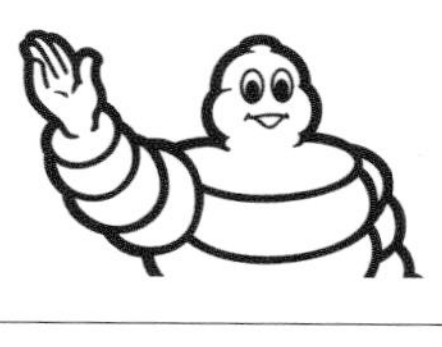

The circuit

Name	Sepang, Kuala Lumpur
Length	5543 meters
Distance	56 laps, 310.408 km
Date	March 21, 2004
Weather	drizzle at the start, warm and humid 34-35°c
Track temperature	40-42°c

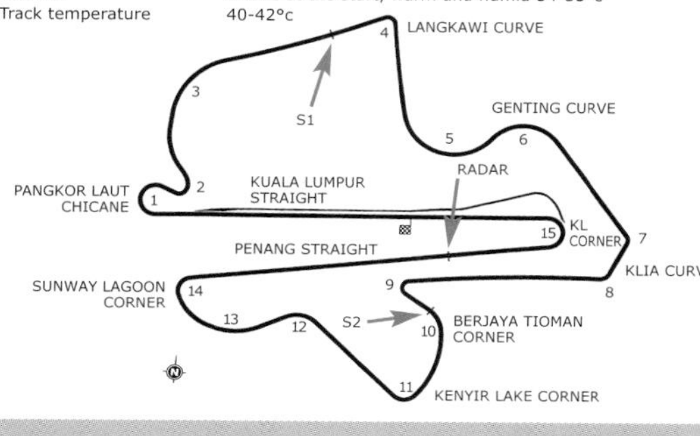

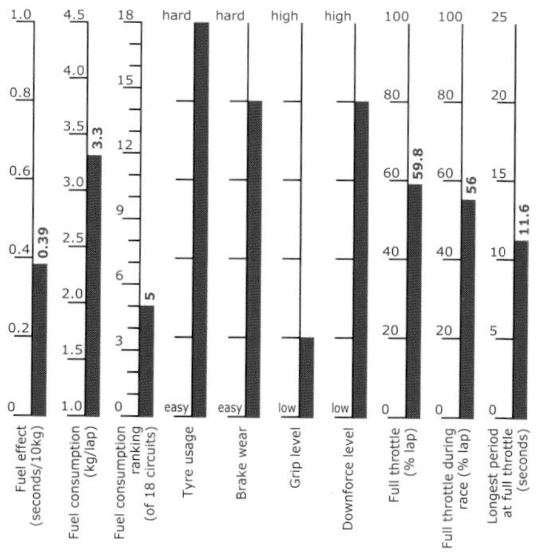

All results : © 2004 Formula One Administration Ltd,
6 Princes Gate, London, SW7 1QJ, England

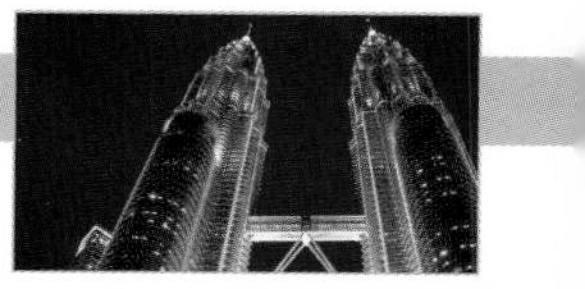

AN OASIS IN THE DESERT

They might be running out of oil in Bahrain, but they are certainly not short of ideas. They persuaded the Formula 1 circus – all it took was money – to come and erect its Big Top in the Middle East and it seemed to work rather well for all parties concerned.

On the track, Michael Schumacher took his third consecutive win from the three races held so far, so the Bahrain Grand Prix confirmed that Williams and McLaren were still struggling. It meant that it was hard to see who might prevent Michael Schumacher running away with a seventh world championship title.

practice

> Michael Schumacher ahead of Juan Pablo Montoya against the spectacular décor of the Bahrain circuit. The former took pole position while the latter was the best of the non-Ferraris.

An all-red front row

> Juan Pablo Montoya was keen on the new circuit and made that clear to his hosts.

The Ferraris claimed the top spots, but they were made to work for it. On Saturday morning, during free practice, they were outpaced by Jenson Button in the BAR and the Williams-BMW duo. In pre-qualifying, to decide the running order for the session proper, the two Williams were again in front.

However, at the end of the only meaningful qualifying session, Michael Schumacher had taken his third consecutive pole position. *"It was not my best lap, I made some mistakes, but it was enough to be in front,"* he said. *"This track is very tricky and very demanding technically. It is really difficult. But, I'm not complaining as we are not here to have an easy time…"*

A serene Michael Schumacher seemed to be gliding over any difficulties this season. With three pole positions from three races, the German was heading for the giddy heights that would not stop until he had a seventh title in his pocket. *"This year, I am more consistent than last, that's for sure,"* he conceded. *"But I think this is down to the car. I feel comfortable with the F2004. it is easy to drive and responds better to set-up changes than the F2003. Having said that, I'm not sure if the fact it is nicer makes me go a*

bit quicker." "We missed out on pole, but I think we will be on the pace in the race," replied Michelin racing boss, Pierre Dupasquier, who could rely on having eight drivers in the top ten places on the grid, all behind the Ferraris. Third on the grid, four tenths

down, Juan Pablo Montoya was thus going to have start in a Ferrari slipstream. *"I had a very good lap, but I lost it all in the last corner,"* he remarked. *"I pushed a bit too hard. I am disappointed, but I think the first corner after the start will be pretty interesting!"*

> Luxury villas on the road from the centre of Manama to the circuit. One unknown factor in Bahrain; the sand storms that could cover the track in a matter of minutes. Bahrain is an island, but the circuit is surrounded by desert. Every morning, sweepers went round the circuit and there were no storms over the race weekend.

Starting grid

*N. HEIDFELD, K. RÄIKKÖNEN et Z. BAUMGARTNER
Penalty for an engine change

Z. BAUMGARTNER
Starts from pit lane

Pos	Driver	Time
19	K. RÄIKKÖNEN*	1:34.584
17	G. BRUNI	1:34.105
15	G. PANTANO	1:32.536
13	F. MASSA	1:31.731
11	G. FISICHELLA	1:31.717
9	C. DA MATTA	1:30.971
7	J. TRULLI	1:30.827
5	T. SATO	1:30.581
3	J.P. MONTOYA	1:30.139 (216,345 km/h)
1	M. SCHUMACHER	

Pos	Driver	Time
20	Z. BAUMGARTNER*	1:35.787
18	N. HEIDFELD*	1:33.506
16	F. ALONSO	1:34.130
14	M. WEBBER	1:32.625
12	C. KLIEN	1:32.332
10	D. COULTHARD	1:31.719
8	O. PANIS	1:31.686
6	J. BUTTON	1:30.856
4	R. SCHUMACHER	1:30.633
2	R. BARRICHELLO	1:30.530

Schumi heading for seventh heaven

Pole position, the win and fastest race lap. From the side of the track it seemed that Schumacher had an easy time of it, on the way to his 73rd grand prix win. However, the man in question denied it had been a stroll in the park. *"Actually it was tough, because the brakes were always right on the limit and I also had to keep an eye on the tyres,"* he commented. *"You had to be very careful not to get off the racing line. In fact, I drove slightly under my limit, taking things gently."* The only scary moment for the six-times world champion came in the braking area for the first corner, when he locked the right front wheel. *"The tyres were still cold, but as I had braked late, I could not afford to lift off the pedal to free the wheel. It caused a flat spot that gave me some vibrations, but luckily I only had nine laps to do before my first pit stop."*

In fact, Michael Schumacher's rivals in Bahrain numbered just one; namely his team-mate, Rubens Barrichello, who spent the entire race around 10 seconds behind the winner. However, the Brazilian had hoped for better. *"At the start, the rain had cooled my brakes a bit too much and I nearly ran into Michael at the first corner,"* he recalled. *"After that, he was going very quickly and he took a couple of seconds off me in just a few corners! Up until the first pit stop, I was not far behind, but I had a problem when they changed the wheels, I lost five seconds and that was pretty much the end of it. When a driver of Michael's class has a ten second lead over you, there is nothing left to do…"*

On the podium, in accordance with Muslim tradition, the usual champagne was replaced with a drink called Warrd, made from fruit juice and specially concocted for the occasion. *"It's not that bad actually,"* joked Michael Schumacher during the press conference. *"At least our race suits don't stink after the podium ceremony!"*

Three weeks later at Imola, Ferrari would be playing in its own backyard, giving Schumacher the opportunity to increase the gap to his pursuers and it was already looking like a real chasm.

^
In a Muslim country, there could be no champagne on the podium, but there was a drink specially prepared for this event, based on fruit juice and called Warrd.

Williams all at sea

Juan Pablo Montoya occupied third place throughout almost the entire race. He was still there with nine laps remaining to the chequered flag and looked set for a podium finish, until a gearbox problem forced him to slow the pace right at the very end of the event.

"At first, I lost seventh gear, then a few more and finally, all of them!" The Colombian finally crossed the line in 13th place, one lap down on the winner. His team-mate, Ralf Schumacher finished seventh after a difficult race, compromised by a collision with the Japanese driver, Takuma Sato on lap 7.

Jenson gets a taste for it

After recording the first podium finish of his career in Malaysia, Jenson Button seemed to have developed a taste for it, as yet again, he finished in third place. *"It's really fantastic! Actually, this podium finish was much harder than my first one. Starting sixth was already not so good, but I was able to make up some places and I had fun. The car was really good and very stable. And the team was fantastic, putting me on a strategy that allowed me to get past Trulli in the pits."*

He had come from a long way back, especially after a hectic start. *"It was a bit of a mess and in fact, I didn't make a very good start. I was stuck behind Ralf, who didn't make a good start either and I lost two places. Then, I realised that the car was understeering and we increased the downforce on the front wing at my first pit stop. It was the right thing to do and the car was perfect after that."*

The Englishman reckoned that the sudden improvement in performance since the last season was easy to explain. *"We worked very hard over the winter and I think we are also benefiting from the experience we gained last season. We've made progress in every area, but we still have a lot more work to do before we fully understand how to get the best out of the car."*

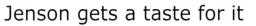

<
It's in the bag! Third win from three grands prix for Michael Schumacher.

"Forza Ferrari!" The Scuderia really does have fans all over the world.
<

Third place for Jenson Button in the desert. The season had got off to a good start for the BAR team and there was more to come…
V

Against the clock

Bahrain won its race against the clock and the Grand Prix weekend ended successfully, with nothing cropping up to spoil the show. In the paddock, Philippe Gurdjian and Martin Whitaker were able to breathe a collective sigh of relief. Packed off in a rush by Bernie Ecclestone in early January to get the construction of the circuit back on track, the two organisational mercenaries won their bet. It was a close run thing as over 3000 people had to work 24 hours a day over the last few months to make up for lost time. *"It was crazy,"* confirmed Gurdjian. *"Only three weeks ago, I thought we would never make it."*

Nevertheless, from the timekeeping to the track marshals, via the security and the décor, everything was impeccable. A good job well done.

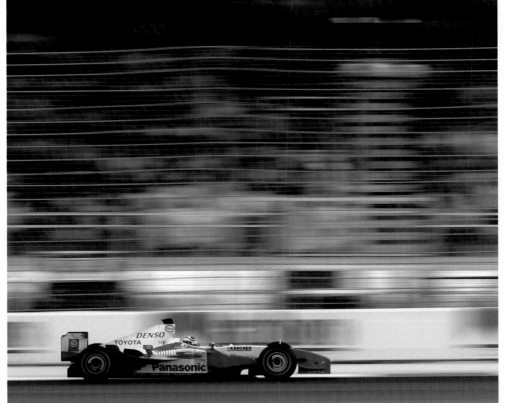

Weekend gossip

> It was the worst kept secret: Ralf Schumacher had signed with Toyota for five years, starting next season, for 85 million Euros. It would make him the best paid driver on the grid barring his brother Michael. Officially of course, the man in question kept denying the move, settling for an admission that *"discussions were taking place"* with the Japanese team.

> With Juan Pablo Montoya having already decided to head for McLaren in 2005, Williams now needed to fill two cockpits. Jenson Button, whose career had begun with the Anglo-German team back in 2000 and who was still under contract to Williams, was one of the men in the frame. However, the young Englishman declined the offer in early April. *"I feel comfortable at BAR and the team is not lacking anything when compared to Williams, so I have no intention of leaving next season."*

> Ferrari had an advantage at this circuit: the track surface had been made by Shell and the tarmac had identical characteristics to that used at Ferrari's Fiorano test track. The team's engineers therefore knew what to expect and the Bridgestone engineers had also been able to adapt easily enough to the surface.

A Grand Prix designed to seduce

"Would those not working on the circuit clear the roads. Let us work hand in hand to assure the success of this Grand Prix." This message came over the radio ever hour and the message was clear: the little kingdom of Bahrain had to do all it could to make a success of the first grand prix to take place in the Middle East.

Everywhere in the town of Manama, dozens of road signs pointed the way to the circuit. The island of Bahrain only measure a few kilometres, so there was no way one could get lost. All along the main streets, the advertising hoardings all spoke of F1 and nothing but F1, be they selling tickets, Toyotas or BMWs, or simply welcoming visitors while advertising banks, everything centred on the Grand Prix.

Bahrain decided to take the plunge into F1 in 1999, when Prince Sheik Salman bin Hamad bin Isa Al Khalifa met Bernie Ecclestone at Monza. He had just commissioned a feasibility study, run by a British business consultancy, that had concluded the best way to put Bahrain on the world map and to attract investors was to stage a Formula 1 race. The prince wanted to put his kingdom on the map, diversifying the economic base of his country which still depended 61% on oil. And oil was getting scarce below ground (Bahrain was the first Arab country to drill for oil back in 1932) and the state was launching itself into other areas such as banking, off-shore companies and insurance.

Designed out in the desert,, the circuit was built in 16 months, using a rotating workforce of 3000. An investment of 130 million Euros was more than enough to get the job done. *"Ever since we decided to stage the Grand Prix, several building projects have taken off in Bahrain,"* confirmed Sheik Fawaz bin Mohammed Al Khalifa, the circuit president.

The drivers were not that enthusiastic about the actual track layout. *"This track looks pretty boring,"* remarked Rubens Barrichello. *"There is a long section of first gear corners which is rubbish. I hope that the long straight will at least allow us to overtake."* Designed inevitably by Hermann Tilke, the German who has designed all the new circuits used over the past few years, the layout, with 15 corners, seemed a bit too twisty to provide a really exciting race and Sunday's event proved that to be the case.

Practice

All the time trials

N°	Driver	N° Chassis - Engine	Practice 1 Friday	Pos.	Practice 2 Friday	Pos.	Practice 3 Saturday	Pos.	Practice 4 Saturday	Pos.	Pre-qual. Saturday	Pos.	Qualif. Saturday	Pos.
1.	Michael Schumacher	Ferrari F2004 234	1:32.158	1	1:31.732	4	1:30.545	3	1:30.407	5	1:30.751	4	1:30.139	1
2.	Rubens Barrichello	Ferrari F2004 236	1:32.651	2	1:31.450	1	1:30.616	4	1:30.513	8	1:31.283	11	1:30.530	2
3.	Juan Pablo Montoya	Williams FW26 05 - BMW	1:33.027	4	1:31.451	2	1:30.121	2	1:29.696	3	1:30.247	2	1:30.581	3
4.	Ralf Schumacher	Williams FW26 03 - BMW	1:34.619	11	1:31.842	6	1:30.651	5	1:29.690	2	1:29.968	1	1:30.633	4
5.	David Coulthard	McLaren MP4-19 03 - Mercedes	1:34.023	6	1:32.495	11	1:31.341	8			1:31.364	13	1:31.719	10
6.	Kimi Räikkönen	McLaren MP4-19 04 - Mercedes	1:34.603	9			1:31.003	6	1:31.320	11	1:30.353	3		
7.	Jarno Trulli	Renault R24-03	1:34.796	12	1:33.437	18	1:31.644	10	1:30.472	6	1:31.103	7	1:30.971	7
8.	Fernando Alonso	Renault R24-02	1:34.810	13	1:32.234	9	1:31.485	9	1:30.774	9	1.31.040	6	1:34.130	17
9.	Jenson Button	B.A.R 006-03 - Honda	1:33.898	5	1:31.879	7	1:30.062	1	1:29.552	1	1:31.131	8	1:30.856	6
10.	Takuma Sato	B.A.R 006-01 - Honda	1:34.610	10	1:32.680	12	1:31.090	7	1:30.239	4	1:31.135	9	1:30.827	5
11.	Giancarlo Fisichella	Sauber C23-04 - Petronas	1:35.388	16	1:33.061	17	1:32.210	14	1:32.433	14	1:31.203	10	1:31.731	11
12.	Felipe Massa	Sauber C23-03 - Petronas	1:34.488	8	1:33.031	15			1:32.557	15	1:32.152	16	1:32.536	13
14.	Mark Webber	Jaguar R5-03	1:35.905	18	1:32.041	8	1:32.276	15	1:31.384	13	1:31.945	15	1:32.625	14
15.	Christian Klien	Jaguar R5-01	1:36.645	21	1:31.789	5	1:31.692	11	1:31.331	12	1:31.868	14	1:32.332	12
16.	Cristiano da Matta	Toyota TF104/02	1:36.359	20	1:32.761	14	1:32.183	13	1:30.499	7	1:31.329	12	1:31.717	9
17.	Olivier Panis	Toyota TF104/03	1:35.981	19	1:33.049	16	1:31.962	12	1:30.934	10	1:31.001	5	1:31.686	8
18.	Nick Heidfeld	Jordan EJ14/03 - Ford	1:34.872	14	1:40.573	24	1:33.404	16	1:32.816	16	1:32.640	17	1:33.506	15
19.	Giorgio Pantano	Jordan EJ14/02 - Ford	1:34.967	15	1:32.708	13	1:33.474	17	1:33.342	17	1:33.598	18	1:34.105	16
20.	Gianmaria Bruni	Minardi PS04B/02 - Cosworth	1:37.347	23	1:34.791	22	1:33.863	18	1:34.590	18	1:34.879	19	1:34.584	18
21.	Zsolt Baumgartner	Minardi PS04B/01 - Cosworth	1:37.049	22	1:34.054	20	1:35.696	19	1:35.901	19	1:35.632	20	1:35.787	19
35.	Anthony Davidson	B.A.R 006-02 - Honda	1:32.958	3	1:31.488	3								
37.	Björn Wirdheim	Jaguar R5-02	1:37.443	24	1:34.317	21								
38.	Ricardo Zonta	Toyota TF104/04	1:34.289	7	1:32.335	10								
39.	Timo Glock	Jordan EJ14/01 - Ford	1:35.760	17	1:33.695	19								
40.	Bas Leinders	Minardi PS04B/04 - Cosworth	1:37.792	25	1:36.248	23								

Maximum speed

N°	Driver	P1 Qualifs	Pos.	P1 Race	Pos.	P2 Qualifs	Pos.	P2 Race	Pos.	Finish Qualifs	Pos.	Finish Race	Pos.	Trap Qualifs	Pos.	Trap Race	Pos.
1.	M. Schumacher	252,2	3	254,1	3	280,8	2	282,2	4	300,7	1	300,7	2	322,5	3	326,4	8
2.	R. Barrichello	250,8	5	255,6	2	277,6	7	283,7	1	297,4	4	301,4	1	319,5	5	330,1	2
3.	J.P. Montoya	252,9	2	253,7	4	276,5	10	282,9	2	298,0	3	298,0	6	323,7	1	323,0	16
4.	R. Schumacher	255,1	1	255,8	1	270,8	13	281,6	5	299,0	2	300,6	3	322,7	2	332,4	1
5.	D. Coulthard	246,1	13	248,9	14	277,0	8	279,1	10	291,1	17	293,7	16	315,2	15	322,9	17
6.	K. Räikkönen	235,0	20	247,9	17	192,3	20	274,2	16			294,9	13	194,3	20	324,0	12
7.	J. Trulli	249,3	7	251,0	9	267,9	16	271,9	17	292,2	14	295,6	11	318,3	9	323,7	14
8.	F. Alonso	246,9	10	251,5	6	271,4	11	282,7	3	291,4	16	294,7	15	318,6	7	323,8	13
9.	J. Button	246,6	11	248,5	16	279,5	4	281,3	7	293,7	9	294,7	14	317,7	10	324,8	11
10.	T. Sato	244,2	15	250,5	10	279,2	5	275,7	14	293,0	10	297,7	8	318,5	8	328,6	5
11.	G. Fisichella	248,7	8	249,8	13	278,1	6	277,5	13	294,5	7	296,5	10	319,8	4	328,5	6
12.	F. Massa	243,9	16	248,7	15	276,9	9	278,7	11	295,5	5	297,8	7	319,0	6	328,8	4
14.	M. Webber	242,2	17	249,9	11	280,0	3	281,5	6	292,5	12	298,9	4	317,0	13	326,4	7
15.	C. Klien	246,9	9	251,1	8	262,8	17	279,7	9	292,2	13	298,9	5	316,0	14	329,2	3
16.	C. Da Matta	249,4	6	251,9	5	281,4	1	280,6	8	294,1	8	295,6	12	317,5	11	325,2	9
17.	O. Panis	251,1	4	251,1	7	270,2	14	274,3	15	294,9	6	297,1	9	314,5	17	325,0	10
18.	N. Heidfeld	241,5	19	247,3	18	271,3	12	277,8	12	292,5	11	292,9	17	314,9	16	322,7	18
19.	G. Pantano	241,8	18	246,9	19	270,0	15	271,9	18	290,8	18	291,6	18	311,3	19	318,5	19
20.	G. Bruni	244,5	14	245,8	20	258,1	19	259,6	20	291,8	15	289,4	20	317,1	12	317,8	20
21.	Z. Baumgartner	246,2	12	249,8	12	260,9	18	267,8	19	290,7	19	291,2	19	313,4	18	323,0	15

Race

Classification & Retirements

Pos.	Driver	Team	Lap	Time	Average
1.	M. Schumacher	Ferrari	57	1:28:34.875	208,976 km/h
2.	R. Barrichello	Ferrari	57	+ 1.367	208,922 km/h
3.	J. Button	B.A.R Honda	57	+ 26.687	207,932 km/h
4.	J. Trulli	Renault	57	+ 32.214	207,717 km/h
5.	T. Sato	B.A.R Honda	57	+ 52.460	206,933 km/h
6.	F. Alonso	Renault	57	+ 53.156	206,906 km/h
7.	R. Schumacher	Williams BMW	57	+ 58.155	206,714 km/h
8.	M. Webber	Jaguar	56	1 lap	205,138 km/h
9.	O. Panis	Toyota	56	1 lap	205,061 km/h
10.	C. Da Matta	Toyota	56	1 lap	204,589 km/h
11.	G. Fisichella	Sauber Petronas	56	1 lap	204,551 km/h
12.	F. Massa	Sauber Petronas	56	1 lap	204,373 km/h
13.	J.P. Montoya	Williams BMW	56	1 lap	203,984 km/h
14.	C. Klien	Jaguar	56	1 lap	203,402 km/h
15.	N. Heidfeld	Jordan Ford	56	1 lap	202,619 km/h
16.	G. Pantano	Jordan Ford	55	2 laps	201,044 km/h
17.	G. Bruni	Minardi Cosworth	52	5 laps	187,620 km/h

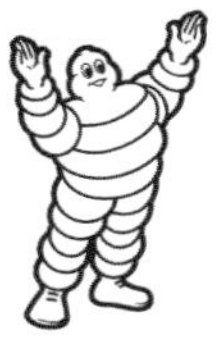

Driver	Team		Reason
D. Coulthard	McLaren Mercedes	51	Loss of pneumatic valve pressure on engine
Z. Baumgartner	Minardi Cosworth	45	Engine problem
K. Räikkönen	McLaren Mercedes	8	Blown engine

Fastest laps

	Driver	Time	Lap	Average
1.	M. Schumacher	1:30.252	7	216,074 km/h
2.	F. Alonso	1:30.654	39	215,116 km/h
3.	R. Schumacher	1:30.781	56	214,815 km/h
4.	R. Barrichello	1:30.876	29	214,591 km/h
5.	J. Button	1:30.960	24	214,393 km/h
6.	J.P. Montoya	1:30.977	28	214,353 km/h
7.	T. Sato	1:31.101	55	214,061 km/h
8.	J. Trulli	1:31.421	24	213,312 km/h
9.	D. Coulthard	1:31.861	19	212,290 km/h
10.	M. Webber	1:32.277	19	211,333 km/h
11.	C. Da Matta	1:32.319	23	211,237 km/h
12.	G. Fisichella	1:32.329	40	211,214 km/h
13.	O. Panis	1:32.401	22	211,049 km/h
14.	C. Klien	1:32.533	38	210,748 km/h
15.	F. Massa	1:32.690	44	210,391 km/h
16.	N. Heidfeld	1:33.284	56	209,051 km/h
17.	K. Räikkönen	1:33.527	7	208,508 km/h
18.	G. Pantano	1:34.032	9	207,388 km/h
19.	Z. Baumgartner	1:34.555	24	206,241 km/h
20.	G. Bruni	1:35.130	40	204,995 km/h

Pit stops

	Driver	Time	Lap	Stop n°
1.	F. Alonso	35.766	1	1
2.	O. Panis	25.888	6	1
3.	C. Da Matta	25.483	7	1
4.	R. Schumacher	28.602	7	1
5.	M. Schumacher	26.629	9	1
6.	M. Webber	27.336	9	1
7.	D. Coulthard	26.476	9	1
8.	F. Massa	27.416	9	1
9.	Z. Baumgartner	26.632	9	1
10.	R. Barrichello	32.668	10	1
11.	J.P. Montoya	27.921	10	1
12.	J. Trulli	25.386	10	1
13.	G. Fisichella	26.866	10	1
14.	C. Klien	27.086	10	1
15.	T. Sato	26.619	11	1
16.	G. Pantano	27.648	11	1
17.	J. Button	30.593	12	1
18.	N. Heidfeld	28.982	13	1
19.	T. Sato	29.505	18	2
20.	C. Klien	26.876	19	2
21.	O. Panis	26.312	20	2
22.	C. Da Matta	26.027	21	2
23.	Z. Baumgartner	27.771	22	2
24.	D. Coulthard	26.425	23	2
25.	M. Webber	26.852	23	2
26.	M. Schumacher	27.443	24	2
27.	R. Schumacher	29.726	24	2
28.	J. Trulli	25.803	25	2
29.	F. Massa	27.293	25	2
30.	G. Pantano	28.400	25	2
31.	J.P. Montoya	26.753	26	2
32.	J. Button	28.672	26	2
33.	G. Fisichella	28.788	26	2
34.	F. Alonso	25.234	26	2
35.	R. Barrichello	26.482	27	2
36.	G. Bruni	37.593	24	1
37.	N. Heidfeld	31.937	34	2
38.	T. Sato	29.039	37	3
39.	O. Panis	27.505	37	3
40.	J. Trulli	27.047	38	3
41.	D. Coulthard	27.879	38	3
42.	M. Webber	30.821	38	3
43.	Z. Baumgartner	30.153	37	3
44.	C. Da Matta	27.544	38	3
45.	J.P. Montoya	26.175	39	3
46.	C. Klien	28.669	39	3
47.	J. Button	27.310	40	3
48.	F. Alonso	26.329	40	3
49.	M. Schumacher	26.862	41	3
50.	G. Pantano	28.002	41	3
51.	R. Barrichello	25.977	43	3
52.	F. Massa	26.263	42	3
53.	G. Bruni	37.611	38	2
54.	G. Fisichella	27.444	43	3
55.	R. Schumacher	25.424	45	3

Race leaders

Driver	Laps in the lead	Nber of Laps
M. Schumacher	1 > 9	9
R. Barrichello	10	1
J. Button	11	1
M. Schumacher	12 > 24	13
R. Barrichello	25 > 27	3
M. Schumacher	28 > 41	14
R. Barrichello	42 > 43	2
M. Schumacher	44 > 57	14

Driver	Nber of Laps	Kilometers
M. Schumacher	50	270,604 km
R. Barrichello	6	32,502 km
J. Button	1	5,417 km

Lap chart

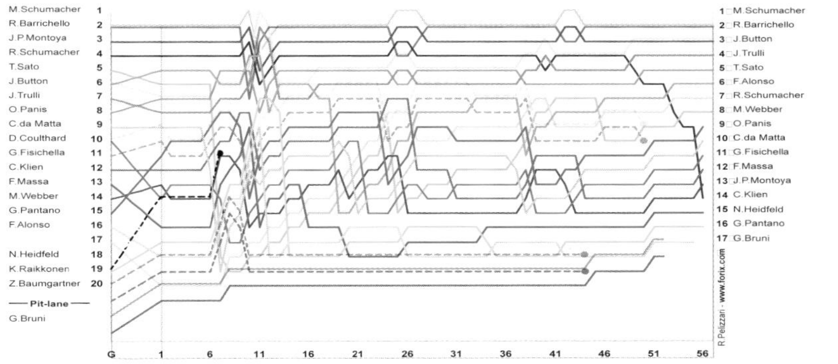

M.Schumacher 1
R.Barrichello 2
J.P.Montoya 3
R.Schumacher 4
T.Sato 5
J.Button 6
J.Trulli 7
O.Panis 8
C.da Matta 9
D.Coulthard 10
G.Fisichella 11
C.Klien 12
F.Massa 13
M.Webber 14
G.Pantano 15
F.Alonso 16
17
N.Heidfeld 18
K.Raikkonen 19
Z.Baumgartner 20
Pit-lane
G.Bruni
1 M.Schumacher
2 R.Barrichello
3 J.Button
4 J.Trulli
5 T.Sato
6 F.Alonso
7 R.Schumacher
8 M.Webber
9 O.Panis
10 C.da Matta
11 G.Fisichella
12 F.Massa
13 J.P.Montoya
14 C.Klien
15 N.Heidfeld
16 G.Pantano
17 G.Bruni
G 1 6 11 16 21 26 31 36 41 46 51 56
R Pelizzari - www.forix.com

Gaps on the leader board

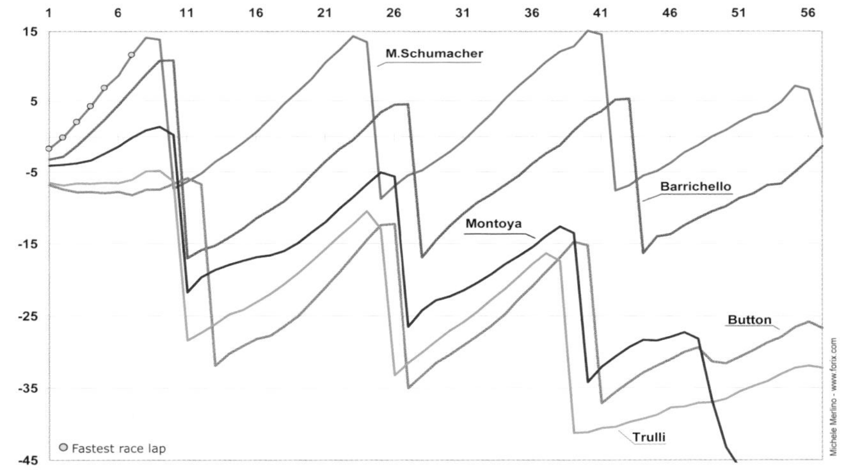

1 6 11 16 21 26 31 36 41 46 51 56
15
5
-5
-15
-25
-35
-45
M.Schumacher
Barrichello
Montoya
Button
Trulli
Fastest race lap
Michele Merlino - www.forix.com

Championship after three rounds

Drivers

1. M. Schumacher ....(3 wins)................30
2. R. Barrichello...21
3. J. Button 15
4. J.P. Montoya 12
5. F. Alonso 11
6. J. Trulli..11
7. R. Schumacher 7
8. T. Sato 4
9. D. Coulthard..4
10. F. Massa 1
11. M. Webber 1
12. C. Da Matta...0
13. O. Panis..0
14. G. Fisichella..0
15. C. Klien 0
16. G. Pantano 0
17. G. Bruni..0
18. N. Heidfeld..0
19. Z. Baumgartner 0

K. Räikkönen ....-

Constructors

1. Scuderia Ferrari Marlboro ......(3 wins) 51
2. Mild Seven Renault F1 Team 22
3. BMW WilliamsF1 Team 19
4. Lucky Strike B.A.R Honda.........................19
5. West McLaren Mercedes............................4
6. Sauber Petronas 1
7. Jaguar Racing..1
8. Panasonic Toyota Racing 0
9. Jordan Ford...0
10. Minardi Cosworth 0

The circuit

Name	Sakhir, Manama
Length	5417 meters
Distance	57 laps, 308.523 km
Date	April 4, 2004
Weather	cloudy and warm, 30-31°c
Track temperature	31-33°c

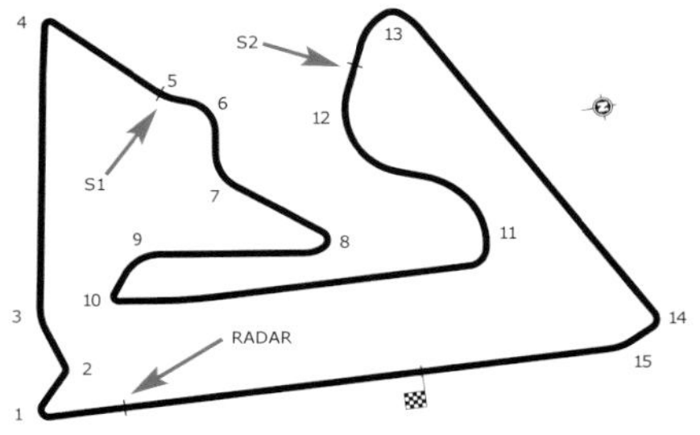

1
2
3
4
5
6
7
8
9
10
11
12
13
14
15
S1
S2
RADAR

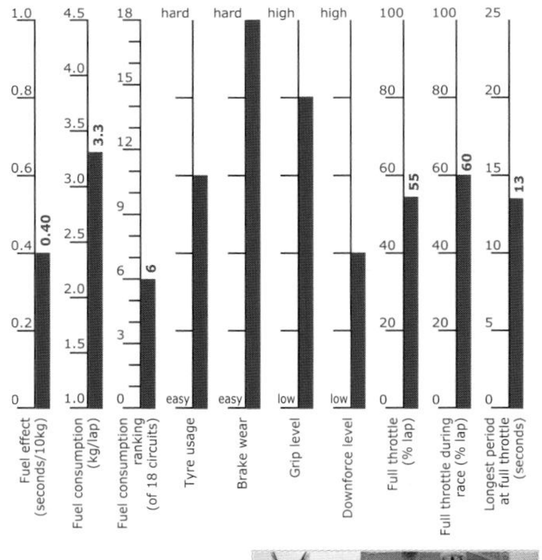

0.40
3.3
6
55
60
13
hard
hard
high
high
easy
easy
low
low
Fuel effect (seconds/10kg)
Fuel consumption (kg/lap)
Fuel consumption ranking (of 18 circuits)
Tyre usage
Brake wear
Grip level
Downforce level
Full throttle (% lap)
Full throttle during race (% lap)
Longest period at full throttle (seconds)

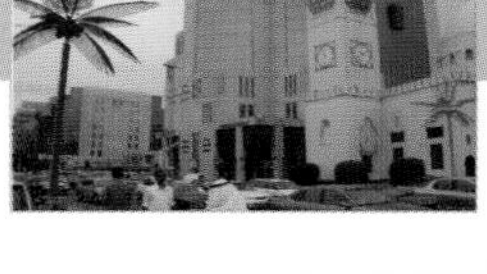

FERRARI SCORES HOME WIN

The reigning world champion pursued his inexorable march towards the 2004 title by winning his fourth grand prix on the trot. Early on he had a brief skirmish with Jenson Button, author of the pole position. The young Englishman managed to open up a gap of 2.7s over Michael at the end of lap 1 but the latter reeled him in and got by during the first round of refuelling stops. Button came home second the best result of his F1 career so far.

Jenson's first pole

Jenson Button made a triumphal return to his pit from the press conference snapped by a myriad of photographers. There he received a rapturous welcome from his team delighted with his performance. After 69 grands prix he had set the first pole position of his career in F1 on the Imola circuit as well as the first for the BAR team created in 1999.

"It's a fantastic feeling to grab pole on Ferrari's home territory and I'm very happy," he laughed. *"It was a great lap. We set up the car for the race as usual but it's working a whole lot better than in the first three grands prix. Quite honestly I can't say why."*

His performance set the gossip mill turning as there were those who said that the BAR team was working a whole lot better since Jacques Villeneuve's departure. That, though, is a very superficial analysis. It is certainly true that the 20 million dollars or thereabouts which the Canadian was paid, would have been much more productive if invested in the development of the car, but it should not be

> Pole position brought Jenson Button instant celebrity. Here he is assailed from all sides by the English journalists after practice.

Ten years ago the San Marino Grand Prix was forever marked by Roland Ratzenberger's fatal accident on Saturday and Ayrton Senna's on Sunday. Various ceremonies were held on the Italian circuit to commemorate this sad anniversary. On Saturday the main grandstand was renamed after Ayrton Senna and there was a parade of cars that used to be driven by the two men.
v

forgotten that the team changed from Bridgestones to Michelins during the winter which helped it gain a few tenths. Michael Schumacher qualified second on a circuit the Scuderia knows like the back of its hand, as it is only about 100 kms from Maranello. His little mistake in the Alta chicane probably cost him pole.

"I pushed a little bit too hard and I was very lucky to keep the car on the track. I don't think it'd have changed anything; I wouldn't have had pole anyway. Jenson put in a super lap. This being said it's going to be an interesting race as there are a few potential winners on the grid." It was the first time this season that Schumacher had not been on pole.

> Juan Pablo Montoya in all-out attack mode on the Dino & Enzo Ferrari Imola circuit. The Colombian ended practice in third place his fourth successive qualification on the second row of the grid.

In brief

> **4:** This was the number of times Takuma Sato exceeded the speed limit in the pit lane leading to a fine of 3500 dollars.

> On Friday the FIA issued a press release containing numerous proposals aimed at reducing speeds from 2008 onwards! It was a question of a completely new Formula 1 replacing the one governed by the Concorde Agreement, which was supposed to put the driver centre stage once again. The engine's cubic capacity was to be reduced to 2.4 litres and manual gearboxes imposed. The teams were asked to give their opinion on the proposals. However, what was really needed was an improved spectacle forthwith.

> Another bad day at the office for Kimi Raïkkönen. He found himself at the back of

the field for the second race in succession due to an engine change. For McLaren the season was turning into a nightmare. As the problems afflicting the MP4-19 seemed insoluble, the team decided to build a new chassis, which was supposed to be ready for the German Grand Prix.

> The GPWC popped up again at Imola. The association made up of BMW, Daimler Chrysler, Ferrari, Ford and Renault threatened to create its own championship in 2008. A communiqué announced that negotiations with Bernie Ecclestone had been broken off. Ron Dennis explained in his inimitable style that the FIA's desire to reduce costs was the wrong way to go. *"The real problem is the quality of the show, not the costs."*

Starting grid

Pos	Driver	Time
2	M. SCHUMACHER	1:20.011
4	R. BARRICHELLO	1:20.451
6	F. ALONSO	1:20.895
8	M. WEBBER	1:20.921
10	C. DA MATTA	1:21.087
12	F. MASSA	1:21.532
14	C. KLIEN	1:21.949
16	N. HEIDFELD	1:23.488
18	G. FISICHELLA	-
20	K. RÄIKKÖNEN*	-

* K. RÄIKKÖNEN et Z. BAUMGARTNER
Penalty for an engine change

Pos	Driver	Time
1	J. BUTTON	1:19.753 (222.672 km/h)
3	J.P. MONTOYA	1:20.212
5	R. SCHUMACHER	1:20.538
7	T. SATO	1:20.913
9	J. TRULLI	1:21.034
11	D. COULTHARD	1:21.091
13	O. PANIS	1:21.558
15	G. PANTANO	1:23.352
17	G. BRUNI	1:26.899
19	Z. BAUMGARTNER*	1:46.299

The Schumacher-Montoya squabble flares up again

When the lights went out Juan Pablo Montoya in third place on the grid did not make the best of starts, but managed to fend off those who were directly behind him and stay in contact with Michael Schumacher. He knew that he had to go for it on the first lap when his Michelin tyres gave him a slight advantage. In the Tossa hairpin he tried to go round the German on the outside. Michael did not expect him there and the two cars touched with the Williams going onto the grass. 'I saw Juan coming on my right," said the Ferrari driver," but I didn't see him again after that and I wasn't expecting him to stay alongside."

The Colombian begged to differ! *"We touched and he forced me off onto the grass. It really is disappointing but not entirely unexpected on his part,"* shot back Montoya. *"The car wasn't damaged. I know it was touch and go but I've already done this kind of thing and I didn't think he'd push me."*

In fact, what really bugged Juan Pablo was that the Stewards of the Meeting did not penalise the German. *"Last year I received a penalty that cost me the world championship for acting in the same way at Indianapolis,"* he growled. *"For once and for all what is allowed and what isn't has to be clearly defined, and the same rules applied to everybody whether his name is Michael Schumacher or not!"* The last spat between the two drivers goes back to the Italian Grand Prix in 2003 when the same type of manoeuvre by the Colombian failed, but they have had other collisions in the past.

With Juan Pablo out of the way Michael began to pull in Jenson Button whom he passed during the latter's first refuelling stop. *"I knew our car would be quicker after a few laps when the tyres had warmed up,"* he said. *"I kept a cool head at the start though I didn't want to lose contact with Jenson. After that all I had to do was to control the race. I didn't have any problems."*

Jenson's second place was the best F1 result of his career so far and his third consecutive rostrum placing. The BAR team was starting to look like being Ferrari's most dangerous rival with a budget much lower than that of Williams or McLaren. After four years in the wilderness the team now knew that it was capable of winning.

His best career result

Jenson set a blinding pace from the start and pulled out a 2.7s lead first time round. *"The early laps were great,"* he stated. *"I wanted to open up a gap right from the start and it worked. After that my rhythm stagnated a little but altogether I was pretty happy. But I don't understand how Michael worked his first refuelling stop. When he rejoined he was well ahead of me: it was a shock."*

As for victory Jenson was honest enough to admit that it isn't for tomorrow. *"My car wasn't really quick enough to win. It's far from perfect and it's still a bit tricky to drive. In the race the Ferraris were uncatachable and I couldn't really hope to* beat Michael. This being said I'm delighted with this second place. The season had got off to a fantastic start for us."*

The next grand prix on the Barcelona circuit looks like favouring the BAR-Hondas as the cars pulverised the record there in testing. *"It's true that we were very fast in private testing but that doesn't mean a lot. You never know what people are doing or what set-up they're using. I must say, though, that we were very quick there over a lap and over a long distance race test, and it's possible that we'll be even closer to Ferrari. Beating them, that's a whole other ballgame."*

Only one point for McLaren

Juan Pablo Montoya came home third following his brush with Michael Schumacher while brother Ralf in the second Williams-BMW finished seventh after losing two places near the end after colliding on lap 50with Fernando Alonso's Renault which came home fourth. They blamed each other for the accident. After the event Race Control summoned them both and concluded that it was a racing incident after hearing the two drivers.

David Coulthard saw the flag in an anonymous twelfth place due an accident in the first corner, which forced him to pit for a new front wing after his McLaren's nasal appendage was torn off.

Kimi Raïkkönen scored his first point of the season thanks to a magnificent climb up from the back of the grid.

^
Yet another Michael Schumacher win allied to Jenson Button's third consecutive rostrum finish so big smiles all round.

<
Jenson Button made an excellent start and led the pack into the first corner.

After winning on the brand-new Bahrain circuit Michael scored a home goal at Imola, in the heart of Ferrari land.
v

Smile you're on camera

This was Schumacher's fourth win in four races
and he let his joy rip when it came to opening
the champagne.

The season was not going all that well for Jordan. At Imola Nick Heidfeld qualified sixteenth and in the race he retired with a transmission problem.

> Pole on Saturday and second on Sunday, a perfect weekend for Button? Well, almost even if he was briefly a wheel short.

Giancarlo Fisichella was just outside the points as he finished under a second behind eight-placed Kimi Raïkkönen. "It's a pity I was distracted by a Minardi and Kimi got past me, as I was much quicker than him. We got into a good rhythm today," said the Italian. Felipe Massa (photo) finished tenth.

The last grand prix at Imola?

Up to the present everybody was happy to see two grands prix on Italian soil thanks to the money it brought in. It seems to be no longer the case. Originally the contract between the Sagis, the company managing the circuit, and Bernie Ecclestone was supposed to run until 2006. Its president then accepted to reduce its length by exchanging the 2005 and 2006 race against a reduction in the price to be paid for the 2002 and 2003 events.
It was not enough as the organisers still had to pay another 5 million dollars to the FOM following the 2000 grand prix, a debt that poisoned the relationship between the two parties.

What Bernie Ecclestone wants to do is to favour events outside the European Union zone due to the forthcoming anti-tobacco legislation so there is not that much going for Imola any longer. With countries like Turkey, India, Mexico and Russia all anxious to have an F1 grand prix the chances of Imola staying on the calendar look slim unless Ecclestone's wish to have twenty races on the calendar is confirmed. "Our priority is to establish a trustworthy relationship with Mr. Ecclestone," said Federico Bendinelli, the Sagis President. "If we want to convince him to continue with us we'll have to invest some twenty million euros to make the paddock and the pits comply with his latest specifications. If the state and the town of Imola don't help us we can't do it, and we're not finding it easy to convince them. This year our aim is to have 100 000 spectators during the weekend otherwise we'll make a loss."

This aim was not easy to attain despite a 10 to 40% reduction in the price of tickets. 2004 was perhaps the last San Marino Grand Prix.

Valentino Rossi astonishes Ferrari!

Luca di Montezemolo, the Ferrari President, had promised him an F1 test. On the Wednesday before the San Marino Grand Prix Valentino Rossi arrived at the Maranello factory around 09h00. He did a few laps of the track, visited the factory and then covered a few more laps. All in all he did a total of thirty-five and his best time was 59.590s, some 3.5 seconds off the lap record held by Michael Schumacher in 55.999s. For someone who had never driven an F1 car before his performance was mind-blowing. In general, a driver who is used to single-seaters needs a whole day to get used to the braking and acceleration of an F1.

On the Wednesday in question Luca Badoer the Ferrari test driver got round in 58.433s, just over a

second quicker than Rossi which only goes to underline the Italian's exploit. Michael Schumacher congratulated him and gave him a signed helmet.

Other top motorbike riders have had a go in an F1. Five years ago Max Biaggi lapped the Fiorano track in 1m 06.580s when Michael held the record in 1m 00.700s. Max was 6 seconds off the record, Rossi only 3.6s.

This performance was the talk of Imola. Would Valentino Rossi take up car racing? "It was a very exciting day, an extraordinary experience," commented the Yamaha rider at the end of his test.

Practice

All the time trials

N°	Driver	N° Chassis - Engine	Practice 1 Friday	Pos.	Practice 2 Friday	Pos.	Practice 3 Saturday	Pos.	Practice 4 Saturday	Pos.	Pre-qual. Saturday	Pos.	Qualif. Saturday	Pos.
1.	Michael Schumacher	Ferrari F2004 234	1:20.084	1	1:21.164	3	1:20.856	1	1:20.125	1	1:20.440	3	1:20.011	2
2.	Rubens Barrichello	Ferrari F2004 236	1:21.443	2	1:22.096	11	1:21.583	3	1:20.996	6	1:20.927	7	1:20.451	4
3.	Juan Pablo Montoya	Williams FW26 05 - BMW	1:22.796	6	1:21.661	7	1:21.764	4	1:20.975	5	1:19.805	1	1:20.212	3
4.	Ralf Schumacher	Williams FW26 07 - BMW	1:22.250	3	1:22.057	10	1:21.864	5	1:21.271	11	1:20.423	2	1:20.538	5
5.	David Coulthard	McLaren MP4-19 03 - Mercedes	1:23.197	11	1:21.795	9	1:22.051	8	1:20.844	4	1:20.566	4	1:21.091	11
6.	Kimi Räikkönen	McLaren MP4-19 04 - Mercedes	1:23.054	8	1:21.586	4	1:22.164	9	1:21.199	9	1:21.181	9		
7.	Jarno Trulli	Renault R24-03	1:22.927	7	1:21.604	5	1:22.462	10	1:21.198	8	1:21.669	12	1:21.034	9
8.	Fernando Alonso	Renault R24-02	1:23.083	9	1:21.788	8	1:21.954	6	1:20.844	3	1.21.799	14	1:20.895	6
9.	Jenson Button	B.A.R 006-05 - Honda	1:22.448	5	1:20.966	1	1:21.165	2	1:20.150	2	1:20.632	5	1:19.753	1
10.	Takuma Sato	B.A.R 006-03 - Honda	1:24.061	16	1:21.159	2	1:22.013	7	1:21.159	7	1:20.984	8	1:20.913	7
11.	Giancarlo Fisichella	Sauber C23-04 - Petronas	1:23.528	13	1:23.335	17	1:22.991	13	1:22.022	14	1:20.716	6	*	
12.	Felipe Massa	Sauber C23-03 - Petronas	1:23.562	14	1:23.043	15	1:23.105	14	1:22.077	15	1:22.154	15	1:21.532	12
14.	Mark Webber	Jaguar R5-03	1:23.417	12	1:22.167	12	1:22.707	11	1:21.393	13	1:21.458	11	1:20.921	8
15.	Christian Klien	Jaguar R5-01	1:25.679	21	1:23.211	16			1:23.222	16	1:22.246	16	1:21.949	14
16.	Cristiano da Matta	Toyota TF104/04	1:24.752	18	1:22.780	14	1:23.482	15	1:21.257	10	1:21.737	13	1:21.087	10
17.	Olivier Panis	Toyota TF104/03	1:23.790	15	1:22.768	13	1:22.885	12	1:21.296	12	1:21.231	10	1:24.558	13
18.	Nick Heidfeld	Jordan EJ14/03 - Ford	1:24.955	19	1:23.866	20	1:24.907	17	1:23.551	17	1:23.055	17	1:23.488	16
19.	Giorgio Pantano	Jordan EJ14/02 - Ford	1:25.375	20	1:24.091	21	1:24.255	16	1:24.736	18	1:24.643	18	1:23.352	15
20.	Gianmaria Bruni	Minardi PS04B/02 - Cosworth	1:27.933	23	1:25.653	22	1:26.783	18	1:26.199	19	1:26.463	19	1:26.899	17
21.	Zsolt Baumgartner	Minardi PS04B/01 - Cosworth	1:29.312	24	1:25.760	23	1:27.539	19	1:27.451	20	1:27.319	20	1:46.299	18
35.	Anthony Davidson	B.A.R 006-02 - Honda	1:22.398	4	1:21.643	6								
37.	Björn Wirdheim	Jaguar R5-02	1:24.152	17	1:23.470	18								
38.	Ricardo Zonta	Toyota TF104/06	1:23.161	10	1:23.500	19								
39.	Timo Glock	Jordan EJ14/01 - Ford	1:26.254	22										
40.	Bas Leinders	Minardi PS04B/04 - Cosworth	1:29.414	25	1:27.025	24								

Maximum speed

N°	Driver	P1 Qualifs	Pos.	P1 Race	Pos.	P2 Qualifs	Pos.	P2 Race	Pos.	Finish Qualifs	Pos.	Finish Race	Pos.	Trap Qualifs	Pos.	Trap Race	Pos.
1.	M. Schumacher	234,9	1	230,4	2	270,6	4	273,9	2	188,7	2	178,9	5	309,8	5	314,6	3
2.	R. Barrichello	231,0	5	230,3	3	271,9	2	276,7	1	187.6	3	180,7	3	313,3	1	318,5	1
3.	J.P. Montoya	233,2	2	229,0	5	271,2	3	271,2	4	187,5	4	178,1	6	309,0	6	312,0	9
4.	R. Schumacher	228,6	7	228,8	6	272,0	1	271,5	3	178,6	16	176,4	7	310,4	3	315,0	2
5.	D. Coulthard	233,0	3	227,2	9	270,5	5	271,0	6	186,2	6	171,8	17	308,8	7	313,8	5
6.	K. Räikkönen	188,3	19	225,6	12	236,4	19	269,3	9			173,9	14	255,0	19	313,1	7
7.	J. Trulli	223,5	12	227,5	8	264,8	14	266,4	15	185,3	7	180,0	4	302,2	14	305,6	17
8.	F. Alonso	228,0	8	230,1	4	266,2	10	269,5	8	188,9	1	181,7	1	303,2	13	309,4	12
9.	J. Button	232,2	4	232,7	1	269,7	6	270,6	7	186,7	5	181,2	2	310,1	4	313,7	6
10.	T. Sato	223,0	13	228,5	7	269,6	7	266,7	14	184,5	8	175,7	9	312,3	2	311,6	10
11.	G. Fisichella			226,0	10			268,5	10			172,9	15			312,8	8
12.	F. Massa	222,5	14	224,8	14	269,5	8	271,0	5	182,1	13	172,3	16	307,5	8	314,5	4
14.	M. Webber	229,2	6	224,2	15	265,6	11	268,1	11	182,9	12	174,5	13	303,4	12	308,7	13
15.	C. Klien	226,1	10	225,3	13	266,6	9	266,8	13	183,1	9	175,5	11	301,5	15	306,4	15
16.	C. Da Matta	225,4	11	224,0	16	265,2	12	265,2	17	183,0	11	176,3	8	305,0	9	307,7	14
17.	O. Panis	227,3	9	225,7	11	263,2	16	266,1	16	183,1	10	175,5	10	300,8	17	306,4	16
18.	N. Heidfeld	220,8	16	223,7	17	263,5	15	267,7	12	182,1	14	175,3	12	304,4	11	310,7	11
19.	G. Pantano	221,3	15	220,0	18	264,8	13	264,5	18	176,0	17	168,0	20	304,4	10	304,3	18
20.	G. Bruni	212,5	17	216,0	20	257,5	18	257,5	20	180,2	15	170,1	19	296,7	18	298,5	20
21.	Z. Baumgartner	209,9	18	217,7	19	262,7	17	263,0	19	173,9	18	170,8	18	301,0	16	303,9	19

Race

Classification & Retirements

Pos.	Driver	Team	Lap	Time	Average
1.	M. Schumacher	Ferrari	62	1:26:19.670	212,405 km/h
2.	J. Button	B.A.R Honda	62	+ 9.702	212,008 km/h
3.	J.P. Montoya	Williams BMW	62	+ 21.617	211,523 km/h
4.	F. Alonso	Renault	62	+ 23.654	211,440 km/h
5.	J. Trulli	Renault	62	+ 36.216	210,931 km/h
6.	R. Barrichello	Ferrari	62	+ 36.683	210,912 km/h
7.	R. Schumacher	Williams BMW	62	+ 55.730	210,144 km/h
8.	K. Räikkönen	McLaren Mercedes	61	1 lap	208,952 km/h
9.	G. Fisichella	Sauber Petronas	61	1 lap	208,913 km/h
10.	F. Massa	Sauber Petronas	61	1 lap	208,406 km/h
11.	O. Panis	Toyota	61	1 lap	207,422 km/h
12.	D. Coulthard	McLaren Mercedes	61	1 lap	207,388 km/h
13.	M. Webber	Jaguar	61	1 lap	207,028 km/h
14.	C. Klien	Jaguar	60	2 laps	204,160 km/h
15.	Z. Baumgartner	Minardi Cosworth	58	4 laps	197,911 km/h
16.	T. Sato	B.A.R Honda	56	6 laps	209,173 km/h Broken engine

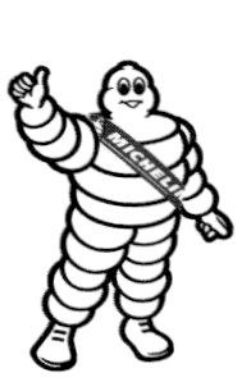

Driver	Team		Reason
N. Heidfeld	Jordan Ford	49	Broken drive shaft
C. Da Matta	Toyota	33	Off-track excursion (forgot to reactivate traction control)
G. Bruni	Minardi Cosworth	23	Brake balance problem
G. Pantano	Jordan Ford	7	Loss of hydraulic fluid from steering system

Fastest laps

	Driver	Time	Lap	Average
1.	M. Schumacher	1:20.411	10	220,850 km/h
2.	J. Button	1:21.201	28	218,701 km/h
3.	F. Alonso	1:21.650	59	217,499 km/h
4.	J. Trulli	1:21.666	11	217,456 km/h
5.	R. Schumacher	1:21.689	30	217,395 km/h
6.	J.P. Montoya	1:21.870	27	216,914 km/h
7.	R. Barrichello	1:21.873	31	216,906 km/h
8.	T. Sato	1:21.929	44	216,758 km/h
9.	K. Räikkönen	1:22.500	39	215,258 km/h
10.	G. Fisichella	1:22.654	60	214,857 km/h
11.	O. Panis	1:22.861	59	214,320 km/h
12.	F. Massa	1:22.895	36	214,232 km/h
13.	M. Webber	1:22.931	55	214,139 km/h
14.	D. Coulthard	1:22.951	42	214,087 km/h
15.	C. Da Matta	1:23.108	25	213,683 km/h
16.	N. Heidfeld	1:23.381	44	212,983 km/h
17.	C. Klien	1:23.647	27	212,306 km/h
18.	G. Pantano	1:25.457	6	207,809 km/h
19.	Z. Baumgartner	1:26.075	58	206,317 km/h
20.	G. Bruni	1:26.857	11	204,460 km/h

Pit stops

	Driver	Time	Lap	Stop n°
1.	D. Coulthard	31.224	1	1
2.	C. Da Matta	26.714	7	1
3.	F. Massa	25.142	7	1
4.	J.P. Montoya	24.127	8	1
5.	M. Webber	25.885	8	1
6.	J. Button	26.571	9	1
7.	R. Schumacher	24.360	9	1
8.	O. Panis	24.586	9	1
9.	C. Klien	28.386	9	1
10.	T. Sato	26.016	10	1
11.	R. Barrichello	24.230	10	1
12.	M. Schumacher	24.371	11	1
13.	F. Alonso	25.084	11	1
14.	J. Trulli	24.760	12	1
15.	G. Bruni	26.800	12	1
16.	N. Heidfeld	24.947	14	1
17.	Z. Baumgartner	24.868	14	1
18.	D. Coulthard	25.734	19	2
19.	G. Fisichella	25.982	20	1
20.	K. Räikkönen	26.180	21	1
21.	C. Da Matta	24.022	23	2
22.	F. Massa	24.578	24	2
23.	M. Webber	25.698	24	2
24.	J.P. Montoya	24.946	25	2
25.	J. Button	25.118	26	2
26.	C. Klien	26.058	25	2
27.	O. Panis	23.538	26	2
28.	M. Schumacher	24.402	27	2
29.	R. Schumacher	24.118	28	2
30.	R. Barrichello	23.933	28	2
31.	F. Alonso	23.617	30	2
32.	Z. Baumgartner	35.378	29	2
33.	J. Trulli	23.685	31	2
34.	C. Da Matta	14.380	32	3
35.	N. Heidfeld	24.042	32	2
36.	F. Massa	26.931	38	3
37.	G. Fisichella	26.222	39	2
38.	D. Coulthard	27.053	40	3
39.	K. Räikkönen	26.692	41	2
40.	M. Webber	30.939	41	3
41.	O. Panis	24.990	42	3
42.	J.P. Montoya	25.137	43	3
43.	R. Barrichello	24.872	43	3
44.	C. Klien	25.270	42	3
45.	J. Button	24.993	44	3
46.	R. Schumacher	23.728	44	3
47.	M. Schumacher	23.946	46	3
48.	J. Trulli	23.019	46	3
49.	Z. Baumgartner	25.062	44	3
50.	F. Alonso	22.619	48	3
51.	N. Heidfeld	25.056	47	3

Race leaders

Driver	Laps in the lead	Nber of Laps
J. Button	1 > 8	8
M. Schumacher	9 > 62	54

Driver	Nber of Laps	Kilometers
M. Schumacher	54	266,382 km
J. Button	8	39,227 km

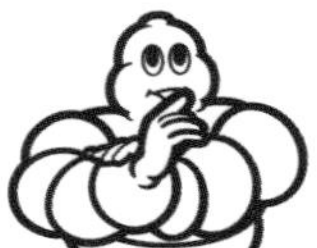

Gaps on the leader board

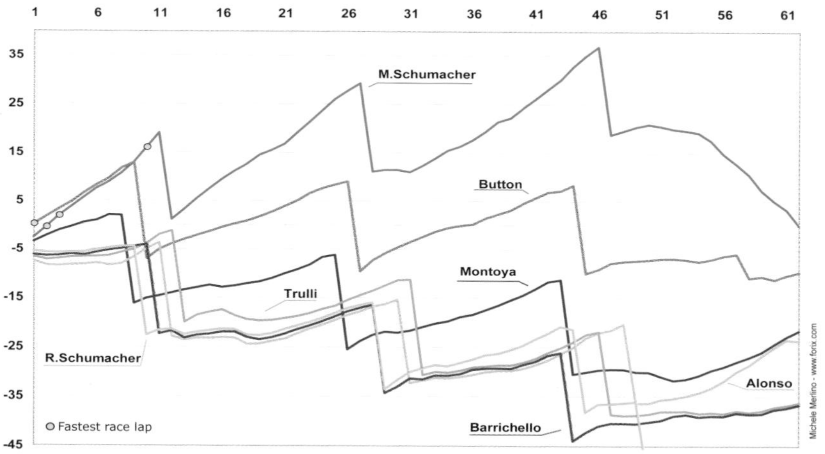

M.Schumacher
Button
Montoya
Trulli
R.Schumacher
Alonso
Barrichello
Fastest race lap
Michele Merlino - www.forix.com

Lap chart

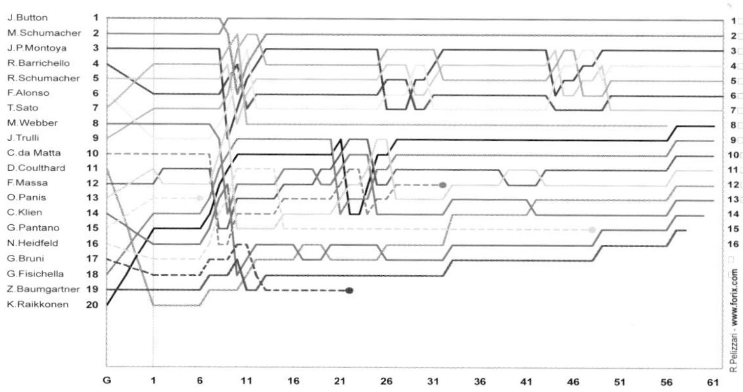

J.Button 1
M.Schumacher 2
J.P.Montoya 3
R.Barrichello 4
R.Schumacher 5
F.Alonso 6
T.Sato 7
M.Webber 8
J.Trulli 9
C.da Matta 10
D.Coulthard 11
F.Massa 12
O.Panis 13
C.Klien 14
G.Pantano 15
N.Heidfeld 16
G.Bruni 17
G.Fisichella 18
Z.Baumgartner 19
K.Raikkonen 20
1 M.Schumacher
2 J.Button
3 J.P.Montoya
4 F.Alonso
5 J.Trulli
6 R.Barrichello
7 R.Schumacher
8 K.Raikkonen
9 G.Fisichella
10 F.Massa
11 O.Panis
12 D.Coulthard
13 M.Webber
14 C.Klien
15 Z.Baumgartner
16 T.Sato
G 1 6 11 16 21 26 31 36 41 46 51 56 61
R.Pelizzari - www.forix.com

Championship after four rounds

Drivers

1. M. Schumacher ....(4 wins)................40
2. R. Barrichello..24
3. J. Button 23
4. J.P. Montoya 18
5. F. Alonso 16
6. J. Trulli...15
7. R. Schumacher 9
8. T. Sato 4
9. D. Coulthard..4
10. F. Massa 1
11. M. Webber 1
12. K. Räikkönen 1
13. G. Fisichella...0
14. C. Da Matta..0
15. O. Panis...0
16. C. Klien 0
17. G. Pantano...0
18. G. Bruni...0
19. Z. Baumgartner 0
20. N. Heidfeld...0

Constructors

1. Scuderia Ferrari Marlboro ......(4 wins) 64
2. Mild Seven Renault F1 Team 31
3. Lucky Strike B.A.R Honda.........................27
4. BMW WilliamsF1 Team 27
5. West McLaren Mercedes............................5
6. Sauber Petronas 1
7. Jaguar Racing..1
8. Panasonic Toyota Racing 0
9. Jordan Ford...0
10. Minardi Cosworth 0

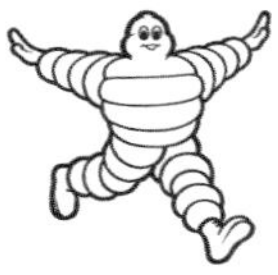

The circuit

Name	Autodromo Enzo & Dino Ferrari, Imola
Length	4933 meters
Distance	62 laps, 305.609 km
Date	April 25, 2004
Weather	sunny, 20-22°c
Track temperature	31-35°c

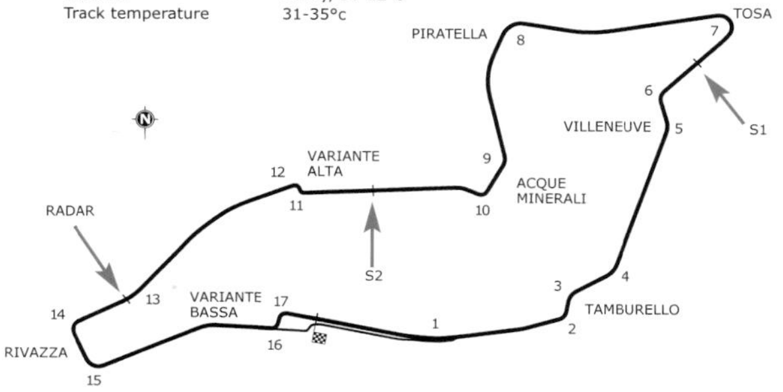

PIRATELLA
TOSA
VILLENEUVE
S1
VARIANTE ALTA
ACQUE MINERALI
RADAR
S2
VARIANTE BASSA
TAMBURELLO
RIVAZZA

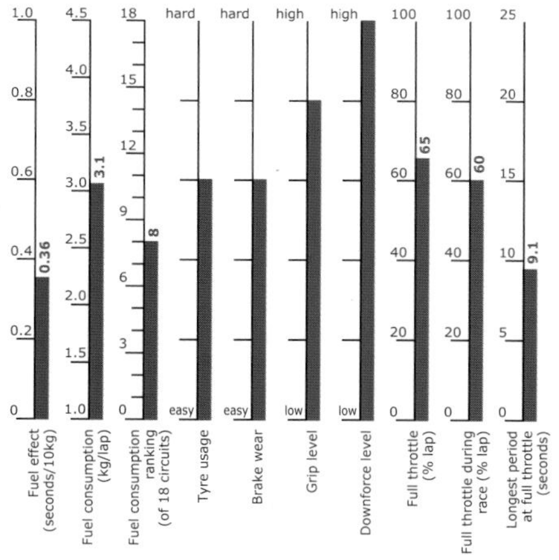

0.36
3.1
8
65
60
9.1
Fuel effect (seconds/10kg)
Fuel consumption (kg/lap)
Fuel consumption ranking (of 18 circuits)
Tyre usage
Brake wear
Grip level
Downforce level
Full throttle (% lap)
Full throttle during race (% lap)
Longest period at full throttle (seconds)

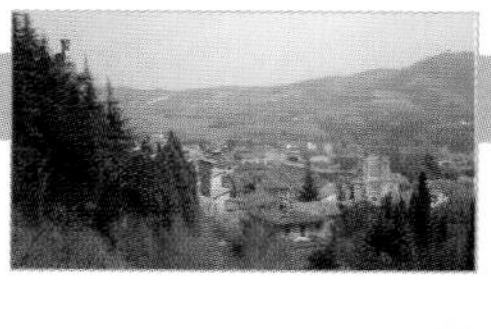

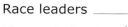

A TENSE VICTORY

Shortly after the start of the race Michael Schumacher's car began to emit a most un-Ferrari like noise due to a broken exhaust. Normally, this kind of problem is terminal. The world champion slowed but he was still fast enough to win! That really says it all concerning the red cars' superiority in relation to their rivals for whom it was yet another smack in the gob as Michael went on to rack up his fifth consecutive victory.

^
In 2003, Fernando Alonso was third quicker in practice. This year he could do no better than eighth.

No repeat performance from Jenson

It was business as usual for the sextuple world champion as he powered his Ferrari to pole on the Barcelona circuit, the 59th of his career. He seemed rather surprised at being so well placed. *"My problem was that I was ninth in prequalifying,"* he grinned, *"so I went out much too early to have ideal track conditions as it was much quicker towards the end. It wasn't perfect but I set good times in the first two sectors and then I just kept it all together in the final one."*

>
The Minardi team had its usual kind of grand prix weekend. The Italian cars qualified 18th and 20th and both retired during the race.

Alongside Michael on the front row was his sparring partner, Juan Pablo Montoya who was over half-a-second behind leaving little doubt to the outcome of the race. *"I'm happy to be on the front row here,"* said the Colombian. *"My car's working well and I think we've got a good chance."*

Once again the BAR team set tongues wagging in practice but this time it was not Jenson Button who was centre stage. He did not manage to reedit his Imola exploit. When he was flat out and as his telemetry showed well placed to go second on the grid, he lost it in corner 7. *"I had to lift off and so I ended up fourteenth,"* he said dolefully. *"It's a pity but that kind of thing can happen. There was a sudden gust of wind that I wasn't expecting which hit me amidships and that was that."* It was his team-mate who outshone him by setting the third fastest time overall and never before had a Japanese been so well placed on the grid of an F1 grand prix.

In Brief

> Once again the McLaren team was in deep trouble with Coulthard in tenth place and Raïkkönen in thirteenth both complaining that the car was dancing all over the place. They ended the session in tenth and thirteenth places respectively. For Ron Dennis and his squad it was the worst start to the season since 1981! It was all the more galling as on Wednesday of the following week Queen Elizabeth was going to open his new factory called Paragon. But Ron Dennis's most pressing problem was not four wheels but four feet. In front of the magnificent bay windows of the building was an immaculate lawn invaded by hundreds of rabbits, which, as is their wont at this time of year, were giving themselves with joyful abandon to activities conducive to the perpetuation of the species. And politically correct Ron did not want the eyes of her gracious majesty to witness such an immoral spectacle! So the problems of making the cars work properly were put on hold and it was Bugs Bunny hunting time at McLaren!

> For the 2004 season Bridgestone built a new 2-storey motor home to keep up with the Joneses, namely, the other teams in the paddock. The problem was that in keeping with an old agreement the tyre manufacturers did not have the right to such a vehicle. Bridgestone should have asked for an authorisation before constructing its new toy but the Japanese forgot!? So at Imola they had to set up their motor home outside the confines of the paddock before Pierre Dupasquier relented and allowed them to erect it inside.

Starting grid

Pos	Driver	Time	Pos	Driver	Time
19	G. PANTANO	1:20.607	20	Z. BAUMGARTNER	1:21.470
17	F. MASSA	1:17.866	18	G. BRUNI	1:19.817
15	N. HEIDFELD	1:17.802	16	C. KLIEN	1:17.812
13	K. RAÏKKÖNEN	1:17.445	14	J. BUTTON	1:17.575
11	C. DA MATTA	1:17.038	12	G. FISICHELLA	1:17.444
9	M. WEBBER	1:16.514	10	D. COULTHARD	1:16.636
7	O. PANIS	1:16.313	8	F. ALONSO	1:16.422
5	R. BARRICHELLO	1:16.272	6	R. SCHUMACHER	1:16.293
3	T. SATO	1:15.809	4	J. TRULLI	1:16.144
1	M. SCHUMACHER	1:15.022 (222,030 km/h)	2	J.P. MONTOYA	1:15.639

Michael Schumacher: five out of five despite problems

There is no better way to stun one's rivals than to win a race with a car that is not 100%. On lap 11 it became obvious for all present that Michael Schumacher's Ferrari's engine was not emitting its usual melodious note. It was an exhaust problem. *"The team told me I had a problem. Ross Brawn, the technical director, asked me over the radio if I felt something. At the start, no, but then the problem got more serious and then I felt it. I reduced the pace a little and accelerated less but fundamentally there wasn't very much I could do,"* the German explained after the race.

Even after slowing down Michael was lapping quicker than his rivals apart from his team-mate Rubens Barrichello. So Ferrari scored its third double of the season without ever being under threat from its rivals. Schumacher led the race almost from start to finish apart from the first eight laps as Jarno Trulli catapulted from his fourth place on the grid to lead into the first corner. *"It's the kind of start that you do once in a lifetime,"* admitted the Italian afterwards. *"I let in the clutch when the lights were still red and the car started just at the very moment they went out. I was very lucky."*

Overall the Renaults had a good day as Jarno finished on the rostrum behind the Ferrari duo and Alonso saw the flag in fourth place. It was the Italian's first finish of the season in the top three and rumour had it that his seat in the French squad was under serious threat.

Anyway he was overjoyed at his rostrum finish. *"Yes because my team and myself have really worked very hard these last few weeks. We've been close to the rostrum on several occasions and finally managing to do is really great."* An emotional Jarno dedicated his third place to Dino, one of the team's aerodynamicist and one of his great friends, who had just been diagnosed with terminal cancer. Sometimes F1 drivers show a human face.

An unexpected guest on the grid!

After the employee fired by Mercedes-Benz in the 2000 German Grand Prix and the rogue priest at Silverstone last year, another unexpected guest jumped over the barriers and appeared on the F1 grid in Spain just as the cars were setting off for their reconnaissance lap.

He was brandishing a banderol, which was upside down so nobody could read what was written on it! He was quickly tackled by the track marshals and spent the rest of his day in the Montmelo police station. The circuit put out a press release stating that the man in question considered himself a *"Professional"* at this kind of thing and it was not his first appearance in public places. He had hid during the morning before jumping over the barrier.

^
Michael Schumacher's usual victory salute. It was five out of five for the German.

^
Rubens Barrichello finished 2nd after starting from 5th on the grid. *"I had to try and get out of the traffic. At Imola I was going crazy being stuck behind the others. My car was perfect and I could do nothing. Here I had the choice. Either I fitted soft tyres on Saturday and went for pole or I used hard ones and stopped one time less in the race. I chose the latter option and it worked perfectly."*

<
The season has got off to a difficult start for Christian Klein. After four finishes outside the top ten he crashed out of the Spanish Grand Prix.

How peaceful it all looks from a height!

Car parks, stands, track and the paddock: it all looks so perfect down there from the air. It really is a beautiful circuit not far from a magnificent town.

paddock

> Only one Williams finished in sixth place (Ralf Schumacher) and both McLarens failed to score. What has happened to these once great teams? Juan Pablo Montoya retired on lap 47 with defective brakes.

The McLarens also ran into problems. Coulthard and Raïkkönen saw the flag in 10th and 11th places respectively. And that result according to both drivers was a pretty fair indication of their present level of competitiveness.

Fernando Alonso: climbing the ladder

Fernando Alonso began his F1 career in a very discreet manner at the wheel of a Minardi in the 2001 Australian Grand Prix. What struck observers at the time was his age – he was only eighteen!

He comes from a modest background and was born in the little town of Oviedo. His father is an explosives specialist and not especially well off so Fernando had to use what he could get to move up the motor sport ladder. During his year with Minardi he was spotted by Flavio Briatore, the Renault F1 boss, who took him under his wing. He decided that the best move would be to give the young Spaniard a year as a Renault test driver. It was the right thing to do and Fernando's talent exploded when Renault gave him his chance. He set pole in only the second race of the season and then went on to win the 2003 Hungarian Grand Prix becoming the youngest ever winner in F1 history. His success fired the hopes of a nation. In 1995, no national TV channel showed F1. Now it is back with a vengeance on the Iberian Peninsula's screens.

Two weeks earlier the San Marino Grand Prix had set a new record as it was seen by 3 600 000 TV viewers. On Saturday traffic jams several kilometres long formed around the Barcelona circuit entry points and the organisers counted no fewer than 93 000 spectators. It is a record for a practice day and for the race itself there were only 750 tickets left. This was a source of worry as traditionally many people come without tickets and buy their seat at the entry to the circuit. It looked like the good weather combined with the wave of enthusiasm created by Alonso were going to pull in a huge crowd. Nobody was complaining, though, as at a moment when people are falling out of love with F1 the Spaniards' passion was a welcome change.

Max Mosley attacks F1 costs

Max Mosley, the FIA President, decided to take the bull by the horns. As he saw for himself the interest in F1 is dwindling again this season due to Michael Schumacher's outrageous domination

The sponsors, who pour huge sums of money, into F1 find it difficult to accept that their investment is not as profitable as before, a feeling shared by the teams that depend on them. Something has to be done. And quickly.

On Tuesday the team bosses met in Monaco under the presidency of Max Mosley to study the measures he had proposed for 2008. *"We reached agreement. For once it was a good meeting,"* commented the FIA President. *"I really want to reduce costs in F1. The engineers explained to us that they spend a billion dollars each year developing F1 engines. This can't go on and I want to reduce this amount by 50%."*

So Max Mosley wants to impose a 2.4 litre 8-cylinder engine. *"I'd like to introduce this measure before 2008, preferably in 2006,"* he explained. In addition, electronic aids like automatic gearboxes and launch controls must go to enhance the role played by the driver. He also wants to have a single tyre supplier thus reducing testing costs.

> The stands were packed with Alonso fans decked out in his colours. On Sunday 108 300 spectators passed through the Catalunya circuit's gates. It was a record number and the combined weekend total was 277 300.

Practice

All the time trials

N°	Driver	N° Chassis - Engine	Practice 1 Friday	Pos.	Practice 2 Friday	Pos.	Practice 3 Saturday	Pos.	Practice 4 Saturday	Pos.	Pre-qual. Saturday	Pos.	Qualif. Saturday	Pos.
1.	Michael Schumacher	Ferrari F2004 234	1:15.658	1	1:16.729	7	1:16.519	5	1:15.025	2	1:16.320	9	1:15.022	1
2.	Rubens Barrichello	Ferrari F2004 236	1:16.033	2	1:16.698	6	1:16.795	8	1:15.540	5	1:16.655	13	1:16.272	5
3.	Juan Pablo Montoya	Williams FW26 06 - BMW	1:17.635	11	1:17.067	12	1:16.048	3	1:15.232	3	1:15.574	1	1:15.639	2
4.	Ralf Schumacher	Williams FW26 07 - BMW	1:17.165	6	1:16.433	4	1:16.233	4	1:16.308	12	1:16.040	4	1:16.293	6
5.	David Coulthard	McLaren MP4-19 03 - Mercedes	1:17.973	13	1:17.069	13	1:17.106	9	1:15.768	7	1:16.465	12	1:16.636	10
6.	Kimi Räikkönen	McLaren MP4-19 04 - Mercedes	1:17.563	10	1:16.798	9	1:17.428	13	1:15.983	11	1:16.240	8	1:17.445	13
7.	Jarno Trulli	Renault R24-03	1:18.341	14	1:16.734	8	1:16.015	2	1:15.457	4	1:16.156	5	1:16.144	4
8.	Fernando Alonso	Renault R24-02	1:17.429	7	1:16.534	5	1:17.294	12	1:15.874	8	1.17.011	15	1:16.422	8
9.	Jenson Button	B.A.R 006-05 - Honda	1:17.060	5	1:15.935	1	1:15.984	1	1:15.627	6	1:16.462	11	1:17.575	14
10.	Takuma Sato	B.A.R 006-03 - Honda	1:17.481	8	1:17.970	18	1:16.685	6	1:14.836	1	1:16.434	10	1:15.809	3
11.	Giancarlo Fisichella	Sauber C23-04 - Petronas	1:18.886	20	1:18.001	19	1:17.277	11	1:17.145	15	1:15.746	2	1:17.444	12
12.	Felipe Massa	Sauber C23-06 - Petronas	1:18.760	19	1:17.906	17	1:17.860	14	1:17.282	16	1:15.771	3	1:17.866	17
14.	Mark Webber	Jaguar R5-03	1:17.763	12	1:17.178	14			1:15.895	9	1:16.212	7	1:16.514	9
15.	Christian Klien	Jaguar R5-01	1:18.615	17			1:19.851	17	1:16.648	13	1:17.863	17	1:17.812	16
16.	Cristiano da Matta	Toyota TF104/04	1:18.362	15	1:16.833	10	1:17.252	10	1:15.895	10	1:16.758	14	1:17.038	11
17.	Olivier Panis	Toyota TF104/03	1:17.489	9	1:16.925	11	1:16.721	7	1:18.392	18	1:16.168	6	1:16.313	7
18.	Nick Heidfeld	Jordan EJ14/03 - Ford	1:19.198	21	1:18.117	20	1:18.643	15	1:16.746	14	1:17.043	16	1:17.802	15
19.	Giorgio Pantano	Jordan EJ14/02 - Ford	1:19.925	22	1:18.726	21	1:19.146	16	1:17.665	17	1:17.965	18	1:20.607	19
20.	Gianmaria Bruni	Minardi PS04B/02 - Cosworth	1:20.858	23	1:19.149	22			1:21.005	20	1:20.372	19	1:19.817	18
21.	Zsolt Baumgartner	Minardi PS04B/01 - Cosworth	1:21.535	25	1:20.313	23	1:19.949	18	1:20.449	19	1:21.620	20	1:21.470	20
35.	Anthony Davidson	B.A.R 006-01 - Honda	1:16.616	3	1:16.188	2								
37.	Björn Wirdheim	Jaguar R5-02	1:18.603	16	1:17.676	16								
38.	Ricardo Zonta	Toyota TF104/06	1:16.639	4	1:16.360	3								
39.	Timo Glock	Jordan EJ14/01 - Ford	1:18.655	18	1:17.608	15								
40.	Bas Leinders	Minardi PS04B/04 - Cosworth	1:21.053	24	1:22.189	24								

Maximum speed

N°	Driver	P1 Qualifs	Pos.	P1 Race	Pos.	P2 Qualifs	Pos.	P2 Race	Pos.	Finish Qualifs	Pos.	Finish Race	Pos.	Trap Qualifs	Pos.	Trap Race	Pos.
1.	M. Schumacher	305,2	1	303,2	1	263,9	13	272,3	12	296,8	1	292,5	5	323,0	3	328,9	7
2.	R. Barrichello	291,8	16	291,4	10	269,2	11	271,3	13	291,1	8	291,5	6	317,9	10	330,3	5
3.	J.P. Montoya	301,3	4	289,0	14	287,0	2	273,5	10	294,1	2	295,4	1	321,7	4	333,6	3
4.	R. Schumacher	301,3	3	295,8	3	273,4	7	275,0	7	291,2	7	294,8	2	318,9	8	331,5	4
5.	D. Coulthard	300,8	6	293,0	6	279,4	4	282,9	2	291,8	6	288,3	15	316,3	12	323,7	15
6.	K. Räikkönen	294,1	12	292,4	9	288,5	1	274,8	9	292,7	5	290,3	9	319,2	7	328,0	10
7.	J. Trulli	299,4	7	294,7	4	280,8	3	284,2	1	289,0	13	288,0	16	312,5	16	319,8	19
8.	F. Alonso	296,0	10	292,6	8	276,7	6	282,0	3	288,5	14	290,7	8	311,2	19	323,0	16
9.	J. Button	303,4	2	290,1	13	251,7	20	275,2	6	293,6	4	292,8	4	324,1	2	334,1	1
10.	T. Sato	301,1	5	296,0	2	264,9	12	280,2	4	293,7	3	293,2	3	325,6	1	333,8	2
11.	G. Fisichella	293,9	13	293,4	5	259,1	17	274,9	8	287,8	17	291,0	7	318,7	9	329,0	6
12.	F. Massa	293,6	14	292,6	7	254,8	18	263,1	17	287,9	16	289,0	14	321,6	5	328,9	8
14.	M. Webber	297,4	8	291,3	11	269,7	10	272,5	11	290,4	9	290,2	10	312,4	17	328,5	9
15.	C. Klien	293,5	15	288,0	15	272,7	8	278,2	5	285,6	19	287,9	17	310,2	20	322,4	17
16.	C. Da Matta	295,6	11	286,0	16	277,9	5	268,7	15	289,8	11	289,6	12	313,4	13	325,3	14
17.	O. Panis	296,7	9	284,8	17	261,0	16	269,4	14	290,0	10	289,7	11	312,3	18	325,5	13
18.	N. Heidfeld	291,5	17	282,0	18	271,0	9	256,1	20	289,5	12	289,3	13	321,1	6	327,6	11
19.	G. Pantano	291,2	18	291,1	12	261,2	15	264,9	16	288,0	15	286,7	18	317,8	11	327,2	12
20.	G. Bruni	284,7	19	281,1	19	252,9	19	259,8	19	286,2	18	281,9	19	312,9	15	321,0	18
21.	Z. Baumgartner	268,6	20	277,2	20	263,3	14	260,9	18	280,8	20	278,9	20	312,9	14	314,9	20

Race

Classification & Retirements

Pos.	Driver	Team	Lap	Time	Average
1.	M. Schumacher	Ferrari	66	1:27:32.841	209,205 km/h
2.	R. Barrichello	Ferrari	66	+ 13.290	208,677 km/h
3.	J. Trulli	Renault	66	+ 32.294	207,926 km/h
4.	F. Alonso	Renault	66	+ 32.952	207,900 km/h
5.	T. Sato	B.A.R Honda	66	+ 42.327	207,532 km/h
6.	R. Schumacher	Williams BMW	66	+ 1:13.804	206,306 km/h
7.	G. Fisichella	Sauber Petronas	66	+ 1:17.108	206,178 km/h
8.	J. Button	B.A.R Honda	65	1 lap	205,732 km/h
9.	F. Massa	Sauber Petronas	65	1 lap	205,082 km/h
10.	D. Coulthard	McLaren Mercedes	65	1 lap	204,416 km/h
11.	K. Räikkönen	McLaren Mercedes	65	1 lap	204,306 km/h
12.	M. Webber	Jaguar	65	1 lap	204,295 km/h
13.	C. Da Matta	Toyota	65	1 lap	204,075 km/h

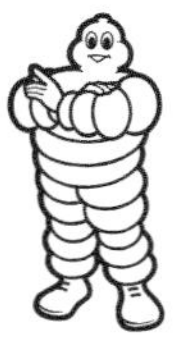

Driver	Team		Reason
G. Pantano	Jordan Ford	52	Hydraulic pressure problem with power assisted steering
J.P. Montoya	Williams BMW	47	Brake cooling problem
C. Klien	Jaguar	44	Throttle pedal problem
O. Panis	Toyota	34	Loss of hydraulic pressure
N. Heidfeld	Jordan Ford	34	Loss of gearbox hydraulic pressure
G. Bruni	Minardi Cosworth	32	Spin caused by brake problems
Z. Baumgartner	Minardi Cosworth	18	Spin after tyres got dirty moving off line to let a Sauber pass

Fastest laps

	Driver	Time	Lap	Average
1.	M. Schumacher	1:17.450	12	215,070 km/h
2.	J. Button	1:17.495	46	214,945 km/h
3.	F. Alonso	1:17.556	27	214,776 km/h
4.	T. Sato	1:17.678	47	214,439 km/h
5.	R. Barrichello	1:17.887	16	213,863 km/h
6.	J. Trulli	1:18.178	12	213,067 km/h
7.	J.P. Montoya	1:18.262	28	212,838 km/h
8.	R. Schumacher	1:18.548	27	212,063 km/h
9.	M. Webber	1:18.617	11	211,877 km/h
10.	F. Massa	1:18.819	43	211,334 km/h
11.	K. Räikkönen	1:18.842	48	211,273 km/h
12.	N. Heidfeld	1:18.971	25	210,928 km/h
13.	G. Fisichella	1:19.062	37	210,685 km/h
14.	C. Da Matta	1:19.112	29	210,552 km/h
15.	C. Klien	1:19.142	18	210,472 km/h
16.	D. Coulthard	1:19.175	38	210,384 km/h
17.	O. Panis	1:19.199	10	210,320 km/h
18.	G. Pantano	1:19.896	27	208,486 km/h
19.	G. Bruni	1:22.323	3	202,339 km/h
20.	Z. Baumgartner	1:23.390	8	199,750 km/h

Pit stops

	Driver	Time	Lap	Stop n°
1.	G. Bruni	25.024	4	1
2.	F. Alonso	21.427	8	1
3.	O. Panis	22.322	8	1
4.	J. Trulli	20.997	9	1
5.	J.P. Montoya	22.742	9	1
6.	K. Räikkönen	23.659	9	1
7.	M. Webber	29.193	9	1
8.	C. Da Matta	28.750	9	1
9.	N. Heidfeld	22.122	9	1
10.	M. Schumacher	22.068	10	1
11.	D. Coulthard	25.497	10	1
12.	R. Schumacher	21.879	10	1
13.	J. Button	24.792	10	1
14.	G. Pantano	23.013	10	1
15.	T. Sato	23.555	11	1
16.	Z. Baumgartner	23.934	12	1
17.	C. Klien	23.237	16	1
18.	R. Barrichello	24.755	17	1
19.	G. Fisichella	24.624	17	1
20.	F. Massa	24.687	18	1
21.	J. Trulli	21.900	23	2
22.	N. Heidfeld	23.017	23	2
23.	M. Schumacher	23.141	25	2
24.	F. Alonso	21.816	25	2
25.	R. Schumacher	25.277	25	2
26.	G. Bruni	25.974	24	2
27.	G. Pantano	23.840	25	2
28.	T. Sato	23.597	26	2
29.	J.P. Montoya	22.687	26	2
30.	O. Panis	24.003	26	2
31.	M. Webber	24.781	26	2
32.	D. Coulthard	24.063	27	2
33.	C. Da Matta	23.026	27	2
34.	J. Button	22.781	28	3
35.	K. Räikkönen	24.370	29	2
36.	O. Panis	12.377	29	3
37.	C. Klien	22.991	32	2
38.	G. Fisichella	25.879	40	2
39.	J. Trulli	24.338	41	3
40.	F. Massa	24.980	41	2
41.	F. Alonso	23.465	42	3
42.	R. Barrichello	27.180	43	2
43.	J.P. Montoya	24.378	43	3
44.	D. Coulthard	25.112	43	3
45.	J. Button	24.109	44	3
46.	M. Schumacher	23.870	45	3
47.	T. Sato	24.238	45	3
48.	R. Schumacher	24.049	45	3
49.	G. Pantano	26.622	44	3
50.	K. Räikkönen	31.696	46	3
51.	C. Da Matta	22.699	46	3
52.	M. Webber	22.028	50	3

Race leaders

Driver	Laps in the lead	Nber of Laps
J. Trulli	1 > 8	8
M. Schumacher	9 > 10	2
R. Barrichello	11 > 17	7
M. Schumacher	18 > 66	49

Driver	Nber of Laps	Kilometers
M. Schumacher	51	235,977 km
J. Trulli	8	36,890 km
R. Barrichello	7	32,389 km

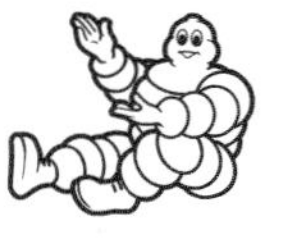

Lap chart

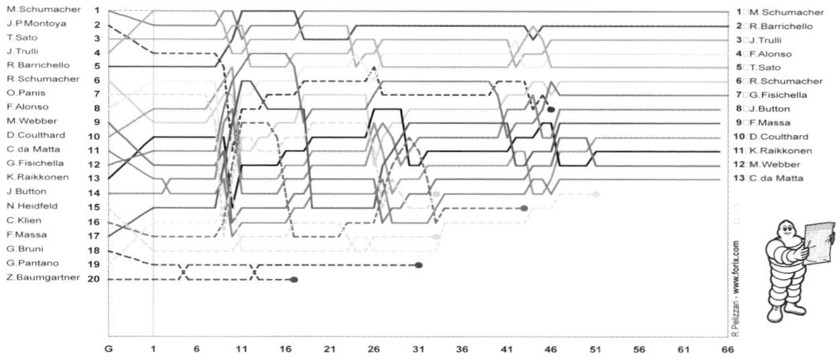

Gaps on the leader board

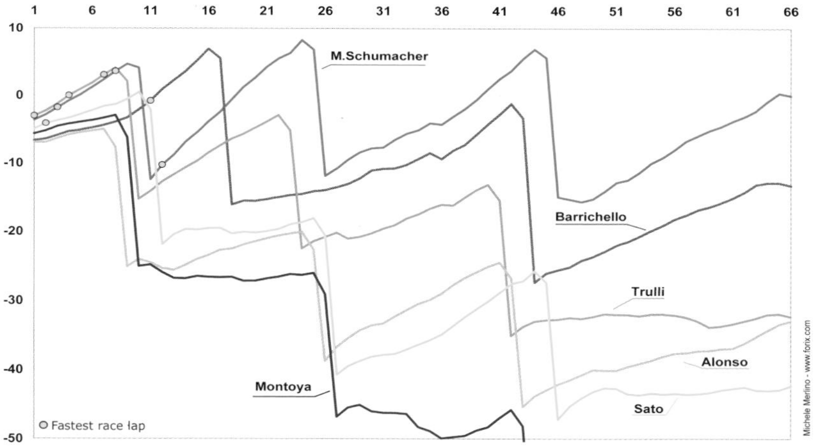

Championship after five rounds

Drivers

1. M. Schumacher ....(5 wins)................50
2. R. Barrichello 32
3. J. Button 24
4. F. Alonso 21
5. J. Trulli..21
6. J.P. Montoya 18
7. R. Schumacher 12
8. T. Sato 8
9. D. Coulthard...4
10. G. Fisichella..2
11. F. Massa 1
12. K. Räikkönen...1
13. M. Webber 1
14. C. Da Matta..0
15. O. Panis...0
16. C. Klien 0
17. G. Pantano...0
18. G. Bruni...0
19. Z. Baumgartner 0
20. N. Heidfeld...0

Constructors

1. Scuderia Ferrari Marlboro ......(5 wins) 82
2. Mild Seven Renault F1 Team 42
3. Lucky Strike B.A.R Honda.........................32
4. BMW WilliamsF1 Team 30
5. West McLaren Mercedes.............................5
6. Sauber Petronas 3
7. Jaguar Racing...1
8. Panasonic Toyota Racing 0
9. Jordan Ford...0
10. Minardi Cosworth......................................0

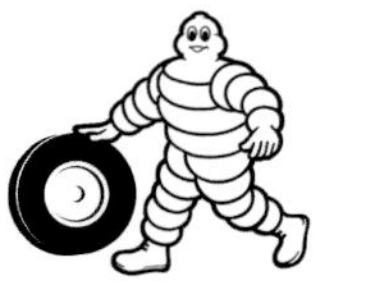

The circuit

Name	Circuit de Catalunya, Montmelo, Barcelone
Length	4627 meters
Distance	66 laps, 305.256 km
Date	May 9, 2004
Weather	Weather sunny and hot, windy, 21-23°c
Track temperature	28-33°c

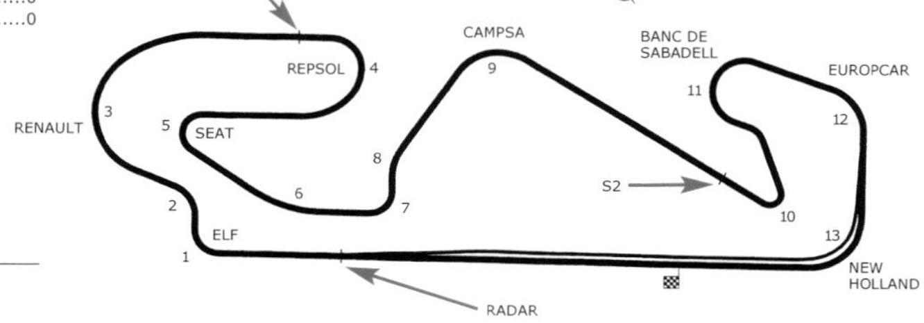

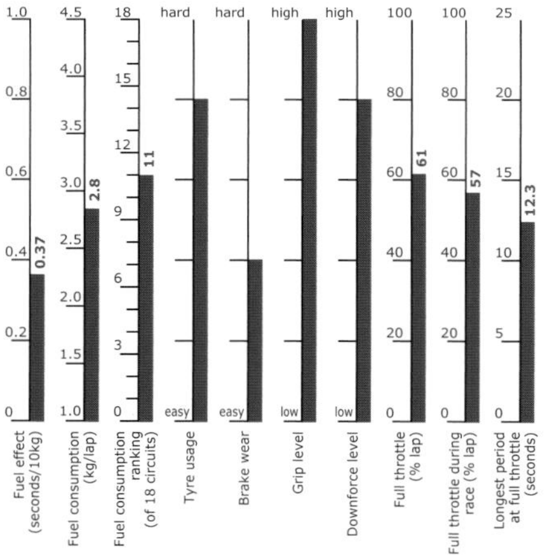

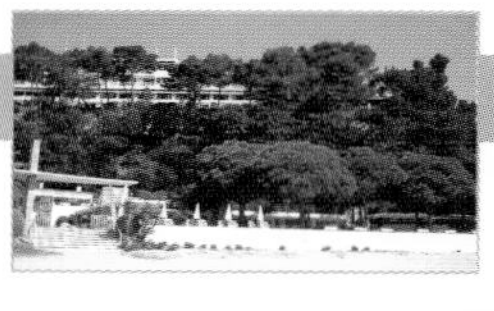

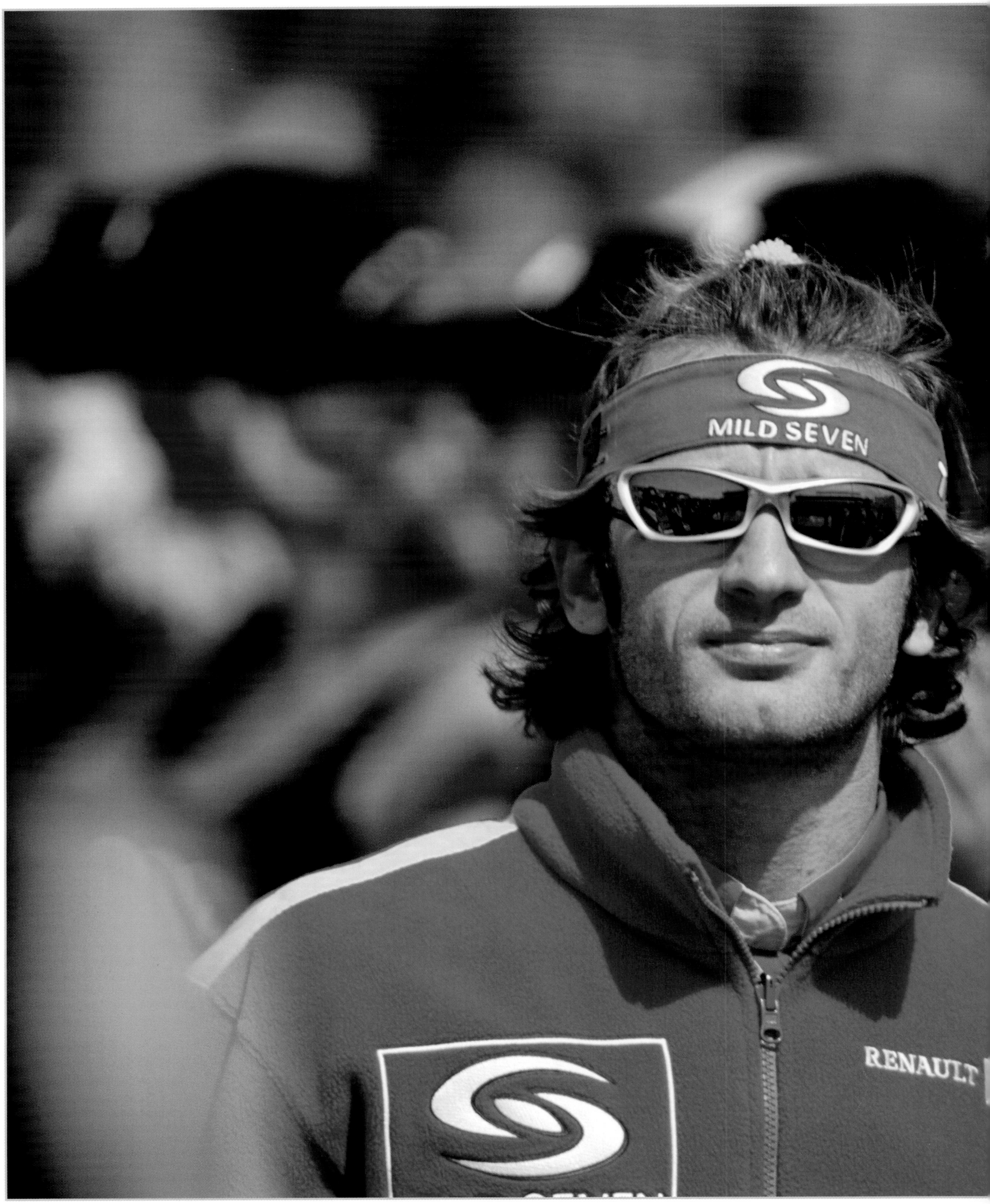
MILD SEVEN
RENAULT

JARNO'S MAIDEN F1 VICTORY

By winning the Monaco Grand Prix Jarno Trulli scored his first ever F1 victory and what a victory, the one all drivers want to add to their laurels. It was also Renault's first and last time on the first step of the rostrum during the 2004 season. It put the French company in a solid second place in the Constructors' Championship. It needed strong nerves to keep it between the hedges over 78 laps of the tight Monaco circuit and a number of accidents marked the race. Giancarlo Fisichella put his Sauber on its roof, Fernando Alonso and Mark Webber both hit the guardrail and Juan Pablo Montoya thumped Michael Schumacher up the rear in the tunnel when they were behind the Safety Car! A first. Jarno was on pole and led almost from start to finish overcoming all the hazards of this particularly tricky race.

Monaco was his dream

"I couldn't have wished for a better place to set my first pole position. All the drivers dream of such a thing happening to them." Jarno Trulli was in seventh heaven when he got out of his car. The Italian was delighted to have grabbed pole in Monaco and was 4/10s ahead of the second man, a country mile in the context of the Monte Carlo toboggan.

"I've been waiting for that pole for a long time and I'm really happy to have done it. Now I'm after my first victory and I'm determined to score it on Sunday. The car is very quick in race set-up and I know I've got the right strategy so I'm very optimistic." Ralf Schumacher set the second quickest time on Saturday but had to start from twelfth place due to an engine change - ten further back in accordance with the new 2004 regulations. On the Monaco circuit where overtaking is practically impossible it was a harsh punishment. *"Starting from twelfth it's not going to be easy,"* he admitted. *"But I'm not too worried. The important thing is that our car's competitive again. It's good for morale."*

Four Michelin-shod cars filled the first four places on the grid so it was obvious that the French rubber was better adapted to the Monaco circuit, which had been the case over the previous three years. *"I have to say that our tyres helped us a lot:* they work really well here,"* said Ralf. *"They don't seem to have found the right rhythm in the Ferrari camp. We'll have to see in the race."*

There were fewer smiling faces than usual at Ferrari. Michael Schumacher (winner of the first five grands prix) was fifth fastest on Saturday but moved up to the second row as a result of his brother's penalty. The German was hoping to pass some of his rivals during the three refuelling stops planned in the race. But like in roulette one never knows what's going to happen until the ball stops spinning.

In brief

> The FIA went back on its decision to outlaw tobacco advertising on the cars from 2006 onwards. *"Everything was going in this direction,"* explained Max Mosley, *"until the European health minister messed things up by advancing the ban to mid-2005. It played hell with the contracts and our decision to ban tobacco advertising was suddenly devoid of sense."* Thus, Ferrari extended its agreement with Philip Morris beyond 2006.

> *"In 1994, we told the teams in F1 that we would not organise the championship in 1995 if they didn't follow us."* This is how Max Mosley explained the fact that after the deaths of Roland Ratzenberger and Ayrton Senna at Imola in 1994 he managed to persuade the teams to reduce the power of their engines in a few weeks. Today, he seems to find it impossible to achieve such a consensus for 2006.

> David Coulthard should know where his future lies in a short time. At present he has not yet signed a contract for 2005 after being dropped by McLaren. The rumour going round the Monaco paddock was that he would be in the Jaguar team with Mark Webber.

> Another rumour, which seemed to have an increasingly solid basis, was that Jacques Villeneuve would be back in F1 in 2005 with the Williams-BMW team. The man from Quebec has consistently repeated that he wants to come back to F1 and that he has been in contact with Frank Williams.

Max attack

On Friday which is a rest day during the Monaco Grand Prix weekend Max Mosley made one of his rare appearances in the press room where he explained his proposals aimed at making F1 more interesting from 2006 onwards. It was too late for next year as most of the teams were already working on their new car.

In 2006, the engines will be limited to 2.4 litres and 8 cylinders (3 litres and 10 cylinders at present). In addition the FIA will impose a single engine management system. It will also enable testing to be limited to a certain number of kilometres fixed in advance and thus reduce their cost.

Mosley also wants to bring back overtaking and make it easier during the race which would mean imposing aerodynamic restrictions. He also wants to attract new small teams by obliging the major manufacturers to sell their chassis to them at reasonable prices.

Another hot topic of discussion in Monaco was the idea of limiting the tyre supply to a single manufacturer from 2006 onwards. The FIA felt that tyres had assumed too much importance in F1 and that their progress was making the cars too quick while their development cost a fortune in terms of testing. Thus, after putting out a tender, a single manufacturer would be chosen (this year) to supply the whole of the field in 2006. *"Apart from the manufacturers themselves everybody agrees with this measure,"* insisted Mosley. *"For me it's fundamental and brooks no question."*

In the past few weeks the Scuderia Ferrari has threatened to withdraw from F1 in 2008 if it reckons that the new regulations did not allow a fair and equal sporting combat.

Max Mosley thought that such a decision would be catastrophic for F1. *"Their withdrawal would be a tragedy for the sport,"* he confirmed. *"There are two names in F1 that are known world wide, Ferrari and the Monaco Grand Prix. Still, I don't think Ferrari will withdraw provided we offer them a level playing field."* These words confirmed as if it were necessary the FIA's natural propensity to favour the Scuderia despite its outrageous domination over the last few years.

∧
Michael was quickest on Thursday but had to be content with fourth place on the grid.

<<
Since qualifying on the first row in Malaysia Mark Webber has never had it so good. In Monaco he started from 11th place.

<
Max Mosley wasn't in Monaco just for the fun of it. On Friday he justified his stance concerning the future F1 regulations.

Starting grid

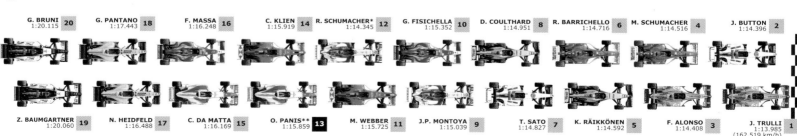

* R. SCHUMACHER
Penalty for an engine change

** O. PANIS
Struggling to get away, he started from pit lane at the second start.

Pos	Driver	Time
20	G. BRUNI	1:20.115
18	G. PANTANO	1:17.443
16	F. MASSA	1:16.248
14	C. KLIEN	1:15.919
12	R. SCHUMACHER*	1:14.345
10	G. FISICHELLA	1:15.352
8	D. COULTHARD	1:14.951
6	R. BARRICHELLO	1:14.716
4	M. SCHUMACHER	1:14.516
2	J. BUTTON	1:14.396
19	Z. BAUMGARTNER	1:20.060
17	N. HEIDFELD	1:16.488
15	C. DA MATTA	1:16.169
13	O. PANIS**	1:15.859
11	M. WEBBER	1:15.725
9	J.P. MONTOYA	1:15.039
7	T. SATO	1:14.827
5	K. RÄIKKÖNEN	1:14.592
3	F. ALONSO	1:14.408
1	J. TRULLI	1:13.985 (162,519 km/h)

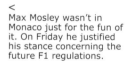

Jarno and Renault come good in an exciting race

While the Renault team has never pretended that it is aiming for the championship in 2004 its drivers have improved with each passing race doing better than Williams and McLaren whose performances have been a major disappointment so far this season. So its Monaco result was a nice surprise.

Jarno Trulli had finished all the races so far in the points and he scored an unchallenged first win in Monaco. Michael Schumacher was never in a position to threaten the Italian and his race ended in a bizarre accident.

Jarno was on pole and led most of the way being headed only because of refuelling stops. On lap 42 the Safety Car came out to neutralise the race after Fernando Alonso's accident. A lap later Trulli took advantage of this and came in to refuel letting Michael Schumacher into the lead. The Safety Car then peeled of at the end of lap 46 when the accident occurred between Schumacher and Montoya (who was a lap behind). The German was heating up his tyres and brakes in

anticipation of the restart and Montoya hit him from behind punting the Ferrari into the guardrail in the tunnel. The F2004's left-hand front wing and suspension were broken and Michael had to retire. To say he was not happy would be a bit of understatement. "*I was in the lead and I was knocked off by a tail-ender,*" he protested on his return to his pit. "*I accelerated and braked behind the Safety Car as one does in these circumstances and as I had done earlier on the same lap.*"

Juan Pablo Montoya considered it a banal racing incident. "*I tried to avoid Michael on the right but it was very tight and we made contact.*" Race Control decided to do nothing about the incident after discussion.

Up front all Trulli had to do was to keep his concentration and stroll on to his first grand prix victory. Jenson Button in second place was close but not close enough to pose a threat unless the Renault driver

slipped up. "*I think it was really a perfect weekend,*" exulted the Italian after the race. Such was his joy that he had difficulty in articulating his words during the press conference. "*I knew I could do it because I knew that I had a car capable of winning. I believed it because you have to believe it, but it never really hits home until you take the chequered flag.*"
He has had to fight hard for that win after a long career that began back in 1997 with Minardi and which has been full of setbacks for a guy who celebrated his thirtieth birthday in July. "*When things go badly you have to remain concentrated and single-minded and believe in yourself. That's what I've done. I feel like I'm on cloud nine. It wasn't easy today because each time I opened up a gap out came the Safety Car. I stayed calm and that's the result.*"

Jarno did not have much time to savour his success as the European Grand Prix was coming up the following weekend and he knew it would be difficult for him to repeat his exploit.

> Jarno Trulli led the pack into the first corner. He set pole, avoided the traps of the Monaco roller coaster and went on to an untroubled victory to celebrate his 119th grand prix.

Weekend echoes

> Michael Schumacher had finished eighteen grands prix in the points until Monaco. His last engine failure went back to the 2001 German Grand Prix.

> "*Ralf slowed to let me past on the entry to the tunnel; then he accelerated and pushed me off the line. There's no grip there and I lost control of the car,*" said Fernando Alonso to explain his accident on lap 42.

> No McLarens saw the flag. David Coulthard was eliminated in Fisichella's accident on lap 3 and Kimi Raïkkönen went out on lap 28 with pneumatic problems in his Mercedes-Benz engine. "*When I saw smoke coming from Sato's car I slowed,*" said the Scot. "*Fisichella was going too fast in such conditions.*"

The most bizarre accident of the season? Juan Pablo Montoya hit the rear of Michael Schumacher's Ferrari when then latter was behind the Safety Car. The Colombian was able to continue but the German retired at his pit with broken suspension and nose damage.
>v

City circuits

This race will leave a pleasant memory in the minds of spectators. The seventy-eight laps of the 2004 Monaco Grand reawakened a passion for Formula 1, which had been stifled because of Michael Schumacher's domination in his Ferrari.

With five victories in five races the 6-times world champion had totally crushed the start of the 2004 season so that the only interest lay in guessing who would finish second. Whatever the layout the Ferrari F2004 in the hands of the German was unbeatable leaving just crumbs for his rivals.

Luckily, the Monaco Grand Prix upset his applecart. The world champion qualified badly and had to fight hard to go into the lead just before he was knocked off. Was it due to bad luck or bad judgement? This grand prix proved that there is a chink in the Scuderia's seemingly impenetrable armour on city circuits.

Many people claim that the latter are totally ill-adapted to modern F1 cars, which push out some 900 bhp and corner at 250 km/h. On the contrary circuits like Monaco are a reminder that they are indispensable for providing exciting races. Certainly some of the Grands Prix in the Principality in the past have been boring but they have also caused memorable battles thanks to the difficulties of the layout. In the past F1 cars raced on city circuits like Long Beach, Detroit, Phoenix and Dallas. They have been abandoned for insipid tracks, which is maybe better from a safety point of view but detrimental to the overall interest of racing.

The 2004 Monaco Grand Prix with all its twists is an invitation to go back to such circuits. It is easy to understand why the drivers consider it as the jewel in the crown.

<
Another great drive from Jenson Button. He started from second place on the grid and finished second for the second time this year.

Sauber leads McLaren in the Constructors' Championship!

With Giancarlo Fisichella in tenth place on the grid Sauber hoped to score some points. And thanks to Brazilian Felipe Massa the Hinwil outfit added another four to its tally.

In fact the Swiss cars could have done even better because of the accidents had Fisichella not been one of the victims. On lap 3 the smoke screen laid down by Sato's exploding engine blinded the Italian. *"I could see nothing,"* said Giancarlo. *"Barrichello and Montoya were in front of me when suddenly I*

saw a McLaren (Coulthard's) and I didn't know what it was doing there. I couldn't avoid it and I heard a big bang and found myself upside down. I waited until I heard no further noise in case the crash was not finished and then I got out of the car."

Without that accident the Italian would probably have finished in fourth place in the grand prix. Felipe Massa came from way back as he was sixteenth on the grid. So the Brazilian did a great job in getting up to fifth by the time the flag fell. His four

points allowed Sauber to take over fifth place in the Constructors' Championship between Williams and McLaren. *"It was a fantastic race for us,"* grinned Peter Sauber. *"But the weekend leaves me with a slight sweet and sour taste. I'm very happy that Giancarlo got out of his accident unhurt but I feel very sorry for him as he did a great job. He qualified with a lot of fuel and I think he'd have racked up a good result."*

<
Felipe Massa in the Monaco tunnel. The little Brazilian came home fifth scoring an additional four points for Peter Sauber.

Exhilerating

The photographers have no better circuit than Monaco on which to exercise their art. They can get close enough to the cars to almost touch them in a dream like environment that enables them to find extraordinary angles. Long live the Monaco Grand Prix!

The Monaco pits up to scratch at last

Juan Pablo Montoya won the race in 2003, a feat he was not able to repeat this year. He finished fourth after starting from ninth on the grid, not a bad performance.

The mechanics loathed Monaco because of its pits. Over the 61 grands prix run in the Principality they worked in burning sun, heavy rain piling up equipment in a ridiculously cramped space that they shared with photographers, journalists, VIPs etc. After each day's practice they had to push the cars back from the pits to the paddock on the quay and while the spectators may have appreciated seeing this parade several times a day it was not in keeping with the standards of modern F1.

In 2003 the Principality filled in around 5000 square metres of the sea after the swimming pool chicane. This enabled the circuit to be moved back ten metres towards the port. The Automobile Club used this space to construct new pits, which measure 15 X 10 metres and allow the mechanics to work in good conditions. Each pit has two storeys so that equipment can be stocked on the first and

the cars installed at ground level. *"It's a pity the spectators won't see the cars passing any more,"* said David Coulthard, *"but it's so much more practical for us."*

The Automobile Club also resurfaced three parts of the track famous for their bumps and new stands were erected in the Rascasse corner. These efforts

show how much the Principality wants to hold on to its grand prix. Every year some drivers and engineers complain how anachronistic the race is. And every year it is on the calendar. The FIA would never dare cancel it as it is the most highly mediatised event of the season. The races are sometimes boring but the magnificent setting of Monaco is ample compensation.

Monaco is very conducive to becoming a Ferrari fan. Some of them seemed hell bent on appearing in the Formula 1 annual while others were out to catch the eye of George Clooney, Brad Pitt and Mark Damon stars of the film *"Oceans 12"* promoted by the Jaguar team in its pit.

results

Practice

All the time trials

N°	Driver	N° Chassis - Engine	Practice 1 Thurday	Pos.	Practice 2 Thurday	Pos.	Practice 3 Saturday	Pos.	Practice 4 Saturday	Pos.	Pre-qual. Saturday	Pos.	Qualif. Saturday	Pos.
1.	Michael Schumacher	Ferrari F2004 234	1:16.502	1	1:14.471	1	1:15.751	1	1:14.014	1	1:15.927	14	1:14.516	5
2.	Rubens Barrichello	Ferrari F2004 235	1:18.621	14	1:15.319	3	1:15.770	2	1:15.174	10	1:15.329	11	1:14.716	7
3.	Juan Pablo Montoya	Williams FW26 06 - BMW	1:17.937	9	1:16.097	10	1:16.559	9	1:14.212	5	1:15.029	9	1:15.039	10
4.	Ralf Schumacher	Williams FW26 07 - BMW		25	1:16.556	12	1:16.863	11	1:14.752	8	1:14.483	1	1:14.345	2
5.	David Coulthard	McLaren MP4-19 03 - Mercedes	1:17.524	5	1:16.229	11	1:16.756	10	1:14.670	7	1:14.728	3	1:14.951	9
6.	Kimi Räikkönen	McLaren MP4-19 04 - Mercedes	1:17.952	10	1:15.479	5	1:16.400	7	1:15.034	9	1:14.659	2	1:14.592	6
7.	Jarno Trulli	Renault R24-03	1:17.856	8	1:15.472	4	1:16.374	5	1:14.016	2	1:14.993	8	1:13.985	1
8.	Fernando Alonso	Renault R24-06	1:17.686	6	1:15.701	9	1:16.386	6	1:14.138	4	1.14.816	6	1:14.408	4
9.	Jenson Button	B.A.R 006-05 - Honda	1:17.339	3	1:15.520	6	1:16.358	4	1:14.646	6	1:14.799	4	1:14.396	3
10.	Takuma Sato	B.A.R 006-04 - Honda	1:17.279	2	1:15.664	7	1:16.540	8	1:14.020	3	1:14.931	7	1:14.827	8
11.	Giancarlo Fisichella	Sauber C23-04 - Petronas	1:18.338	11	1:16.748	14	1:17.209	12	1:15.709	11	1:14.814	5	1:15.352	11
12.	Felipe Massa	Sauber C23-06 - Petronas	1:19.335	16	1:17.422	17		20	1:16.332	14	1:15.436	12	1:16.248	16
14.	Mark Webber	Jaguar R5-02	1:19.261	15			1:16.273	3	1:17.173	18	1:16.161	15	1:15.725	12
15.	Christian Klien	Jaguar R5-01	1:19.487	17	1:17.988	20	1:18.390	16	1:16.101	13	1:16.379	16	1:15.919	14
16.	Cristiano da Matta	Toyota TF104/04	1:18.889	13	1:16.743	13	1:17.409	13	1:15.861	12	1:15.738	13	1:16.169	15
17.	Olivier Panis	Toyota TF104/07	1:19.218	14	1:17.007	15	1:18.299	15	1:16.431	16	1:15.125	10	1:15.859	13
18.	Nick Heidfeld	Jordan EJ14/03 - Ford	1:21.141	21	1:17.873	19	1:19.221	17	1:16.385	15	1:16.914	17	1:16.488	17
19.	Giorgio Pantano	Jordan EJ14/02 - Ford	1:20.528	18	1:17.309	16	1:18.117	14	1:16.700	17	1:17.674	18	1:17.443	18
20.	Gianmaria Bruni	Minardi PS04B/02 - Cosworth	1:21.201	22	1:18.822	21		19			1:20.740	20	1:20.115	20
21.	Zsolt Baumgartner	Minardi PS04B/01 - Cosworth	1:22.203	23	1:18.829	22	1:23.963	18	1:19.467	19	1:20.468	19	1:20.060	19
35.	Anthony Davidson	B.A.R 006-02 - Honda	1:17.791	7	1:15.141	2								
37.	Björn Wirdheim	Jaguar R5-04	1:20.680	20		24								
38.	Ricardo Zonta	Toyota TF104/03	1:17.426	4	1:15.690	8								
39.	Timo Glock	Jordan EJ14/01 - Ford	1:20.534	19	1:17.756	18								
40.	Bas Leinders	Minardi PS04B/04 - Cosworth	1:23.361	24	1:20.370	23								

Maximum speed

N°	Driver	P1 Qualifs	Pos.	P1 Race	Pos.	P2 Qualifs	Pos.	P2 Race	Pos.	Finish Qualifs	Pos.	Finish Race	Pos.	Trap Qualifs	Pos.	Trap Race	Pos.
1.	M. Schumacher	213,2	3	211,7	4	230,1	1	232,7	1	269,9	3	274,6	3	295,8	1	303,0	1
2.	R. Barrichello	213,1	4	208,2	8	222,2	5	219,6	5	269,7	4	273,6	4	294,7	4	301,6	2
3.	J.P. Montoya	201,6	18	209,9	6	218,0	8	215,2	7	272,9	2	275,9	1	293,7	5	299,2	7
4.	R. Schumacher	212,4	7	202,1	14	220,4	6	208,5	12	274,1	1	275,2	2	295,1	3	295,0	11
5.	D. Coulthard	212,8	5	191,9	17	218,9	7	203,1	16	268,7	7	268.8	12	292,8	8	294,6	13
6.	K. Räikkönen	206,1	14	204,2	11	222,5	4	220,1	4	269,2	5	271,6	6	293,3	7	299,3	6
7.	J. Trulli	212,0	9	215,0	1	213,1	14	223,6	2	266,9	13	271,3	8	290,4	13	299,5	4
8.	F. Alonso	214,7	2	214,0	2	209,9	16	213,4	8	265,9	15	269,8	11	291,7	11	299,4	5
9.	J. Button	211,8	10	209,6	7	225,0	2	221,3	3	269,1	6	271,6	5	293,3	6	298,5	9
10.	T. Sato	216,6	1	197,3	16	223,4	3	205,5	14	268,7	8	254,4	19	292,6	9	276,9	18
11.	G. Fisichella	212,7	6	187,4	19	214,5	11	195,6	17	267,5	11	268,4	13	291,9	10	290,5	16
12.	F. Massa	210,8	13	210,9	5	217,2	10	218,1	6	268,6	9	270,6	10	295,8	2	300,0	3
14.	M. Webber	212,3	8	204,8	10	213,1	13	204,9	15	264,3	17	266,8	16	288,3	17	294,5	14
15.	C. Klien	205,0	17	153,7	20	217,8	9			263,6	18			285,4	20		
16.	C. Da Matta	210,9	12	212,0	3	205,2	18	211,5	9	267,1	12	270,9	9	291,2	12	298,8	8
17.	O. Panis	211,6	11	207,0	9	210,3	15	211,3	10	267,8	10	271,5	7	289,1	14	286,0	17
18.	N. Heidfeld	205,7	15	203,0	12	209,6	17	207,2	13	265,9	14	267,7	15	288,6	15	295,1	10
19.	G. Pantano	205,6	16	202,3	13	213,9	12	210,7	11	265,0	16	268,1	14	288,5	16	294,9	12
20.	G. Bruni	188,8	20	189,6	18	186,1	20	181,8	19	262,4	20	254,5	18	285,7	19	276,9	19
21.	Z. Baumgartner	198,3	19	200,1	15	193,4	19	194,7	18	262,9	19	265,0	17	286,3	18	290,7	15

Race

Classification & Retirements

Pos.	Driver	Team	Lap	Time	Average	
1.	J. Trulli	Renault	77	1:45:46.601	145,880 km/h	
2.	J. Button	B.A.R Honda	77	+ 0.497	145,869 km/h	
3.	R. Barrichello	Ferrari	77	+ 1:15.766	144,159 km/h	
4.	J.P. Montoya	Williams BMW	76	1 lap	143,439 km/h	
5.	F. Massa	Sauber Petronas	76	1 lap	142,370 km/h	
6.	C. Da Matta	Toyota	76	1 lap	142,367 km/h	
7.	N. Heidfeld	Jordan Ford	75	2 laps	140,505 km/h	
8.	O. Panis	Toyota	74	3 laps	139,196 km/h	
9.	Z. Baumgartner	Minardi Cosworth	71	6 laps	134,411 km/h	
10.	R. Schumacher	Williams BMW	69	8 laps	138,674 km/h	Gearbox stuck in 4th gear

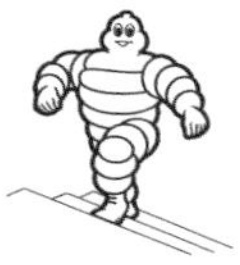

Driver	Team		Reason
M. Schumacher	Ferrari	46	Hit from behind by Montoya, hit barrier in tunnel
F. Alonso	Renault	42	Hit barrier in tunnel
K. Räikkönen	McLaren Mercedes	28	Engine pneumatic system
G. Bruni	Minardi Cosworth	16	Gearbox problem
G. Pantano	Jordan Ford	13	Gearbox stuck in 4th gear
M. Webber	Jaguar	12	Engine broken
T. Sato	B.A.R Honda	3	Blown engine
D. Coulthard	McLaren Mercedes	3	Hit from behind by Fisichella
G. Fisichella	Sauber Petronas	3	Blinded by smoke from Sato's engine, hit from behind by Coulthard and rolled
C. Klien	Jaguar	1	No front wing, goes straight on into the tyres at Loews

Fastest laps

Driver	Time	Lap	Average
M. Schumacher	1:14.439	23	161,528km/h
J. Trulli	1:14.870	22	160,598 km/h
J. Button	1:15.220	40	159,851 km/h
F. Alonso	1:15.226	23	159,838 km/h
J.P. Montoya	1:15.395	41	159,480 km/h
R. Barrichello	1:15.763	16	158,705 km/h
K. Räikkönen	1:16.203	15	157,789 km/h
C. Da Matta	1:16.232	22	157,729 km/h
O. Panis	1:16.494	57	157,188 km/h
F. Massa	1:17.151	23	155,850 km/h
M. Webber	1:17.466	11	155,216 km/h
R. Schumacher	1:17.588	18	154,972 km/h
N. Heidfeld	1:18.262	35	153,637 km/h
G. Pantano	1:19.415	10	151,407 km/h
D. Coulthard	1:20.560	2	149,255 km/h
G. Fisichella	1:20.804	2	148,804 km/h
T. Sato	1:21.368	2	147,773 km/h
G. Bruni	1:21.592	10	147,367 km/h
Z. Baumgartner	1:21.886	2	146,838 km/h

Pit stops

	Driver	Time	Lap	Stop n°
1.	R. Schumacher	36.610	3	1
2.	N. Heidfeld	26.328	4	1
3.	J.P. Montoya	27.591	13	1
4.	J. Button	26.169	18	1
5.	K. Räikkönen	27.122	19	1
6.	R. Barrichello	26.511	20	1
7.	F. Massa	25.615	21	1
8.	C. Da Matta	25.943	23	1
9.	Z. Baumgartner	26.394	22	1
10.	J. Trulli	25.622	24	1
11.	O. Panis	27.335	24	1
12.	F. Alonso	25.287	25	1
13.	M. Schumacher	26.936	26	1
14.	N. Heidfeld	26.549	31	2
15.	R. Schumacher	27.958	37	2
16.	J. Button	26.992	42	2
17.	F. Massa	26.350	41	2
18.	Z. Baumgartner	27.023	39	2
19.	C. Da Matta	47.844	42	2
20.	N. Heidfeld	24.478	41	3
21.	J.P. Montoya	26.146	42	2
22.	J. Trulli	24.131	43	2
23.	C Da Matta	14.836	52	3
24.	R. Barrichello	23.856	55	2
25.	O. Panis	25.026	55	2

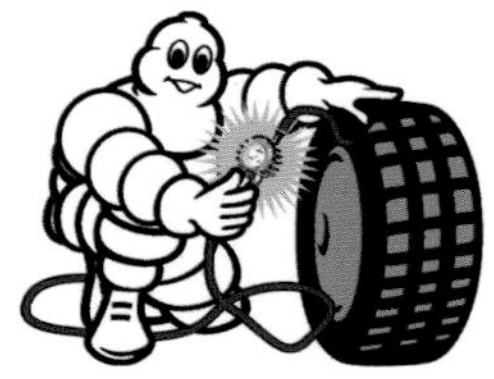

Race leaders

Driver	Laps in the lead	Nber of Laps
J. Trulli	1 > 23	23
F. Alonso	24	1
M. Schumacher	25	1
J. Trulli	26 > 42	17
M. Schumacher	43 > 45	3
J. Trulli	46 > 77	32

Driver	Nber of Laps	Kilometers
J. Trulli	72	240,480 km
M. Schumacher	4	13,360 km
F. Alonso	1	3,340 km

Lap chart

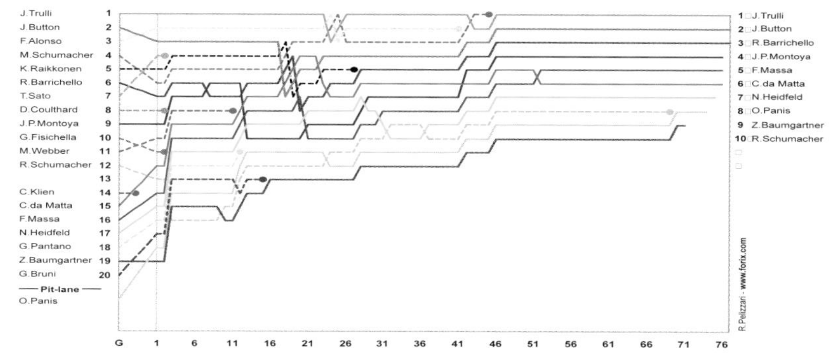

Gaps on the leader board

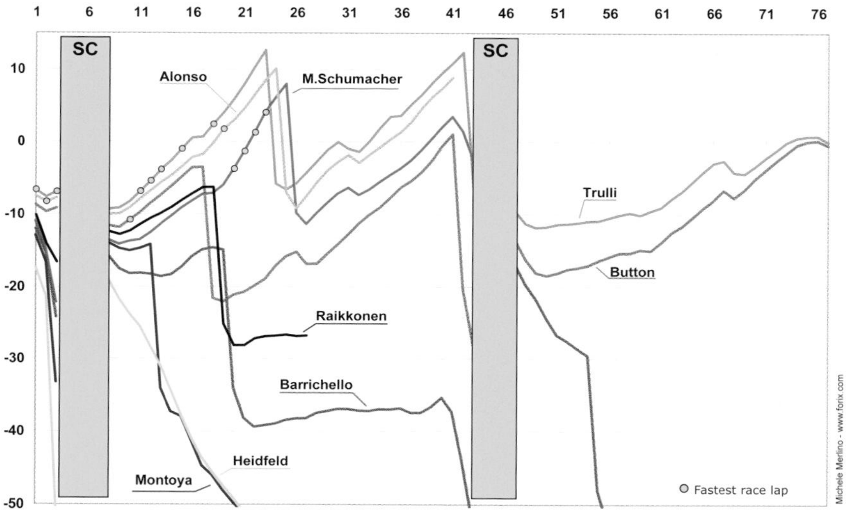

Championship after six rounds

Drivers

1. M. Schumacher ....(5 wins)................50
2. R. Barrichello..38
3. J. Button 32
4. J. Trulli ....(1 win) 31
5. J.P. Montoya 23
6. F. Alonso 21
7. R. Schumacher 12
8. T. Sato 8
9. F. Massa 5
10. D. Coulthard...4
11. C. Da Matta..3
12. G. Fisichella...2
13. N. Heidfeld...2
14. O. Panis...1
15. K. Räikkönen...1
16. M. Webber 1
17. Z. Baumgartner 0
18. C. Klien 0
19. G. Pantano..0
20. G. Bruni..0

Constructors

1. Scuderia Ferrari Marlboro ......(5 wins) 88
2. Mild Seven Renault F1 Team ..(1 win).........52
3. Lucky Strike B.A.R Honda.........................40
4. BMW WilliamsF1 Team 35
5. Sauber Petronas 7
6. West McLaren Mercedes.............................5
7. Panasonic Toyota Racing 4
8. Jordan Ford..2
9. Jaguar Racing...1
10. Minardi Cosworth.....................................0

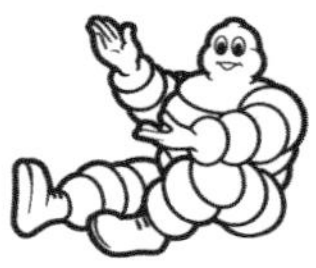

The circuit

Name	Monaco, Monte-Carlo
Length	3340 meters
Distance	78 laps scheduled, 77 completed, 257.180 km
Date	May 23, 2004
Weather	sunny, warm, 23-25°c
Track temperature	36-39°c

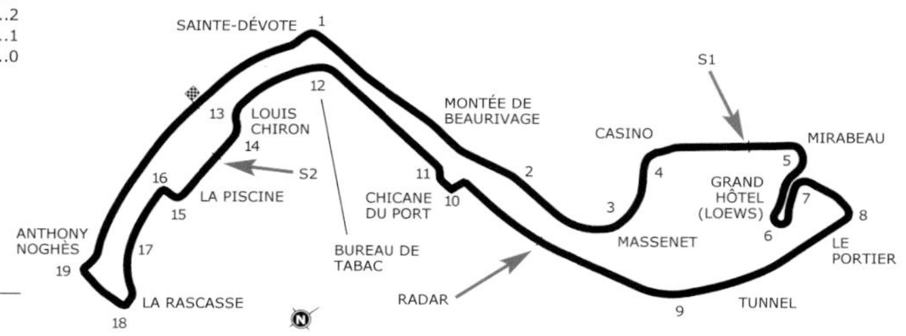

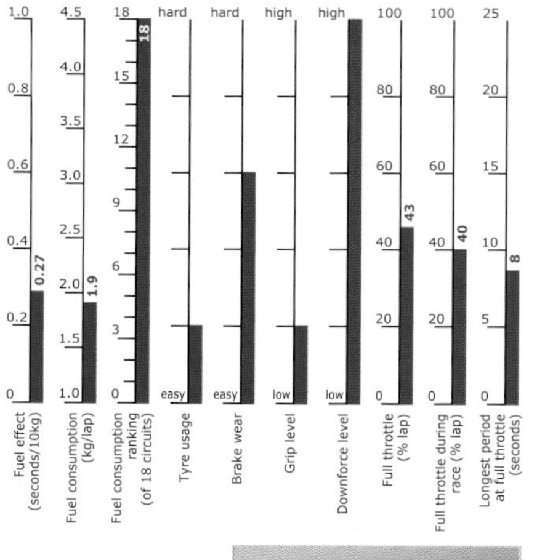

All results : © 2004 Formula One Administration Ltd,
6 Princes Gate, London, SW7 1QJ, England

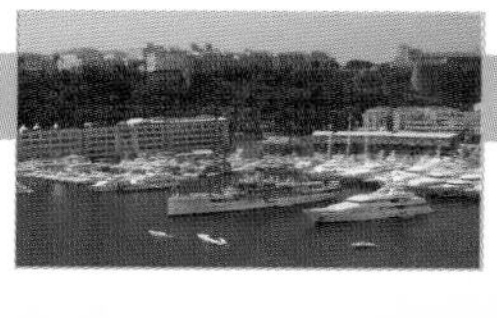

FERRARI BACK ON TOP

The Monaco Grand Prix was but a brief interlude in Ferrari's triumphal march forward to both 2004 titles. Just a week after the Monaco Grand Prix the Scuderia scored its fourth double of the season and Michael Schumacher notched up win number six in seven races.

∧
At night the temperature on the Nürburgring was 2°C! And during the day it reached the dizzy height of 14°C. It was the coldest t race of the season but this did not really change anything. In practice Michael Schumacher set pole once again which he followed up with an easy victory.

Banzaï

Michael Schumacher set his fifth pole of the year on the Nürburgring. It was the sixtieth of his career. And it was a dominant one as his nearest challenger was over 6/10s behind. *"I expected us to be competitive here so I'm not that surprised to be on pole,"* was his analysis, *"but I don't really understand why the others are so far behind."*

Leading the *"others"* was none other than Takuma Sato who second quickest behind the Ferrari. It was the first time ever that a Japanese driver was on the front row for an F1 World Championship Grand Prix and Takuma was over the moon. *"It's really incredible. I did a perfect lap. In Monaco I didn't get very far as my engine blew at the start of the race. I hope it'll last longer here."*

Jarno Trulli, the Monaco winner, was third on the grid. David Coulthard set the fourth-quickest time in prequalifying and was then obliged to park his McLaren on the grass out on the circuit when the engine let go. His team had to change it and the Scot did not take part in qualifying. It was certainly not the best place for McLaren to run into problems, as all the Mercedes big wigs were present. Immediately crazy rumours began circulating concerning Ron Dennis's retirement and the buy out of the McLaren team. The future would prove them false.

>
Takuma Sato was on the front row! The BARs were really beginning to shine and the Japanese's confidence was blossoming.

Starting grid

*Z. BAUMGARTNER, G. FISICHELLA, G. BRUNI et D. COULTHARD Start from the pit lane with his spare car.	G. BRUNI* 19 —	Z. BAUMGARTNER* 17 1:34.398	G. PANTANO 15 1:31.979	N. HEIDFELD 13 1:31.604	C. DA MATTA 11 1:29.706	R. SCHUMACHER 9 1:29.459	R. BARRICHELLO 7 1:29.353	J. BUTTON 5 1:29.245	J. TRULLI 3 1:29.135	M. SCHUMACHER 1 1:28.351 (209,763 km/h)
	D. COULTHARD* 20 —	G. FISICHELLA* 18 —	F. MASSA 16 1:31.982	M. WEBBER 14 1:31.797	C. KLIEN 12 1:31.431	O. PANIS 10 1:29.697	J.P. MONTOYA 8 1:29.354	F. ALONSO 6 1:29.313	K. RÄIKKÖNEN 4 1:29.137	T. SATO 2 1:28.986

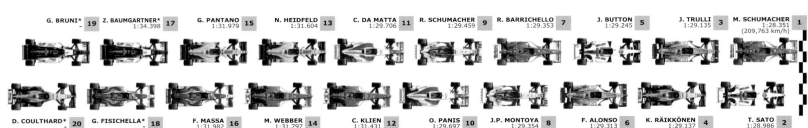

Ferrari doubles up again as Michael scores another victory

The German Grand Prix could hardly be described as a nerve tingling race apart from the last ten laps. While Michael Schumacher strolled on to an easy victory there was a real scrap for second place.

The man who really provided the excitement was Takuma Sato. Jarno Trulli's fast starting Renault passed the Japanese on the front row when the lights went out. Tako hit back on the run down to turn 1 and repassed but in the next two bends there was a lot of pushing and shoving which cost Sato dear as both Kimi Raïkkönen and Alonso nipped past the BAR-Honda. Up front Michael sailed serenely away while Raïkkönen held up the pack until he came in for fuel on lap 9. When the first round of stops was over Rubens Barrichello was in second place but soon

came under severe threat from Sato who was thrashing his car really hard to try and pull out a big enough advantage to refuel and grab second. It was nearly, nearly but not quite! When he came in on lap 44 his mechanics turned him around very quickly, but not quickly enough and just as he rejoined the red scut of Barrichello's F2004 shot tantalisingly past. Did this discourage Takuma? Did it, hell! As the two cars powered into the bend at the end of the pits straight he went down the inside of the Ferrari to Barrichello's astonishment and the two cars touched. Result: one BAR minus its front wing. Hardly had it been replaced than Sato's engine felt it was time to erupt which it did in a huge cloud of smoke as had happened in Monaco the week before. "It's really disappointing," groaned the Japanese. "The car was

great and I thought I could pass Rubens and finish second before we collided. I saw an opening and I went for it."

Finally, Jenson Button came home third after trying to catch Barrichello. "My car was working really well, there's nothing to say. I lost too much time behind Kimi at the start of the race to hope for a better result," he commented. "Towards the end I pushed hard to try and catch Rubens but I had to both try and accelerate and nurse my engine which ain't easy."

Ferrari's fresh double more or less wrapped up the season. "Apart from Rubens I can't see anybody beating Michael," stated Button, third in the world championship ratings.

∧
Juan Pablo Montoya was involved in a collision in the first corner and had to come in to have his front wing changed. He scored only a single point.

<
An accident in the first corner caused the retirement of Ralf Schumacher and Cristiano da Matta.

The collision

The tight first corners at the Nürburgring are often the theatre of first lap incidents. This year the action was in the mid-field. Juan Pablo Montoya was at it again and caught in a sandwich between Ralf Schumacher and Olivier Panis's Toyota he locked up under braking and hit his team-mate. "I was just behind Rubens Barrichello and I was about to turn in when Olivier Panis arrived and thumped my front wheel which punted me into Ralf," explained the Colombian. The German's version was not exactly the same. "Juan Pablo braked too late to try and gain a few places at the end of the straight," accused Ralf.

Weekend gossip

> Smiles were fast becoming a rarity in the McLaren-Mercedes camp while in those of their rivals there was more than the odd snigger. On the manufacturer's home territory both cars suffered blown engines a recurrent problem since the start of the season. Kimi Raïkkönen went out on lap 10 and David Coulthard on lap 26 after a fabulous comeback. Both drivers were shattered but the inimitable Ron justified these reliability problems by saying that *"they were linked to the efforts of the team to make the cars more competitive!"*

> Giancarlo Fisichella drove a great race. He started from the second last row and it did not look like he would score any points. However, thanks to a two-stop strategy he crossed the line in sixth place scoring another three. The Hinwil team now had twice as many points as McLaren! Not bad for the Swiss outfit which Ron Dennis had written off in February as not being a rival worthy of consideration

> The Agnelli family was in mourning after the loss of Umberto Agnelli, Gianni's brother (the latter died in 2003). *"This death touches us very deeply,* said Jean Todt, the Ferrari team manager. *We've tried to work normally today but our thoughts are with the Agnelli family."*

> Thus neither of the Ferrari drivers squirted the champagne on the rostrum. *"I'm sorry for the fans but I didn't feel like doing it,"* Michael Schumacher declared. *"I hope people will understand that Umberto Agnelli's death was a big shock for us. He was a great supporter of the team and I'd like to dedicate this victory to him."*

> Patrick Head, co-owner of the Williams team since its creation in 1977, decided to hand over the role of technical director to Sam Michael, the young engineer (33) who up to now was in charge of race engineering the cars at the grands prix. Henceforth Patrick's job will be to look after the personnel and long-term technical development.

> Like every year Michael Schumacher invited the whole Ferrari team – bosses, engineers, mechanics and chefs – to his Kart track in

Kerpen to the north of the Nürburgring. This is where Michael honed his skills. *"For me Ferrari is like a second family. Its members give their all for me, so it's normal that I give something in return by inviting them here,"* explained the world champion.

> And what about Jacques Villeneuve? The Canadian was supposed to test a Williams in

the near future following a conversation between himself and the team's technical director. As Mika Häkkinen also wanted to make a come back would the pair find themselves together in the Williams team in 2005? Juan Pablo Montoya brought up the subject during a press conference but his mocking smile was stronger than a thousand words!

results

Practice

All the time trials

N°	Driver	N° Chassis - Engine	Practice 1 Friday	Pos.	Practice 2 Friday	Pos.	Practice 3 Saturday	Pos.	Practice 4 Saturday	Pos.	Pre-qual. Saturday	Pos.	Qualif. Saturday	Pos.
1.	Michael Schumacher	Ferrari F2004 239	1:29.631	2	1:30.227	9	1:30.418	5	1:29.064	2	1:28.278	2	1:28.351	1
2.	Rubens Barrichello	Ferrari F2004 235	1:29.865	3	1:29.943	6	1:30.681	9	1:29.545	5	1:29.014	7	1:29.353	7
3.	Juan Pablo Montoya	Williams FW26 06 - BMW	1:31.782	11	1:30.337	11	1:30.101	4		20	1:29.092	9	1:29.354	8
4.	Ralf Schumacher	Williams FW26 07 - BMW	1:31.680	8	1:29.677	3	1:30.192	2	1:30.176	9	1:28.655	3	1:29.459	9
5.	David Coulthard	McLaren MP4-19 05 - Mercedes	1:32.301	13	1:29.700	4		20	1:29.955	7	1:28.717	4		
6.	Kimi Räikkönen	McLaren MP4-19 04 - Mercedes	1:31.643	6	1:29.355	1	1:30.532	6	1:29.354	4	1:28.897	6	1:29.137	4
7.	Jarno Trulli	Renault R24-03	1:32.696	15	1:29.919	5	1:30.551	7	1:30.986	13	1:29.905	13	1:29.135	3
8.	Fernando Alonso	Renault R24-06	1:31.768	9	1:30.163	8	1:30.600	8	1:29.555	6	1:29.069	8	1:29.313	6
9.	Jenson Button	B.A.R 006-05 - Honda	1:31.770	10	1:29.618	2	1:29.485	1	1:28.827	1	1:28.816	5	1:29.245	5
10.	Takuma Sato	B.A.R 006-03 - Honda	1:32.500	14	1:30.283	10	1:30.261	3	1:29.127	3	1:27.691	1	1:28.986	2
11.	Giancarlo Fisichella	Sauber C23-03 - Petronas		25	1:30.974	16	1:31.816	12	1:30.519	11	1:29.327	12		
12.	Felipe Massa	Sauber C23-06 - Petronas	1:31.673	7	1:32.310	20	1:32.206	13	1:31.504	15	1:31.879	16	1:31.982	16
14.	Mark Webber	Jaguar R5-04	1:31.448	4	1:30.466	12	1:32.596	14	1:30.867	12	1:30.579	14	1:31.797	14
15.	Christian Klien	Jaguar R5-01	1:34.402	19	1:32.217	19	1:33.917	19	1:31.061	14	1:30.933	15	1:31.431	12
16.	Cristiano da Matta	Toyota TF104/04	1:32.915	16	1:30.531	14	1:31.814	11	1:30.316	10	1:29.272	11	1:29.706	11
17.	Olivier Panis	Toyota TF104/07	1:31.910	12	1:30.497	13	1:31.248	10	1:30.277	9	1:29.243	10	1:29.697	10
18.	Nick Heidfeld	Jordan EJ14/03 - Ford	1:33.971	18	1:33.175	23	1:32.692	15	1:31.956	16	1:32.216	18	1:31.604	13
19.	Giorgio Pantano	Jordan EJ14/02 - Ford	1:34.488	20	1:33.393	24	1:33.226	17	1:33.383	19	1:31.928	17	1:31.979	15
20.	Gianmaria Bruni	Minardi PS04B/02 - Cosworth	1:35.455	23	1:32.643	21	1:33.499	18	1:32.894	18	1:33.077	20		
21.	Zsolt Baumgartner	Minardi PS04B/01 - Cosworth	1:35.186	22	1:32.986	22	1:32.898	16	1:32.753	17	1:33.061	19	1:34.398	17
35.	Anthony Davidson	B.A.R 006-04 - Honda	1:29.447	1	1:30.028	7								
37.	Björn Wirdheim	Jaguar R5-02	1:35.043	21	1:31.780	17								
38.	Ricardo Zonta	Toyota TF104/03	1:31.587	5	1:30.949	15								
39.	Timo Glock	Jordan EJ14/01 - Ford	1:33.925	17	1:32.080	18								
40.	Bas Leinders	Minardi PS04B/04 - Cosworth	1:37.609	24	1:34.538	25								

Maximum speed

N°	Driver	P1 Qualifs	Pos.	P1 Race	Pos.	P2 Qualifs	Pos.	P2 Race	Pos.	Finish Qualifs	Pos.	Finish Race	Pos.	Trap Qualifs	Pos.	Trap Race	Pos.
1.	M. Schumacher	283,0	1	280,7	1	237,4	1	239,3	1	261,5	1	260,9	2	311,7	1	321,2	1
2.	R. Barrichello	280,8	3	284,0	1	233,8	4	238,2	2	260,8	2	262,0	1	310,0	3	320,7	2
3.	J.P. Montoya	279,2	4	278,2	6	235,6	3	233,8	6	259,0	4	257,6	3	307,6	5	317,6	4
4.	R. Schumacher	281,0	2			232,6	5			258,1	5			306,4	8		
5.	D. Coulthard			278,2	8			229,9	15			256,5	4			316,9	7
6.	K. Räikkönen	274,7	12	279,5	4	230,0	9	233,3	10	260,1	3	255,5	9	309,4	4	314,3	11
7.	J. Trulli	277,4	7	277,4	11	227,4	14	233,7	8	254,5	11	255,2	12	304,3	13	312,5	15
8.	F. Alonso	276,0	9	276,8	14	227,1	15	235,1	5	257,1	7	255,8	8	302,7	16	311,8	17
9.	J. Button	278,2	6	278,4	5	231,2	6	237,7	3	256,1	9	254,1	14	307,6	6	312,7	14
10.	T. Sato	278,5	5	276,9	12	236,2	2	236,8	4	257,5	6	256,1	7	311,3	2	315,5	10
11.	G. Fisichella			278,2	7			233,7	7			256,2	6			316,1	8
12.	F. Massa	274,3	13	276,9	13	230,5	7	233,7	9	253,6	14	254,7	13	305,4	10	315,6	9
14.	M. Webber	272,8	15	277,7	10	227,7	13	233,0	11	251,5	16	253,5	15	302,6	17	317,4	5
15.	C. Klien	271,8	17	273,6	17	226,9	16	231,5	13	251,9	16	253,4	16	305,3	11	314,2	12
16.	C. Da Matta	273,3	14			228,9	11			256,6	8			304,2	15		
17.	O. Panis	275,2	10	275,2	15	230,2	8	230,2	14	255,3	10	255,4	10	304,7	12	312,2	16
18.	N. Heidfeld	275,1	11	278,6	4	229,0	10	232,6	12	254,3	12	256,3	9	306,3	9	317,1	6
19.	G. Pantano	276,2	8	278,1	9	227,7	12	228,9	16	253,8	13	255,5	11	307,2	7	318,4	3
20.	G. Bruni	272,7	16	273,9	16	222,1	18	223,5	18	253,5	15	252,3	18	304,2	14	313,7	13
21.	Z. Baumgartner	269,2	18	272,1	18	223,0	17	227,0	17	251,6	17	252,5	17	299,5	19	309,8	18

Race

Classification & Retirements

Pos.	Driver	Team	Lap	Time	Average
1.	M. Schumacher	Ferrari	60	1:32:35.101	200,159 km/h
2.	R. Barrichello	Ferrari	60	+ 17.989	199,513 km/h
3.	J. Button	B.A.R Honda	60	+ 22.533	199,350 km/h
4.	J. Trulli	Renault	60	+ 53.673	198,244 km/h
5.	F. Alonso	Renault	60	+ 1:00.987	197,985 km/h
6.	G. Fisichella	Sauber Petronas	60	+ 1:13.448	197,547 km/h
7.	M. Webber	Jaguar	60	+ 1:16.206	197,450 km/h
8.	J.P. Montoya	Williams BMW	59	1 lap	196,410 km/h
9.	F. Massa	Sauber Petronas	59	1 lap	195,355 km/h
10.	N. Heidfeld	Jordan Ford	59	1 lap	195,343 km/h
11.	O. Panis	Toyota	59	1 lap	194,421 km/h
12.	C. Klien	Jaguar	59	1 lap	194,167 km/h
13.	G. Pantano	Jordan Ford	58	2 laps	192,416 km/h
14.	G. Bruni	Minardi Cosworth	57	3 laps	188,344 km/h
15.	Z. Baumgartner	Minardi Cosworth	57	3 laps	187,596 km/h

Driver	Team		Reason
T. Sato	B.A.R Honda	48	Blown engine
D. Coulthard	McLaren Mercedes	26	Blown engine
K. Räikkönen	McLaren Mercedes	10	Blown engine
R. Schumacher	Williams BMW	1	Contact with Montoya which pushes him into Da Matta
C. Da Matta	Toyota	1	Hit by Ralf Schumacher

Fastest laps

	Pilote	Temps	Tour	Moyenne
1.	M. Schumacher	1:29.468	7	207,144 km/h
2.	T. Sato	1:30.004	11	205,910 km/h
3.	R. Barrichello	1:30.101	14	205,689 km/h
4.	J. Button	1:30.457	13	204,879 km/h
5.	F. Alonso	1:31.065	29	203,511 km/h
6.	J. Trulli	1:31.131	30	203,364 km/h
7.	G. Fisichella	1:31.413	23	202,737 km/h
8.	J.P. Montoya	1:31.424	43	202,712 km/h
9.	K. Räikkönen	1:31.670	2	202,168 km/h
10.	M. Webber	1:31.893	37	201,678 km/h
11.	N. Heidfeld	1:32.121	55	201,178 km/h
12.	D. Coulthard	1:32.337	14	200,708 km/h
13.	O. Panis	1:32.506	12	200,341 km/h
14.	F. Massa	1:32.729	37	199,859 km/h
15.	G. Pantano	1:32.772	27	199,767 km/h
16.	C. Klien	1:32.804	14	199,698 km/h
17.	Z. Baumgartner	1:34.666	46	195,770 km/h
18.	G. Bruni	1:35.555	7	193,949 km/h

Pit stops

Driver	Time	Lap	Stop n°
1. J.P. Montoya	30.703	1	1
2. M. Schumacher	25.178	8	1
3. K. Räikkönen	24.216	9	1
4. J. Trulli	24.075	9	1
5. F. Alonso	24.342	10	1
6. O. Panis	24.548	10	1
7. T. Sato	22.866	12	1
8. G. Pantano	25.153	12	1
9. G. Bruni	24.946	12	1
10. N. Heidfeld	24.664	14	1
11. Z. Baumgartner	25.078	14	1
12. R. Barrichello	25.067	15	1
13. C. Klien	25.342	16	1
14. M. Webber	25.771	18	1
15. F. Massa	26.318	18	1
16. D. Coulthard	24.890	20	2
17. J.P. Montoya	24.500	22	2
18. O. Panis	24.082	23	2
19. G. Fisichella	26.917	24	2
20. G. Pantano	24.338	25	2
21. T. Sato	24.575	26	2
22. M. Schumacher	24.870	28	2
23. J. Trulli	23.403	28	2
24. G. Bruni	24.593	27	2
25. F. Alonso	22.962	30	2
26. N. Heidfeld	24.345	30	2
27. Z. Baumgartner	24.525	29	2
28. C. Klien	26.506	36	2
29. R. Barrichello	26.588	38	2
30. M. Webber	26.729	38	2
31. F. Massa	26.826	40	2
32. J.P. Montoya	25.463	41	3
33. F. Alonso	22.888	42	3
34. O. Panis	24.818	42	2
35. M. Schumacher	24.945	44	3
36. T. Sato	23.722	44	3
37. G. Pantano	33.629	43	3
38. J. Trulli	23.935	44	3
39. G. Fisichella	25.035	44	3
40. G. Bruni	24.914	42	3
41. T. Sato	30.972	46	4
42. Z. Baumgartner	24.332	44	3
43. N. Heidfeld	27.798	47	3
44. G. Pantano	13.885	48	3

Race leaders

Driver	Laps in the lead	Nber of Laps
M. Schumacher	1 > 8	8
F. Alonso	9	1
T. Sato	10 > 11	2
R. Barrichello	12 > 15	4

Driver	Laps in the lead	Nber of Laps
M. Schumacher	16 > 60	45

Driver	Nber of Laps	Kilometers
M. Schumacher	53	272,827 km
R. Barrichello	4	20,592 km
T. Sato	2	10,296 km
F. Alonso	1	5,148 km

Lap chart

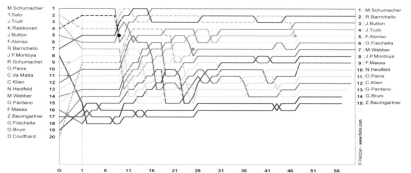

1. M.Schumacher
2. R.Barrichello
3. J.Button
4. J.Trulli
5. F.Alonso
6. G.Fisichella
7. M.Webber
8. J.P.Montoya
9. F.Massa
10. N.Heidfeld
11. O.Panis
12. C.Klien
13. G.Pantano
14. G.Bruni
15. Z.Baumgartner

Gaps on the leader board

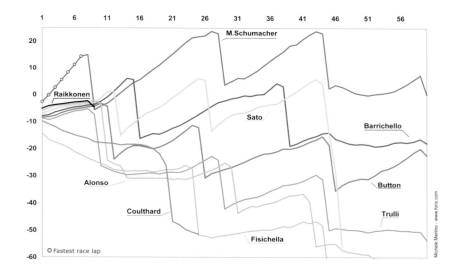

⊙ Fastest race lap

Championship after seven rounds

Drivers

1. M. Schumacher ....(6 wins)................60
2. R. Barrichello.......................................46
3. J. Button...38
4. J. Trulli ....(1 win) 36
5. F. Alonso 25
6. J.P. Montoya 24
7. R. Schumacher 12
8. T. Sato 5
9. F. Massa 5
10. G. Fisichella...5
11. D. Coulthard..4
12. C. Da Matta 3
13. M. Webber 3
14. N. Heidfeld 3
15. O. Panis 2
16. K. Räikkönen 1
17. Z. Baumgartner...................................0
18. C. Klien 0
19. G. Pantano 0
20. G. Bruni 0

Constructors

1. Scuderia Ferrari Marlboro ......(6 wins) 106
2. Mild Seven Renault F1 Team ...(1 win).........61
3. Lucky Strike B.A.R Honda........................46
4. BMW WilliamsF1 Team 36
5. Sauber Petronas 10
6. West McLaren Mercedes............................5
7. Panasonic Toyota Racing 4
8. Jaguar Racing...3
9. Jordan Ford...2
10. Minardi Cosworth......................................0

The circuit

Name	Nürburgring
Length	5148 meters
Distance	60 laps, 308.863 km
Date	May 30, 2004
Weather	Weather slightly cloudy, 21-22°c
Track temperature	34-40°c

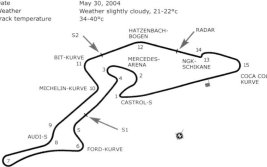

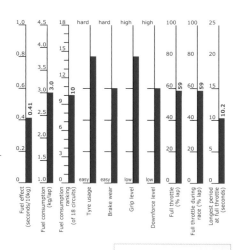

MICHAEL'S SEVENTH LUCKY CHARM

Whether he starts from sixth on the grid or from pole position, the result is still the same: Michael Schumacher can extricate himself from any situation. He won the Canadian Grand Prix, adopting a daring two stop strategy. He really did seem unbeatable.

> First (and last) pole of the season for Ralf Schumacher; a pole taken by a whisker from Jenson Button.

Ralf Schumacher on pole. His brother is sixth.

Ralf Schumacher proved to be quickest in qualifying for the Canadian Grand Prix. At the wheel of his Williams-BMW, the German lapped the Gilles Villeneuve circuit in a time of 1m12.275, thus robbing Jenson Button of the chance of a second pole after the one he secured in San Marino.

The Rue Sainte-Catherine is the busiest in Montreal and a delight for shopaholics and those who like bars and pretty girls.
∨

The gap between the two men was just 0.066 seconds and it was Ralf Schumacher's first pole since the 2003 French Grand Prix. *"I am very surprised,"* he said and he sounded it. *"The weekend had got off to a bad start with brake problems. The team did a lot of work, but I did not expect to find myself on pole."*

Worried? Michael Schumacher? In Montreal, the world champion qualified sixth, his worst grid position, not counting those caused by problems in China and Brazil. Luckily for him, it all came good in the race.
∨

As for the six times world champion, he was only sixth at Montreal. The track temperature was relatively high (46 degrees) and it definitely seemed to favour the Michelin runners, unless it was a case of Ferrari running with a very heavy fuel load for the start of the race. *"I don't think the Ferraris can be a second off our pace all of a sudden,"* was Ralf Schumacher's analysis. His brother Michael confirmed it: *"we will have to wait and see how our tyres work in the race,"* he remarked.

In brief

> *"Jacques will get his chance,"* was the headline in Friday's daily, *"Le Journal de Montreal,"* all written in quirky French-Canadian of course. Frank Williams had apparently confirmed that he would give the 1997 world champion a run in his car in early September.

> Following a problem with his personal sponsors, who had apparently not coughed up the money to the Jordan team, or according to others, it was a case of a harsh words between his father and the team boss, Italy's Giorgio Pantano was replaced for the weekend by the team's test driver, Timo Glock. Pantano had made the trip to Montreal, but he left before practice and hoped to

be back on track a week later in the United States Grand Prix.

> 11,200 tyres! That's the number of race tyres that Michelin produced for this busy weekend of 13th June. Apart from the Canadian Grand Prix, 128 of the French company's staff were working at the Le Mans 24 Hours, the Catalunya motorcycle grand prix and a motocross round in Italy.

> Rumour had it that Eddie Jordan had sold his team to a consortium of oil barons for the modest sum of 30 million pounds. The man in question denied the story, but confirmed he was in discussion with the oil Emirs regarding investing in his team that was in dire financial states.

Starting grid

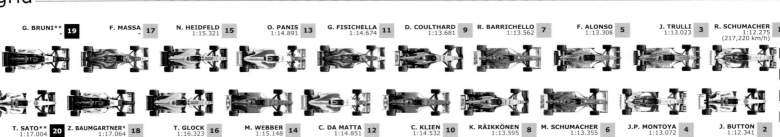

*Z. BAUMGARTNER et G. BRUNI — Penalty for an engine change

**G. BRUNI et T. SATO — Starts from pit lane

Pos	Driver	No	Time
	G. BRUNI**	19	-
	F. MASSA	17	1:15.321
	N. HEIDFELD	15	1:14.891
	O. PANIS	13	1:14.674
	G. FISICHELLA	11	1:13.681
	D. COULTHARD	9	1:13.562
	R. BARRICHELLO	7	1:13.308
	F. ALONSO	5	1:13.023
	J. TRULLI	3	1:12.275 (217,220 km/h)
	R. SCHUMACHER	1	
	T. SATO**	20	1:17.004
	Z. BAUMGARTNER*	18	1:17.064
	T. GLOCK	16	1:16.323
	M. WEBBER	14	1:15.148
	C. DA MATTA	12	1:14.851
	C. KLIEN	10	1:14.532
	K. RÄIKKÖNEN	8	1:13.595
	M. SCHUMACHER	6	1:13.355
	J.P. MONTOYA	4	1:13.072
	J. BUTTON	2	1:12.341

7th win of the season, 7th win in Montreal, 77th win of his career

Edouard Michelin himself had made the trip to Montreal. Five of his cars were on the first five places on the grid and Michael Schumacher was only sixth. It looked as though there was a good chance he would witness a Michelin victory in the Canadian Grand Prix.

But this did not take into account Ferrari's strategic skills. On Saturday morning, the Scuderia men discussed race tactics with the drivers. They opted to refuel twice rather than the more obvious three and thus sacrifice qualifying performance. It was an especially risky strategy as the length of the pit lane meant that refuelling stops did not take long in Montreal. Apart from Renault and Sauber, all the other teams thus opted for three stops. At the start, Ralf Schumacher tore off into the lead, while in fifth place, Michael Schumacher bided his time. After the first run of stops, the German was up to third, behind his brother and Jenson Button. On lap 33, Michael moved into the lead, handing it back to his little brother for just one lap. As far as Michael

Schumacher was concerned, the biggest threat came from his own team-mate, Rubens Barrichello. "*It was a good race,*" said the Brazilian. "*I had a bit less fuel than Michael and my tyres were working better. But my only chance would have been if he had made a mistake.*" In the end, it was Barrichello who got it wrong, which allowed Ralf Schumacher to take second in his Williams-BMW. However, he was later disqualified as his car did not conform to the technical regulations (see opposite.)

He did not seem too happy with second place. "*It's better than we had hoped for, but it is still disappointing,*" reckoned Ralf. "*Starting second is not your target when you start from pole! At one point, when I was leading Michael by nine seconds, I thought I could win. But in fact, Ferrari's strategy was obvious. They are a second quicker than us in terms of race pace and we really have to improve our car to get to their level.*"

In the end, this latest win for Michael Schumacher meant he extended his lead in the championship, while thanks to Rubens Barrichello's second place, Ferrari now had twice as many points as its nearest rival, Renault. Edouard Michelin would have to visit another grand prix to see his tyres win.

Williams and Toyota disqualified!
Ferrari take a one-two in the stewards room.

Around four hours after the finish, news broke that both the Williams and both the Toyotas had been disqualified as the size of their brake cooling ducts was outside the permitted dimensions. This handed Ferrari another one-two in Montreal, as Rubens Barrichello was promoted to second after Ralf Schumacher's disqualification. The Saubers also picked up two extra points, as Giancarlo Fisichella was promoted to fourth. Jordan benefited too with both its drivers now finishing in the points, which was a great result for the yellow team.

All for nothing

Juan Pablo Montoya in action at the Gilles Villeneuve circuit in Montreal. As he took the chequered flag, the Colombian was fifth, but four hours later he was disqualified.

In search of the lost millions

> David Coulthard can afford to smile again. The Scotsman finished sixth in Montreal, thus scoring points for the first time in six grands prix.

What had happened to Montreal's enthusiasm for its grand prix? Usually all the downtown shops dressed their windows with team paraphernalia, stickers here, banners and slick tyres there.

This year, it seemed the passion had died. For much of the summer of 2003, it looked as though the grand prix would not take place. In the end, it was only just confirmed on the calendar in October, after the city of Montreal promised to reimburse the teams for this race, considered as the 18th grand prix of the season. Although the race went ahead, it seemed that Montreal's love affair with F1 had died. Hotels that used to be fully booked over the race weekend were now only eighty percent full. *"It's still better than nothing!"* thundered grand prix organiser, Norman Legault, the man who had fought to save the event. At a Wednesday night party in a Montreal restaurant to celebrate his success, he seemed somewhat despondent. *"I fought like mad to save the grand prix, but something has gone and it will never be repaired,"* he admitted.

> *"Get your T-shirts here."* In Montreal, the sellers had to face unfair competition.
> v

On the financial front, the grand prix was on a suspended sentence. Air Canada, its principal sponsor for the past few years had pulled out and there were no obvious signs of a replacement on the horizon. It meant that four million Canadian dollars were missing

from the coffers, although it was said that the Belgian brewery firm, Interbrew, that owned Becks and Labatt, might increase its contribution. It meant that, in order to save the race, the Canadian government had to pay the teams several million dollars. It hoped to recoup much of the sum through additional VAT revenues generated over the weekend. But it was not prepared to do the same every year. Not all tickets were sold in advance, whereas traditionally, the Canadian Grand Prix had always been a sell-out.

The Canadian Grand Prix was in trouble and struggling to find a budget. It really needed Jacques Villeneuve to make a comeback, as the return of the Caanadian would bring with it a revival in local interest and no doubt local sponsors.

However, come Sunday night, the organisers could breathe a sigh of relief as the crowds had come and the event was a success.

Jacques and the demands of Frank Williams

"But where's Jacques?" This was the main topic of conversation in the Ile Notre Dame paddock. According to some, he was in Montreal and according to a joke article in the *"La Presse"* newspaper, he had been spotted buying fruit and veg in a market. Others said he was hiding away in Monaco, or maybe Villars sur Ollon. One thing was certain, contrary to popular rumour, he would not be racing this weekend. He was not even going to turn up and give his former BAR colleagues a cheery wave. There would be no announcement about his future for several weeks.

The Williams team had let it be known that it would not announce its 2005 driver line-up until the end of July. With two seats up for grabs, the Grove squad held the key to the driver transfer market. For Villeneuve, it also represented his most interesting option for a big F1 comeback. Williams had so far not won a single race this season, but it was still one of the major challengers to Ferrari's dominance.

The problem was that Frank Williams was playing for very high stakes. *"We are mainly looking for experienced drivers who have already won races,"* he explained. *"But the amount of money we have from our sponsors means we are looking for drivers who are prepared to work hard for our investors."* Ouch! This was not Jacques' strong point, as he was known to always try and get away with the minimum number of contractual days dedicated to sponsor appearances and public relations activities.

"We are also looking for someone who is very hard working," continued Frank Williams. *"The driver must be prepared to make sacrifices in terms of his free time to help the team move forward with the car as quickly as possible."* Ouch again! Villeneuve had never been keen on testing, which he preferred to leave to the test drivers. Two months earlier, the Canadian had gone to England to meet Frank Williams to try and reconcile his demands with those of the team boss. No one knows what took place at this meeting, but no contract had been signed.

Villeneuve maintained he was ready to drive for Williams on a money-for-points basis only, which must have stood him in good stead. Furthermore, Williams reckoned his former driver had never been as fit as he was now. Villeneuve had been training for several hours a day prior to the promise of a test in a Williams. But he still had to convince the team and that would be no picnic.

Weekend gossip

> Sauber's Felipe Massa had a big accident on lap 63, having lost his right rear wheel, probably because of a suspension failure. *"I have no idea what happened,"* commented the Brazilian. *"I was just a passenger in the car. I went to the hospital, just to check my left elbow, but everything is okay."*

> And it's another one-two! If they can't do it on the track, then the Stewards are always on hand to help. There were some murmurings that FIA stood for *"Ferrari International Assistance."*

> 114,000: that is the number of spectators who made the trip to the Circuit Gilles Villeneuve in Montreal on Sunday. It meant the Canadian Grand Prix was the second best attended event of the year. Over the three days, 317,000 were counted coming through the gates.

> Although well placed on the grid, neither Renault saw the chequered flag. Jarno Trulli's race did not even last three hundred metres. Back in the paddock, the Italian was distraught, explaining he had been put out

by a transmission problem. Team-mate Fernando Alonso suffered the same fate on lap 45, when he was running fourth.

> Takuma Sato's run of misfortune continued. In Montreal, his engine exploded in a spectacular cloud of smoke, for the third time in a row. The Honda engineers wondered if the Japanese driver was using too many revs, even though, in theory, a rev-limiter should have stopped him giving the V10 a hard time.

> Less scary than it looked. Jordan's refueller, Mick Gomm, was knocked down in the pits during Nick Heidfeld's refuelling, but he got up with nothing more than some bruising. There had been a misunderstanding with the team and the German driver had tried to pull away while the fuel nozzle was still locked onto the tank.

Practice

All the time trials

N°	Driver	N° Chassis - Engine	Practice 1 Friday	Pos.	Practice 2 Friday	Pos.	Practice 3 Saturday	Pos.	Practice 4 Saturday	Pos.	Pre-qual. Saturday	Pos.	Qualif. Saturday	Pos.
1.	Michael Schumacher	Ferrari F2004 239	1:14.013	1	1:14.535	3	1:13.865	1	1:13.420	1	1:13.463	8	1:13.355	6
2.	Rubens Barrichello	Ferrari F2004 235	1:14.291	2	1:14.705	5	1:14.284	4	1:13.904	9	1:13.782	11	1:13.562	7
3.	Juan Pablo Montoya	Williams FW26 06 - BMW	1:15.928	8	1:16.564	20	1:15.067	8	1:13.320	5	1:12.746	2	1:13.072	4
4.	Ralf Schumacher	Williams FW26 07 - BMW	1:15.948	9	1:15.803	14	1:15.191	9	1:14.697	12	1:12.441	1	1:12.275	1
5.	David Coulthard	McLaren MP4-19 05 - Mercedes	1:16.947	16	1:15.164	9	1:14.747	7	1:13.686	8	1:13.595	8	1:13.681	9
6.	Kimi Räikkönen	McLaren MP4-19 04 - Mercedes	1:16.570	13	1:14.581	4	1:14.584	6	1:13.566	7	1:13.602	9	1:13.681	8
7.	Jarno Trulli	Renault R24-03	1:15.428	5	1:15.492	11	1:14.421	5	1:12.629	1	1:13.149	5	1:13.023	3
8.	Fernando Alonso	Renault R24-02	1:15.606	6	1:14.426	2	1:13.946	2	1:12.901	2	1:12.826	3	1:13.308	5
9.	Jenson Button	B.A.R 006-05 - Honda	1:15.905	7	1:15.152	8	1:14.047	3	1:13.026	3	1:13.333	7	1:12.341	2
10.	Takuma Sato	B.A.R 006-03 - Honda	1:16.655	14	1:14.086	1		20	1:13.235	4	1:12.989	4	1:17.004	17
11.	Giancarlo Fisichella	Sauber C23-04 - Petronas	1:16.240	11	1:15.293	10	1:15.290	10	1:14.902	14	1:13.663	10	1:14.674	11
12.	Felipe Massa	Sauber C23-06 - Petronas	1:17.447	18	1:16.119	16	1:15.764	12	1:15.332	16	1:14.392	14		
14.	Mark Webber	Jaguar R5-04	1:16.820	15	1:15.926	15	1:15.854	14	1:14.835	13	1:14.715	15	1:15.148	14
15.	Christian Klien	Jaguar R5-01	1:18.463	20	1:16.815	21	1:15.843	13	1:14.340	10	1:14.751	16	1:15.164	13
16.	Cristiano da Matta	Toyota TF104/04	1:16.475	12	1:15.146	14	1:15.573	11	1:14.521	11	1:13.807	12	1:14.851	12
17.	Olivier Panis	Toyota TF104/03	1:15.997	10	1:15.538	13	1:15.843	11	1:14.916	15	1:14.166	13	1:14.891	13
18.	Nick Heidfeld	Jordan EJ14/03 - Ford	1:17.135	17	1:16.475	12	1:15.492	15	1:14.751	18	1:15.657	17	1:15.321	15
39/19.	Timo Glock	Jordan EJ14/02 - Ford	1:17.890	19	1:16.508	18	1:16.305	16	1:15.987	17	1:15.657	17	1:15.321	15
20.	Gianmaria Bruni	Minardi PS04B/02 - Cosworth	1:18.828	21	1:16.235	17	1:16.928	17	1:16.417	18	1:16.865	18	1:16.323	16
21.	Zsolt Baumgartner	Minardi PS04B/01 - Cosworth	1:18.959	22	1:16.981	22	1:18.409	18	1:18.711	19		20		20
35.	Anthony Davidson	B.A.R 006-04 - Honda	1:14.519	3	1:15.513	12					1:17.903	19	1:17.064	18
37.	Björn Wirdheim	Jaguar R5-05			1:14.260	24								
38.	Ricardo Zonta	Toyota TF104/07	1:14.952	4	1:14.871	6								
40.	Bas Leinders	Minardi PS04B/03 - Cosworth			1:17.697	23								

Maximum speed

N°	Driver	P1 Qualifs	Pos.	P1 Race	Pos.	P2 Qualifs	Pos.	P2 Race	Pos.	Finish Qualifs	Pos.	Finish Race	Pos.	Trap Qualifs	Pos.	Trap Race	Pos.
1.	M. Schumacher	275,2	6	278,8	2	303,2	4	306,5	4	303,1	6	304,5	4	340,9	1	344,6	3
2.	R. Barrichello	276,8	3	280,0	1	303,3	3	307,9	3	305,4	3	307,1	3	334,4	6	347,9	1
3.	J.P. Montoya	277,8	2	278,4	3	304,3	2	309,8	1	306,3	2	310,5	1	336,9	3	344,0	4
4.	R. Schumacher	275,7	4	275,9	4	306,8	1	308,8	2	306,9	1	307,2	2	337,5	2	341,9	6
5.	D. Coulthard	274,9	7	272,7	8	299,8	8	301,7	10	301,3	9	303,2	7	332,7	8	339,9	7
6.	K. Räikkönen	272,8	8	272,2	10	300,4	6	301,5	11	300,1	11	300,0	12	330,2	12	333,8	11
7.	J. Trulli	271,9	10			299,2	10			302,0	7			329,8	13		
8.	F. Alonso	272,8	9	272,6	9	299,8	9	304,7	5	303,7	4	304,3	5	333,8	7	335,7	8
9.	J. Button	275,5	5	275,0	6	302,8	5	302,7	9	303,3	5	303,1	8	336,4	4	334,7	9
10.	T. Sato	278,2	1	271,4	12	300,4	7	304,0	6	301,8	8	302,0	10	331,6	9	334,6	10
11.	G. Fisichella	270,9	11	275,3	5	299,0	11	303,5	7	300,7	10	303,2	6	334,8	5	342,3	5
12.	F. Massa	240,4	19	271,7	11	293,5	17	302,7	8			302,1	9	186,3	20	344,9	2
14.	M. Webber	267,6	16	263,7	17	290,6	19	293,4	19	293,6	18	291,4	19	321,3	18	324,0	19
15.	C. Klien	268,2	14	270,4	14	294,4	14	297,5	16	295,5	15	297,0	16	326,2	16	331,6	14
16.	C. Da Matta	270,8	12	273,2	7	296,8	12	301,5	12	297,6	12	298,8	14	327,4	14	330,9	17
17.	O. Panis	264,4	18	261,9	18	295,2	13	299,2	15	295,5	16	298,5	15	326,5	15	330,2	18
18.	N. Heidfeld	267,6	15	270,9	13	294,1	15	299,2	14	297,1	13	300,5	11	330,7	10	333,7	12
19.	T. Glock	268,4	13	264,8	15	294,2	16	295,2	13	295,3	14	299,7	13	332,3	14		
20.	G. Bruni	193,6	20	258,1	19	226,5	20	294,8	18			294,2	17	217,2	19	332,0	15
21.	Z. Baumgartner	265,1	17	263,9	16	292,3	18	295,0	17	295,4	17	293,7	18	326,1	17	332,3	13

Race

Classification & Retirements

Pos.	Driver	Team	Lap	Time	Average
1.	M. Schumacher	Ferrari	70	1:28:24.803	207,165 km/h
2.	R. Barrichello	Ferrari	70	+ 5.108	206,966 km/h
3.	J. Button	B.A.R Honda	70	+ 20.409	206,371 km/h
4.	G. Fisichella	Sauber Petronas	69	1 lap	203,433 km/h
5.	K. Räikkönen	McLaren Mercedes	69	1 lap	202,663 km/h
6.	D. Coulthard	McLaren Mercedes	69	1 lap	202,418 km/h
7.	T. Glock	Jordan Ford	68	2 laps	199,538 km/h
8.	N. Heidfeld	Jordan Ford	68	2 laps	199,525 km/h
9.	C. Klien	Jaguar	67	3 laps	196,860 km/h
10.	Z. Baumgartner	Minardi Cosworth	66	4 laps	193,104 km/h

Driver	Team	Lap	Reason
F. Massa	Sauber Petronas	63	Crash due to broken suspension
T. Sato	B.A.R Honda	49	Engine broken
F. Alonso	Renault	45	Left drive shaft broken
G. Bruni	Minardi Cosworth	31	Gearbox problem
M. Webber	Jaguar	7	Rear suspension damaged after collision at start
J. Trulli	Renault	1	Broken drive shaft
(2.) R. Schumacher	Williams BMW	70	+ 1.062 — 207,123 km/h — Disqualified*
(5.) J.P. Montoya	Williams BMW	70	+ 21.200 — 206,340 km/h — Disqualified*
(8.) C. Da Matta	Toyota	69	1 lap — 202,494 km/h — Disqualified*
(10.) O. Panis	Toyota	69	1 lap — 201,653 km/h — Disqualified*

(*) Brake cooling ducts do not comply with article 11.4 of the technical regulations.

Fastest laps

	Driver	Time	Lap	Average
1.	R. Barrichello	1:13.622	68	213,246 km/h
2.	M. Schumacher	1:13.630	18	213,222 km/h
3.	R. Schumacher	1:14.040	70	212,042 km/h
4.	F. Alonso	1:14.179	41	211,644 km/h
5.	J. Button	1:14.246	68	211,453 km/h
6.	J.P. Montoya	1:14.295	69	211,314 km/h
7.	K. Räikkönen	1:14.752	44	210,022 km/h
8.	T. Sato	1:15.076	25	209,116 km/h
9.	G. Fisichella	1:15.078	47	209,110 km/h
10.	D. Coulthard	1:15.478	55	208,002 km/h
11.	F. Massa	1:15.560	25	207,776 km/h
12.	C. Da Matta	1:15.652	39	207,523 km/h
13.	C. Klien	1:15.731	45	207,307 km/h
14.	N. Heidfeld	1:15.890	18	206,873 km/h
15.	O. Panis	1:16.045	23	206,451 km/h
16.	T. Glock	1:16.300	42	205,761 km/h
17.	M. Webber	1:16.739	6	204,584 km/h
18.	Z. Baumgartner	1:17.516	64	202,533 km/h
19.	G. Bruni	1:18.025	25	201,212 km/h

Pit stops

	Driver	Time	Lap	Stop n°		Driver	Time	Lap	Stop n°
1.	M. Webber	40.494	1	1	24.	J.P. Montoya	25.063	30	2
2.	D. Coulthard	25.908	11	1	25.	K. Räikkönen	24.878	30	3
3.	K. Räikkönen	25.373	12	1	26.	J. Button	26.553	31	2
4.	J. Button	24.416	13	1	27.	D. Coulthard	25.830	32	2
5.	J.P. Montoya	26.203	13	1	28.	R. Schumacher	23.941	33	2
6.	R. Schumacher	25.521	15	1	29.	N. Heidfeld	30.106	40	2
7.	F. Alonso	34.123	15	1	30.	T. Sato	28.044	42	2
8.	C. Da Matta	27.528	17	1	31.	R. Barrichello	27.537	44	2
9.	T. Glock	28.974	17	1	32.	O. Panis	28.560	43	2
10.	C. Klien	28.054	17	1	33.	T. Glock	28.336	43	2
11.	R. Barrichello	26.946	18	1	34.	C. Da Matta	27.832	44	2
12.	Z. Baumgartner	27.948	17	1	35.	Z. Baumgartner	28.544	42	2
13.	M. Schumacher	28.169	19	1	36.	K. Räikkönen	28.691	45	4
14.	C. Klien	31.728	18	2	37.	M. Schumacher	26.565	47	2
15.	K. Räikkönen	14.730	19	2	38.	R. Schumacher	27.042	48	3
16.	N. Heidfeld	1:12.616	19	1	39.	J. Button	24.904	49	3
17.	C. Klien	30.627	20	3	40.	J.P. Montoya	26.872	49	3
18.	O. Panis	26.539	21	1	41.	G. Fisichella	25.882	49	2
19.	G. Bruni	35.933	22	1	42.	C. Klien	27.273	49	4
20.	T. Sato	25.696	23	1	43.	D. Coulthard	25.388	53	3
21.	G. Fisichella	27.392	25	1	44.	F. Massa	27.381	55	3
22.	F. Massa	47.746	26	1	45.	K. Räikkönen	28.682	60	5
23.	F. Massa	26.307	28	2					

Race leaders

Driver	Laps in the lead	Nber of Laps	Driver	Laps in the lead	Nber of Laps	Driver	Nber of Laps	Kilometers
R. Schumacher	1 > 14	14	M. Schumacher	33 > 46	14	M. Schumacher	39	170,079 km
F. Alonso	15 > 16	2	R. Schumacher	47	1	R. Schumacher	29	126,469 km
M. Schumacher	17 > 18	2	M. Schumacher	48 > 70	23	F. Alonso	2	8,722 km
R. Schumacher	19 > 32	14						

Lap chart

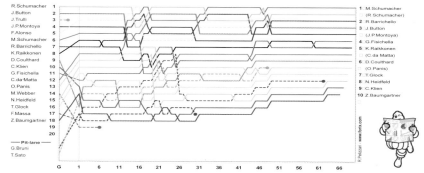

Gaps on the leader board

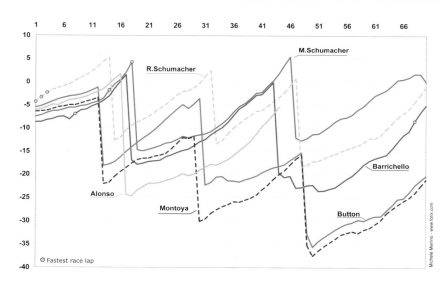

Championship after eight rounds

Drivers

1. M. Schumacher ....(7 wins) 70
2. R. Barrichello 54
3. J. Button 44
4. J. Trulli ....(1 win) 36
5. F. Alonso 25
6. J.P. Montoya 24
7. R. Schumacher 12
8. G. Fisichella 10
9. T. Sato 8
10. D. Coulthard 7
11. F. Massa 5
12. K. Räikkönen 5
13. C. Da Matta 3
14. M. Webber 3
15. N. Heidfeld 2
16. T. Glock 2
17. O. Panis 1
18. Z. Baumgartner 0
19. G. Bruni 0
20. G. Pantano 0
21. G. Bruni 0

Constructors

1. Scuderia Ferrari Marlboro ......(7 wins) 124
2. Mild Seven Renault F1 Team ..(1 win) 61
3. Lucky Strike B.A.R Honda 52
4. BMW WilliamsF1 Team 36
5. Sauber Petronas 15
6. West McLaren Mercedes..........................12
7. Jordan Ford 5
8. Panasonic Toyota Racing 4
9. Jaguar Racing 3
10. Minardi Cosworth.............................0

The circuit

Name	Gilles Villeneuve, Montréal
Length	4361 meter
Distance	70 laps, 305.270 km
Date	June 13, 2004
Weather	sunny, 25-27°c
Track temperature	37-41°c

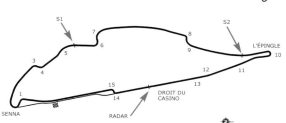

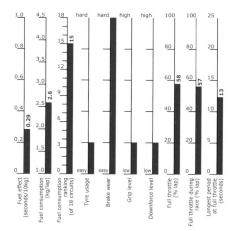

FERNANDO THE MAGNIFICENT

A fantastic performance from Fernando Alonso at Magny Cours with the Spaniard hoisting his Renault up to pole position come the end of qualifying. In the race, while all the other drivers pitted three times, as is the norm at Magny Cours, Michael Schumacher outwitted his rivals by making four refuelling stops. It was a daring move and he still had to find the speed to back it up. He did and he won.

8 FERNA DO

^
The Renault drivers certainly looked the part! Fernando Alonso on pole and Jarno Trulli fifth on the grid. The atmosphere was tense in the blue camp.

Fernando takes pole in front of 6000 admirers

The Michelin tyres turned out to be very much on the pace at Magny Cours. Based a short distance from the circuit, in Clermont Ferrand, the tyre company got no benefit from this proximity, as private testing is banned at the Nevers track. *"But to be honest, it's true that we are perfectly au fait with all the subtleties of Magny Cours,"* commented Pierre Dupasquier. *"Magny Cours is like three circuits in one and the trick is to find the right compromise to maximise performance over a whole lap, rather than in the individual sectors."*

Michelin was hoping to get its own back here. As did Fernando Alonso. In the last two grands prix, in Canada and the United States, the young Spaniard was eliminated by mechanical problems. *"Since Monaco, I have been really unlucky,"* he reckoned. *"But I am sure that my luck will turn at last and I will be able to finish the race here."*

Fernando Alonso went at his qualifying lap like a man with a chainsaw, on a track with a peculiar surface which is unforgiving. *"My lap was nearly perfect,"* he revealed. *"This morning I had set-up problems and I had to push myself to find the right line. In the final chicane before the straight, it's not very easy and you*

often get crossed up. But I managed to set the quickest time, even if it was a bit of a surprise. Of course, it's great news for all the Renault team."

The French marque had an improved version of its engine here and that might have made the difference.

In brief

> A Renault, a Ferrari, a McLaren and a BAR-Honda in the first four places. The grid seemed to prove that the pack was closing up as the season approached its halfway point. There were no less than 11 drivers qualified in the same second.

> McLaren-Mercedes turned up with the "B" version of its disastrous MP4/19. The car had, to use a euphemism, not given satisfaction since the start of the season. Engine problems ended several races prematurely, but the chassis also proved impossible to set-up. The hope was that the new MP4/19B would wipe away those memories. It was a completely new design and it seemed to be living up to expectations. On Friday morning, in free practice, Kimi Raikkonen was quickest, while

Pole came at just the right time, given that there were 6000 Renault employees expected for race day. Several of the grandstands were therefore decked out in blue and yellow.

in the afternoon, David Coulthard qualified third.

> Juan Pablo Montoya had a serious crash on Friday morning when rain made the track very slippery. His Williams was badly damaged and 15 mechanics went at it for two hours to replace the gearbox, bodywork and suspension on the FW26.

> The organisers took part in an initiative with the ICM, the institute for brain and spinal illnesses. Michael Schumacher is a patron of the institute and he did two laps of the circuit in a Ferrari road car with one lucky passenger selected by a lucky dip aimed at raising money for the ICM, at the circuit.

Starting grid

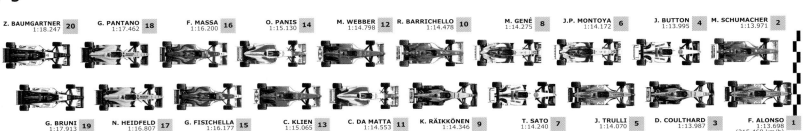

Z. BAUMGARTNER 20 1:18.247	G. PANTANO 18 1:17.462	F. MASSA 16 1:16.200	O. PANIS 14 1:15.130	M. WEBBER 12 1:14.798	R. BARRICHELLO 10 1:14.478	M. GENÉ 8 1:14.275	J.P. MONTOYA 6 1:14.172	J. BUTTON 4 1:13.995	M. SCHUMACHER 2 1:13.971

G. BRUNI 19 1:17.913	N. HEIDFELD 17 1:16.807	G. FISICHELLA 15 1:16.177	C. KLIEN 13 1:15.065	C. DA MATTA 11 1:14.553	K. RÄIKKÖNEN 9 1:14.346	T. SATO 7 1:14.240	J. TRULLI 5 1:14.070	D. COULTHARD 3 1:13.987	F. ALONSO 1 1:13.698 (215,468 km/h)

^
The grid just before the start of the formation lap. Always an exciting moment.

Michael Schumacher strikes four times

"Before the race, I was not very optimistic. But our strategy and the way the mechanics carried it out was absolutely perfect today." Michael Schumacher was all smiles after the race, brimming with compliments for one and all.

It was after his second visit to pit lane that Ferrari decided to go for a total of four stops, a strategy that had not yet been tried this season. *"I did not have much to say after the team told me to up the pace. I had nothing to lose and it was a bit of case of he who risks nothing has nothing. In fact, I was not sure of winning until five laps before my final stop, when I realised I had a big enough lead to stop again."*

The world champion admitted that he might have been able to win on a three stop strategy. *"But I would have to pass a lot of cars on the track and that was more risky,"* concluded the German. So ended another win for Schumi: his ninth in ten races. However, it was Fernando Alonso who had led from

One corner away from the podium

After Michael Schumacher's fourth stop, the top eight places seemed settled. But then, Rubens Barrichello had a last-ditch attack up his sleeve. In fourth place, he had been tailing Jarno Trulli since lap 53, but he waited for the penultimate corner of the race to go past.

Having started tenth on the grid, the Brazilian therefore finished a miraculous third to stand on the podium! *"I really enjoyed myself in the race,"* he beamed. *"The car was fantastic, especially just before the pit stops. I had some problems with Jarno, because he had very good traction and so it was difficult to keep up with him coming out of corners. But on the very last lap, he*

the start. At the first corner, he was followed by Michael Schumacher and Jarno Trulli, who surprisingly had shot up from fifth on the grid to third.

The race was run at a cracking pace, until the first pit stops began as early as lap 11. Fernando Alonso managed to hang onto the lead after the first run of stops, but Michael Schumacher went past the Spaniard at his second stop and was leading just before half-distance. Once in the lead, the Ferrari driver constantly extended his lead before making

slowed a bit too much at the exit to the Chateau d'Eau corner and I was able to get alongside. I tried an 85% attack and when I saw I had a chance, I added 20% to be at 105% of what I could do. And it worked!"

Judging by the way he punched the air as he crossed the line, this third place was as good as a win for the Brazilian. Over in the Renault camp, Jarno Trulli was distraught. *"I am really annoyed to have lost this place at the very end of the race,"* he moaned. *"I defended as*

his third stop on lap 42. Against all expectation, he then upped the pace yet again, instead of simply managing his lead. Then he came in for a fourth stop on lap 58.

Fernando Alonso ended up second and stood on the podium for the first time since the Australian Grand Prix. *"I'd been waiting for that for a long time,"* he admitted. *"I could have been on the podium in the last two races if my car hadn't picked up mechanical problems. Anyway, no regrets. Michael was stronger than us today."*

<
It was the mistake of the year. At the very last corner of the grand prix, Jarno Trulli is caught napping by Rubens Barrichello. Flavio Briatore would never forgive his driver.

well as I could. I tried to shut the door, but it was not on. I am very disappointed, but I will have to get over it for the coming races."

More than that, he would have to face up to a very angry Flavio Briatore. His boss was visibly furious to have lost out on getting both his drivers onto the podium in front of all the Renault bosses, including company president, Louis Schweitzer, who had made the trip to Magny Cours.

Welcome to Formula 1

In Magny-Cours, Marc Gene stood in for Ralf Schumacher at Williams. He qualified eight and had plenty of time to enjoy the pleasure and pain of Formula 1.

Max Mosley sums up his thoughts and hands in his notice

Max Mosley has never ceased to evolve in motor sport. Co-owner of the March team at the start of the 70s, he then became Bernie Ecclestone's lawyer. When he was elected president of the FIA in 1991, their relationship led to suggestions that *"uncle Bernie would now have total control over Formula 1."*

That failed to take into account Mosley's subtlety and intelligence and he fulfilled his role in an irreproachable manner. Re-elected several times, he had decided to resign his pro bono job in favour of a well deserved retirement.

"There is no special reason for my retirement," he stressed in a Magny Cours press conference. I am in good health and I have not been offered another well paid job! It's simply that I no longer find it satisfying to spend hours in meetings with the team owners who agree on something and then change their mind as soon as they get home. It's frustrating and tiring. There comes a time when one gets bored with that attitude. And one should not do this job if it doesn't inspire one. I reached all the goals I had set myself when I was elected and now I think I would be better off on a beach, reading a good book rather than taking part in meetings with team bosses. It is a demanding job that keeps me busy from morning to night and I've had enough."

Although his arguments were convincing, they were met with some suspicion. Why was Max Mosley throwing in the towel in such a hurry as his term of office was due to come to an end quite soon in 2005? The explanation he gave concerning the lack of credibility of the team owners meetings was all the more surprising given that Mosley had attended them for several years, so their attitude was hardly a surprise. *"I am not a team owner. I do not change my mind every two minutes,"* he even added when he was asked if he might change his mind about retiring in October – an ironic remark given what would happen later...

Apart from announcing his retirement, Mosley also laid out the decisions reached earlier in the week by the FIA world council. The teams now had two months in which to come up with proposals to reduce the speed of the F1 cars for the 2005 season. If they could not agree on a series of measures, which seemed likely, it would be down to the FIA to decide on the new rules for 2005.

Ralf out of action for 11 weeks

11th lap of the United States Grand Prix. Because of a puncture, Ralf Schumacher's Williams shot off line and slammed into the concrete wall at very high speed. It was an extremely hard impact, which according to sensors on the car reached 78 G! The car stood up well and ended up parked in the middle of the straight. At first the driver appeared to be unconscious and was stuck in his car for several minutes until the safety cars arrived.

He was taken to an Indianapolis hospital where doctors diagnosed nothing worse than a few bruises. However, with pains in his back, Ralf decided to see specialists when he returned to Europe. This visit revealed a double fracture to the spine, which meant that the world champion's little brother would be out of action for at least three months, or maybe even the rest of the season. It also meant there might be an element of doubt over his contract with Toyota.

Practice

All the time trials

N°	Driver	N° Chassis - Engine	Practice 1 Friday	Pos.	Practice 2 Friday	Pos.	Practice 3 Saturday	Pos.	Practice 4 Saturday	Pos.	Pre-qual. Saturday	Pos.	Qualif. Saturday	Pos.
1.	Michael Schumacher	Ferrari F2004 239	1:15.713	2	1:16.397	5	1:14.944	1	1:14.571	3	1:13.541	2	1:13.971	2
2.	Rubens Barrichello	Ferrari F2004 240	1:15.487	1	1:17.094	10	1:15.500	6	1:14.817	5			1:14.478	10
3.	Juan Pablo Montoya	Williams FW26 06 - BMW		23	1:17.556	13	1:15.529	7	1.21.458	20	1:13.377	1	1:14.172	6
4.	Marc Gené	Williams FW26 05 - BMW	1:19.348	3	1:17.688	14	1:16.608	13	1:15.179	11	1:14.133	9	1:14.275	8
5.	David Coulthard	McLaren MP4-19B 02 - Mercedes		22	1:16.464	7	1.15.402	2	1:14.977	8	1:13.649	3	1.13.987	3
6.	Kimi Räikkönen	McLaren MP4-19B 01 - Mercedes		24	1:16.794	9		20	1:14.513	1	1:13.736	4	1:14.346	9
7.	Jarno Trulli	Renault R24-03	1:39.392	18	1:16.206	2	1:15.423	3	1:15.033	9	1:13.949	7	1:14.070	5
8.	Fernando Alonso	Renault R24-02		20	1:16.454	6	1:15.434	4	1:15.096	10	1.13.750	5	1:13.698	1
9.	Jenson Button	B.A.R 006-05 - Honda	1:28.317	12	1:16.397	4	1:16.304	10	1:14.568	2	1:13.772	6	1:13.995	4
10.	Takuma Sato	B.A.R 006-03 - Honda	1:30.092	16	1:17.967	17	1:16.569	12	1:14.711	4	1:14.130	8	1:14.240	7
11.	Giancarlo Fisichella	Sauber C23-04 - Petronas		21	1:17.324	12	1:15.910	9	1:16.161	15	1:15.793	15	1.16.177	15
12.	Felipe Massa	Sauber C23-01 - Petronas		19	1:18.614	18	1:16.619	14	1:16.062	14	1:14.627	12	1:16.200	16
14.	Mark Webber	Jaguar R5-05		25	1:16.745	8	1:15.907	8	1:15.350	12	1:15.332	14	1:14.798	12
15.	Christian Klien	Jaguar R5-01	1:29.626	14	1:17.936	16	1:16.669	15	1:15.449	13	1:15.205	13	1:15.065	13
16.	Cristiano da Matta	Toyota TF104/04	1:26.757	10	1:15.518	1	1:16.384	11	1:14.885	7	1:14.245	10	1:14.553	11
17.	Olivier Panis	Toyota TF104/03	1:27.449	11	1:17.303	11	1:15.478	5	1:14.883	6	1:14.540	11	1:15.130	14
18.	Nick Heidfeld	Jordan EJ14/03 - Ford	1:20.531	6	1:19.270	21	1:17.846	19	1:17.162	18	1:16.366	17	1:16.807	17
19.	Giorgio Pantano	Jordan EJ14/02 - Ford	1:19.466	5	1:18.711	19	1:17.399	17	1:17.104	17	1:15.913	16	1:17.462	18
20.	Gianmaria Bruni	Minardi PS04B/02 - Cosworth	1:21.203	7	1:19.349	22	1:17.174	16	1:19.401	19	1:18.070	18	1.17.913	19
21.	Zsolt Baumgartner	Minardi PS04B/01 - Cosworth	1:29.877	15	1:19.636	24	1:17.731	18	1:16.861	16	1:18.108	19	1:18.247	20
35.	Anthony Davidson	B.A.R 006-04 - Honda	1:26.552	9	1:16.231	3								
37.	Björn Wirdheim	Jaguar R5-02	1:30.204	17	1:19.179	20								
38.	Ricardo Zonta	Toyota TF104/07	1:29.085	13	1:17.735	15								
39.	Timo Glock	Jordan EJ14/01 - Ford	1:19.428	4	1:19.490	23								
40.	Bas Leinders	Minardi PS04B/03 - Cosworth	1:22.267	8	1:19.914	25								

Maximum speed

N°	Driver	P1 Qualifs	Pos.	P1 Race	Pos.	P2 Qualifs	Pos.	P2 Race	Pos.	Finish Qualifs	Pos.	Finish Race	Pos.	Trap Qualifs	Pos.	Trap Race	Pos.
1.	M. Schumacher	172,1	11	180,7	12	291,4	3	294,6	1	155,2	13	158,6	3	318,8	2	323,7	2
2.	R. Barrichello	170,4	14	174,8	18	290,0	4	293,8	3	159,1	6	157,2	6	316,0	5	324,4	1
3.	J.P. Montoya	181,6	3	182,8	6	292,0	2	291,7	5	157,4	9	154,7	14	317,4	3	320,6	8
4.	M. Gené	169,8	16	186,5	4	292,9	1	294,4	2	151,4	19	156,0	11	320,3	1	321,4	6
5.	D. Coulthard	186,0	1	182,3	8	289,9	5	291,0	7	164,6	2	157,8	4	316,0	6	322,9	3
6.	K. Räikkönen	175,9	6	179,9	14	288,2	8	291,1	6	161,3	4	157,1	8	314,1	9	319,9	11
7.	J. Trulli	184,1	2	181,3	11	289,1	7	290,1	8	157,5	8	160,5	2	314,2	7	315,6	17
8.	F. Alonso	180,3	4	195,7	1	289,6	6	288,9	12	165,6	1	161,3	1	314,1	8	314,6	18
9.	J. Button	172,3	10	184,1	5	284,2	18	287,6	15	162,3	3	157,7	5	310,8	14	317,5	14
10.	T. Sato	173,2	8	177,2	17	286,0	13	286,8	18	156,4	11	152,8	18	316,6	4	316,0	16
11.	G. Fisichella	178,2	5	194,6	2	287,0	11	292,4	4	156,6	10	157,2	7	312,0	13	322,1	5
12.	F. Massa	170,9	12	181,6	10	286,6	12	287,3	16	159,5	5	154,8	12	313,3	10	316,7	15
14.	M. Webber	175,4	7	182,5	7	287,3	10	289,9	9	152,3	17	156,7	10	312,1	12	322,2	4
15.	C. Klien	161,1	20	189,8	3	287,7	9	289,1	11	155,0	15	154,5	16	312,5	11	321,2	7
16.	C. Da Matta	170,9	13	179,9	15	285,9	14	288,7	13	158,6	7	156,9	9	309,5	17	319,7	12
17.	O. Panis	172,4	9	182,2	9	285,6	16	288,6	14	154,7	16	154,6	15	310,3	15	318,4	13
18.	N. Heidfeld	164,8	19	174,7	19	285,5	17	289,4	10	155,1	14	153,5	17	309,5	16	320,0	10
19.	G. Pantano	169,5	17	180,5	13	285,6	15	286,8	17	156,3	12	154,8	13	308,2	19	320,2	9
20.	G. Bruni	169,8	15	179,3	16	283,1	20	283,1	20	151,4	18	148,0	20	309,3	18	311,3	20
21.	Z. Baumgartner	169,4	18	173,8	20	283,2	19	283,6	19	149,5	20	149,1	19	306,0	20	312,8	19

Race

Classification & Retirements

Pos.	Driver	Team	Lap	Time	Average	
1.	M. Schumacher	Ferrari	70	1:30:18.133	205,035 km/h	
2.	F. Alonso	Renault	70	+ 8.329	204,720 km/h	
3.	R. Barrichello	Ferrari	70	+ 31.622	203,845 km/h	
4.	J. Trulli	Renault	70	+ 32.082	203,828 km/h	
5.	J. Button	B.A.R Honda	70	+ 32.484	203,813 km/h	
6.	D. Coulthard	McLaren Mercedes	70	+ 35.520	203,700 km/h	
7.	K. Räikkönen	McLaren Mercedes	70	+ 36.230	203,673 km/h	
8.	J.P. Montoya	Williams BMW	70	+ 43.419	203,405 km/h	
9.	M. Webber	Jaguar	70	+ 52.394	203,071 km/h	
10.	M. Gené	Williams BMW	70	+ 58.166	202,857 km/h	
11.	C. Klien	Jaguar	69	1 lap	201,728 km/h	
12.	G. Fisichella	Sauber Petronas	69	1 lap	200,690 km/h	
13.	F. Massa	Sauber Petronas	69	1 lap	200,182 km/h	
14.	C. Da Matta	Toyota	69	1 lap	199,833 km/h	
15.	O. Panis	Toyota	68	2 laps	198,423 km/h	
16.	N. Heidfeld	Jordan Ford	68	2 laps	196,849 km/h	
17.	G. Pantano	Jordan Ford	67	3 laps	195,529 km/h	
18.	G. Bruni	Minardi Cosworth	65	5 laps	192,569 km/h	Gearbox oil leak

Driver	Team		Reason
Z. Baumgartner	Minardi Cosworth	32	Off track and stuck in the gravel trap
T. Sato	B.A.R Honda	16	Engine broken

Fastest laps

	Driver	Time	Lap	Average
1.	M. Schumacher	1:15.377	32	210,669 km/h
2.	F. Alonso	1:15.551	34	210,183 km/h
3.	K. Räikkönen	1:15.791	30	209,518 km/h
4.	M. Webber	1:15.956	53	209,063 km/h
5.	J. Button	1:15.971	50	209,021 km/h
6.	R. Barrichello	1:16.035	50	208,845 km/h
7.	M. Gené	1:16.070	56	208,749 km/h
8.	J.P. Montoya	1:16.140	48	208,557 km/h
9.	J. Trulli	1:16.248	15	208,262 km/h
10.	D. Coulthard	1:16.303	11	208,112 km/h
11.	G. Fisichella	1:16.699	22	207,037 km/h
12.	T. Sato	1:16.809	14	206,741 km/h
13.	C. Klien	1:16.852	37	206,625 km/h
14.	C. Da Matta	1:16.937	49	206,397 km/h
15.	O. Panis	1:17.069	53	206,043 km/h
16.	F. Massa	1:17.388	23	205,194 km/h
17.	G. Pantano	1:17.641	15	204,525 km/h
18.	N. Heidfeld	1:18.627	26	201,961 km/h
19.	G. Bruni	1:18.932	52	201,180 km/h
20.	Z. Baumgartner	1:19.659	13	199,344 km/h

Pit stops

	Driver	Time	Lap	Stop n°
1.	M. Schumacher	20.443	11	1
2.	K. Räikkönen	20.516	11	1
3.	M. Gené	22.405	11	1
4.	C. Da Matta	21.341	11	1
5.	Z. Baumgartner	21.728	11	1
6.	D. Coulthard	21.175	12	1
7.	R. Barrichello	20.675	12	1
8.	J. Trulli	20.891	13	1
9.	J.P. Montoya	20.964	13	1
10.	G. Pantano	23.123	13	1
11.	O. Panis	24.668	13	1
12.	G. Bruni	21.956	13	1
13.	F. Alonso	21.305	14	1
14.	J. Button	21.313	14	1
15.	T. Sato	20.746	15	1
16.	M. Webber	21.049	15	1
17.	C. Klien	21.121	16	1
18.	N. Heidfeld	21.230	18	1
19.	G. Fisichella	20.593	20	1
20.	F. Massa	23.124	21	1
21.	K. Räikkönen	21.838	28	1
22.	M. Schumacher	19.425	29	2
23.	D. Coulthard	22.150	29	2
24.	J. Button	20.958	30	2
25.	C. da Matta	20.463	30	2
26.	J. Trulli	19.951	31	2
27.	R. Barrichello	20.179	31	2
28.	J.P. Montoya	21.458	31	2
29.	Z. Baumgartner	25.702	30	2
30.	F. Alonso	19.791	32	2
31.	G. Pantano	22.546	31	2
32.	O. Panis	21.806	32	2
33.	M. Webber	20.643	33	2
34.	M. Gené	21.270	33	2
35.	G. Bruni	21.656	32	2
36.	C. Klien	21.747	35	2
37.	N.Heidfeld	11.042	35	2
38.	N.Heidfeld	21.622	36	3
39.	G. Fisichella	21.063	37	2
40.	M. Schumacher	19.641	42	3
41.	F. Alonso	22.102	46	3
42.	F. Massa	22.805	45	2
43.	K. Räikkönen	22.382	47	3
44.	C. da Matta	20.897	47	3
45.	D. Coulthard	21.514	48	3
46.	J. Trulli	20.667	49	3
47.	G. Pantano	22.691	48	3
48.	J.P. Montoya	21.498	50	3
49.	R. Barrichello	20.529	51	3
50.	M. Webber	20.891	51	3
51.	N.Heidfeld	21.661	50	4
52.	J. Button	21.861	52	3
53.	O. Panis	25.822	51	3
54.	G. Fisichella	20.392	52	3
55.	G. Bruni	21.334	50	3
56.	C. Klien	21.263	53	3
57.	G. Pantano	11.084	52	4
58.	M. Gené	20.517	54	3
59.	M. Schumacher	19.036	58	4

Race leaders

Driver	Laps in the lead	Nber of Laps
F. Alonso	1 > 32	32
M. Schumacher	33 > 42	10
F. Alonso	43 > 46	4
M. Schumacher	47 > 70	24

Driver	Nber of Laps	Kilometers
F. Alonso	36	158,612 km
M. Schumacher	34	149,974 km

Gaps on the leader board

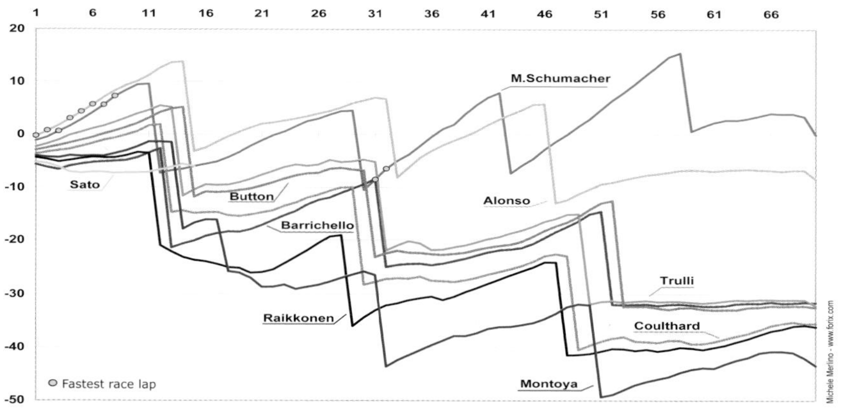

1 6 11 16 21 26 31 36 41 46 51 56 61 66
20 10 0 -10 -20 -30 -40 -50
M.Schumacher
Sato
Button
Barrichello
Alonso
Trulli
Raikkonen
Coulthard
Montoya
Fastest race lap
Michele Merlino - www.forix.com

Lap chart

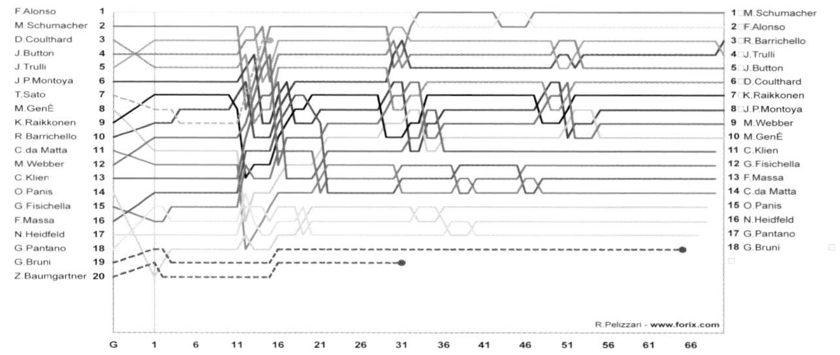

F.Alonso 1
M.Schumacher 2
D.Coulthard 3
J.Button 4
J.Trulli 5
J.P.Montoya 6
T.Sato 7
M.GenÉ 8
K.Raikkonen 9
R.Barrichello 10
C.da Matta 11
M.Webber 12
C.Klien 13
O.Panis 14
G.Fisichella 15
F.Massa 16
N.Heidfeld 17
G.Pantano 18
G.Bruni 19
Z.Baumgartner 20
1 M.Schumacher
2 F.Alonso
3 R.Barrichello
4 J.Trulli
5 J.Button
6 D.Coulthard
7 K.Raikkonen
8 J.P.Montoya
9 M.Webber
10 M.GenÉ
11 C.Klien
12 G.Fisichella
13 F.Massa
14 C.da Matta
15 O.Panis
16 N.Heidfeld
17 G.Pantano
18 G.Bruni
R.Pelizzari - www.forix.com
G 1 6 11 16 21 26 31 36 41 46 51 56 61 66

Championship after ten rounds

Drivers

1. M. Schumacher ....(9 wins)................90
2. R. Barrichello 68
3. J. Button 48
4. J. Trulli.......................(1 win) 46
5. F. Alonso 33
6. J.P. Montoya 25
7. T. Sato 14
8. R. Schumacher 12
9. D. Coulthard 12
10. G. Fisichella..10
11. K. Räikkönen 10
12. F. Massa 5
13. O. Panis 5
14. C. Da Matta..3
15. M. Webber 3
16. N. Heidfeld...3
17. T. Glock 2
18. Z. Baumgartner 1
19. C. Klien 0
20. M. Gené..0
21. G. Pantano..0
22. G. Bruni..0

Constructors

1. Scuderia Ferrari Marlboro ......(9 wins) 158
2. Mild Seven Renault F1 Team ..(1 win) 79
3. Lucky Strike B.A.R Honda 62
4. BMW WilliamsF1 Team..............................37
5. West McLaren Mercedes............................22
6. Sauber Petronas 15
7. Panasonic Toyota Racing 8
8. Jordan Ford 5
9. Jaguar Racing 3
10. Minardi Cosworth.......................................1

The circuit

Name	Magny-Cours, Nevers
Length	4411 meters
Distance	70 laps, 308.586 km
Date	July 4, 2004
Weather	sunny and warm, 27-31°c
Track temperature	38-43°c

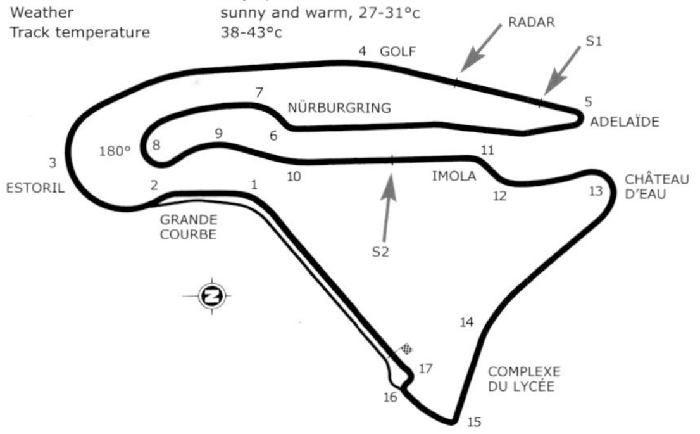

RADAR
S1
4 GOLF
5
ADELAÏDE
7
NÜRBURGRING
6
9
8
180°
3
ESTORIL
2
1
10
IMOLA
11
12
13
CHÂTEAU D'EAU
GRANDE COURBE
S2
14
17
16
15
COMPLEXE DU LYCÉE

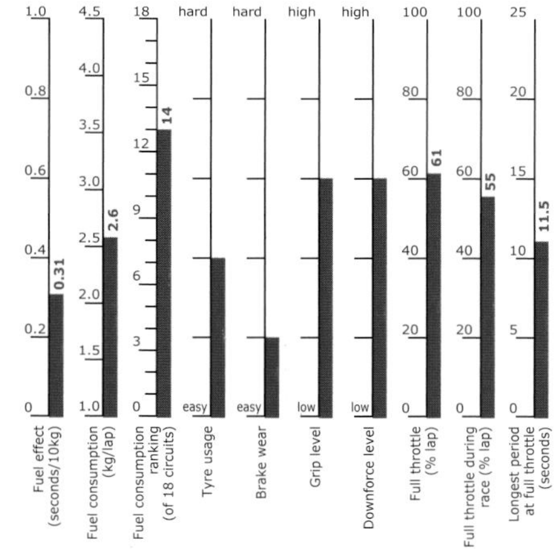

Fuel effect (seconds/10kg) 0.31
Fuel consumption (kg/lap) 2.6
Fuel consumption ranking (of 18 circuits) 14
Tyre usage
Brake wear
Grip level
Downforce level
Full throttle (% lap) 61
Full throttle during race (% lap) 55
Longest period at full throttle (seconds) 11.5
hard
easy
high
low

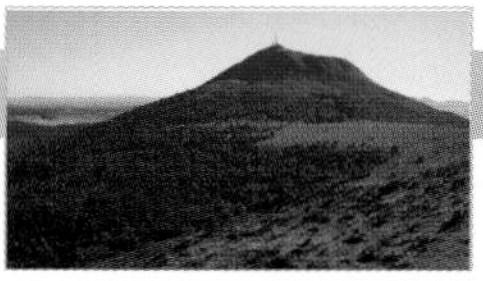

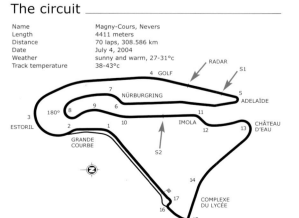

KIMI BACK ON TRACK

In 2003, Kimi Raikkonen was in the running for the title right down to the final race. This year was proving a nightmare. On the eve of the British Grand Prix, he was only eleventh in the championship and, as from Magny Cours, he was definitely out of the title fight. At Silverstone, the McLaren team managed to stage something of a comeback on home turf. Kimi Raikkonen took pole position and went on to finish second in the race. Once again, the top step of the podium was occupied by Michael Schumacher, who took his tenth win from eleven races.

A farcical pre-qualifying

> First pole of the season for Kimi Raikkonen. The "B" version of the MP4-19 seems to be working miracles.

It all began with a spin from Michael Schumacher. The world champion was not in the habit of making this sort of mistake. Then, a few moments later, Rubens Barrichello staged a pseudo off-track excursion that raised a few eyebrows in the media centre. Subsequently, several cars went round at a snails pace and pre-qualifying turned into a farce.

The teams' weather experts all reckoned that sooner or later, rain was due to hit the track, so they were all keen to start the actual qualifying as early as possible, hence the need to be slowest in the first session. *"Our forecast was for rain in the second half of qualifying, so we did not want to be out on track at that time,"* explained Ross Brawn, who had called the Ferrari strategy. *"We tried to hide our intentions from the other teams, but they all had the same idea."*

McLaren adopted the same tactic, with their drivers crawling round the track. *"Of course the spectators here did not know what was going on, but it was only in pre-qualifying,"* was David Coulthard's justification for his actions. *"Mind you, with all the pit stops in the races, I don't suppose they have a better idea of what's going on then either!"* As far as Ron Dennis, the boss of the Anglo-German team was concerned, there was no other option. *"We were constantly tracking the arrival of the rain on our radar and we knew the showers would hit during the qualifying session. So it was normal to want to be first out on track. That's part of the game. In fact, it rained exactly as predicted and it was very heavy, except that it was 8 kilometres away from the circuit. Our tactics were therefore perfectly justifiable. We preferred to be honest about it rather than by pretending to go off the track, like some others!"*

Solitude at Silverstone. It is a tradition that the English circuit is always at risk of being defeated by its archaic layout. The British Grand Prix looked like heading for more modern surroundings, such as the centre of London. v

Against all expectation, the rain never actually made it to Silverstone and Kimi Raikkonen ended up with his first pole position of the season. It seemed that the "B" version of the McLaren MP4-19, which had made its debut a week earlier in Magny Cours, was doing the business. *"Yes it is definitely more stable,"* confirmed the Finn. *"As soon as we ran it for the first time, here at this track six weeks ago, it has worked really well."*

London wants a grand prix

Above the main entrance to Silverstone there is a large sign bearing the legend, *"The Home of British Motor Racing"* which greets spectators. The Northamptonshire circuit, around 100 kilometres to the north of London had staged the British Grand Prix 37 times since 1950. It seemed unthinkable that the circuit could lose its main attraction. However, Silverstone came in for heavy criticism from Bernie Ecclestone, the F1 commercial rights holder. In the week leading up to the race, he even sent the circuit an ultimatum, giving it until 30th September to sign a contract for the 2005 and 2006 races, at a much higher price than in the past.

It was against this backdrop that the city of London planned to launch its own bid. On Tuesday a Formula 1 demonstration run had been staged in the capital, with eight F1 cars running at much reduced speeds through the streets. There was a Ferrari, driven by Luca Badoer, a McLaren, a Williams, a BAR and a Jordan, driven by Nigel Mansell no less! The cars ran down Regent Street between Oxford Street and Piccadilly Circus and they drew a crowd estimated at 300,000. It prompted Mayor of London, Ken Livingstone to promote the idea of staging a race in the city. *"A London Grand Prix would be amazing. It's exactly what one needs to get a city talked about. I have spoken to Buckingham Palace and the Queen's people and they are in favour of the project."* A poll revealed that 90% of Londoners would be in favour of staging the race, which was a much bigger figure than the 67% who supported an Olympic bid.

On Thursday, the British press had gone to town, proposing no less than five different track layouts, including three based around Hyde Park which would be used as the pits and paddock. The worked needed to resurface the roads, to build the grandstands and a paddock was estimated to cost around 13 million Euros, which would need to be added to the 21 million that Bernie Ecclestone would charge to bring the circus to town and that would be split between the teams. *"The money spent on organising the race would be paid back several times over by the spectators filling our hotel rooms and our restaurants,"* continued Livingstone. *"I reckon the event could draw a crowd of two million people."* It seemed that Silverstone and its reputation for ancient pits, chaotic access and muddy car parks could not match this dynamic challenge emanating from London.

Starting grid

* F. ALONSO, G. BRUNI, Z. BAUMGARTNER et G. FISICHELLA
Penalty for an engine change

** O. PANIS
Time cancelled because he blocked F. Massa on his qualifying lap.

Pos	Driver	Time
19	Z. BAUMGARTNER*	1:24.117
17	O. PANIS**	- (1:20.335)
15	N. HEIDFELD	1:22.677
13	C. KLIEN	1:21.559
11	M. GENÉ	1:20.335
9	M. WEBBER	1:20.004
7	J.P. MONTOYA	1:19.378
5	J. TRULLI	1:18.715
3	J. BUTTON	1:18.580
1	K. RÄIKKÖNEN	1:18.233 (236,570 km/h)
20	G. FISICHELLA*	-
18	G. BRUNI*	1:23.437
16	F. ALONSO*	1:18.811
14	G. PANTANO	1:22.458
12	C. DA MATTA	1:20.545
10	F. MASSA	1:20.202
8	T. SATO	1:19.688
6	D. COULTHARD	1:19.148
4	M. SCHUMACHER	1:18.710
2	R. BARRICHELLO	1:18.305

Four or two stops, Michael is still king

It really did seem to be the case that everyone was powerless against Michael Schumacher. Fourth on the grid, behind team-mate Rubens Barrichello, the world champion knew he would have to run a tactically sound race to take his tenth win of the season. *"Michael was not very happy with the handling of his car before qualifying,"* explained Ross Brawn after the race. *"We therefore opted to put him on a more conservative strategy. We wanted to be more aggressive as far as Rubens (Barrichello) was concerned, but in fact, it turned out that the opposite of what we had expected actually worked better."*

Indeed, refuelling three times, the Brazilian finished third, behind the German. *"If I had known, with hindsight I would have done better to chose the other strategy!"* admitted Rubens with a weary smile. Starting with more fuel than most of his rivals, Michael Schumacher waited patiently for everyone else to pit before stepping up the pace and building up an enough of a gap to emerge in the lead after his own pit stop. *"I am amazed at how things worked out,"* he confessed. *"I thought we had a good strategy, sacrificing qualifying for the race, but I did not expect to see it pay off so easily. The car was perfect."*

The only glitch in the world champion's plans was the arrival of the safety car on lap 40, which meant his rivals could make their third stops without losing time. *"It wiped out my advantage,"* he confirmed. *"On top of that, the Safety Car was going so slowly that my tyres lost too much temperature. Despite trying everything, they still took three laps to warm up again."*

Once the race was underway again, Schumacher was never really threatened from then on. As he took the chequered flag however, his lead over Kimi

Raikkonen had come down to just two seconds, with a total of twelve drivers finishing on the same lap. *"It's clear that the superiority we enjoyed in the early part of the season has been worn away,"* felt the winner. *"In Melbourne, we could do as we pleased. Today, we had to pull out all the strategic tricks to*

win." 26 points ahead of Rubens Barrichello and almost double that number over Jenson Button, Michael Schumacher still had nothing much to worry about. It was now only a question of weeks before he would take his seventh drivers' world championship title.

^
"I'm glad you're back!" Michael Schumacher congratulates Kimi Raikkonen on his first podium finish of the season.

Jarno Trulli escapes unscathed from a terrible crash

Lap 40: the race is well underway when Jarno Trulli has a huge accident at the wheel of his Renault and the organisers have to bring out the Safety Car. The Italian was taken to the circuit medical centre and eventually emerged unscathed after piling into the

tyre barriers at 250 km/h, spinning several times before rolling the car. *"It all happened very quickly,"* he recounted. *"It was a big accident, but I immediately indicated to the marshals that I was okay. I think the suspension broke, but we won't be

able to confirm that until the car is back at the factory. Anyway, apart from that, things were not going too well. The car was vicious to drive and I had to fight to keep my position."*

^
Start: The Finn surges into the lead, but he would be powerless against Ferrari's strategy.

The loneliness of the F1 driver

Juan Pablo Montoya and Ralf Schumacher have never been out for a night on the town together, but they work in tandem for the greater good of the Williams car. With the German on sick leave, set up responsibilities rested on Montoya's shoulders, in what was proving to be a lacklustre season for the English team. At Silverstone, Marc Gené, 12th, couldn't help him that much...

paddock

Saubers breeze along

The new Hinwil wind tunnel was working rather well thank you very much. Ever since it had been brought into service back in March, it never ceased to surprise the team's engineers. *"We are surprised to see how quickly we have been able to exploit our new wind tunnel,"* confirmed Sauber''s technical director, Willy Rampf.

A month earlier, in Canada, new brake cooling ducts made their first appearance. A week earlier in Magny Cours, it was time for a new front wing. And here in Silverstone, a new engine cover put in an appearance, which followed the chassis contours more closely, was more rounded, featured exhausts that emerged ten centimetres higher and it also boasted a small central wing.

They were essentially minor modifications, but the results were excellent. The new engine cover was used for the first time on Friday and Felipe Massa was the first to try it, coming back to the pits singing its praises. *"Felipe immediately said that it was an enormous step forward,"* explained team spokesman Hanspeter Brack.

Fitted to Giancarlo Fisichella's car and combined with the new "B" spec Ferrari engine that the team was using for the first time here, it helped the Roman driver to set the second fastest time on Friday. *"It is*

really a big improvement," he confirmed. *"Frankly, the progress we have made since the first grand prix is incredible, but today's step is definitely the most important."*

Both the C23 drivers reckoned the car was now more stable in high speed corners and definitely better balanced.

Unfortunately, an engine problem meant that Fisichella's car had to be fitted with a new V10 on Saturday. He would therefore start from the back of the grid, but even that did not dent his optimism. *"We had the same problem at the Nurburgring, where I still managed to score points. So I am still optimistic!"* He had reason to be. From last on the grid, *"Fisi"* staged an incredible climb through the

field to finish sixth, just twelve seconds down on the winner, scoring three points. He did it despite an air pressure problem on the engine. His mechanics tried to fix it at his second and final pit stop. *"I was really confident in the car,"* declared the Italian. *"I knew it was very quick and I was able to overtake everyone before making my first pit stop. Without that engine problem, I would have finished ahead of Montoya."*

For his part, Peter Sauber had mixed feelings after the race. *"Everything worked against us this weekend: Giancarlo's engine problem, Felipe's problem with Panis in qualifying, a problem with the engine in the race... Scoring three points in these circumstances proves we now have an excellent car, driver and tyre package."*

Kimi climbs back

At Silverstone, Kimi Raikkonen finished on the podium for the first time since the 2003 Japanese Grand Prix. Finally! *"Usually, I'm not very happy to finish second, but today, I'm almost pleased!"* he joked. *"We are experiencing a really difficult season. The whole team is working very hard to fix it and now, with the MP4-19B, we are finally beginning to move in the right direction. Being second is better than fighting for 7th or 8th place, but I'll be even happier when I'm fighting for the win. Well, we can't do everything all at once and there is still work to do."*

On the first lap, the Finn had carved out a lead of 3.5 seconds, before looking in his mirrors and seeing the Ferraris close on him. For a short while, he believed he could win. *"Of course, I always thought I could win, right up to the last metre. At the start, I pushed as hard as I could because we thought that Michael would actually be quicker over the race distance, so I tried to build a gap at the start. Unfortunately, it wasn't enough."*

Weekend gossip

> It was not Olivier Panis' weekend. On Saturday, he was disqualified for blocking Felipe Massa on his qualifying lap. Starting from 17th on the grid, Panis posted the first retirement on lap 17, after his fire extinguisher went off in the cockpit, just after his pit stop. A very unusual occurrence! *"The foam went everywhere, on the wheels and on my visor. I couldn't see anything and ended up in the gravel."*

> On Thursday, Jackie Stewart, president of the BRDC, the club that owns Silverstone, declared that Bernie Ecclestone had gone back on his promise to stage the British Grand Prix at this circuit in 2005 and 2006. *"Going back on my word is not my way of doing things,"* thundered Ecclestone. *"If I see Jackie Stewart in the paddock, I'll strangle him with his kilt."* Just to be on the safe side, the Scottish former racer made sure he was wearing trousers.

> It's done: Mark Webber had signed a contract for 2005 with the Williams team, for a fee of 11 million pounds. He thus rejected Toyota's even juicier salary offer.

> *"Jarno made a beginner's mistake, that someone of his experience should not do,"* let slip Renault's director of race engineering, Pat Symonds on the subject of Jarno Trulli's gaffe in Magny Cours.

> *"These cars aren't powerful enough!"* commented Nigel Mansell after driving the Jordan through the streets of London. *"With all the electronics, anyone could get one of these cars off the line. All you have to do is lift off the clutch."*

> It is confirmed: Ralf Schumacher had signed with Toyota for three seasons, from 2005 to 2007, for a sum of 80 million Euros.

Practice

All the time trials

N°	Driver	N° Chassis - Engine	Practice 1 Friday	Pos.	Practice 2 Friday	Pos.	Practice 3 Saturday	Pos.	Practice 4 Saturday	Pos.	Pre-qual. Saturday	Pos.	Qualif. Saturday	Pos.
1.	Michael Schumacher	Ferrari F2004 239	1:19.214	2	1:19.162	3	1:19.571	3	1:18.951	8	1:30.293	14	1:18.710	4
2.	Rubens Barrichello	Ferrari F2004 240	1:19.138	1	1:19.473	6	1:19.585	4	1:18.623	3	1:24.817	12	1:18.305	2
3.	Juan Pablo Montoya	Williams FW26 06 - BMW	1:19.502	3	1:19.746	11	1:19.699	5	1.18.912	6	1:34.386	15	1:19.378	8
4.	Marc Gené	Williams FW26 07 - BMW	1:19.687	4	1:19.540	7	1:20.552	10	1:18.832	5	1:34.981	16	1:20.335	13
5.	David Coulthard	McLaren MP4-19B 02 - Mercedes	1:20.021	6	1:19.287	4	1.19.979	7	1:18.919	7	1:23.521	11	1.19.148	7
6.	Kimi Räikkönen	McLaren MP4-19B 01 - Mercedes	1:20.633	9	1:18.655	1	1:19.315	1	1:18.280	1	1:21.639	6	1:18.233	1
7.	Jarno Trulli	Renault R24-03	1:21.792	15	1:19.601	8	1:19.966	6	1:18.694	4	1:21.496	5	1:18.715	5
8.	Fernando Alonso	Renault R24-02	1:22.003	16	1:19.874	12	1:20.482	9	1:19.169	9	1.21.923	7	1:18.811	6
9.	Jenson Button	B.A.R 006-05 - Honda	1:20.866	10	1:19.401	5	1:19.468	2	1:18.414	2	1:18.872	1	1:18.580	3
10.	Takuma Sato	B.A.R 006-04 - Honda	1:21.285	13	1:19.611	9	1:20.177	8	1:20.837	16	1:28.910	13	1:19.688	9
11.	Giancarlo Fisichella	Sauber C23-03 - Petronas	1.20.446	8	1:18.660	2	1:20.759	12	1:19.895	10		19		20
12.	Felipe Massa	Sauber C23-01 - Petronas	1:20.430	7	1:19.676	10	1:20.685	11	1:20.281	12	1:19.317	2	1:20.202	11
14.	Mark Webber	Jaguar R5-05	1:21.520	14	1:21.352	18	1:21.295	14	1:20.310	13	1:35.853	17	1:20.004	10
15.	Christian Klien	Jaguar R5-01	1:22.279	17	1:21.073	17	1:21.706	16	1:20.913	17	1:38.648	18	1:21.559	15
16.	Cristiano da Matta	Toyota TF104/04	1:22.466	18	1:20.829	15	1:21.017	13	1:20.183	11	1:22.507	8	1:20.545	14
17.	Olivier Panis	Toyota TF104/03	1:22.520	19	1:20.489	14	1:21.416	15	1:20.531	14	1:19.697	3	1:20.335	12
18.	Nick Heidfeld	Jordan EJ14/03 - Ford	1:22.716	21	1:22.365	20	1:22.503	18	1:20.726	15		20	1:22.677	17
19.	Giorgio Pantano	Jordan EJ14/02 - Ford	1:22.664	20	1:22.586	23	1:21.984	17	1:22.014	19	1:21.350	4	1:22.458	16
20.	Gianmaria Bruni	Minardi PS04B/02 - Cosworth	1:23.663	23	1:22.516	22			1:23.941	20	1:22.529	9	1.23.437	18
21.	Zsolt Baumgartner	Minardi PS04B/01 - Cosworth	1:23.715	24	1:23.436	25			1:21.980	18	1:23.116	10	1:24.117	19
35.	Anthony Davidson	B.A.R 006-03 - Honda	1:19.748	5	1:20.861	16								
37.	Björn Wirdheim	Jaguar R5-05	1:21.277	12	1:21.353	19								
38.	Ricardo Zonta	Toyota TF104/07	1:21.095	11	1:20.095	13								
39.	Timo Glock	Jordan EJ14/01 - Ford	1:23.149	22	1:22.500	21								
40.	Bas Leinders	Minardi PS04B/03 - Cosworth	1:24.887	25	1:22.792	24								

Maximum speed

N°	Driver	P1 Qualifs	Pos.	P1 Race	Pos.	P2 Qualifs	Pos.	P2 Race	Pos.	Finish Qualifs	Pos.	Finish Race	Pos.	Trap Qualifs	Pos.	Trap Race	Pos.
1.	M. Schumacher	309,8	4	319,2	7	274,3	6	276,0	6	304,3	1	303,5	4	275,0	10	289,5	1
2.	R. Barrichello	311,2	2	323,6	1	273,9	8	273,1	11	304,3	2	306,0	2	278,9	2	283,7	7
3.	J.P. Montoya	307,2	11	320,4	5	277,9	2	279,0	4	301,9	4	301,0	10	278,7	3	287,7	2
4.	M. Gené	307,6	10	319,1	8	281,3	1	281,9	1	302,9	3	303,2	5	280,0	1	282,7	8
5.	D. Coulthard	307,9	7	321,8	3	272,0	11	275,2	8	300,3	6	301,7	8	271,6	12	286,0	4
6.	K. Räikkönen	309,3	5	316,5	11	275,7	4	270,7	14	300,5	5	306,0	1	265,8	14	284,1	6
7.	J. Trulli	309,1	6	312,4	19	277,7	3	274,3	10	295,3	14	299,3	13	277,8	5	282,3	9
8.	F. Alonso	302,6	16	321,5	4	274,8	5	275,7	7	296,7	11	301,0	11	278,6	4	285,4	5
9.	J. Button	312,2	1	315,1	14	271,1	14	268,7	17	296,8	10	298,5	15	275,9	9	279,2	12
10.	T. Sato	306,6	12	315,7	13	273,9	7	271,5	13	296,3	12	297,4	16	276,6	8	279,8	10
11.	G. Fisichella			323,7	1			272,3	12			301,8	7			272,5	15
12.	F. Massa	310,7	3	320,0	6	271,8	12	276,6	5	297,8	9	304,5	3	266,3	13	277,4	13
14.	M. Webber	307,6	9	318,8	9	270,6	15	280,5	2	298,6	7	303,1	6	276,9	7	279,8	11
15.	C. Klien	305,4	13	318,2	10	272,8	10	274,9	9	296,2	13	299,1	14	277,2	6	286,7	3
16.	C. Da Matta	298,4	19	312,6	18	271,6	13	279,2	3	293,8	17	297,0	17	265,2	15	276,9	14
17.	O. Panis	304,4	14	313,2	16	273,0	9	260,3	18	291,8	19	296,2	18	272,5	11	266,4	19
18.	N. Heidfeld	303,9	15	316,1	12	262,2	17	270,0	16	298,5	8	301,4	9	257,2	17	268,2	16
19.	G. Pantano	307,9	8	314,7	15	263,0	16	270,0	15	295,3	15	299,9	12	255,9	18	266,9	17
20.	G. Bruni	299,4	17	307,3	20	249,8	19	252,5	20	294,0	16	294,0	20	258,6	16	266,6	18
21.	Z. Baumgartner	299,2	18	312,7	17	250,1	18	256,0	19	293,1	18	294,9	19	247,1	19	258,3	20

Race

Classification & Retirements

Pos.	Driver	Team	Lap	Time	Average
1.	M. Schumacher	Ferrari	60	1:24:42.700	218,403 km/h
2.	K. Räikkönen	McLaren Mercedes	60	+ 2.130	218,311 km/h
3.	R. Barrichello	Ferrari	60	+ 3.114	218,269 km/h
4.	J. Button	B.A.R Honda	60	+ 10.683	217,945 km/h
5.	J.P. Montoya	Williams BMW	60	+ 12.173	217,881 km/h
6.	G. Fisichella	Sauber Petronas	60	+ 12.888	217,850 km/h
7.	D. Coulthard	McLaren Mercedes	60	+ 19.668	217,561 km/h
8.	M. Webber	Jaguar	60	+ 23.701	217,389 km/h
9.	F. Massa	Sauber Petronas	60	+ 24.023	217,375 km/h
10.	F. Alonso	Renault	60	+ 24.835	217,341 km/h
11.	T. Sato	B.A.R Honda	60	+ 33.736	216,963 km/h
12.	M. Gené	Williams BMW	60	+ 34.303	216,939 km/h
13.	C. Da Matta	Toyota	59	1 lap	213,201 km/h
14.	C. Klien	Jaguar	59	1 lap	213,156 km/h
15.	N. Heidfeld	Jordan Ford	59	1 lap	212,792 km/h
16.	G. Bruni	Minardi Cosworth	56	4 laps	202,652 km/h

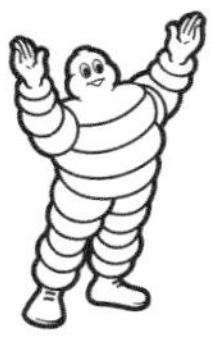

Driver	Team		Reason
G. Pantano	Jordan Ford	48	Spin
J. Trulli	Renault	40	Big crash after left rear suspension failure
Z. Baumgartner	Minardi Cosworth	30	Engine problem
O. Panis	Toyota	17	Fire extinguisher goes off in cockpit

Fastest laps

	Driver	Time	Lap	Average
1.	M. Schumacher	1:18.739	14	235,049 km/h
2.	R. Barrichello	1:19.296	8	233,398 km/h
3.	J. Button	1:19.488	10	232,835 km/h
4.	K. Räikkönen	1:19.554	10	232,641 km/h
5.	G. Fisichella	1:19.813	22	231,887 km/h
6.	J.P. Montoya	1:19.968	26	231,437 km/h
7.	M. Gené	1:20.434	58	230,096 km/h
8.	F. Alonso	1:20.442	39	230,073 km/h
9.	F. Massa	1:20.484	58	229,953 km/h
10.	D. Coulthard	1:20.547	25	229,773 km/h
11.	J. Trulli	1:20.655	34	229,466 km/h
12.	M. Webber	1:20.768	11	229,145 km/h
13.	C. Da Matta	1:20.768	35	229,145 km/h
14.	T. Sato	1:20.790	12	229,082 km/h
15.	C. Klien	1:20.956	10	228,613 km/h
16.	N. Heidfeld	1:21.720	17	226,475 km/h
17.	G. Pantano	1:22.146	13	225,301 km/h
18.	O. Panis	1:23.131	4	222,631 km/h
19.	G. Bruni	1:24.296	33	219,554 km/h
20.	Z. Baumgartner	1:24.317	12	219,500 km/h

Pit stops

	Driver	Time	Lap	Stop n°
1.	F. Alonso	22.597	8	1
2.	R. Barrichello	23.380	9	1
3.	M. Gené	22.260	9	1
4.	D. Coulthard	23.634	10	1
5.	K. Räikkönen	22.474	11	1
6.	J. Button	21.972	11	1
7.	J.P. Montoya	22.191	11	1
8.	G. Bruni	23.853	11	1
9.	J. Trulli	22.512	13	1
10.	Z. Baumgartner	23.221	13	1
11.	G. Pantano	25.495	14	1
12.	M. Schumacher	24.277	15	1
13.	T. Sato	23.314	15	1
14.	C. Da Matta	24.836	15	1
15.	K. Klien	24.540	15	1
16.	M. Webber	24.183	16	1
17.	F. Massa	24.940	16	1
18.	O. Panis	25.011	16	1
19.	N. Heidfeld	23.686	18	1
20.	G. Fisichella	23.599	23	1
21.	F. Alonso	21.228	25	2
22.	M. Gené	22.243	25	2
23.	G. Bruni	12.429	25	2
24.	J. Button	21.968	27	2
25.	K. Räikkönen	21.710	28	2
26.	R. Barrichello	21.489	28	2
27.	Z. Baumgartner	23.075	27	2
28.	J.P. Montoya	21.908	29	2
29.	D. Coulthard	22.410	30	2
30.	G. Bruni	1:11.727	29	3
31.	J. Trulli	20.997	32	2
32.	T. Sato	25.357	35	2
33.	M. Schumacher	24.692	37	2
34.	K. Klien	24.542	36	2
35.	G. Pantano	25.120	36	2
36.	M. Webber	24.664	37	2
37.	C. Da Matta	25.025	37	2
38.	N. Heidfeld	25.601	37	2
39.	F. Massa	26.633	38	2
40.	K. Räikkönen	23.013	41	3
41.	R. Barrichello	22.884	41	3
42.	J. Button	23.724	41	3
43.	G. Fisichella	26.554	41	2
44.	J.P. Montoya	22.754	41	3
45.	D. Coulthard	22.130	41	3
46.	G. Bruni	24.024	38	4
47.	F. Alonso	21.604	41	3
48.	M. Gené	24.352	41	3

Race leaders

Driver	Laps in the lead	Nber of Laps
K. Räikkönen	1 > 11	11
M. Schumacher	12 > 60	49

Driver	Nber of Laps	Kilometers
M. Schumacher	49	251,909 km
K. Räikkönen	11	56,446 km

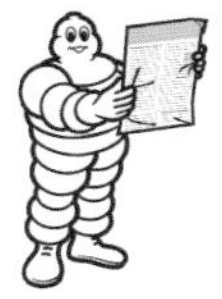

Lap chart

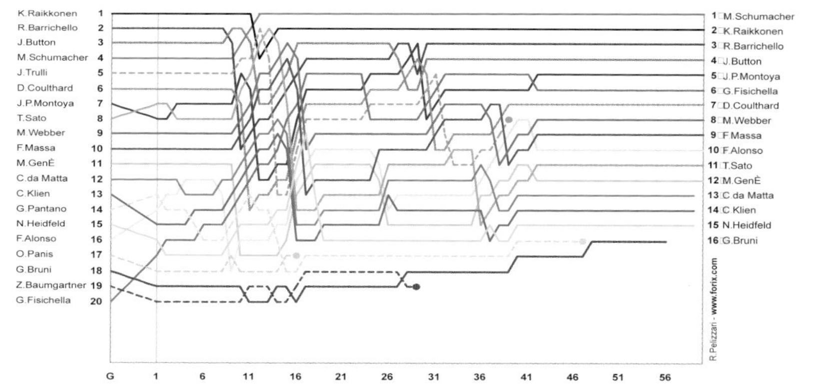

Gaps on the leader board

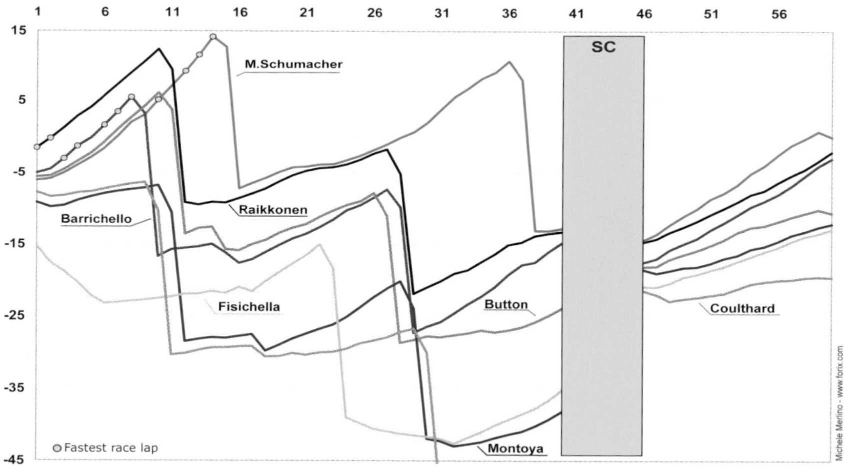

Championship after eleven rounds

Drivers

1. M. Schumacher ....(10 wins) 100
2. R. Barrichello 74
3. J. Button 53
4. J. Trulli ....(1 win) 46
5. F. Alonso 33
6. J.P. Montoya 29
7. K. Räikkönen 18
8. T. Sato 14
9. D. Coulthard 14
10. G. Fisichella 13
11. R. Schumacher 12
12. F. Massa 5
13. O. Panis 5
14. M. Webber 4
15. C. Da Matta 3
16. N. Heidfeld 3
17. T. Glock 2
18. Z. Baumgartner 1
19. C. Klien 0
20. M. Gené 0
21. G. Pantano 0
22. G. Bruni 0

Constructors

1. Scuderia Ferrari Marlboro ......(10 wins) 174
2. Mild Seven Renault F1 Team ..(1 win) 79
3. Lucky Strike B.A.R Honda 67
4. BMW WilliamsF1 Team.................................41
5. West McLaren Mercedes 32
6. Sauber Petronas..18
7. Panasonic Toyota Racing 8
8. Jordan Ford 5
9. Jaguar Racing 4
10. Minardi Cosworth 1

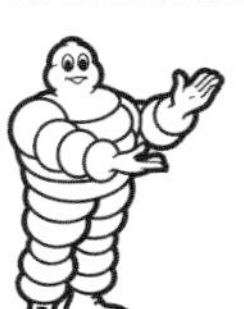

The circuit

Name	Silverstone
Length	5141 meters
Distance	60 laps, 308.355 km
Date	July 11, 2004
Weather	Weather overcast, 17-18°c
Track temperature	27-30°c

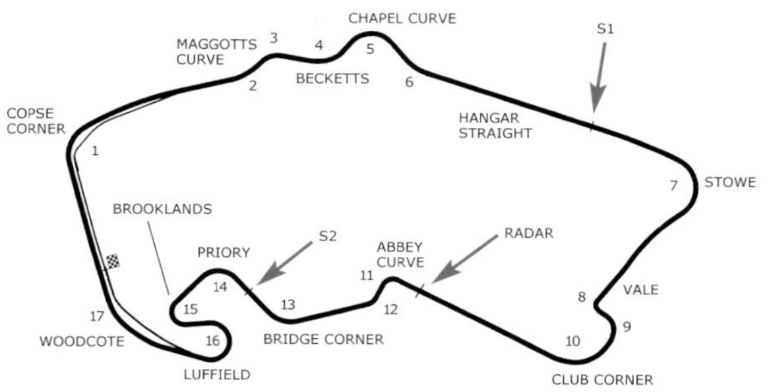

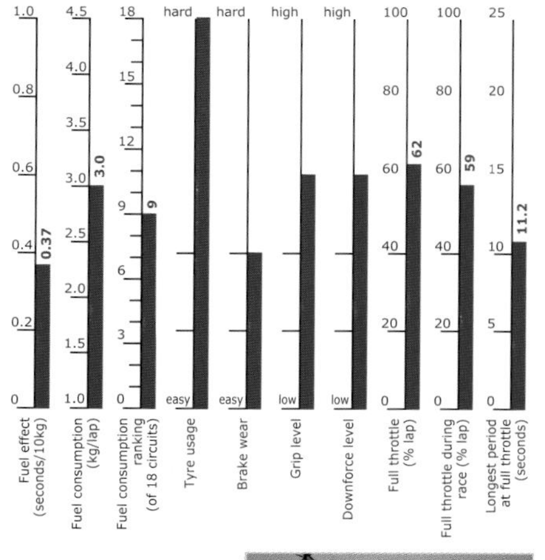

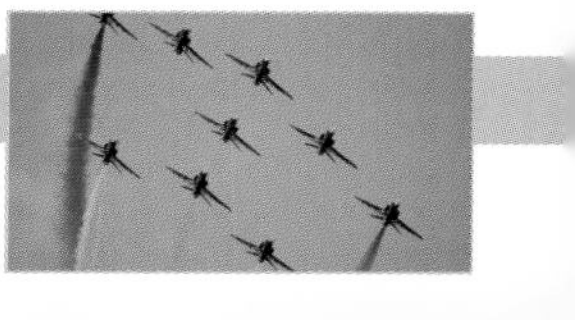

WINNING AT HOME

The atmosphere was highly charged in the Hockenheim grandstands at the finish of the German Grand Prix, as Michael Schumacher took an eleventh win of the season on home turf. He was never really threatened, although the battle raged behind him.

A front row start for Juan Pablo Montoya, who had won at this circuit in 2003. >

Michael takes pole and conserves his tyres

For the first time since the European Grand Prix back in May, Michael Schumacher took pole position. In front of a rapturous home crowd, he outpaced Juan Pablo Montoya's Williams by almost 4 tenths of a second. It was a stunning performance, which led his rivals to think the Ferrari must have been running very light, with the attached hope that its soft tyres would soon lose their edge. Even on his quickest lap, the German had to conserve his tyres in the first sector so that they would last for the final two!

> The Minardis usually qualify on the back row of the grid, but that's no reason for the team not to get fired up.

On Saturday morning, Rubens Barrichello checks over his car, having had a puncture. In the race, he tangled with David Coulthard and lost a lot of time, before finishing a modest twelfth.
>v

Jenson Button was third quickest on the stopwatch, but an engine change relegated him to 13th place on the start grid. In the end, it was all for the best, as his climb through the field was one of the highlights of the season.
v

BAR-Honda continues

In Hockenheim, the BAR team held a press conference to announce that its partnership with engine supplier Honda had been extended, *"at least until the end of the 2007 season."* *"It is now five years that Honda had been back in Formula 1 for our third period in the sport,"* commented Honda managing director, Takanobu Ito. *"We are beginning to see positive results and now we are aiming for our first win. This new agreement with BAR stipulates that, not only will we supply the engine, but we will also collaborate on the design of the chassis."* Several Japanese engineers were therefore due to set up camp in the BAR factory at Brackley.

In brief

> 360,000 Euros per race is what Eddie Jordan had asked Frank Williams to pay in exchange for the *"loan"* of Nick Heidfeld for the remaining races of the season. Unhappy with Marc Gene's performance, Williams found the bill a bit steep and in the end, he put Antonio Pizzonia in the vacant Ralf Schumacher car.

> In a complete turnaround from what he had announced in style at Magny Cours three weeks earlier, Max Mosley would no longer be retiring in October 2004. He had decided to delay his departure by a year.

> 46664 was the number written on the side pods of the two Jordans in Hockenheim. As part of his deal with the Bahrain circuit, Eddie Jordan had agreed to carry a different humanitarian message on the cars at every race. In this case, it was the number of Nelson Mandela's cell number during his 18 year incarceration in South Africa. The previous month, the president had launched an anti-Aids campaign called *"46664: the message"* which Eddie was supporting on his cars.

> Michael Schumacher had lost his lucky charm pendant at Silverstone, a small square inscribed with the initials of his wife and children. English newspaper *"The Sun"* launched a campaign to find the totemic item. The next day, an English cameraman said he had found the pendant in the Silverstone paddock, but did not know to whom it belonged. So on Friday in Germany, the Sun journalist handed it back to the world champion, who was happier than if he had won a race.

> Ferrari supplier Shell had come up with a new fuel for the German Grand Prix. *"It should help us get more power out of the engine,"* explained Jean Todt.

Starting grid

*J. BUTTON
Penalty for an engine change

**O. PANIS
Struggling to get away, he started from pit lane at the second start.

Pos	Driver	Time
19	G. BRUNI	1:18.055
17	G. PANTANO	1:16.192
15	C. DA MATTA	1:15.454
13	J. BUTTON*	1:13.674
11	M. WEBBER	1:14.802
9	O. PANIS**	1:14.368
7	R. BARRICHELLO	1:14.278
5	F. ALONSO	1:13.874
3	K. RÄIKKÖNEN	1:13.690
1	M. SCHUMACHER	1:13.306 (224,625 km/h)
20	Z. BAUMGARTNER	1:18.400
18	N. HEIDFELD	1:16.310
16	F. MASSA	1:15.616
14	G. FISICHELLA	1:15.395
12	C. KLIEN	1:15.011
10	A. PIZZONIA	1:14.556
8	T. SATO	1:14.287
6	J. TRULLI	1:14.134
4	D. COULTHARD	1:13.821
2	J.P. MONTOYA	1:13.668

< Michael Schumacher passes Juan Pablo Montoya. The race ended with another win for the former and a meagre fifth place for the latter, even though the Colombian had qualified on the front row.

Eleventh victory: a dream weekend for Michael Schumacher

"It was a perfect weekend. Pole position yesterday, the win today, it's a dream. I can't find the words to describe how I feel." Michael Schumacher is certainly used to being on the top step of the podium, as this was his 81st win, but this time he seemed as emotional as if it had been his first victory. *"I have not been that successful on this track in the past (he had only won here twice before) and it's fantastic. I could feel the support of the fans in the cockpit as they drowned out the engine noise as I came across the finish line."*

No doubt the tension on the day added to the emotion. Because, although the *"Kaiser"* led for almost all the race, barring a few laps during the pit stops, he came up against some strong opposition. *"It*

was a very tough race," he confirmed. *"I was always under pressure from Kimi, Jenson or Fernando."* This sixth consecutive win was also the third anniversary of his last mechanical failure, here at Hockenheim in 2001! *"Yes, it's true, I've just done 50 grands prix without any problems, which says a great deal about the strength of the team,"* he said. Flat out from start to finish, Schumacher might not have won this race if Kimi Raikkonen had made it to the finish, or if Jenson Button had not started from 13th on the grid.

Because, putting the winner to one side, this German Grand Prix was very closely contested, with several passing moves and, above all, a breathtaking duel for second place between Fernando Alonso and Jenson

Button. After several attempts, the Englishman eventually got the upper hand, when the Spaniard encountered a problem. *"With 16 laps to go, the car didn't want to turn into the corners,"* recounted Alonso. *"I thought I had lost my front wing. I called the pits to warn them I was going to come in. They told me to stay out on track so as not to lose any points. Then, after three laps, I rode over a kerb and everything was fine again. Something must have been stuck under the floor of the car."*

Michael Schumacher could now see the world title beckoning. He could already win it in Belgium in a month's time, while Ferrari could take the Constructors' crown in three weeks time in Budapest.

13th to 2nd for Jenson Button. And one-handed too!

What a comeback. Starting down in 13th spot on the grid, having had to change an engine, Jenson Button managed to haul his way up to the second step on the podium. It was an incredible exploit. *"Yes, there's no doubt it was the best race of my Formula 1 career,"* he admitted. *"It was not easy to work my way through the field. Before the start, I knew our car would be on the pace, but I thought maybe I could finish fifth at best. In fact, I'm happy, but I'm also a bit disappointed. If I had started from third, where I qualified, it would have been a very different story. I could have put Michael under a lot more pressure and who knows what could have happened. But I'm sure I'll get another chance before the end of the season."*

Seen from the side of the track, the most difficult part of his day seemed to have been the duel with Fernando Alonso, as the two men passed and re-passed one another several times. *"Yes, Fernando had incredible traction coming out of the hairpin. He would drop me every time before I could catch up going down the next straight. I tried to pass him several times, but it seemed there was no way round. Finally, I dived down the inside, I held on and it worked."*

At the end of the race, the Brit seemed in agony. He was even holding his helmet going down the straights, as if he was finding it difficult to hold his head up. *"Actually, the strap on my helmet had come loose. When this happens, the helmet tends to be sucked upwards down the straights and I had to hold it in place as it was choking me. I had to drive one-handed for most of the time!"*

It was just another facet of a great drive. Hardly surprising therefore that Jenson was being courted by both BAR and Williams for 2005.

Kimi loses his rear wing

Lap 14. Kimi Raikkonen has just set the fastest lap, which would not be beaten and he was running right behind Michael Schumacher when he veered violently off the track as his rear wing suddenly flew off as he was going down the pit straight. *"I was just a passenger in the car,"* commented the Finn. He was very disappointed,

as he felt he was in with a chance of winning the race. *"I was quicker than Michael after my first pit stop and in just a few more laps, I could have tried to pass him. It is always disappointing to retire, but at least we are now convinced we have the necessary pace to win races."*

Jenson Button was the star attraction in the German Grand Prix, especially when he attacked Fernando Alonso. The Englishman finished a magnificent second.
v

All smiles

Michael Schumacher often displays all the exuberance of youth on the podium. He takes a visible pleasure in winning, but this victory was special, as the world champion won in front of his favourite Hockenheim crowd, which he had not done too often in the past.

Williams in search of its glory days

Six points from the last five races! This was the miserable result of the Williams team's efforts going into the German Grand Prix. The team was but a shadow of its former self, of the one that harried Michael Schumacher in 2003.

Several factors combined to produce this disaster. The FW26 was far from a success. Its front suspension with its twin keel meant the engineers could not put enough ballast at the front end, which upset the balance of the car. On top of that, its shark shaped nose was more prone to being caught out by sidewinds, hence making the car unstable at some tracks. *"We suffer both from turn-in understeer and oversteer from the apex onwards,"* complained Juan Pablo Montoya. Over the past few years, any inadequacies on the chassis side had been masked by the power of the BWM engine. The

Munich V10 had been the most powerful in the field, but that was no longer the case in 2004.

Faced with similar problems, the McLaren team had come up with its "B" chassis three weeks earlier. Williams had also made changes notably to the underside of the car. But while McLaren made a step forward, the stopwatch did not reveal a similar story for the FW26. Its designers had thought about changing the nose during the season, but it was deemed too risky and the idea was shelved.

Nevertheless, the team was not taking this lying down. A new technical director, Sam Michael, had been put in to succeed Patrick Head, who had been in the job since 1977. The team had also just completed a new 35 million Euro wind tunnel and Frank Williams had sold his

private jet to pay for it. On the technical front, the team was paying the price for adopting too conservative a philosophy. While other teams played with the rules, using flexible wings or cars that ran underweight in between refuelling stops, nothing of the sort ever happened at Williams. *"It's true that we have never been good at exploiting the grey areas in the regulations,"* admitted Frank Williams. He has never been much good at looking after his drivers either. His two seats were still vacant therefore for next season, while he just missed out on getting Giancarlo Fisichella on board (see below.) On track, Ralf Schumacher was still on sick leave, so Juan Pablo Montoya was faced with doing most of the set-up work; not exactly his strong point, And in any case, he was simply biding his time before switching to McLaren in 2005.

Chassis, rules, drivers, management: there were plenty of areas that could do with improvement in the Williams-BMW camp.

An excellent driver would certainly be the first step on the road back to the top in 2005. Frank Williams had been unable to hang onto his existing drivers and he had also been unable to find new ones. It's a shame the Englishman had not learnt from past mistakes.

Pizzonia replaces Gene

Antonio Pizzonia was not shown lacking in his first grand prix at the wheel of a Williams-BMW. On Friday, when Juan Pablo Montoya was third, the young Brazilian posted the fifth quickest time and went on to qualify tenth. *"It's the first time I have driven an F1 car on this circuit and I spent most of the day learning its secrets and understanding how the FW26 reacted to it,"* he explained. *"But it's nice to be racing again and I thank the team for giving me this opportunity."*

It's over for Trulli

The decree nisi has been signed between Jarno Trulli and Flavio Briatore. As the latter was no longer the former's manager since the end of the 2004 season, because the driver had not wanted to extend the relationship, there was no reason for Briatore to keep him in his team. Especially as the fiery team boss had still not got over the way his driver had been caught out over the last two corners of the French Grand Prix. Sacked from the team he had been with since 2002, Trulli was no doubt going to end up at Toyota. Renault did not hesitate and immediately signed up Giancarlo Fisichella. The Roman driver had preferred to go for this option rather than wait and see if Frank Williams eventually came up with an offer. In fact, "Fisico" had already driven for the Renault team, in its Benetton days, from 1998 to 2001.

Practice

All the time trials

N°	Driver	N° Chassis - Engine	Practice 1 Friday	Pos.	Practice 2 Friday	Pos.	Practice 3 Saturday	Pos.	Practice 4 Saturday	Pos.	Pre-qual. Saturday	Pos.	Qualif. Saturday	Pos.
1.	Michael Schumacher	Ferrari F2004 239	1:15.864	2	1:15.001	1	1:15.066	1	1:14.459	7	1:14.042	11	1:13.306	1
2.	Rubens Barrichello	Ferrari F2004 240	1:16.493	7	1:15.738	9	1:15.354	3	1:14.393	6	1:14.111	12	1:14.278	8
3.	Juan Pablo Montoya	Williams FW26 06 - BMW	1:16.795	9	1:15.167	3	1:15.277	2	1.13.976	2	1:13.391	1	1:13.668	2
4.	Antonio Pizzonia	Williams FW26 07 - BMW	1:16.845	10	1:15.470	5	1:16.151	8	1:14.766	9	1:13.422	2	1:14.556	11
5.	David Coulthard	McLaren MP4-19B 03 - Mercedes	1:16.916	11	1:16.265	11	1.15.919	7	1:14.064	3	1:13.640	5	1.13.821	5
6.	Kimi Räikkönen	McLaren MP4-19B 01 - Mercedes	1:16.318	3	1:15.045	2	1:15.626	4	1:14.100	4	1:13.842	8	1:13.690	4
7.	Jarno Trulli	Renault R24-04	1:17.487	15	1:16.660	14	1:16.334	10	1:14.468	8	1:13.737	7	1:14.134	7
8.	Fernando Alonso	Renault R24-02	1:17.142	13	1:15.677	8	1:16.462	12	1:14.320	5	1.13.582	4	1:13.874	6
9.	Jenson Button	B.A.R 006-05 - Honda	1:16.544	8	1:15.379	4	1:15.839	5	1:13.676	1	1:13.535	3	1:13.674	3
10.	Takuma Sato	B.A.R 006-04 - Honda	1:17.526	16	1:15.657	7		20			1:14.465	13	1:14.287	9
11.	Giancarlo Fisichella	Sauber C23-04 - Petronas	1.16.451	5	1:17.026	17	1:16.232	9	1:15.572	14	1:13.914	10	1.15.395	14
12.	Felipe Massa	Sauber C23-01 - Petronas	1:17.361	14	1:16.865	16	1:16.532	13	1:15.588	15	1:13.899	9	1:15.616	16
14.	Mark Webber	Jaguar R5-05		25	1:16.514	13	1:16.961	15	1:15.000	12	1:15.093	15	1:14.802	12
15.	Christian Klien	Jaguar R5-01	1:18.810	20	1:16.854	15	1:16.650	14	1:15.481	13	1:15.090	14	1:15.011	13
16.	Cristiano da Matta	Toyota TF104/10B	1:17.111	12	1:17.300	18	1:16.457	11	1:14.791	10	1:15.119	16	1:15.454	15
17.	Olivier Panis	Toyota TF104/09B	1:16.484	6	1:17.419	19	1:15.882	6	1:14.953	11	1:13.641	6	1:14.368	10
18.	Nick Heidfeld	Jordan EJ14/03 - Ford	1:18.257	18	1:18.243	24	1:17.369	16	1:16.832	16	1:16.538	18	1:16.310	18
19.	Giorgio Pantano	Jordan EJ14/02 - Ford	1:20.029	24	1:17.869	21	1:18.914	18			1:16.167	17	1:16.192	17
20.	Gianmaria Bruni	Minardi PS04B/02 - Cosworth	1:19.088	21	1:18.309	25	1:18.198	17	1:18.227	17	1:17.283	19	1.18.055	19
21.	Zsolt Baumgartner	Minardi PS04B/01 - Cosworth	1:19.959	23	1:18.098	22	1:21.288	19	1:18.691	18	1:17.515	20	1:18.400	20
35.	Anthony Davidson	B.A.R 006-03 - Honda	1:15.756	1	1:15.576	6								
37.	Björn Wirdheim	Jaguar R5-02	1:17.714	17	1:16.342	12								
38.	Ricardo Zonta	Toyota TF104/03	1:16.340	4	1:16.200	10								
39.	Timo Glock	Jordan EJ14/01 - Ford	1:18.768	19	1:17.724	20								
40.	Bas Leinders	Minardi PS04B/03 - Cosworth	1:19.270	22	1:18.224	23								

Maximum speed

N°	Driver	P1 Qualifs	Pos.	P1 Race	Pos.	P2 Qualifs	Pos.	P2 Race	Pos.	Finish Qualifs	Pos.	Finish Race	Pos.	Trap Qualifs	Pos.	Trap Race	Pos.
1.	M. Schumacher	222,3	3	224,0	3	274,1	2	276,2	3	277,7	1	281,5	5	331,7	1	332,0	14
2.	R. Barrichello	219,5	12	224,1	1	271,3	4	276,3	2	277,2	3	281,3	6	325,5	4	337,1	6
3.	J.P. Montoya	222,3	4	223,8	4	267,9	8	273,3	6	277,2	2	281,5	4	326,5	3	336,2	7
4.	A. Pizzonia	222,5	2	223,2	5	269,1	5	273,3	8	275,1	8	282,2	1	324,9	7	335,7	9
5.	D. Coulthard	223,6	1	222,6	7	268,3	7	273,9	4	277,2	4	281,9	3	325,1	6	338,0	5
6.	K. Räikkönen	221,3	6	222,2	10	269,0	6	273,6	5	275,6	7	280,2	9	321,5	13	329,8	16
7.	J. Trulli	220,6	7	222,1	11	266,7	13	270,2	16	271,4	16	277,6	18	321,5	14	332,1	13
8.	F. Alonso	219,7	11	222,3	9	267,8	9	271,5	12	274,1	10	279,9	11	323,8	10	330,4	15
9.	J. Button	220,0	10	221,6	13	274,3	1	278,1	1	276,8	5	281,9	2	329,2	2	339,0	4
10.	T. Sato	219,3	13	221,4	14	273,0	3	273,3	7	276,3	6	279,7	12	324,3	8	339,9	3
11.	G. Fisichella	215,7	18	222,8	6	266,3	14	272,8	9	274,1	9	281,3	7	324,0	9	340,5	1
12.	F. Massa	218,7	14	218,5	18	264,3	17	269,6	17	272,4	13	277,9	16	321,5	12	340,3	2
14.	M. Webber	218,4	16	218,9	17	267,0	11	272,7	10	273,9	11	280,0	10	320,0	15	334,8	10
15.	C. Klien	220,3	9	220,9	15	267,0	12	272,7	11	271,3	17	278,7	13	318,3	16	333,4	12
16.	C. Da Matta	220,3	8	221,6	12	265,0	16	270,8	15	269,2	18	277,8	17	312,5	19	328,7	18
17.	O. Panis	221,4	5	224,0	2	267,3	10	270,9	14	273,4	12	281,1	8	316,6	17	328,8	17
18.	N. Heidfeld	218,4	15	219,2	16	262,3	18	267,5	18	272,3	14	277,9	15	325,2	5	333,9	11
19.	G. Pantano	217,6	17	222,4	8	265,3	15	271,3	13	271,7	15	278,4	14	322,6	11	336,0	8
20.	G. Bruni	213,1	20	214,0	20	257,4	19	260,3	19	264,8	19	267,4	20	313,5	18	321,8	20
21.	Z. Baumgartner	213,3	19	216,6	19	255,3	20	259,9	20	264,7	20	269,3	19	310,6	20	327,1	19

Race

Classification & Retirements

Pos.	Driver	Team	Lap	Time	Average
1.	M. Schumacher	Ferrari	66	1:23.54.848	215,852 km/h
2.	J. Button	B.A.R Honda	66	+ 8.388	215,493 km/h
3.	F. Alonso	Renault	66	+ 16.351	215,153 km/h
4.	D. Coulthard	McLaren Mercedes	66	+ 19.231	215,030 km/h
5.	J.P. Montoya	Williams BMW	66	+ 23.055	214,868 km/h
6.	M. Webber	Jaguar	66	+ 41.108	214,103 km/h
7.	A. Pizzonia	Williams BMW	66	+ 41.956	214,068 km/h
8.	T. Sato	B.A.R Honda	66	+ 46.842	213,842 km/h
9.	G. Fisichella	Sauber Petronas	66	+ 1:07.102	213,013 km/h
10.	C. Klien	Jaguar	66	+ 1:08.578	212,951 km/h
11.	J. Trulli	Renault	66	+ 1:10.258	212,881 km/h
12.	R. Barrichello	Ferrari	66	+ 1:13.252	212,756 km/h
13.	F. Massa	Sauber Petronas	65	1 lap	211,734 km/h
14.	O. Panis	Toyota	65	1 lap	211,134 km/h
15.	G. Pantano	Jordan Ford	63	3 laps	205,888 km/h
16.	Z. Baumgartner	Minardi Cosworth	62	4 laps	202,278 km/h
17.	G. Bruni	Minardi Cosworth	62	4 laps	199,821 km/h

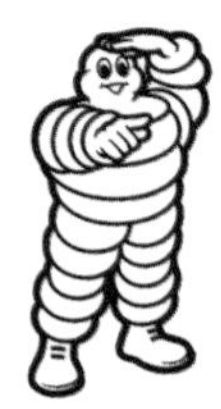

Driver	Team		Reason
N. Heidfeld	Jordan Ford	43	Car undriveable because of balance problem
C. Da Matta	Toyota	39	Right rear tyre blow-out, crash
K. Räikkönen	McLaren Mercedes	14	Rear wing flap pulled off, crash

Fastest laps

	Driver	Time	Lap	Average
1.	K. Räikkönen	1:13.780	10	223,182 km/h
2.	M. Schumacher	1:13.783	5	223,173 km/h
3.	J. Button	1:14.117	11	222,167 km/h
4.	O. Panis	1:14.247	59	221,778 km/h
5.	F. Alonso	1:14.265	8	221,724 km/h
6.	J. Trulli	1:14.386	9	221,364 km/h
7.	J.P. Montoya	1:14.446	10	221,185 km/h
8.	D. Coulthard	1:14.558	8	220,853 km/h
9.	T. Sato	1:14.585	29	220,773 km/h
10.	A. Pizzonia	1:14.586	65	220,770 km/h
11.	M. Webber	1:14.883	65	219,895 km/h
12.	R. Barrichello	1:14.963	59	219,660 km/h
13.	C. Klien	1:15.045	33	219,420 km/h
14.	C. Da Matta	1:15.145	20	219,128 km/h
15.	G. Fisichella	1:15.635	39	217,708 km/h
16.	G. Pantano	1:16.058	63	216,497 km/h
17.	F. Massa	1:16.248	61	215,958 km/h
18.	N. Heidfeld	1:16.903	20	214,119 km/h
19.	G. Bruni	1:18.372	52	210,105 km/h
20.	Z. Baumgartner	1:18.760	18	209,070 km/h

Pit stops

	Driver	Time	Lap	Stop n°
1.	R. Barrichello	25.075	1	1
2.	F. Alonso	21.514	9	2
3.	A. Pizzonia	21.090	9	1
4.	M. Schumacher	23.811	10	1
5.	J. Trulli	21.552	10	1
6.	D. Coulthard	21.693	10	1
7.	T. Sato	21.676	10	1
8.	C. Da Matta	20.981	10	1
9.	K. Räikkönen	23.225	11	1
10.	J.P. Montoya	21.886	11	1
11.	O. Panis	21.985	11	1
12.	M. Webber	21.433	12	1
13.	G. Pantano	23.490	12	1
14.	C. Klien	22.013	13	1
15.	J. Button	21.768	14	1
16.	Z. Baumgartner	23.690	15	1
17.	G. Bruni	1:14.061	16	1
18.	N. Heidfeld	23.180	18	1
19.	G. Fisichella	22.658	21	1
20.	C. Da Matta	21.655	22	2
21.	F. Massa	23.278	23	1
22.	R. Barrichello	22.751	23	2
23.	J.P. Montoya	21.335	27	2
24.	T. Sato	22.077	27	2
25.	M. Schumacher	22.015	28	2
26.	D. Coulthard	21.429	28	2
27.	J. Trulli	28.281	28	2
28.	A. Pizzonia	21.558	28	2
29.	F. Alonso	21.585	29	2
30.	M. Webber	20.860	29	2
31.	O. Panis	21.623	29	2
32.	G. Pantano	23.462	29	2
33.	K. Klien	21.456	31	2
34.	Z. Baumgartner	22.814	30	2
35.	J. Button	20.490	34	2
36.	G. Bruni	23.250	32	2
37.	N. Heidfeld	25.110	38	2
38.	N. Heidfeld	24.164	39	3
39.	G. Fisichella	22.989	44	2
40.	M. Webber	22.563	45	3
41.	J. Trulli	21.286	45	3
42.	F. Massa	22.074	45	2
43.	A. Pizzonia	22.636	46	3
44.	R. Barrichello	22.176	46	3
45.	M. Schumacher	23.665	47	3
46.	F. Alonso	21.197	47	3
47.	D. Coulthard	22.529	47	3
48.	G. Pantano	32.268	46	3
49.	J.P. Montoya	21.813	48	3
50.	T. Sato	22.219	48	3
51.	K. Klien	21.958	48	3
52.	O. Panis	22.348	48	3
53.	Z. Baumgartner	23.261	46	3
54.	J. Button	20.821	50	3
55.	G. Bruni	25.066	49	3
56.	O. Panis	19.895	57	4
57.	G. Pantano	22.790	60	4

Race leaders

Driver	Laps in the lead	Nber of Laps
M. Schumacher	1 > 10	10
K. Räikkönen	11	1
J. Button	12 > 14	3
M. Schumacher	15 > 28	14
F. Alonso	29	1
J. Button	30 > 34	5
M. Schumacher	35 > 47	13
J. Button	48 > 50	3
M. Schumacher	51 > 66	16

Driver	Nber of Laps	Kilometers
M. Schumacher	53	242,422 km
J. Button	11	50,314 km
K. Räikkönen	1	4,574 km
F. Alonso	1	4,574 km

Gaps on the leader board

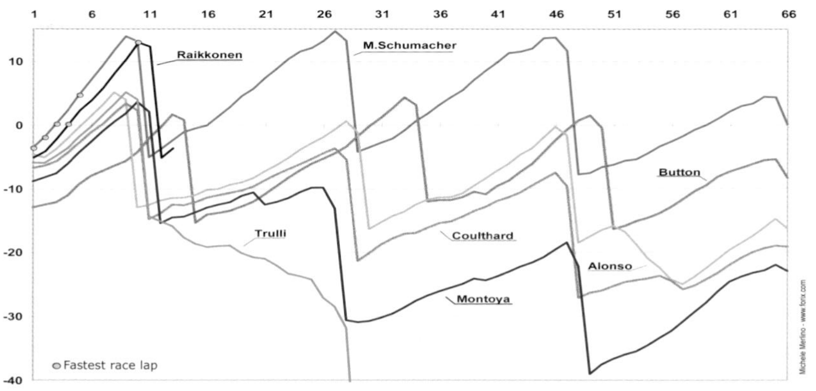

Lap chart

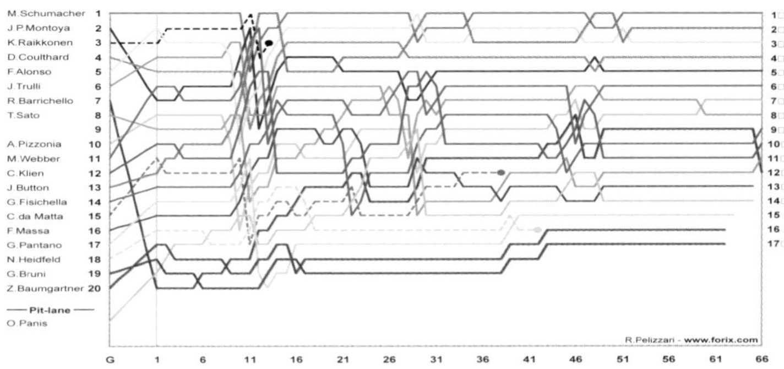

Championship after twelve rounds

Drivers

1. M. Schumacher ....(11 wins) 110
2. R. Barrichello 74
3. J. Button 61
4. J. Trulli ....(1 win) 46
5. F. Alonso 39
6. J.P. Montoya 33
7. D. Coulthard 19
8. K. Räikkönen 18
9. T. Sato..15
10. G. Fisichella 13
11. R. Schumacher 12
12. M. Webber 7
13. F. Massa 5
14. O. Panis 5
15. C. Da Matta..3
16. N. Heidfeld 3
17. T. Glock 2
18. A. Pizzonia 2
19. Z. Baumgartner 1
20. C. Klien 0
21. M. Gené..0
22. G. Pantano 0
23. G. Bruni 0

Constructors

1. Scuderia Ferrari Marlboro ......(11 wins) 184
2. Mild Seven Renault F1 Team ..(1 win) 85
3. Lucky Strike B.A.R Honda 76
4. BMW WilliamsF1 Team.................................47
5. West McLaren Mercedes 37
6. Sauber Petronas...18
7. Panasonic Toyota Racing 8
8. Jaguar Racing 7
9. Jordan Ford 5
10. Minardi Cosworth 1

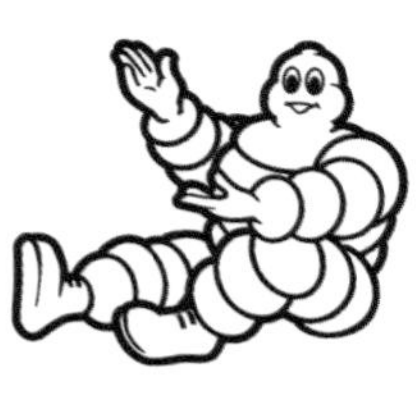

The circuit

Name	Hockenheimring
Length	4574 meters
Distance	67 laps scheduled, 66 completed, 301.884 km
Date	July 25, 2004
Weather	sunny and warm, 27-29°c
Track temperature	41-46°c

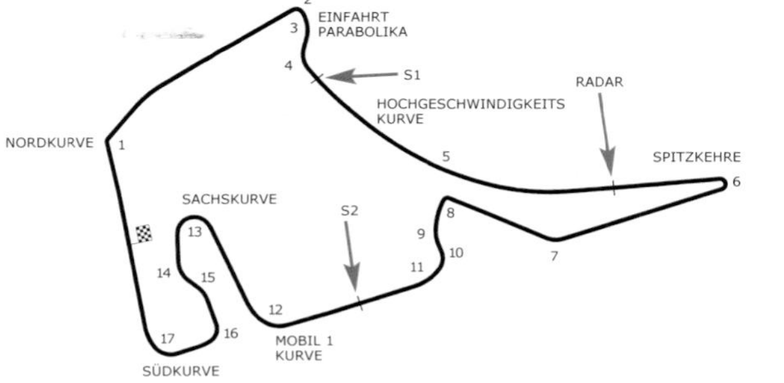

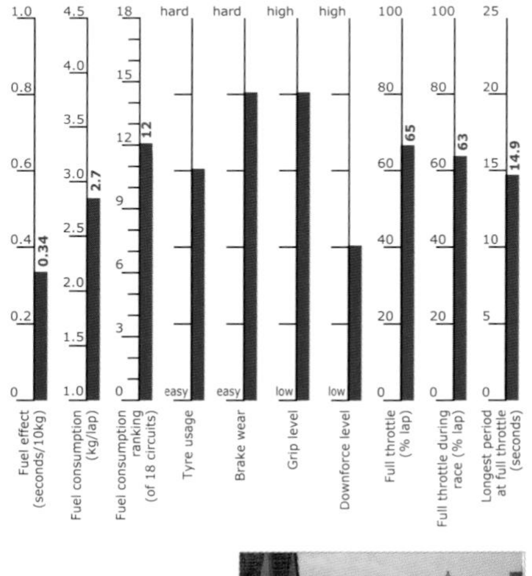

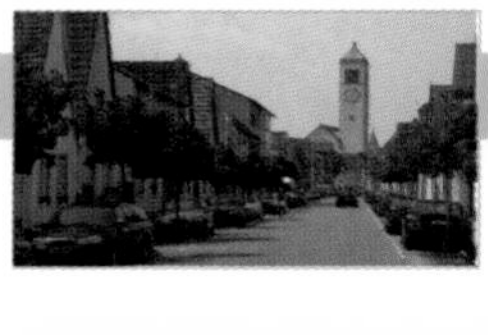

CRUMBS
FOR RENAULT

Once again Ferrari was unbeatable.
On the Budapest circuit where they
had been humbled in 2003 the
Scuderia's cars scored another
double. Michael Schumacher set
pole and led from start to finish to
rack up his twelfth victory of the
season in thirteen races. Thanks to
Rubens's second place Ferrari won
the Constructors' Championship for
the sixth year running, a record.
For their rivals it was just a question
of picking up the crumbs. Alonso
was the best of the rest with a
third- place finish.

> Michael Schumacher comes back into his pit after his quick lap giving him yet another pole position.

> What's Jarno Trulli up to? He was fired by Renault and then found a place at Toyota. However, being dismissed by one's team is never very pleasant. The Italian had been almost voiceless throughout the summer. When he signed with Toyota he suddenly found his powers of speech again!

All red front row in Budapest

Last year Michael Schumacher finished eighth on the same circuit, a lap behind the winner: it was an affront to Ferrari's pride. This year the Scuderia was out for revenge. In 2003, the main problem was the Bridgestone tyres which had suffered from the high temperatures reigning on the Hungarian circuit - over 50°C. The Japanese manufacturer did a lot of work on the rubber used in such heat although on Saturday the temperature did not exceed 25°C on what was a cloudy day.

The result was that both Ferraris were on the front row of the grid over half-a-second ahead of their rivals. *"The new Bridgestones have given us a big advantage,"* said Michael Schumacher on pole. *"They were really exceptional over a lap."*

Both Saubers profited from the Japanese rubber with Giancarlo Fisichella eighth on the grid his best qualifying performance of the season so far. *"What a change in relation to yesterday,"* crowed a delighted Roman. *"We've really improved the car's balance and I felt much more confident in going for it. This being said it won't be easy to score points in the race."*

In brief

> In the Toyota camp Cristiano da Matta was replaced by the team's test driver Brazilian Ricardo Zonta. Thus on Friday the third car was driven by Ryan Briscoe who also has a test contract with the Japanese team. The young Australian took it easy on Friday setting the 21st time.

> Corsican Ange Pasquali the Toyota team manager was fired at the start of the week. He counter-attacked on Friday by distributing a discreet press release: *"I was shocked and surprised to learn that I could no longer fulfil my role as Toyota team manager,"* he stated. He was with the Japanese team for seven years and was given the boot without any explanation. He will certainly attack his former employer for abusive dismissal.

> Kimi Raïkkönen married Jennie, his girl friend and former Miss Scandinavia, in secret. The only visible sign was her huge engagement ring.

Starting grid

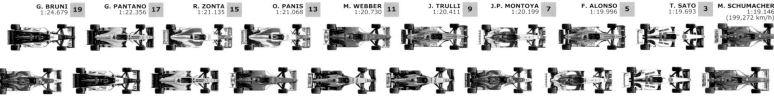

* Z. BAUGARTNER
Starts from pit lane

** F. MASSA
Penalty for an engine change

Pos	Driver	Time
19	G. BRUNI	1:24.679
17	G. PANTANO	1:22.356
15	R. ZONTA	1:21.135
13	O. PANIS	1:21.068
11	M. WEBBER	1:20.730
9	J. TRULLI	1:20.411
7	J.P. MONTOYA	1:20.199
5	F. ALONSO	1:19.996
3	T. SATO	1:19.693
1	M. SCHUMACHER	1:19.146 (199,272 km/h)
20	F. MASSA**	-
18	Z. BAUMGARTNER*	1:24.329
16	N. HEIDFELD	1:22.180
14	C. KLIEN	1:21.118
12	D. COULTHARD	1:20.897
10	K. RÄIKKÖNEN	1:20.570
8	G. FISICHELLA	1:20.324
6	A. PIZZONIA	1:20.170
4	J. BUTTON	1:19.700
2	R. BARRICHELLO	1:19.323

<
A delighted Michael
Schumacher sprayed the
whole Ferrari team from
the rostrum in Hungary.

Michael Schumacher's round dozen

Nobody got near Michael Schumacher during his triumphal march towards victory in Budapest. He didn't even lose his lead during refuelling. But was it a doddle for the German? *"It looked easy from the outside,"* he stated, *"but this wasn't really the case as the circuit is very demanding. You've no time to relax and I could only ease off after the final refuelling stop."*

Ferrari's uncontested supremacy made for a very boring race but a frenzied atmosphere reigned in the paddock after the finish.

Ferrari and Bridgestone were delighted with this new Constructors' Championship. Elsewhere there

were long faces because the previous year the fact that Ferrari finished a lap behind gave its rivals hope that here at least they could beat the Scuderia. Some hope!

The ambience in the Renault camp, winners in 2003, was more sombre than elsewhere. Flavio Briatore fired off a volley in front of his motor home. *"How do you expect us to win with such tyres,"* he thundered repeating the words of his driver? *" We're second in the championship but we're a little bit far away from the tyre point of view,"* Alonso had said during the press conference.

The winners admitted that their success was due in large part to the new Bridgestones. *"We had a big

test session on the Jerez circuit which enabled us to choose the right mixtures for here,"* declared Michael Schumacher. *"On Friday I knew I'd be in the ballpark."* With five grand prix to go to the end of the season the German was thirty-eight points ahead of his team-mate who was the only one, mathematically speaking, able to stop him from being crowned for the seventh time.

A win in Belgium would give him the title; if not he would have to wait until the Italian Grand Prix. *"Both circuits have a special meaning for me,"* he commented. *"I'll do what I can. As long as I enjoy driving and winning, I'll continue."*

Fernando Alonso
finished third for
the second race
in succession.
∨

A word from Jean Todt after Ferrari's sixth consecutive title

In Budapest the Scuderia won its sixth Constructors' World Championship title on the trot, beating its own records. *"It's true,"* smiled Jean Todt after the race. *"Today we've written a new page in Ferrari's extraordinary history: a sixth constructors' title and the certainty that we'll win the drivers' one too. We owe this triumph not only to our drivers but also to the whole team as it has done a remarkable job. And of course, our suppliers especially Bridgestone which has played a key role in helping us attain our goal."*

The Scuderia boss underlined the fact that there would be no letting up. *" Ferrari is more than just a team; it's a legend that Enzo Ferrari created.*
Tomorrow we'll celebrate out title at the factory with the whole staff and the President Luca di Montezemolo: a title is always special. The day we get used to it we'll probably not be as competitive." The next day at 18h00 the Maranello factory rang to the sounds of celebration.

Hello Planet earth!

Sometimes in the garages the ambience is more space conquest than motor sport. But it's all part of the magic of F1!

> Olivier Panis had a fairly anonymous race. He qualified thirteenth and finished eleventh.

Fisichella qualified eighth and finished in the same place giving Sauber a precious point. "*A point's not a lot, but I'm very happy to have scored it,*" he said. "*The race went exactly as planned from start to finish. The car perfectly well balanced and I didn't make a mistake.*"

∨

Nick Heidfeld qualified sixteenth and finished twelfth.

∨

A wasted meeting in Budapest

To everybody's surprise given Michael Schumacher's domination the F1 Grand Prix TV audience is slightly up during the summer in relation to 2003. However, all the protagonists admit that something has to be done to add spice to the races, which have become increasingly processional.

To achieve this both the FIA and some teams have made proposals. The latest from Tony Purnell, the Jaguar boss, suggests replacing the present qualify system with mini 10 lap races. From a technically point of view the engineers speak about reducing overall grip through modifying the front and rear wings which would enable the cars to follow each other more closely in corners thus facilitating overtaking.

The FIA wants to reduce the teams' budgets and the speed of the cars. This season has seen a fall in lap times of around two or three seconds which calls the drivers' safety into question and the Federation wants to reduce performances to a more reasonable level. In F1 any regulation change requires the unanimous agreement of the teams. This is impossible to achieve when it comes to reconciling interests as diverse as those of Minardi or Ferrari; the former's budget is around 43 million dollars while the latter's is in the region of 400 million! Thus the Scuderia refuses to limit testing between races – all the more so as it has two circuits, Fiorano and Mugello – while the other teams favour such a limitation. As unanimity could not be reached these changes could not be applied. A final meeting was held on Sunday in Budapest but once again it was a setback, like the one at Hockenheim. "*At least we've progressed on one point,*" quipped Flavio Briatore. "*In the past it took five hours to come up with nothing. Now it takes only two!*"

If no agreement is found the FIA will impose its own ideas which risks making a lot of people very unhappy. But if that's what F1 requires...!

Jenson Button keeps mum about his future

Jenson Button was invited to the Thursday press conference along with Mark Webber. He did not give any information about his future with either Williams-BMW or BAR both of which claim to have a contract with him for 2005. "*I've had some good times with BAR,*" he muttered. "*The ambience in the team is still good. We talk to each other. We're there to do a job, to try and win the Hungarian Grand Prix, and we're going to do it.*"

Technically the Williams had a new more conventional nose replacing the 'walrus' used up to then.

Practice

All the time trials

N°	Driver	N° Chassis - Engine	Practice 1 Friday	Pos.	Practice 2 Friday	Pos.	Practice 3 Saturday	Pos.	Practice 4 Saturday	Pos.	Pre-qual. Saturday	Pos.	Qualif. Saturday	Pos.
1.	Michael Schumacher	Ferrari F2004 239	1:21.552	1	1:21.009	2	1:20.216	1	1:19.747	2	1:19.107	2	1:19.146	1
2.	Rubens Barrichello	Ferrari F2004 240	1:21.938	2	1:21.712	9	1:20.830	5	1:19.768	3	1:18.436	1	1:19.323	2
3.	Juan Pablo Montoya	Williams FW26 06 - BMW	1:23.753	6	1:21.185	3	1:20.696	3	1.20.480	8	1:19.821	6	1:20.199	7
4.	Antonio Pizzonia	Williams FW26 07 - BMW	1:24.381	16	1:21.574	7	1:20.482	2	1:19.913	4	1:20.019	9	1:20.170	6
5.	David Coulthard	McLaren MP4-19B 03 - Mercedes	1:23.100	5	1:21.203	4	1.21.555	8	1:20.914	12	1:21.192	16	1.20.897	12
6.	Kimi Räikkönen	McLaren MP4-19B 01 - Mercedes	1:23.024	4	1:20.884	1	1:21.825	10	1:20.614	10	1:20.066	10	1:20.570	10
7.	Jarno Trulli	Renault R24-05	1:24.124	9	1:22.788	17	1:21.257	6	1:20.130	5	1:19.879	8	1:20.411	9
8.	Fernando Alonso	Renault R24-04	1:24.191	11	1:21.948	10	1:21.392	7	1:20.363	7	1.20.135	11	1:19.996	5
9.	Jenson Button	B.A.R 006-05 - Honda	1:24.140	10	1:21.685	8	1:20.731	4	1:19.556	1	1:19.878	7	1:19.700	4
10.	Takuma Sato	B.A.R 006-06 - Honda	1:25.071	19	1:21.364	6		20	1:20.363	6	1:19.695	5	1:19.693	3
11.	Giancarlo Fisichella	Sauber C23-04 - Petronas	1.24.198	12	1:22.743	16	1:22.013	13	1:21.165	14	1:19.668	4	1.20.324	8
12.	Felipe Massa	Sauber C23-01 - Petronas	1:25.218	20	1:23.188	22	1:21.593	9	1:21.989	17	1:19.658	3		20
14.	Mark Webber	Jaguar R5-05		25	1:21.999	11	1:22.068	14	1:21.112	13	1:21.452	17	1:20.730	11
15.	Christian Klien	Jaguar R5-01	1:25.834	21	1:23.003	20	1:22.421	15	1:21.390	15	1:21.510	18	1:21.118	14
16.	Ricardo Zonta	Toyota TF104/10B	1:24.236	13	1:22.808	18	1:21.927	12	1:20.606	9	1:20.199	12	1:21.135	15
17.	Olivier Panis	Toyota TF104/09B	1:23.827	7	1:21.352	5	1:21.838	11	1:20.689	11	1:20.491	14	1:21.068	13
18.	Nick Heidfeld	Jordan EJ14/03 - Ford	1:24.462	17	1:22.651	14	1:23.242	18	1:21.712	16	1:20.439	13	1:22.180	16
19.	Giorgio Pantano	Jordan EJ14/02 - Ford	1:24.353	15	1:22.937	19	1:22.709	16	1:23.083	18	1:21.187	15	1:22.356	17
20.	Gianmaria Bruni	Minardi PS04B/02 - Cosworth	1:28.893	24	1:26.365	25	1:23.112	17	1:23.979	19	1:23.362	19	1.24.479	19
21.	Zsolt Baumgartner	Minardi PS04B/01 - Cosworth	1:28.296	23	1:25.450	24	1:24.233	19	1:24.522	20	1:24.656	20	1:24.329	18
35.	Anthony Davidson	B.A.R 006-04 - Honda	1:21.951	3	1:22.356	12								
37.	Björn Wirdheim	Jaguar R5-03	1:24.265	14	1:22.559	13								
38.	Ryan Briscoe	Toyota TF104/07	1:24.108	8	1:23.170	21								
39.	Timo Glock	Jordan EJ14/01 - Ford	1:24.843	18	1:22.697	15								
40.	Bas Leinders	Minardi PS04B/03 - Cosworth	1:26.074	22	1:25.339	23								

Maximum speed

N°	Driver	P1 Qualifs	Pos.	P1 Race	Pos.	P2 Qualifs	Pos.	P2 Race	Pos.	Finish Qualifs	Pos.	Finish Race	Pos.	Trap Qualifs	Pos.	Trap Race	Pos.
1.	M. Schumacher	299,8	1	303,3	2	248,9	4	250,8	4	260,1	1	263,6	2	300,3	1	313,8	1
2.	R. Barrichello	298,9	2	304,1	1	249,3	3	253,2	1	259,8	2	265,0	1	299,1	4	313,6	2
3.	J.P. Montoya	297,8	6	300,8	10	245,1	10	251,1	3	256,8	9	258,9	8	298,7	5	309,0	6
4.	A. Pizzonia	298,0	5	301,5	6	247,1	8	249,3	7	257,0	8	260,0	5	296,9	7	308,3	8
5.	D. Coulthard	298,0	4	301,5	5	244,5	11	245,1	15	257,7	4	261,5	3	299,7	2	306,3	13
6.	K. Räikkönen	297,7	7	301,5	7	244,5	12	249,1	10	257,2	6	257,8	12	298,6	6	307,3	9
7.	J. Trulli	294,9	11	301,8	4	242,0	15	243,6	18	254,9	11	257,2	14	295,0	10	306,2	14
8.	F. Alonso	295,7	10	299,8	12	245,6	9	247,1	13	257,1	7	259,9	6	295,0	9	311,0	4
9.	J. Button	296,0	8	298,9	14	252,1	1	252,3	2	256,7	10	257,4	13	292,6	14	303,7	18
10.	T. Sato	295,8	9	297,7	16	234,7	17	250,6	5	259,7	3	258,3	11	295,8	8	304,2	17
11.	G. Fisichella	298,4	3	302,6	3	250,0	2	249,1	9	257,7	5	260,8	4	299,2	3	309,4	5
12.	F. Massa			301,5	8			248,1	11			259,8	7			312,0	3
14.	M. Webber	293,2	13	299,5	13	248,0	6	249,9	6	253,5	13	258,8	9	294,1	12	308,7	7
15.	C. Klien	291,7	15	300,2	11	240,8	16	247,3	12	252,3	16	254,9	17	294,2	11	306,9	10
16.	F. Zonta	291,5	16	295,0	17	243,4	13	243,8	17	253,5	14	256,2	16	289,0	18	306,9	11
17.	O. Panis	289,6	17	294,0	18	247,2	7	249,2	8	254,6	12	258,6	10	292,1	15	304,6	16
18.	N. Heidfeld	293,1	14	298,4	15	248,4	5	245,8	14	252,9	15	256,4	15	293,6	13	305,1	15
19.	G. Pantano	293,6	12	301,0	9	242,3	14	244,6	16	251,1	17	254,8	18	291,4	16	306,5	12
20.	G. Bruni	283,4	19	286,3	20	233,8	19	234,3	20	246,4	19	248,6	20	288,3	19	296,5	20
21.	Z. Baumgartner	288,1	18	288,2	19	234,0	18	238,4	19	251,0	18	250,0	19	290,7	17	298,0	19

Race

Classification & Retirements

Pos.	Driver	Team	Lap	Time	Average
1.	M. Schumacher	Ferrari	70	1:35.26.131	192,798 km/h
2.	R. Barrichello	Ferrari	70	+ 4.696	192,640 km/h
3.	F. Alonso	Renault	70	+ 44.599	191,307 km/h
4.	J.P. Montoya	Williams BMW	70	+ 1:02.613	190,712 km/h
5.	J. Button	B.A.R Honda	70	+ 1:07.439	190,553 km/h
6.	T. Sato	B.A.R Honda	69	1 lap	190,027 km/h
7.	A. Pizzonia	Williams BMW	69	1 lap	189,990 km/h
8.	G. Fisichella	Sauber Petronas	69	1 lap	189,136 km/h
9.	D. Coulthard	McLaren Mercedes	69	1 lap	189,068 km/h
10.	M. Webber	Jaguar	69	1 lap	188,215 km/h
11.	O. Panis	Toyota	69	1 lap	187,685 km/h
12.	N. Heidfeld	Jordan Ford	68	2 laps	186,220 km/h
13.	C. Klien	Jaguar	68	2 laps	184,979 km/h
14.	G. Bruni	Minardi Cosworth	66	4 laps	179,260 km/h
15.	Z. Baumgartner	Minardi Cosworth	65	5 laps	177,838 km/h

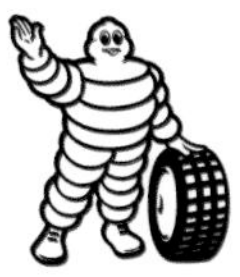

Driver	Team		Reason
G. Pantano	Jordan Ford	49	Gearbox failure
J. Trulli	Renault	42	Drop of engine oil pressure
R. Zonta	Toyota	32	Loss of power because of electrical problems
F. Massa	Sauber Petronas	22	Brake problems
K. Räikkönen	McLaren Mercedes	14	Engine cuts out with electrical problem

Fastest laps

	Driver	Time	Lap	Average
1.	M. Schumacher	1:19.071	29	199,461 km/h
2.	R. Barrichello	1:19.213	29	199,103 km/h
3.	F. Alonso	1:20.275	49	196,469 km/h
4.	J. Button	1:20.425	47	196,103 km/h
5.	A. Pizzonia	1:20.501	48	195,918 km/h
6.	J. Trulli	1:20.705	10	195,422 km/h
7.	J.P. Montoya	1:20.715	49	195,398 km/h
8.	M. Webber	1:20.825	45	195,132 km/h
9.	G. Fisichella	1:21.022	53	194,658 km/h
10.	T. Sato	1:21.030	10	194,639 km/h
11.	D. Coulthard	1:21.134	67	194,389 km/h
12.	O. Panis	1:21.310	50	193,968 km/h
13.	N. Heidfeld	1:21.518	68	193,473 km/h
14.	K. Räikkönen	1:21.678	6	193,094 km/h
15.	F. Massa	1:21.856	14	192,674 km/h
16.	R. Zonta	1:22.525	13	191,112 km/h
17.	C. Klien	1:22.530	45	191,101 km/h
18.	G. Pantano	1:22.927	43	190,186 km/h
19.	G. Bruni	1:24.601	65	186,423 km/h
20.	Z. Baumgartner	1:24.855	63	185,865 km/h

Pit stops

	Driver	Time	Lap	Stop n°
1.	F. Alonso	21.033	1	1
2.	G. Fisichella	21.677	9	1
3.	R. Barrichello	21.330	9	1
4.	J.P. Montoya	21.858	10	1
5.	J. Button	21.464	10	1
6.	J. Trulli	21.008	10	1
7.	D. Coulthard	21.813	10	1
8.	R. Zonta	21.944	10	1
9.	M. Schumacher	20.989	11	1
10.	T. Sato	21.251	11	1
11.	K. Räikkönen	24.834	11	1
12.	O. Panis	21.602	12	1
13.	F. Massa	21.909	12	1
14.	G. Bruni	22.695	13	1
15.	G. Pantano	22.466	14	1
16.	A. Pizzonia	21.211	15	1
17.	N. Heidfeld	22.916	16	1
18.	C. Klien	24.140	18	1
19.	M. Webber	22.260	21	1
20.	Z. Baumgartner	22.166	22	1
21.	F. Massa	41.537	23	2
22.	R. Zonta	21.652	23	2
23.	T. Sato	20.605	27	2
24.	F. Alonso	21.826	27	2
25.	N. Heidfeld	28.684	28	2
26.	J.P. Montoya	21.501	28	2
27.	J. Button	21.044	28	2
28.	G. Fisichella	22.478	28	2
29.	R. Barrichello	21.701	29	2
30.	J. Trulli	21.724	29	2
31.	M. Schumacher	21.805	29	2
32.	M. Webber	21.242	31	2
33.	O. Panis	23.675	30	2
34.	D. Coulthard	21.712	34	2
35.	G. Bruni	22.551	32	2
36.	G. Pantano	22.116	38	2
37.	A. Pizzonia	20.623	39	2
38.	K. Klien	21.774	44	2
39.	Z. Baumgartner	30.540	45	2
40.	J. Trulli	20.694	45	3
41.	M. Webber	22.495	45	3
42.	T. Sato	22.545	46	3
43.	J. Button	23.149	46	3
44.	R. Barrichello	21.365	47	3
45.	G. Pantano	23.476	47	3
46.	A. Pizzonia	24.191	47	3
47.	M. Schumacher	21.983	46	3
48.	N. Heidfeld	21.868	48	3
49.	K. Klien	22.927	48	3
50.	F. Alonso	21.373	48	3
51.	G. Bruni	22.514	48	3
52.	G. Fisichella	21.532	46	3
53.	O. Panis	21.061	50	3
54.	J.P. Montoya	21.809	49	3
55.	D. Coulthard	21.263	57	3
56.	Z. Baumgartner	22.147	60	3

Race leader

Driver	Laps in the lead	Nber of Laps
M. Schumacher	1 > 70	70

Driver	Nber of Laps	Kilometers
M. Schumacher	70	306,663 km

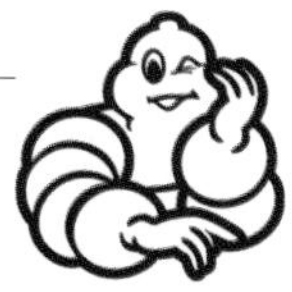

Lap chart

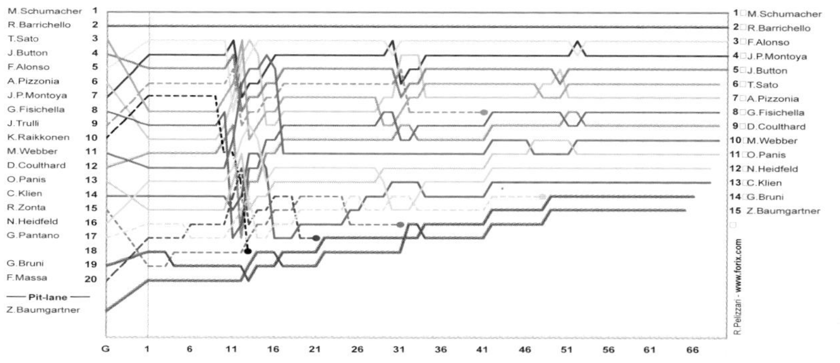

Gaps on the leader board

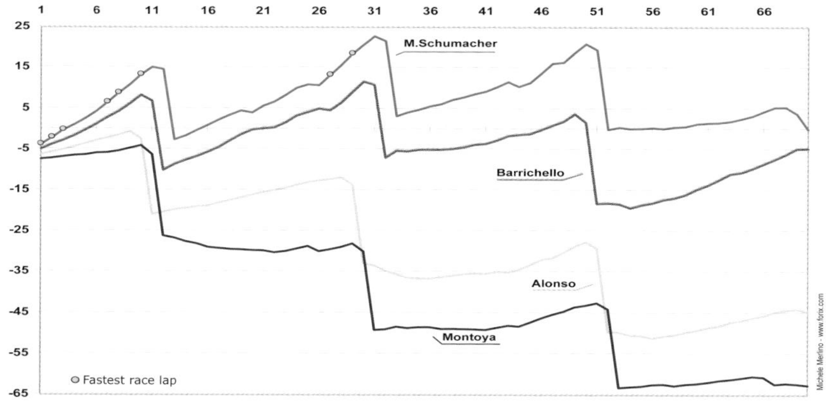

Championship after thirteen rounds

Drivers

1. M. Schumacher ....(12 wins) 120
2. R. Barrichello 82
3. J. Button 65
4. J. Trulli ....(1 win) 46
5. F. Alonso 45
6. J.P. Montoya 38
7. D. Coulthard 19
8. K. Räikkönen 18
9. T. Sato 18
10. G. Fisichella 14
11. R. Schumacher 12
12. M. Webber 7
13. F. Massa 5
14. O. Panis 5
15. A. Pizzonia 4
16. C. Da Matta 3
17. N. Heidfeld 3
18. T. Glock 2
19. Z. Baumgartner 1
20. C. Klien 0
21. M. Gené 0
22. G. Pantano 0
23. G. Bruni 0

Constructors

1. **Scuderia Ferrari Marlboro** .(12 wins) 202
2. Mild Seven Renault F1 Team ..(1 win) 91
3. Lucky Strike B.A.R Honda 83
4. BMW WilliamsF1 Team.................................54
5. West McLaren Mercedes 37
6. Sauber Petronas...19
7. Panasonic Toyota Racing 8
8. Jaguar Racing 7
9. Jordan Ford 5
10. Minardi Cosworth 1

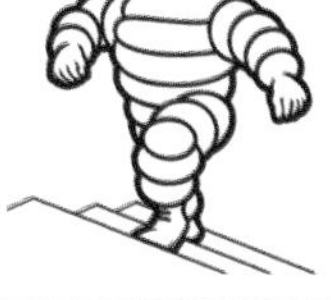

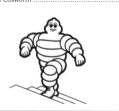

The circuit

Name	Hungaroring, Budapest
Length	4381 meters
Distance	70 laps, 306.663 km
Date	August 15, 2004
Weather	sunny and warm, 25-27°c
Track temperature	37-48°c

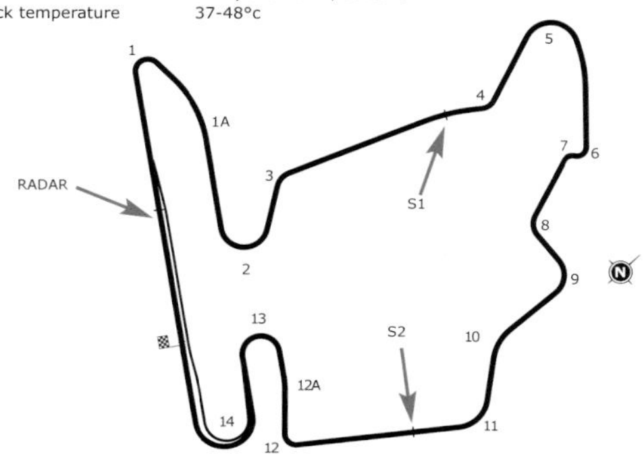

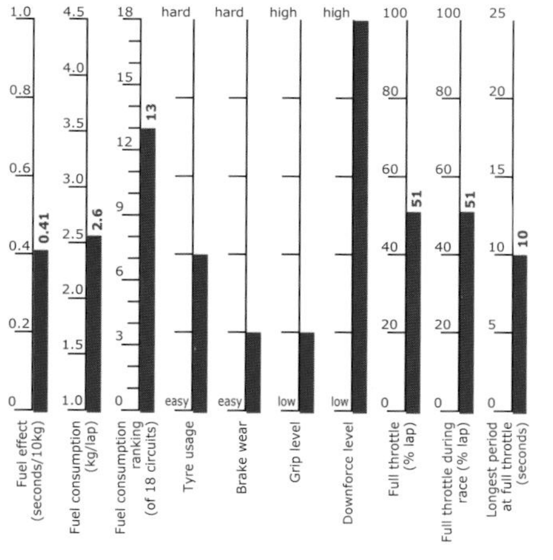

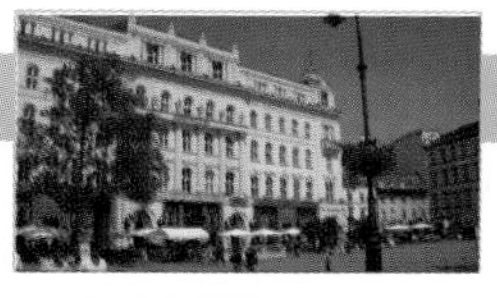

KIMI ON TOP

The magnificent Spa-Francorchamps circuit. Three safety car periods, half the field eliminated and a winner who started from tenth place on the grid. The Belgian Grand Prix was the most closely contested of the year and at the flag, both Kimi Raikkonen and Michael Schumacher were crowned. There were two winners at the end of a classic race.

>
A new hairstyle for Jarno Trulli and a pole position in his pocket. It was partly down to luck, as the Italian was the first to be able to switch to dry weather tyres on a drying track.

Number 7 in the Spa lottery

"It's always a gamble in the rain." After qualifying, Michael Schumacher preferred to take the philosophical approach rather than curse the elements, which did not help him at all. He was last out on track, when the downpour was at its strongest. Earlier in the session, several drivers had been able to run intermediate tyres and make the most of a lull in the rain.

In fact, given the awful conditions when he was on his quick lap, the German drove exceptionally to secure himself a ticket for a front row start. *"It's true that in a way it is quite an achievement,"* he admitted without any false modesty. *"But my lap was not fantastic and the car slid in turn 5...with the tyres Jarno (Trulli) used, he had better grip under braking and acceleration. So, in one sense, I am happy with second in these conditions. Luck played a big part, but I'm not complaining."* The lottery picked up number 7, which belonged to Jarno Trulli. Naturally, the Renault driver was delighted with the way things worked out. He had cocked a snook at his team that had just sacked him, bringing in Giancarlo Fisichella for the next season. Never one to feel embarrassed, his boss Flavio Briatore still hugged him to his bosom after qualifying in celebration of this pole position. *"This pole comes at just the right time,"* admitted the little Italian, all smiles. *"I like Monaco, where I took pole back in May and I like Spa, which is one of my favourite circuits. But I have to say I was a bit pumped up today. At the very last moment, I decided to fit intermediate tyres. It was the right choice and then, as luck would have it, it started to rain again after my quick lap. It didn't make life easy for those running after me."*

The rain really started to come down during Juan Pablo Montoya's lap. Those who came after the Colombian; the two Saubers, the two Ferraris and Kimi Raikkonen were forced to fit extreme wets, which meant they had no chance of beating the Renault.

>
Heavy rain and persistent fog forced the stewards to delay the Saturday morning session, so that only 15 minutes of track time were available. This much shortened practice was reduced still further when Antonio Pizzonia and Gianmaria Bruni went off the road at the same time, at opposite ends of the track. It brought the wettest session of the year to a premature end.

Starting grid

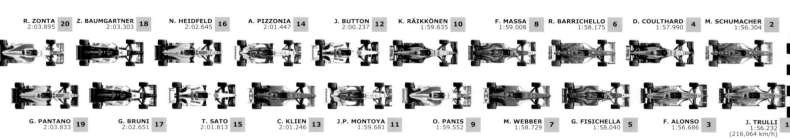

R. ZONTA 20	Z. BAUMGARTNER 18	N. HEIDFELD 16	A. PIZZONIA 14	J. BUTTON 12	K. RÄIKKÖNEN 10	F. MASSA 8	R. BARRICHELLO 6	D. COULTHARD 4	M. SCHUMACHER 2
2:03.895	2:03.303	2:02.645	2:01.447	2:00.237	1:59.635	1:59.008	1:58.175	1:57.990	1:56.304

G. PANTANO 19	G. BRUNI 17	T. SATO 15	C. KLIEN 13	J.P. MONTOYA 11	O. PANIS 9	M. WEBBER 7	G. FISICHELLA 5	F. ALONSO 3	J. TRULLI 1
2:03.833	2:02.651	2:01.813	2:01.246	1:59.681	1:59.552	1:58.729	1:58.040	1:56.686	1:56.232 (216,064 km/h)

A crazy grand prix at Spa. Kimi wins, Michael is champion

It was all over. With a 40 point lead over Rubens Barrichello and with four grands prix remaining, mathematically, Michael Schumacher could not be caught and therefore he took his seventh world championship title here in Spa.

All he needed to do was to score two more points than his team-mate. It was almost all over right at the start, as the Brazilian was caught up in the opening lap mayhem. At the first corner there were two collisions, one involving Kimi Raikkonen and Felipe Massa and the other, Giancarlo Fisichella and Olivier Panis. One corner further on, Takuma Sato got it all wrong and it

Michael in seventh heaven

In Spa, Michael Schumacher took his seventh world championship title, thus extending the record he held already still further. *"You never get used to this sort of thing,"* he commented. *"Each title has brought me different emotions. Today is really very special. To become champion here at Spa, a circuit that means so much to me and to do it in Ferrari's 700th grand prix, is really special. I made my F1 debut here, I took my first win here and it now feels as though it has come full circle. I am trying to stay calm, but I think we will have a big party tonight."*

Paradoxically, it had been the first time he had not won, apart from the accident in Monaco. *"It was a tough fight. I would have preferred to take my seventh title with a win, but today, we just weren't quick enough. We have won so much so far that it had to happen one day. Kimi was the best here, but the race was made a bit more complicated with the three Safety Car periods."*

provoked a chain reaction that also eliminated Mark Webber, Gianmaria Bruni and Giorgio Pantano. Also hit, Rubens Barrichello pitted at the end of the opening lap to change tyres, thinking he had a puncture. Then he came in again next time round to change his rear wing. *"It was a difficult moment,"* he recalled. *"I was not thinking about the consequences. The team was talking to me during these stops as if I was sitting quietly at home in the lounge. They told me to get going again and to push hard. And that's what I did."*

The Brazilian battled hard and worked his way through the field from last to third, profiting from the retirement of many of those ahead of him.
In the end, it was Kimi Raikkonen, charging off from

the depths of tenth place on the grid, who took the win. By lap 6 he was up to third.. From then on, he just had to wait for the two Renaults to retire. Jarno Trulli kindly obliged after his first pit stop and Fernando Alonso did the same with oil on his tyres. However, Raikkonen did not have an easy time of it. *"Just after I passed Michael, I had a problem with the gearbox. Every time I changed down, the car accelerated and I had to fight it for all the race and was quite slow at times."*

It was the Finn's first win of the year and the second of his career. At least the McLarens now seemed to be on the pace. *"It's an excellent day for us,"* he concluded. *"Now, we have solved our problems and I hope we will be able to win other races and fight against Michael next season."*

The Spa waters

Spa is a water town, what with its mineral waters and its eternal rain. Hardly a day goes by in this part of the Ardennes that it does not rain and the 2004 race weekend was no exception. Saturday morning practice was almost a complete wash out because of the terrible conditions on track. Then, in the afternoon, it was Jarno Trulli who got the best of the weather, to put himself on pole.

Nine points for Sauber

Felipe Massa fourth, Giancarlo Fisichella fifth: the Sauber team left Belgium with nine unexpected points.

Things had got off to a bad start for Massa, who saw his front wing fly off after a collision at the first corner, with eventual winner, Kimi Raikkonen. The Brazilian was forced to pit at the end of the opening lap for repairs and then he had to stop again one lap later, because of serious vibrations coming up through the steering wheel. Having changed the wheel, he rejoined the race one from last.

Luckily, the Safety Car had slowed the field. With the race underway again, the Sauber driver began to attack and moved up the order. *"I was so disappointed after the start,"* he said. *"I had not seen Kimi, who was coming down the outside and then Sato hit me hard from behind! After that, the car was vibrating a lot, but at least I could push on. Without that accident, maybe I could have got on the podium. I was lucky really. It makes up for all the bad luck I had in the last five races."*

Team-mate Giancarlo Fisichella finished fifth. He was also involved in an accident at the first corner. *"Someone ran into me from behind (it was Olivier Panis) and after that, my car lost grip."* A further minor off-track excursion on lap 20, which broke a front wing deflector, aggravated the situation. With both his cars in the points, Peter Sauber could not be happier. *"We showed what we can do if we don't give up,"* he concluded.

Weekend gossip

> The 2005 regulations were the subject of much debate. From a technical point of view, the engineers were complaining that they still did not know what rules governed the design of their 2005 cars. *"It was very urgent four months ago,"* said a bitterly ironic Geoff Willis, the BAR technical director. As for Williams, there were even suggestions that the FIA was colluding with the Renault and Ferrari teams, the English team claiming that these two were the only ones to know the specifications for the 2005 cars.

> Maybe it was married life that had given Jarno Trulli wings during qualifying. The Italian revealed he had secretly got married to Barbara, his long time girlfriend. *"Actually, it* was unplanned,*"* he said. *"Barbara and me just thought it was a good time to get married. But as the season still has a long way to go, we have not celebrated yet. The party will have to wait."*

> Spa was Ferrari's 700th grand prix. On Saturday, Rubens Barrichello appeared to have got hold of the wrong end of the stick, when he explained in a press conference, that the Scuderia was celebrating its 700th birthday!

> Three of the most competitive teams of the moment, Renault, BAR and Williams, all failed to score points in Spa, testifying to a race rich in incident.

results

Practice

All the time trials

N°	Driver	N° Chassis - Engine	Practice 1 Friday	Pos.	Practice 2 Friday	Pos.	Practice 3 Saturday	Pos.	Practice 4 Saturday	Pos.	Pre-qual. Saturday	Pos.	Qualif. Saturday	Pos.
1.	Michael Schumacher	Ferrari F2004 239	1:45.408	2	1:45.137	3	cancelled:		1:57.906	2	1:53.755	1	1:56.304	2
2.	Rubens Barrichello	Ferrari F2004 240	1:45.605	3	1:45.625	8	bad conditions		1:57.085	1	1:54.913	2	1:58.175	6
3.	Juan Pablo Montoya	Williams FW26 06 - BMW	1:47.560	12	1:45.678	10	meteorological		2:02.559	14	1:56.842	6	1:59.681	11
4.	Antonio Pizzonia	Williams FW26 07 - BMW	1:47.083	9	1:45.559	7	(fog and rain)		2:07.337	19	1:59.100	12	2:01.447	14
5.	David Coulthard	McLaren MP4-19B 03 - Mercedes	1:47.650	15	1:45.507	6			1:58.434	5	1:56.994	7	1.57.990	4
6.	Kimi Räikkönen	McLaren MP4-19B 01 - Mercedes	1:46.674	5	1:44.701	1			1:57.975	3	1:55.371	3	1:59.635	10
7.	Jarno Trulli	Renault R24-05	1:47.829	17	1:46.912	16			1:59.519	8	1:58.606	9	1:56.232	1
8.	Fernando Alonso	Renault R24-04	1:46.679	6	1:45.658	9			2:01.475	10	1.58.242	8	1:56.686	3
9.	Jenson Button	B.A.R 006-05 - Honda	1:47.511	11	1:45.015	2			1:59.182	7	1:58.837	10	1:00.237	12
10.	Takuma Sato	B.A.R 006-06 - Honda	1:47.618	13	1:45.451	5			2:00.088	9	1:58.929	11	2:01.813	15
11.	Giancarlo Fisichella	Sauber C23-04 - Petronas	1:47.648	14	1:45.978	12			1:58.138	4	1:56.068	5	1:58.040	5
12.	Felipe Massa	Sauber C23-01 - Petronas	1:47.765	16	1:45.960	11			1:58.864	6	1:56.057	4	1:59.008	8
14.	Mark Webber	Jaguar R5-05	1:46.782	7	1:46.471	13			2:02.501	13	1:59.437	13	1:58.729	7
15.	Christian Klien	Jaguar R5-01	1:46.809	8	1:47.370	18			2:02.411	12	1:59.997	15	2:01.246	13
16.	Ricardo Zonta	Toyota TF104/10B	1:48.642	18	1:46.902	15			2:02.175	11		20	2:03.895	20
17.	Olivier Panis	Toyota TF104/09B	1:48.834	19	1:46.528	14			2:02.592	15	2:01.472	18	1:59.552	9
18.	Nick Heidfeld	Jordan EJ14/03 - Ford	1:50.805	24	1:48.803	21			2:03.556	16	2:00.166	16	2:02.645	16
19.	Giorgio Pantano	Jordan EJ14/02 - Ford	1:50.165	20	1:48.962	23			2:04.131	17	1:59.442	14	2:03.833	19
20.	Gianmaria Bruni	Minardi PS04B/02 - Cosworth	1:50.531	23	1:49.742	25			2:05.485	18	2:03.226	19	2:02.651	17
21.	Zsolt Baumgartner	Minardi PS04B/01 - Cosworth	1:50.950	25	1:48.687	20			2:09.428	20	2:01.195	17	2:03.303	18
35.	Anthony Davidson	B.A.R 006-04 - Honda	1:45.104	1	1:45.437	4								
37.	Björn Wirdheim	Jaguar R5-03	1:46.658	4	1:47.265	17								
38.	Ryan Briscoe	Toyota TF104/04	1:47.506	10	1:47.634	19								
39.	Timo Glock	Jordan EJ14/01 - Ford	1:50.317	22	1:48.817	22								
40.	Bas Leinders	Minardi PS04B/03 - Cosworth	1:50.311	21	1:49.480	24								

Maximum speed

N°	Driver	P1 Qualifs	Pos.	P1 Race	Pos.	P2 Qualifs	Pos.	P2 Race	Pos.	Finish Qualifs	Pos.	Finish Race	Pos.	Trap Qualifs	Pos.	Trap Race	Pos.
1.	M. Schumacher	318,3	6	336,3	4	182,3	5	204,1	12	270,4	7	281,2	2	286,4	3	320,0	3
2.	R. Barrichello	315,9	7	337,8	1	183,1	3	208,9	2	270,0	8	283,0	1	282,8	6	313,2	9
3.	J.P. Montoya	305,1	16	336,8	2	178,3	13	203,5	13	272,6	3	280,7	4	276,2	14	319,9	4
4.	A. Pizzonia	320,0	4	335,0	7	178,6	12	205,4	10	271,0	5	280,9	3	281,3	8	321,4	1
5.	D. Coulthard	320,9	3	335,6	6	186,9	1	207,3	4	272,7	2	280,1	5	291,8	1	320,2	2
6.	K. Räikkönen	199,9	20	326,6	12			209,3	1			279,2	7	229,2	20	318,7	6
7.	J. Trulli	308,9	13	328,9	10	180,9	9	206,6	7	271,0	6	278,0	9	272,4	15	311,0	11
8.	F. Alonso	321,9	2	330,7	9	186,7	2	208,0	3	273,0	1	279,5	6	281,6	7	316,7	7
9.	J. Button	322,4	1	336,5	3	173,6	18	207,0	5	272,3	4	278,7	8	286,6	2	319,4	5
10.	T. Sato	318,6	5			181,6	8			269,2	10			282,9	5	232,5	17
11.	G. Fisichella	310,7	12	333,9	8	181,9	7	202,9	14	265,4	12	277,6	11	283,0	4	314,7	8
12.	F. Massa	314,0	8	335,6	5	182,0	6	204,9	11	264,7	13	276,2	14	277,4	12	311,2	10
14.	M. Webber	312,8	9			175,0	17			269,4	9			276,7	13	197,3	20
15.	C. Klien	308,6	14	327,9	11	182,9	4	206,6	8	264,5	14	277,8	10	270,8	16	310,7	14
16.	F. Zonta	312,7	10	325,3	14	180,0	10	205,9	9	263,6	16	275,4	15	256,0	18	310,7	12
17.	O. Panis	312,2	11	324,5	15	177,6	15	206,7	6	266,4	11	276,3	13	279,5	10	310,7	13
18.	N. Heidfeld	304,8	17	325,7	13	177,8	14	202,0	15	263,8	15	276,5	12	278,5	11	297,0	16
19.	G. Pantano	305,8	15			172,3	19			260,1	19			280,5	9	212,2	18
20.	G. Bruni	297,0	19			175,9	16			262,7	17			254,1	19	208,4	19
21.	Z. Baumgartner	299,5	18	322,6	16	179,0	11	198,3	16	261,8	18	271,7	16	269,5	17	305,9	15

Race

Classification & Retirements

Pos.	Driver	Team	Lap	Time	Average	
1.	K. Räikkönen	McLaren Mercedes	44	1:32.35.274	198,898 km/h	
2.	M. Schumacher	Ferrari	44	+ 3.132	198,786 km/h	
3.	R. Barrichello	Ferrari	44	+ 4.371	198,742 km/h	
4.	F. Massa	Sauber Petronas	44	+ 12.504	198,452 km/h	
5.	G. Fisichella	Sauber Petronas	44	+ 14.104	198,395 km/h	
6.	C. Klien	Jaguar	44	+ 14.614	198,376 km/h	
7.	D. Coulthard	McLaren Mercedes	44	+ 17.970	198,257 km/h	
8.	O. Panis	Toyota	44	+ 18.693	198,231 km/h	
9.	J. Trulli	Renault	44	+ 22.115	198,110 km/h	
10.	R. Zonta	Toyota	41	3 laps	196,438 km/h	Engine broken
11.	N. Heidfeld	Jordan Ford	40	4 laps	180,039 km/h	

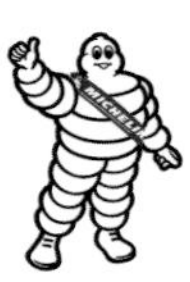

Driver	Team		Reason
J.P. Montoya	Williams BMW	38	Car damaged after right rear puncture
A. Pizzonia	Williams BMW	32	Gearbox stuck in 3rd gear
J. Button	B.A.R Honda	30	Right rear puncture, hits Baumgartner
Z. Baumgartner	Minardi Cosworth	29	Hit by a spinning Button
F. Alonso	Renault	12	Spin, rear tyre covered in oil from a leak
M. Webber	Jaguar	1	Collision with Sato
T. Sato	B.A.R Honda	1	Collision with Webber
G. Bruni	Minardi Cosworth	1	Hit from behind by Baumgartner, spins and his collected by Pantano
G. Pantano	Jordan Ford	1	Hits a spinning Bruni

Fastest laps

	Driver	Time	Lap	Average
1.	K. Räikkönen	1:45.108	42	238,931 km/h
2.	M. Schumacher	1:45.503	28	238,036 km/h
3.	R. Barrichello	1:45.666	43	237,669 km/h
4.	F. Alonso	1:45.870	9	237,211 km/h
5.	J. Trulli	1:45.898	9	237,148 km/h
6.	J.P. Montoya	1:46.547	36	235,704 km/h
7.	D. Coulthard	1:46.579	11	235,633 km/h
8.	A. Pizzonia	1:46.740	26	235,278 km/h
9.	G. Fisichella	1:46.758	11	235,238 km/h
10.	J. Button	1:47.151	26	234,375 km/h
11.	C. Klien	1:47.509	11	233,595 km/h
12.	R. Zonta	1:47.576	26	233,449 km/h
13.	F. Massa	1:47.624	29	233,345 km/h
14.	O. Panis	1:47.765	29	233,040 km/h
15.	N. Heidfeld	1:50.471	40	227,332 km/h
16.	Z. Baumgartner	1:51.031	25	226,185 km/h

Pit stops

	Driver	Time	Lap	Stop n°		Driver	Time	Lap	Stop n°
1.	J. Button	35.343	1	1	21.	F. Massa	32.630	19	3
2.	F. Massa	37.441	1	1	22.	O. Panis	32.769	19	2
3.	Z. Baumgartner	35.584	1	1	23.	C. Klien	32.557	20	2
4.	R. Barrichello	33.423	1	1	24.	J. Button	32.701	21	2
5.	N. Heidfeld	36.952	1	1	25.	J. Trulli	34.734	22	2
6.	O. Panis	33.287	1	1	26.	R. Barrichello	36.181	23	3
7.	F. Massa	1:57.323	2	2	27.	G. Fisichella	38.562	26	2
8.	R. Barrichello	2:46.531	2	2	28.	K. Räikkönen	34.458	29	2
9.	C. Klien	32.402	9	1	29.	J.P. Montoya	33.713	29	2
10.	J. Trulli	33.009	10	1	30.	C. Klien	32.696	29	3
11.	D. Coulthard	35.212	12	1	31.	D. Coulthard	33.816	29	2
12.	K. Räikkönen	34.302	13	1	32.	M. Schumacher	32.582	30	2
13.	G. Fisichella	33.885	14	1	33.	A. Pizzonia	32.495	30	2
14.	J.P. Montoya	32.868	15	1	34.	R. Zonta	32.373	30	2
15.	M. Schumacher	32.971	16	1	35.	F. Massa	32.002	30	4
16.	R. Zonta	32.556	16	1	36.	O. Panis	32.541	30	3
17.	Z. Baumgartner	34.325	16	2	37.	N. Heidfeld	32.296	29	4
18.	N. Heidfeld	37.085	16	2	38.	N. Heidfeld	4:46.457	35	5
19.	A. Pizzonia	33.627	17	1	39.	D. Coulthard	41.524	39	3
20.	N. Heidfeld	31.609	18	3					

Race leaders

Driver	Laps in the lead	Nber of Laps
J. Trulli	1 > 9	9
F. Alonso	10 > 11	2
K. Räikkönen	12 > 13	2
J.P. Montoya	14	1
M. Schumacher	15	1
A. Pizzonia	16	1
K. Räikkönen	17 > 29	13
M. Schumacher	30	1
K. Räikkönen	31 > 44	14

Driver	Nber of Laps	Kilometers
K. Räikkönen	29	202,304 km
J. Trulli	9	62,767 km
F. Alonso	2	13,952 km
M. Schumacher	2	13,952 km
J.P. Montoya	1	6,976 km
A. Pizzonia	1	6,976 km

Lap Chart

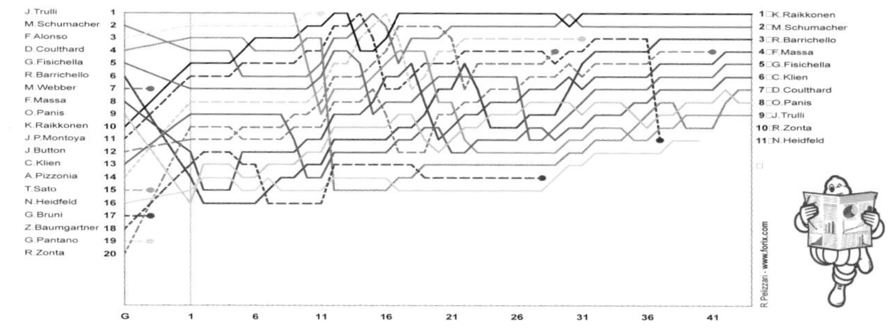
J.Trulli
M.Schumacher
F.Alonso
D.Coulthard
G.Fisichella
R.Barrichello
M.Webber
F.Massa
O.Panis
K.Raikkonen
J.P.Montoya
J.Button
C.Klien
A.Pizzonia
T.Sato
N.Heidfeld
G.Bruni
Z.Baumgartner
G.Pantano
R.Zonta
1 K.Raikkonen
2 M.Schumacher
3 R.Barrichello
4 F.Massa
5 G.Fisichella
6 C.Klien
7 D.Coulthard
8 O.Panis
9 J.Trulli
10 R.Zonta
11 N.Heidfeld
G
1
6
11
16
21
26
31
36
41
R.Pelzer - www.forix.com

Gaps on the leader board

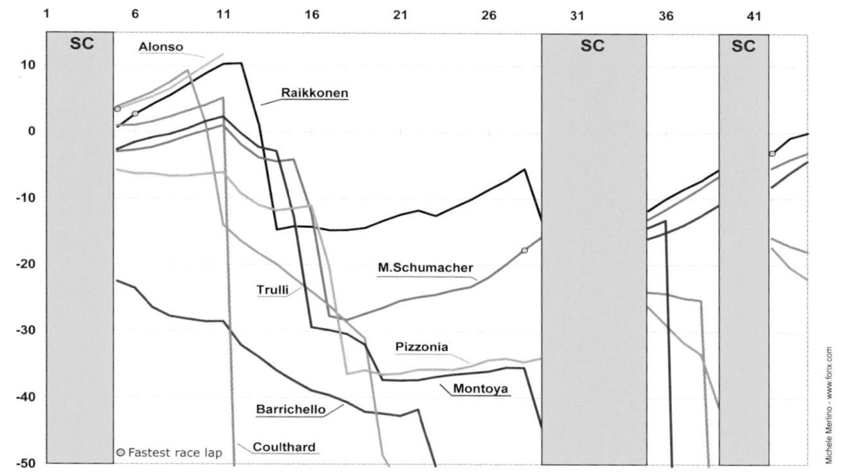
1
6
11
16
21
26
31
36
41
10
0
-10
-20
-30
-40
-50
SC
SC
SC
Alonso
Raikkonen
M.Schumacher
Trulli
Pizzonia
Montoya
Barrichello
Coulthard
Fastest race lap
Michele Merlino - www.forix.com

Championship after fourteen rounds

Drivers

1. **M. Schumacher** ....(12 wins) 128
2. R. Barrichello 88
3. J. Button 65
4. J. Trulli ....(1 win) 46
5. F. Alonso 45
6. J.P. Montoya 38
7. K. Räikkönen ....(1 win) 28
8. D. Coulthard 21
9. T. Sato 18
10. G. Fisichella 18
11. R. Schumacher 12
12. F. Massa 10
13. M. Webber 7
14. O. Panis 6
15. A. Pizzonia 4
16. C. Klien 3
17. C. Da Matta 3
18. N. Heidfeld 3
19. T. Glock 2
20. Z. Baumgartner 1
21. M. Gené 0
22. R. Zonta 0
23. G. Pantano 0
24. G. Bruni 0

Constructors

1. **Scuderia Ferrari Marlboro** .(12 wins) 216
2. Mild Seven Renault F1 Team ..(1 win) 91
3. Lucky Strike B.A.R Honda 83
4. BMW WilliamsF1 Team.................................54
5. West McLaren Mercedes ....(1 win) 49
6. Sauber Petronas 28
7. Jaguar Racing 10
8. Panasonic Toyota Racing 9
9. Jordan Ford 5
10. Minardi Cosworth 1

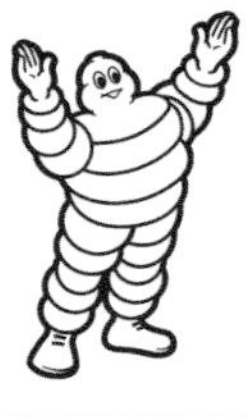

The circuit

Name	Spa-Francorchamps
Length	6976 meters
Distance	44 laps, 306,927 km
Date	August 29, 2004
Weather	overcast, 18-21°c
Track temperature	20-27°c

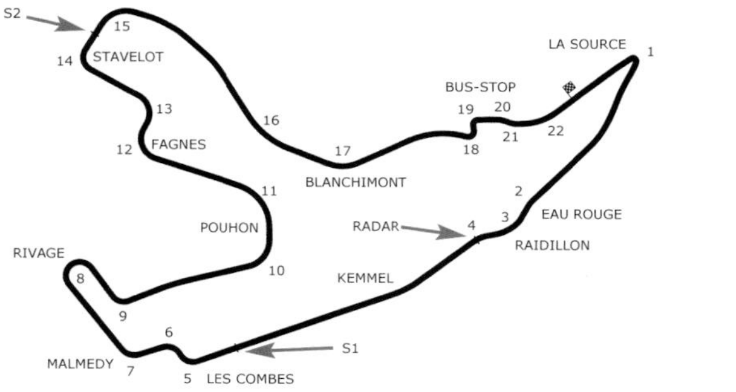
S2
15
14
STAVELOT
13
12
FAGNES
16
17
BLANCHIMONT
11
POUHON
10
RIVAGE
8
9
6
7
MALMEDY
5
LES COMBES
S1
KEMMEL
RADAR
4
3
2
EAU ROUGE
RAIDILLON
BUS-STOP
19
20
18
21
22
LA SOURCE
1

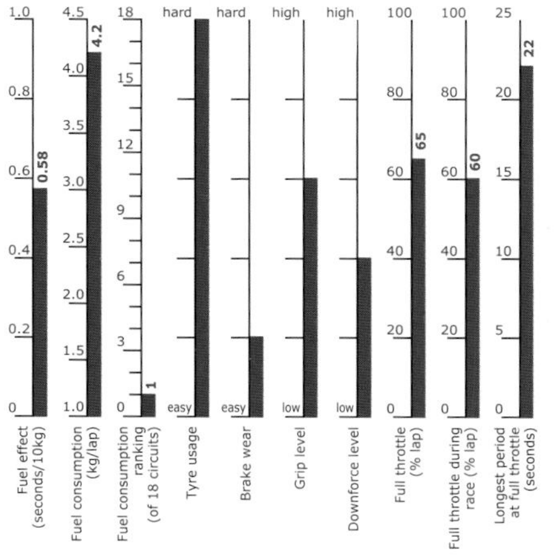
1.0
0.8
0.6
0.4
0.2
0
0.58
4.5
4.0
3.5
3.0
2.5
2.0
1.5
1.0
4.2
18
15
12
9
6
3
0
1
hard
easy
hard
easy
high
low
high
low
100
80
60
40
20
0
65
100
80
60
40
20
0
60
25
20
15
10
5
0
22
Fuel effect (seconds/10kg)
Fuel consumption (kg/lap)
Fuel consumption ranking (of 18 circuits)
Tyre usage
Brake wear
Grip level
Downforce level
Full throttle (% lap)
Full throttle during race (% lap)
Longest period at full throttle (seconds)

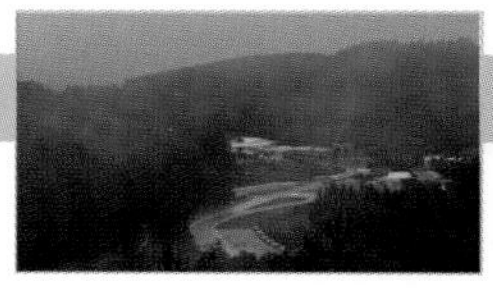

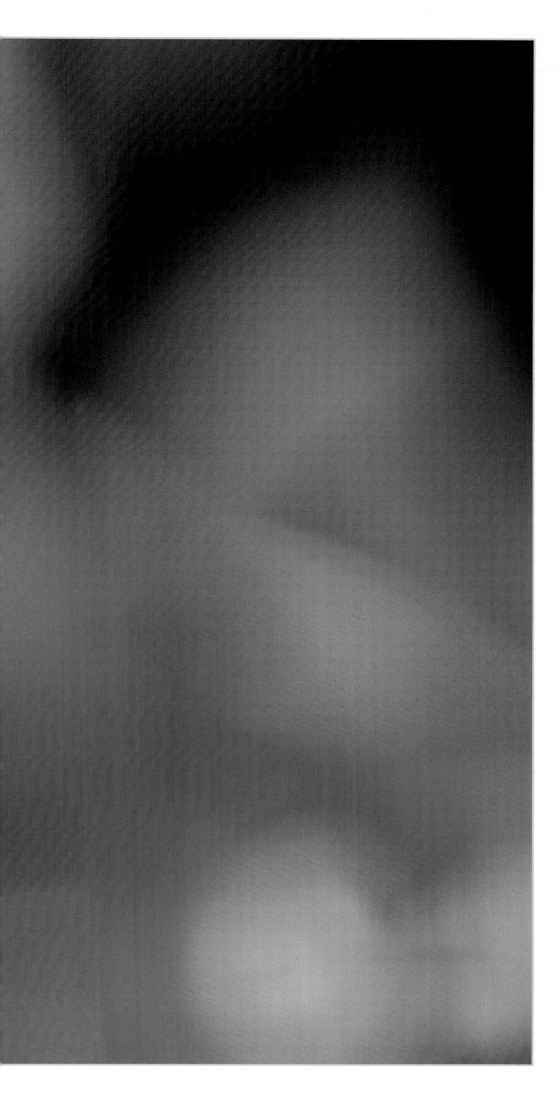

FERRARI PULLS A DOUBLE OUT OF THE HAT !

Rubens Barrichello scored his first victory of the season at Monza from Michael Schumacher. His win was not without problems as at the end of lap 6 the Ferraris were ninth and eleventh positions respectively. They then caught and passed all their rivals underlining yet again their superiority.

> Juan Pablo Montoya was on the front once again for the third time this season. He had to wait until the last race to score his first and only victory in 2004.

Rubens Barrichello on pole: Juan Pablo Montoya, fastest!

The Tifosi were scarcer than usual on the Monza Autodromo. However, this did not prevent each passage of a Ferrari to be greeted with shouts of joy equalled by the roars of the local commentator whose chauvinism left no doubt as to which team he was rooting for!

> Mike Gascoyne and Olivier Panis in deep conversation on the grid. The Frenchman had just announced his retirement from racing at the end of the 2004 season after which he would act as a consultant for Toyota. It was the end of a chapter in French motor sport.

The Tifosi's cup was filled to overflowing when the last car crossed the line and it was announced that Rubens Barrichello was on pole in a time of 1m 20.098s, a speed of over 260 km/h, the quickest ever in the history of F1. *"I'm so happy,"* gushed Rubens. *"The car was great and I managed to get everything out of it. The important thing on the Monza circuit is not so much finding the limit but not making any mistakes. If you make one in the first chicane, for example, it's half-a-second gone. The most difficult thing is to time your acceleration on the exit of the second Lesmo as it precedes a long straight. I don't think I've ever timed it as well as this afternoon."*

The fastest driver of the day, however, was Juan Pablo Montoya who, on his prequalification run, lapped at over 262 km/h in his Williams-BMW, a feat he did not manage to emulate during his qualifying lap and he finished the day in second place. *"I made too many mistakes to be able to beat Rubens,"* he admitted. *"We knew Ferrari would be very quick in qualifying and that it would be difficult to beat them. In the race, though, we're pretty fast over long distances."*

It was a hotly disputed practice session as witnessed by the fact that the first ten cars were grouped in the same second. Michael Schumacher in third said he lost a little time in the Parabolica. *"My lap got off to a good start but I messed up in the last corner. But really, I can't complain. Third isn't too bad? I didn't really expect to qualify so well. Rubens put in a perfect lap and I couldn't do anything about him."* Thanks to his third place the world champion would start on the clean side of the track leaving him ideally placed to slice past his old friend Montoya when the lights went out.

In brief

> *"Formula 1 really is a rotten system. It all has to be changed. It's the end of an era."* Luca di Montezemolo made no bones about saying what he thought of the present organisation of the grands prix on Saturday in the Monza paddock. He then went off to the big party organised by the Scuderia to celebrate both the drivers' and constructors' titles.

> The Sauber team announced the arrival of three new sponsors on the cars for the Italian Grand Prix. They were not that big and were only for one race; just about enough to pay for the mechanics' coffee. *"Let's just say that we take whatever we can. We're delighted with these contracts,"* the team explained

Starting grid

*D. COULTHARD
Change his strategy and take the start from his box

**G. BRUNI et Z. BAUMGARTNER
Penalty for an engine change

***N. HEIDFELD
Penalty for an engine change and take the start from pit lane

Driver	Time	Pos
Z. BAUMGARTNER**	1:25.808	19
G. PANTANO	1:23.239	17
G. FISICHELLA	1:22.239	15
O. PANIS	1:21.841	13
R. ZONTA	1:21.520	11
J. TRULLI	1:21.027	9
K. RÄIKKÖNEN	1:20.877	7
T. SATO	1:20.715	5
M. SCHUMACHER	1:20.637	3
R. BARRICHELLO	1:20.089 (226,172 km/h)	1
N. HEIDFELD***	1:22.301	20
G. BRUNI**	1:24.940	18
F. MASSA	1:22.287	16
C. KLIEN	1:21.989	14
M. WEBBER	1:21.602	12
D. COULTHARD*	1:21.049	10
A. PIZZONIA	1:20.888	8
J. BUTTON	1:20.786	6
F. ALONSO	1:20.645	4
J.P. MONTOYA	1:20.620	2

An unexpected double. The Scuderia scales the heights once again

On lap 43 Rubens Barrichello came out of his pit in the lead after his last stop while behind him Michael Schumacher drifted past Jenson Button on the long pits straight. The Ferraris were running in one-two formation and that was how it stayed until the flag.

In the paddock Pierre Dupasquier, the Michelin competitions manager, took off his cap and burst out laughing. On lap 10 cars fitted with his tyres were in the first eight places. Thirty-three laps later the Ferraris had reversed the situation. *"They can do whatever they like, have a bite to eat, wash the cars and then rejoin, they'll still win,"* he said ironically.

In fact at Monza the Ferraris had all their work cut out. When the sun shone again at the start Rubens

Barrichello made the wrong tyre choice and shod wets. They heated up very quickly and he had to change them on lap 5. Michael Schumacher spun on the first lap after contact with Jenson Button and restarted in fifteenth place *"Fifteenth, it might as well have been last,"* he commented. *"I had to let everybody past. Honestly, after that I never thought I'd finish second. I didn't think we were capable of overtaking the front runners."*

Rubens found himself in ninth place after his tyre change. Schumacher passed him pushing him back to tenth spot. *"At that precise moment Pizzonia really came back at me very quickly and also overtook me,"* remembered the Brazilian. *"I thought it was all over and then as the drivers in front came in to refuel I was given the signal P4. I was in fourth place and I could see the first three*

in front of me so hope sprang afresh." Rubens then threw caution to the winds and went flat out and managed to come out in first place after his second stop. The game was over and Ferrari stunned all its rivals by lapping a good second quicker each time round. It was a humiliation not a punishment that the Scuderia inflicted at Monza.

It was the Brazilian's first win of the season after spending most of it in Michael Schumacher's shadow. *"I honestly think it's my best season in Formula One,"* was Rubens' analysis. *"All I needed was a win to round it off. The way in which Michael and the team have dominated the season is absolutely fantastic. You know, in an hour we're having a meeting to prepare the Chinese Grand Prix. We never stop working."* And the results were there to prove it.

Rubens made it difficult for himself

The Italian Grand Prix got off to a bad start for the future winner. Rubens opted for rain tyres, which was not the case for most of his rivals. *"It was a difficult decision to take as it was still very wet at the start. The sun reappeared and I knew that the track was going to dry out quicker than I expected (!) but I hoped to be able to open up a big gap thanks to my rain tyres before this happened. When the race got under way it was a bit confused on the radio. The team told me that Alonso was very quick and that I had to come. Then it was 'Stay out.' I really feel I should have pitted a lap earlier."*

Rubens constructed his victory during his last but one stint as he built up enough of a gap over Button to be able to refuel and emerge ahead of the Brit. *"In fact, I didn't know my position when I came out of the pits and I pushed as hard as I could. The car wasn't great over the first three or four laps on new tyres and I tried to compensate by adjusting the settings from the cockpit. I asked my engineers where I was and I heard nothing on the radio. And then suddenly 'Rubens calm down, you're in the lead.' I didn't believe it and I shouted something in Portuguese which propriety forbids me from repeating! It was sheer magic under the rostrum. I saw the crowd stretching as far as the eye could see. You know the Italians are like the Brazilians, they've got a lot of heart."*

<
"Thank you God!" Rubens Barrichello praises the heavens after winning his first race of the season.

Takuma Sato:
Japanese coming man

The Japanese drivers who raced in Formula 1
never left much of a trace. Until Takuma Sato arrived.
He is something special and some say he is quicker
than Jenson Button. He finished in the points again
at Monza, fourth behind his team-mate.

> Christian Klien in maximum attack mode. The Austrian doesn't know it yet but the Monza weekend was the last relatively calm one for the Jaguar team. Its withdrawal was announced a few days later.

No agreement among the teams so Max Mosley imposes his law

On Friday afternoon at 16h00 Max Mosley arrived in the press room to bring everybody up to date on the evolution of the regulations for the coming seasons. Several months ago the FIA rang the warning bell stating that the cars were getting too fast, some one or two seconds per lap in relation to last year. Following Ralf Schumacher's accident in the USA Grand Prix the FIA World Council decided to adopt an emergency procedure. At the French Grand Prix at the beginning of July Max Mosley gave the teams two months to come up with a set of proposals aimed at reducing speed.

In addition, he also wanted to improve the show and used safety as a pretext to get his changes through. Normally speaking within the framework of the famous Concorde Agreement, which governs F1, any rule change requires the unanimous agreement of all the teams, an impossibility in practical terms, as there are too many divergent interests at stake.

However, in case of danger when the FIA judges that speeds must be reduced immediately, an emergency procedure can be invoked as happened in 1994 following the death of Ayrton Senna. This was the path that the FIA followed in July which allowed it to impose regulation changes at very short notice. The two months in question came to an end on 6th September. As Mosley anticipated the teams were incapable of reaching agreement as three of them (Williams, McLaren and BAR) refused to sign the proposal accepted by the other seven. So the FIA offered a set of three propositions among which the teams had to make

their choice. If within forty-five days eight out of the ten had not agreed to one then the FIA would impose its own choice. Whatever the choice adopted a certain number of measures would be taken for 2005 concerning the aerodynamics (reduction of the dimensions of the wings) and tyres (limited to three sets per weekend) one for Friday and one for Saturday morning plus one for qualifying and the race. In 2006 the engines would be 2.4 litres V8s as against the present V10 3-litre configuration and a standard engine management system would be imposed. In his usual brilliant style Max Mosley gave the team managers a

severe dressing down because of their inability to reach agreement among themselves. *"We want to improve the show in F1. These gentlemen think they know what the public wants. They're all over fifty, multimillionaires who watch the race from the pits. But the fans are generally under fifty; not many of them are millionaires and they watch the race on TV. They're the ones we have to listen to, not the former!"* It still remains to be seen if the FIA's measures will improve the spectacle – without even thinking about reducing the speeds. In F1 nothing should ever be taken for granted.

Les échos du week-end

> It was a catastrophic weekend for Renault. Not only did neither of the blue and yellow cars finish in the points but the team also lost second place in the Constructors' Championship to BAR-Honda. Fernando Alonso gave his employers a brief ray of hope by leading for a few laps at the start before spinning off while Jarno Trulli was never in the hunt and came home in an anonymous tenth place.

> Antonio Pizzonia reached a speed of 369,9 km/h at the end of the pits straight, the quickest in the race.

> *"Eh no,"* was all Jenson Button said when asked if he regretted wanting to go to Williams in 2005 while Monza showed that the BAR-Hondas were much quicker than the Anglo-German machines.

> It was a catastrophic weekend for Renault. Not only did neither of the blue and yellow cars finish in the points but the team also lost second place in the Constructors' Championship to BAR-Honda. Fernando Alonso gave his employers a brief ray of hope by leading for a few laps at the start before spinning off while Jarno Trulli was never in the hunt and came home in an anonymous tenth place.

> Antonio Pizzonia reached a speed of 369,9 km/h at the end of the pits straight, the quickest in the race. *"Eh no,"* was all Jenson Button said when asked if he regretted wanting to go to Williams in 2005 while Monza showed that the BAR-Hondas were much quicker than the Anglo-German machines.

> Kimi Raïkkonen's engine explodes and out goes the winner of the Belgian Grand Prix. David Coulthard came home in sixth place scoring three points.

Practice

All the time trials

N°	Driver	N° Chassis - Engine	Practice 1 Friday	Pos.	Practice 2 Friday	Pos.	Practice 3 Saturday	Pos.	Practice 4 Saturday	Pos.	Pre-qual. Saturday	Pos.	Qualif. Saturday	Pos.
1.	Michael Schumacher	Ferrari F2004 239	1:20.526	1	1:21.080	3	1:21.962	6	1:20.898	7	1:20.528	9	1:20.637	3
2.	Rubens Barrichello	Ferrari F2004 240	1:20.861	2	1:20.899	2	1:21.855	4	1:20.555	1	1:20.552	10	1:20.089	1
3.	Juan Pablo Montoya	Williams FW26 05 - BMW	1:22.232	10	1:21.419	7	1:21.700	1	1:20.653	2	1:19.525	1	1:20.620	2
4.	Antonio Pizzonia	Williams FW26 07 - BMW	1:22.259	9	1:21.264	5	1:21.723	3	1:20.921	8	1:19.671	2	1:20.888	8
5.	David Coulthard	McLaren MP4-19B 03 - Mercedes	1:22.248	12	1:22.052	10	1:22.097	9	1:21.058	9	1:20.414	7	1.21.049	10
6.	Kimi Räikkönen	McLaren MP4-19B 01 - Mercedes	1:21.637	4	1:20.846	1	1:22.018	7	1:20.856	6	1:20.501	8	1:20.877	7
7.	Jarno Trulli	Renault R24-01	1:22.052	7	1:22.191	11	1:22.774	12	1:21.506	10	1:21.011	12	1:21.027	9
8.	Fernando Alonso	Renault R24-02	1:21.778	5	1:21.630	9	1:21.705	2	1:20.773	4	1.20.341	5	1:20.645	4
9.	Jenson Button	B.A.R 006-05 - Honda	1:21.904	6	1:21.124	4	1:22.062	8	1:20.734	3	1:19.856	4	1:20.786	6
10.	Takuma Sato	B.A.R 006-06 - Honda	1:22.245	11	1:21.313	6	1:21.867	5	1:20.805	5	1:19.733	3	1:20.715	5
11.	Giancarlo Fisichella	Sauber C23-04 - Petronas	1:22.460	14	1:22.302	15	1:22.369	11	1:21.929	13	1:20.357	6	1:22.239	15
12.	Felipe Massa	Sauber C23-01 - Petronas	1:22.259	13	1:22.258	13	1:22.284	10	1:21.859	11	1:20.571	11	1:22.287	16
14.	Mark Webber	Jaguar R5-05	1:23.071	18	1:22.392	17	1:22.784	13	1:22.490	16	1:21.783	13	1:21.602	12
15.	Christian Klien	Jaguar R5-01	1:23.723	21	1:23.199	20	1:23.332	16	1:22.230	15	1:22.114	15	1:21.989	14
16.	Ricardo Zonta	Toyota TF104/10B	1:22.607	16	1:22.298	14	1:22.867	14	1:22.114	14	1:21.829	14	1:21.520	11
17.	Olivier Panis	Toyota TF104/09B	1:22.487	15	1:22.813	18	1:23.103	15	1:21.889	12	1:22.169	16	1:21.841	13
18.	Nick Heidfeld	Jordan EJ14/03 - Ford	1:24.000	22		25	1:24.669	19	1:23.146	17			1:22.301	17
19.	Giorgio Pantano	Jordan EJ14/02 - Ford	1:24.412	23	1:23.818	21	1:24.526	18			1:23.264	17	1:23.239	18
20.	Gianmaria Bruni	Minardi PS04B/02 - Cosworth	1:26.062	24	1:24.225	24	1:24.411	17	1:23.794	18	1:23.963	18	1:24.940	19
21.	Zsolt Baumgartner	Minardi PS04B/01 - Cosworth	1:26.161	25	1:24.063	23	1:26.114	20			1:25.082	19	1:25.808	20
35.	Anthony Davidson	B.A.R 006-04 - Honda	1:20.902	3	1:21.544	8								
37.	Björn Wirdheim	Jaguar R5-02	1:22.065	8	1:22.914	19								
38.	Ryan Briscoe	Toyota TF104/07	1:22.815	17	1:22.197	12								
39.	Timo Glock	Jordan EJ14/01 - Ford	1:23.333	19	1:22.332	16								
40.	Bas Leinders	Minardi PS04B/03 - Cosworth	1:23.696	20	1:24.045	22								

Maximum speed

N°	Driver	P1 Qualifs	Pos.	P1 Race	Pos.	P2 Qualifs	Pos.	P2 Race	Pos.	Finish Qualifs	Pos.	Finish Race	Pos.	Trap Qualifs	Pos.	Trap Race	Pos.
1.	M. Schumacher	346,1	5	349,7	3	346,4	5	350,8	7	328,6	3	333,9	1	363,1	2	367,3	2
2.	R. Barrichello	345,1	6	348,6	7	343,8	10	350,0	9	327,3	7	330,3	6	360,4	8	364,0	8
3.	J.P. Montoya	343,6	10	346,1	10	343,9	9	348,8	10	327,6	6	328,7	11	356,7	10	363,6	9
4.	A. Pizzonia	344,6	9	349,9	2	345,4	7	351,4	4	327,9	4	332,4	2	360,2	9	369,9	1
5.	D. Coulthard	346,8	3	348,1	8	347,3	2	350,0	8	326,7	8	330,1	7	361,6	4	365,3	5
6.	K. Räikkönen	347,3	1	348,7	6	346,0	6	351,3	5	326,6	9	328,4	12	361,0	6	360,2	10
7.	J. Trulli	347,0	2	351,5	1	347,0	4	353,7	2	330,2	1	329,2	9	363,1	1	365,2	7
8.	F. Alonso	344,7	8	348,8	5	347,2	3	351,5	3	329,2	2	330,4	5	361,0	7	365,7	3
9.	J. Button	339,8	11	341,6	14	340,9	11	343,4	14	325,3	11	326,6	14	353,0	11	356,3	15
10.	T. Sato	338,9	13	342,8	11	340,0	12	345,7	13	324,4	13	329,0	10	352,9	12	358,2	14
11.	G. Fisichella	344,7	7	349,1	4	345,0	8	354,7	1	325,6	10	332,4	3	362,0	3	365,3	6
12.	F. Massa	346,2	4	347,1	9	347,7	1	351,2	6	327,6	5	329,3	8	361,4	5	365,4	4
14.	M. Webber	339,5	12	340,9	15	337,3	13	345,7	12	324,6	12	331,0	4	351,1	15	358,6	13
15.	C. Klien	336,5	15	342,4	12	335,1	19	345,9	11	322,1	15	328,2	13	348,6	18	358,8	12
16.	F. Zonta	336,9	14	339,5	17	336,4	15	342,3	15	322,5	14	322,0	16	351,3	14	355,3	16
17.	O. Panis	333,2	19	263,8	20	336,1	16			321,3	17			349,5	17	203,3	20
18.	N. Heidfeld	333,6	18	333,3	19	335,4	18	337,0	19	322,0	16	320,5	18	348,0	19	350,9	19
19.	G. Pantano	334,7	16	342,2	13	335,6	17	342,0	16	320,0	18	324,4	15	351,4	13	355,0	17
20.	G. Bruni	329,4	20	335,1	18	332,0	20	337,2	18	316,1	20	320,0	19	343,9	20	352,9	18
21.	Z. Baumgartner	333,8	17	339,8	16	336,6	14	339,7	17	319,2	19	321,1	17	350,1	16	359,4	11

Race

Classification & Retirements

Pos.	Driver	Team	Lap	Time	Average
1.	R. Barrichello	Ferrari	53	1:15:18.448	244,374 km/h
2.	M. Schumacher	Ferrari	53	+ 1.347	244,301 km/h
3.	J. Button	B.A.R Honda	53	+ 10.197	243,823 km/h
4.	T. Sato	B.A.R Honda	53	+ 15.370	243,545 km/h
5.	J.P. Montoya	Williams BMW	53	+ 32.352	242,636 km/h
6.	D. Coulthard	McLaren Mercedes	53	+ 33.439	242,578 km/h
7.	A. Pizzonia	Williams BMW	53	+ 33.752	242,562 km/h
8.	G. Fisichella	Sauber Petronas	53	+ 35.431	242,472 km/h
9.	M. Webber	Jaguar	53	+ 56.761	241,342 km/h
10.	J. Trulli	Renault	53	+ 1:06.316	240,839 km/h
11.	R. Zonta	Toyota	53	+ 1:22.531	239,990 km/h
12.	F. Massa	Sauber Petronas	52	1 lap	239,556 km/h
13.	C. Klien	Jaguar	52	1 lap	238,608 km/h
14.	N. Heidfeld	Jordan Ford	52	1 lap	237,241 km/h
15.	Z. Baumgartner	Minardi Cosworth	50	3 laps	230,246 km/h

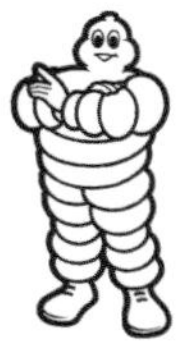

Driver	Team		Reason
F. Alonso	Renault	41	Spins, marshals refuse to push him
G. Pantano	Jordan Ford	34	Spin
G. Bruni	Minardi Cosworth	30	Choking on smoke from car catching fire at 2nd pit stop
K. Räikkönen	McLaren Mercedes	14	Engine coolant leak
O. Panis	Toyota	1	Stuck in gravel trap after collision with Pizzonia

Fastest laps

	Driver	Time	Lap	Average
1.	R. Barrichello	1:21.046	41	257,320 km/h
2.	M. Schumacher	1:21.361	35	256,324 km/h
3.	A. Pizzonia	1:22.246	32	253,566 km/h
4.	G. Fisichella	1:22.615	51	252,433 km/h
5.	T. Sato	1:22.660	32	252,296 km/h
6.	J. Button	1:22.671	13	252,262 km/h
7.	J. Trulli	1:22.855	52	251,702 km/h
8.	F. Alonso	1:22.881	31	251,623 km/h
9.	D. Coulthard	1:22.889	24	251,599 km/h
10.	J.P. Montoya	1:22.929	32	251,477 km/h
11.	F. Massa	1:22.941	50	251,441 km/h
12.	M. Webber	1:23.090	53	250,990 km/h
13.	K. Räikkönen	1:23.365	11	250,162 km/h
14.	R. Zonta	1:23.410	52	250,027 km/h
15.	C. Klien	1:23.432	29	249,961 km/h
16.	G. Pantano	1:24.061	13	248,091 km/h
17.	N. Heidfeld	1:24.166	23	247,781 km/h
18.	Z. Baumgartner	1:26.356	31	241,497 km/h
19.	G. Bruni	1:26.371	24	241,456 km/h

Pit stops

	Driver	Time	Lap	Stop n°
1.	R. Barrichello	25.981	5	1
2.	F. Massa	26.189	5	1
3.	G. Bruni	27.482	7	1
4.	F. Massa	29.248	8	2
5.	F. Alonso	27.640	10	1
6.	C. Klien	27.702	11	1
7.	M. Webber	27.759	12	1
8.	J. Trulli	28.086	12	1
9.	J.P. Montoya	29.404	13	1
10.	T. Sato	27.128	13	1
11.	R. Zonta	26.819	13	1
12.	Z. Baumgartner	37.905	13	1
13.	J. Button	27.969	14	1
14.	G. Pantano	27.504	14	1
15.	M. Schumacher	27.759	15	1
16.	A. Pizzonia	27.067	16	1
17.	G. Fisichella	26.766	19	1
18.	N. Heidfeld	31.386	24	1
19.	D. Coulthard	30.209	26	1
20.	R. Barrichello	24.557	29	2
21.	C. Klien	28.061	31	2
22.	M. Webber	27.063	32	2
23.	F. Alonso	26.780	33	2
24.	J.P. Montoya	28.390	33	2
25.	T. Sato	28.675	33	2
26.	R. Zonta	27.642	33	2
27.	F. Massa	27.250	33	3
28.	Z. Baumgartner	29.488	32	2
29.	J. Button	27.507	34	2
30.	G. Pantano	28.188	33	2
31.	J. Trulli	26.415	34	2
32.	A. Pizzonia	27.688	35	2
33.	M. Schumacher	25.766	36	2
34.	C. Klien	15.321	36	3
35.	G. Fisichella	26.229	37	2
36.	R. Barrichello	23.487	42	3

Race leaders

Driver	Laps in the lead	Nber of Laps
R. Barrichello	1 > 4	4
F. Alonso	5 > 10	6
J. Button	11 > 34	24
M. Schumacher	35 > 36	2
R. Barrichello	37 > 53	17

Driver	Nber of Laps	Kilometers
J. Button	24	139,032 km
R. Barrichello	21	121,344 km
F. Alonso	6	34,458 km
M. Schumacher	2	11,586 km

Lap Chart

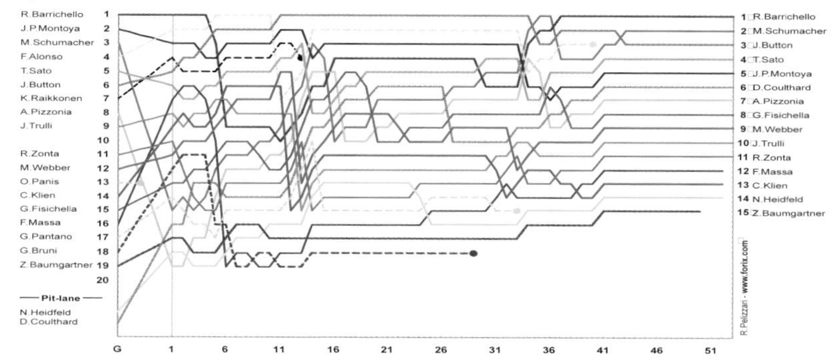

Gaps on the leader board

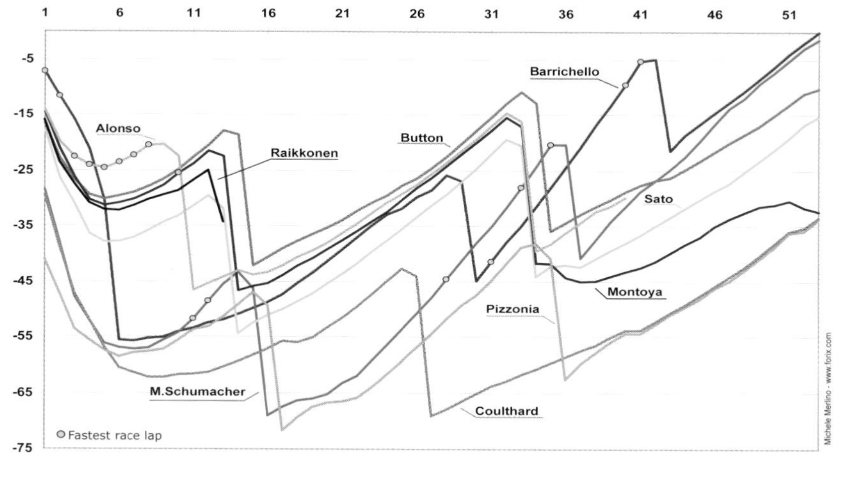

Championship after fifteen rounds

Drivers

1. **M. Schumacher** ....(12 wins) 136
2. R. Barrichello ....(1 win) 98
3. J. Button 71
4. J. Trulli.....................(1 win) 46
5. F. Alonso 45
6. J.P. Montoya 42
7. K. Räikkönen ....(1 win) 28
8. D. Coulthard 24
9. T. Sato 23
10. G. Fisichella..19
11. R. Schumacher 12
12. F. Massa..10
13. M. Webber 7
14. O. Panis..6
15. A. Pizzonia 6
16. C. Klien 3
17. C. Da Matta...3
18. N. Heidfeld..3
19. T. Glock 2
20. Z. Baumgartner 1
21. R. Zonta 0
22. M. Gené..0
23. G. Pantano 0
24. G. Bruni..0

Constructors

1. **Scuderia Ferrari Marlboro** .(13 wins) 234
2. Lucky Strike B.A.R Honda 94
3. Mild Seven Renault F1 Team ..(1 win) 91
4. BMW WilliamsF1 Team...............................60
5. West McLaren Mercedes ....(1 win) 52
6. Sauber Petronas..29
7. Jaguar Racing 10
8. Panasonic Toyota Racing 9
9. Jordan Ford 5
10. Minardi Cosworth 1

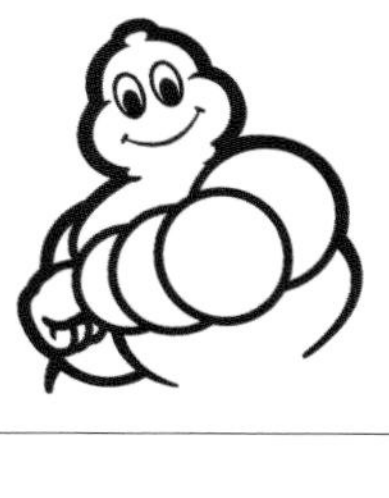

The circuit

Name	Autodromo nazionale Monza
Length	5793 meters
Distance	53 laps, 306,720 km
Date	September 12, 2004
Weather	overcast, start on wet track, 22-23°c
Track temperature	25-28°c

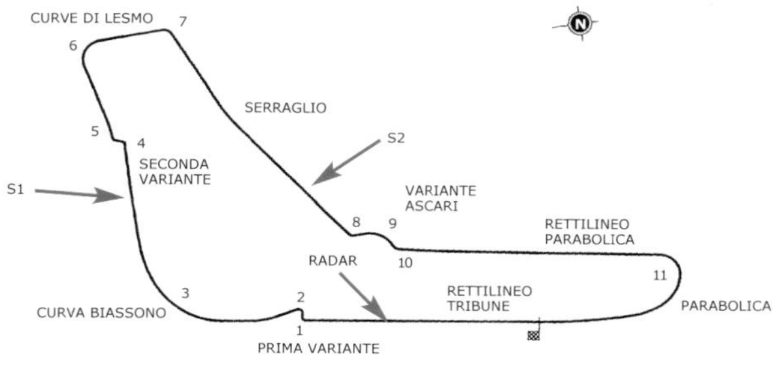

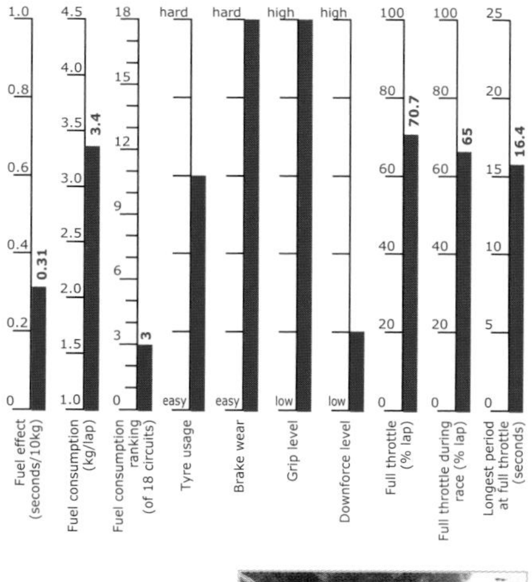

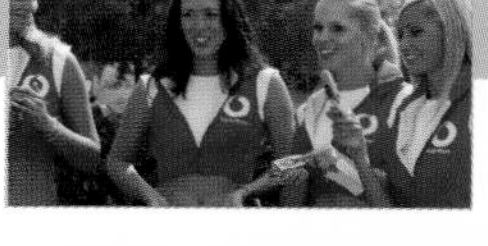

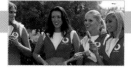

BUTTON SECOND AGAIN

For once Michael Schumacher was in difficulty but thanks to his team-mate Ferrari won the inaugural Chinese Grand Prix. Barrichello resisted intense pressure from his rivals and secured his runner-up spot in the Drivers' World Championship. Jenson Button finished second again which put the BAR-Honda team in an ideal position to clinch second in the Constructors' title chase.

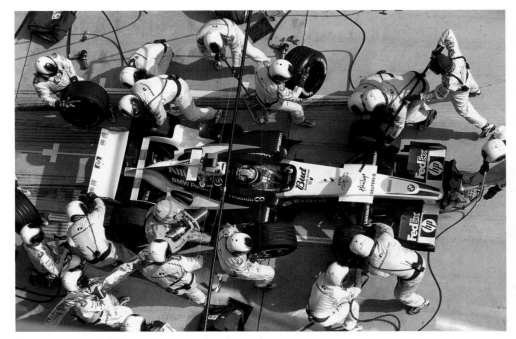

> Juan Pablo Montoya found it difficult to get to grips with the Shanghai circuit and ended up tenth on the grid.

A Sauber on the second row!

The two Saubers had their best qualifying session of the season, which must have gladdened the heart of Jacques Villeneuve (see sidebar) who had just signed a 2-year contract with the Swiss team. Felipe Massa was on the second row after being fourth quickest and on the fourth row in seventh place was his team-mate, Giancarlo Fisichella. *"It's really great starting from fourth,"* enthused the Brazilian. *"It was an almost perfect qualifying session. The new Bridgestones worked well straight away and I managed a whole lap without graining (balls of rubber forming on the tread). I know it'll go even better in the race. It's a fantastic result for the team."*

This performance confirmed the progress made by the new version of the C23. The new engine cover, which appeared at Silverstone in July, was obviously a big help. The new wind tunnel at Hinwil – the most sophisticated in Europe – is now working full time and a plethora of new parts are appearing on the Saubers. *"However, we've got nothing new here,"* remarked Peter Sauber.

The BAR cars were dressed in 555 livery, the brand of cigarettes sold by the BAT group in China.
>∨

It was a busy week for Jacques Villeneuve as hardly had he signed his contract with Peter Sauber when he replaced Jarno Trulli for the last three races of the season.
∨

On pole was Rubens Barrichello while at the back of the grid was his illustrious team-mate who spun at the very start of his timed lap ending up in eighteenth spot. *"I really don't know what happened,"* he said. *"We'll have to examine the telemetry readings. If we find nothing then it's the fault of what is between fuel tank and the steering wheel (could that mean the driver!). I don't know what I can do starting so far back; it's a big challenge."*

Jacques Villeneuve is back

Only Villeneuve's real fans believed in him. Since the spring the man from Quebec has been telling anybody who would listen that he would do anything to get back into F1. He had a few openings: BAR, Williams or Renault but they all snapped shut one after the other. In August he went to visit the Swiss team in Hinwil. It took him just three hours to make up his mind. *"I was very impressed with the professionalism in the factory,"* he said afterwards, *" and I'm looking forward to see what'll come out of the new wind tunnel."*

Following several days' discussion with Peter Sauber's lawyers the contract was signed between the Swiss outfit and the ex-world champion a few days after the Italian Grand Prix. Jacques won his bet even if his salary had undergone a big squeeze – the word was a retainer of 3 million dollars plus a fixed bonus per point. And there was more good news for the Canadian; after a couple of days intensive testing on the Silverstone circuit where Villeneuve covered over 700 kms he was confirmed as a Renault team driver for the last three races. He was delighted. *"I worked on my driving position for a day and half before going for a time. The Renault people were great."*

Renault's (and Villeneuve's aim) was to score the maximum number of points to try and wrest second place from BAR in the Constructors' Championship.

Starting grid

 T. SATO** 19 1:34.993

 M. SCHUMACHER* 17 -

C. KLIEN 15 1:36.535

R. ZONTA 13 1:35.410

M. WEBBER 11 1:35.286

D. COULTHARD 9 1:35.029

G. FISICHELLA 7 1:34.951

R. SCHUMACHER 5 1:34.891

J. BUTTON 3 1:34.295

R. BARRICHELLO 1 1:34.012 (208,735 km/h)

Z. BAUMGARTNER** 20 1:40.240

G. BRUNI 18 -

T. GLOCK 16 1:37.140

N. HEIDFELD 14 1:36.507

J. VILLENEUVE 12 1:35.384

J.P. MONTOYA 10 1:35.245

O. PANIS 8 1:34.975

F. ALONSO 6 1:34.917

F. MASSA 4 1:34.759

K. RÄIKKÖNEN 2 1:34.178

Second win on the trot for Barrichello

Formula 1 had a touch of magic for the tens of thousands of Chinese massed round the Shanghai circuit. It is only two years since the grands prix have been shown on TV on the Chinese mainland. This weekend was the first time ever that they could see F1 in steel and carbon fibre as it were as motor sport is virtually non-existent in a country where only 2% of the inhabitants have a vehicle.

The Chinese are avid consumers of anything modern and F1, which is the vanguard in this field, filled all its promises. The race was hotly contested with a top class battle for victory while Michael Schumacher had the greatest difficult in hewing his way up through the field thus the Chinese Grand Prix was one of the most exciting races of the season.

Although Rubens Barrichello led almost from start to finish he was under constant threat from Kimi Raïkkönen first of all and then Jenson Button, who went for a two-stop strategy, which nearly paid off

Michael's dreadful weekend!

Overall the Chinese Grand Prix was a nightmare for Michael Schumacher. It began with a spin just when he started his qualifying lap so he found himself on the back of the grid. His team decided to change strategy and installed a new engine in his F2004, thus he had to start from the pit lane. In the race he collided with Christian Klien's Jaguar and then he spun when following Fernando Alonso very closely (loss of aerodynamic grip at the front). And to cap it all his car suffered a puncture. *"At least all the bad luck was concentrated in one weekend. I'm Ok for the rest of the season,"* Michael commented. He finished twelfth his worst result since his Monaco retirement.

Coulthard launches a Kamikaze attack!

On lap 36, Ralf Schumacher in seventh place was fighting off David Coulthard. Then at the end of the straight the Scot launched a Kamikaze attack against the German. The cars collided and the Williams driver was eliminated: *"I think David was just a tad optimistic,"* said Ralf. When the German got back to his pit he thought the suspension had been broken in the impact. *"In fact, it was only a puncture,"* he went on. *"By the time my mechanics found out two laps had passed. It wasn't worth going back out."*

David Coulthard did not make any excuses. *"I'm sorry for Ralf, but the accident also screwed up my race. I could've scored some points had I not be obliged to change my front wheel."*

as he finished just one second behind the Ferrari. In addition, Rubens had problems with his front tyres, which were graining.

"It wasn't easy," said a very relieved Brazilian when he left the rostrum. *"It was very difficult to keep Kimi behind. I though he'd go a bit quicker at the start of the race, but afterwards we were racing at about the same speed."*

This win gave him the runner-up spot in the Drivers' World Championship. *"Frankly, it's been a difficult season,"* he stated. *"I've spent months trying to reach Michael's level. He made a very strong start to the year and I couldn't follow his rhythm and I don't really know why. At the moment things are going well so let's hope I can keep it up till Brazil."*

Jenson Button's second place was due in part to a daring strategy. It was his ninth rostrum finish of the year but he is still after that elusive victory. *"We have work to do on our starts. If we can improve them, we should be able to battle for first place,"* was how he summed it up.

When the race was over the Chinese spectators left the circuit to go home having lived in another world for an all too brief couple of hours.

^
Rubens Barrichello was one happy bunny due to his second victory of the season. He also clinched the runner up spot in the drivers' championship.

<
Rubens takes the chequered flag ahead of Mark Webber whom he has just lapped.

Praise all round

The first Chinese Grand Prix was a big success thanks to impeccable organisation. It was a great race on a beautiful circuit, a real eye-opener.

paddock

The incredible Shanghai circuit installations with its two suspended bridges on the ninth floor and the covered main grandstand, which turned out to be a great resonance chamber the cars roaring down the main straight.

A magnificent achievement

The world is full of contradictions and so is motor sport. At the very moment when Ford decided to stop its participation in F1 with Jaguar no expenses were spared to organise a grand prix on the other end of the world. Attracting the F1 circus became a point of honour for Shanghai and its 14 million inhabitants to stake their claim mark on the sporting map of the world as its main rival, Peking, is organising the 2008 Olympic Games. A grand prix seemed the right way to go as the F1 World Championship attracts the third largest TV audience after the Olympic Games and the Football World Cup.

Excessive is probably the best adjective to describe Shanghai with its huge skyscrapers, infernal traffic and unbreathable air. It used to be one of the centres of the opium trade but today it has dethroned Hong Kong as the economic capital of

Asia. The Chinese government has invested billions to achieve this result. Today the town looks like a huge building site – the inhabitants all say that one-third of the world's skyscraper cranes work here. An airport that cost two billion dollars has just been opened and a suspended railway travelling at 430 km/h will soon link it to the city centre. Shanghai built a grand prix circuit in keeping with its ambitions. The SIC (Shanghai International Circuit) is the most spectacular even seen in F1 with its fourteen corners and beautiful layout but above all for its mind-boggling installations. The paddock consists of magnificent pagodas on a pond and there is a huge control tower containing a press room overlooking the track from the ninth floor. It cost around 260 million euros making it the most expensive circuit on the planet.

Weekend Gossip

> The Jordan team was in a sorry state and it was rumoured that its Silverstone factory had already closed. The trip to Shanghai was supposed to have been paid by Timo Glock's sponsors, which explained why the German replaced Giorgio Pantano. So the team had a new test driver, Robert Doornbos from Monaco.

> Ralf Schumacher was back after recovering from his spinal column injuries following his Indianapolis accident.

> The Shanghai circuit stands can hold 200 000 people but the number was limited to

150 000 for the race which was a sell-out as the last tickets went two months earlier.

> The Chinese drive like madmen and Europeans cannot get behind the wheel without a special licence. On Sunday morning the Williams minibus collided with a car coming in the opposite direction at high speed on a four-lane highway! Four members of the team were injured and taken to the Shanghai hospital.

Shanghai's different faces. The old town with its narrow streets, dreadful smells and its charm still intact on the one side, and on the other the skyscrapers surrounding the People's park.
v

Jaguar withdraws from F1. What a waste

The Jaguar team has never won anything and now it has lost everything. Just before the Chinese Grand Prix the Cat announced its retirement from racing at the end of 2004. The team was up for sale as was its engine manufacturer Cosworth. After over forty years the blue oval was about to disappear from the F1 scene.

A quick flashback. When the little world of F1 got off their planes for the 2000 Australian Grand Prix they were by fans wielding banners saying, *"Jaguar is back."* The Cat had decided to make a splash for its first grand prix. Throughout the season it was the PR champion as its drivers spent hours charming sponsors and appearing on TV programmes.

While the Jaguar team was a redoubtable opponent in the alleyways of F1 – it was the first to erect a chateau-like motor home at the circuits – it missed its mark on the track. Its highest place in the Constructors' Championship in five years was seventh (out of ten). Its claws never left much of a trace the team made a lot of mistakes. Its Mexican army style management was the laughing stock of the paddock through which a whole stream of bosses passed to explain why its results were not up to scratch. Neil Ressler, Bobby Rahal, Wolfgang Reitzl, Niki Lauda, Tony Purnell, David Pitchford, John Hogan or even Franz Kafka (!) would have been at a loss to explain the goings-on. Ford, Jaguar's owner since 1989, also decided to close the Browns Lane factory in Coventry in Great Britain. In addition the Detroit giant confirmed the sale of race engine manufacturer Cosworth. *"F1 is too expensive and does not evolve quickly enough,"* explained Richard Parry-Jones, the group's vice-president. *"We're not accusing anybody, That's just how it is. We tried to change F1 and we failed."*

This dig was directed at Bernie Ecclestone, the F1 commercial rights holder who is accused of not giving the teams enough money from the advertising income. Ford was now on the look out for a buyer, and two months later it was confirmed that the Red Bull Company had purchased the team. Five seasons and not a single victory the big cat sheathed its claws, but what a waste!

results

Practice

All the time trials

N°	Driver	N° Chassis - Engine	Practice 1 Friday	Pos.	Practice 2 Friday	Pos.	Practice 3 Saturday	Pos.	Practice 4 Saturday	Pos.	Pre-qual. Saturday	Pos.	Qualif. Saturday	Pos.
1.	Michael Schumacher	Ferrari F2004 239	1:37.300	15	1:34.776	8	1:34.844	3	1:33.448	1	1:33.185	1		19
2.	Rubens Barrichello	Ferrari F2004 240	1:36.660	7	1:34.448	5	1:34.854	4	1:33.796	2	1:33.787	4	1:34.012	1
3.	Juan Pablo Montoya	Williams FW26 05 - BMW	1:35.761	3	1:35.646	14	1:34.679	2	1:34.458	7	1:34.016	7	1:35.245	11
4.	Ralf Schumacher	Williams FW26 07 - BMW	1:35.455	2	1:34.714	7	1:34.380	1	1:34.769	12	1:33.849	6	1:34.891	5
5.	David Coulthard	McLaren MP4-19B 03 - Mercedes	1:37.976	18	1:34.362	4	1:35.930	9	1:34.470	8	1:34.355	12	1.35.029	10
6.	Kimi Räikkönen	McLaren MP4-19B 01 - Mercedes	1:37.102	11	1:34.289	3	1:35.532	6	1:34.042	3	1:33.499	2	1:34.178	2
7.	Jacques Villeneuve	Renault R24-08	1:37.240	14	1:35.851	15	1:35.965	10	1:35.309	15	1:34.425	13	1:35.384	13
8.	Fernando Alonso	Renault R24-07	1:36.884	8	1:35.514	13	1:36.243	13	1:34.627	11	1.34.599	14	1:34.917	6
9.	Jenson Button	B.A.R 006-05 - Honda	1:36.475	6	1:34.174	2	1:35.660	8	1:34.233	4	1:34.273	10	1:34.295	3
10.	Takuma Sato	B.A.R 006-06 - Honda	1:37.438	16		25	1:36.226	12	1:35.155	13	1:34.051	8	1:34.993	9
11.	Giancarlo Fisichella	Sauber C23-04 - Petronas	1:36.944	9	1:34.680	6	1:35.049	5	1:34.286	5	1:33.738	3	1:34.951	7
12.	Felipe Massa	Sauber C23-03 - Petronas	1:36.086	4	1:34.959	12	1:36.539	14	1:34.607	10	1:33.816	5	1:34.759	4
14.	Mark Webber	Jaguar R5-05	1:38.761	21	1:35.886	16	1:36.002	11	1:35.354	16	1:34.334	11	1:35.286	12
15.	Christian Klien	Jaguar R5-06	1:38.504	20	1:37.111	20	1:37.160	16	1:35.869	17	1:35.447	17	1:36.535	16
16.	Ricardo Zonta	Toyota TF104/10B	1:36.970	10	1:34.868	9	1:35.597	7	1:34.518	9	1:34.958	16	1:35.410	14
17.	Olivier Panis	Toyota TF104/09B	1:37.191	13	1:34.870	10	1:36.623	15	1:35.211	14	1:34.153	9	1:34.975	8
18.	Nick Heidfeld	Jordan EJ14/03 - Ford	1:38.132	19	1:36.630	18	1:37.166	17	1:34.404	6	1:34.808	15	1:36.507	15
19.	T. Glock	Jordan EJ14/02 - Ford	1:37.587	17	1:37.728	22	1:38.128	20	1:37.158	19	1:37.143	19	1:37.140	17
20.	Gianmaria Bruni	Minardi PS04B/02 - Cosworth	1:38.805	22	1:37.431	21	1:37.533	18	1:36.748	18	1:36.623	18		20
21.	Zsolt Baumgartner	Minardi PS04B/04 - Cosworth	1:42.795	25	1:37.076	19	1:37.552	19	1:38.014	20	1:37.510	20	1:40.240	18
35.	Anthony Davidson	B.A.R 006-04 - Honda	1:35.369	1	1:33.289	1								
37.	Björn Wirdheim	Jaguar R5-01	1:37.142	12	1:36.363	17								
38.	Ryan Briscoe	Toyota TF104/11B	1:36.394	5	1:34.881	11								
39.	Robert Doornbos	Jordan EJ14/02 - Ford	1:39.244	23	1:39.051	24								
40.	Bas Leinders	Minardi PS04B/03 - Cosworth	1:39.529	24	1:38.522	23								

Maximum speed

N°	Driver	P1 Qualifs	Pos.	P1 Race	Pos.	P2 Qualifs	Pos.	P2 Race	Pos.	Finish Qualifs	Pos.	Finish Race	Pos.	Trap Qualifs	Pos.	Trap Race	Pos.
1.	M. Schumacher	282,8	19	299,5	2	272,7	19	290,7	2	259,8	20	275,3	2	313,1	20	337,6	6
2.	R. Barrichello	298,0	1	298,5	3	289,7	1	290,1	3	272,3	1	275,6	1	326,9	5	338,0	5
3.	J.P. Montoya	295,8	4	300,0	1	287,9	4	290,8	1	269,8	2	273,7	5	328,5	4	338,1	4
4.	R. Schumacher	295,2	5	296,9	6	286,9	6	289,5	4	269,5	4	274,7	3	324,6	6	335,9	7
5.	D. Coulthard	291,8	13	295,2	9	285,7	11	285,6	12	267,0	11	271,6	12	316,8	17	330,6	14
6.	K. Räikkönen	294,9	6	293,7	13	286,1	9	287,4	7	269,6	3	274,7	4	319,9	13	330,3	15
7.	J. Villeneuve	292,4	11	293,8	12	283,3	13	285,8	11	266,6	12	271,0	13	323,8	8	332,1	11
8.	F. Alonso	294,0	8	294,7	10	286,4	8	286,8	9	267,2	10	272,1	9	323,5	9	329,0	18
9.	J. Button	293,2	10	294,2	11	285,7	10	286,6	10	268,9	5	273,6	6	324,4	7	333,2	10
10.	T. Sato	291,9	12	293,3	14	282,8	14	285,2	13	267,9	8	272,5	8	319,3	15	331,8	12
11.	G. Fisichella	296,0	3	295,2	8	288,6	2	288,8	5	268,9	6	271,8	11	329,2	3	340,8	1
12.	F. Massa	296,8	2	297,4	4	287,5	5	288,3	6	267,3	9	272,9	7	330,3	1	339,7	2
14.	M. Webber	291,6	14	292,6	15	283,4	12	283,0	15	266,4	13	267,9	17	319,8	14	330,7	13
15.	C. Klien	291,2	15	288,3	19	282,7	15	280,5	18	264,5	16	266,0	18	315,5	18	333,8	9
16.	F. Zonta	293,2	9	296,9	5	288,0	3	284,9	14	266,2	14	268,6	15	321,2	10	338,2	3
17.	O. Panis	294,5	7	295,4	7	286,5	7	287,3	8	268,4	7	271,9	10	329,3	2	334,9	8
18.	N. Heidfeld	290,6	16	290,6	17	280,1	17	282,5	16	263,6	17	268,9	14	320,5	12	329,0	19
19.	T. Glock	290,5	17	290,7	16	280,7	16	282,1	17	265,0	15	268,5	16	318,6	16	330,0	16
20.	G. Bruni	274,0	20	287,0	20	269,1	20	275,7	20	260,1	19	261,8	20	314,3	19	325,5	20
21.	Z. Baumgartner	290,4	18	289,9	18	279,2	18	279,5	19	261,3	18	263,8	19	320,8	11	329,5	17

Race

Classification & Retirements

Pos.	Pilote	Equipe	Tour	Temps	Moyenne
1.	R. Barrichello	Ferrari	56	1:29:12.420	205,185 km/h
2.	J. Button	B.A.R Honda	56	+ 1.035	205,145 km/h
3.	K. Räikkönen	McLaren Mercedes	56	+ 1.469	205,128 km/h
4.	F. Alonso	Renault	56	+ 32.510	203,946 km/h
5.	J.P. Montoya	Williams BMW	56	+ 45.193	203,467 km/h
6.	T. Sato	B.A.R Honda	56	+ 54.791	203,106 km/h
7.	G. Fisichella	Sauber Petronas	56	+ 1:05.464	202,705 km/h
8.	F. Massa	Sauber Petronas	56	+ 1:20.080	202,160 km/h
9.	D. Coulthard	McLaren Mercedes	56	+ 1:20.619	202,140 km/h
10.	M. Webber	Jaguar	55	1 lap	201,514 km/h
11.	J. Villeneuve	Renault	55	1 lap	201,508 km/h
12.	M. Schumacher	Ferrari	55	1 lap	201,147 km/h
13.	N. Heidfeld	Jordan Ford	55	1 lap	200,476 km/h
14.	O. Panis	Toyota	55	1 lap	200,446 km/h
15.	T. Glock	Jordan Ford	55	1 lap	199,310 km/h
16.	Z. Baumgartner	Minardi Cosworth	53	3 laps	191,107 km/h

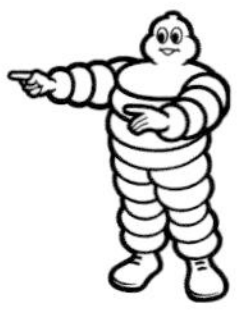

Driver	Team		Reason
G. Bruni	Minardi Cosworth	39	Loses left front wheel because of a mechanical problem
R. Schumacher	Williams BMW	38	Loses too much time having car checked, following puncture caused by collision with Coulthard
R. Zonta	Toyota	36	Loss of 5th gear
C. Klien	Jaguar	12	Right rear suspension damaged after colliding with M Schum.

Fastest laps

	Driver	Time	Lap	Average
1.	M. Schumacher	1:32.238	55	212,749 km/h
2.	R. Barrichello	1:32.455	28	212,250 km/h
3.	K. Räikkönen	1:32.876	53	211,288 km/h
4.	J. Button	1:32.935	33	211,154 km/h
5.	J.P. Montoya	1:33.108	34	210,761 km/h
6.	F. Massa	1:33.483	43	209,916 km/h
7.	G. Fisichella	1:33.520	25	209,833 km/h
8.	T. Sato	1:33.533	36	209,804 km/h
9.	R. Schumacher	1:33.546	31	209,774 km/h
10.	F. Alonso	1:33.625	55	209,597 km/h
11.	D. Coulthard	1:33.727	26	209,369 km/h
12.	R. Zonta	1:34.269	24	208,165 km/h
13.	O. Panis	1:34.603	51	207,431 km/h
14.	N. Heidfeld	1:34.717	55	207,181 km/h
15.	M. Webber	1:34.893	32	206,797 km/h
16.	T. Glock	1:34.931	54	206,714 km/h
17.	J. Villeneuve	1:34.950	55	206,672 km/h
18.	C. Klien	1:36.888	10	202,539 km/h
19.	G. Bruni	1:37.377	23	201,521 km/h
20.	Z. Baumgartner	1:37.578	51	201,106 km/h

Pit stops

	Driver	Time	Lap	Stop n°
1.	F. Massa	25.026	10	1
2.	O. Panis	24.158	10	1
3.	G. Bruni	28.603	10	1
4.	G. Fisichella	25.455	11	1
5.	D. Coulthard	24.922	11	1
6.	R. Zonta	23.534	11	1
7.	R. Barrichello	25.155	12	1
8.	K. Räikkönen	25.623	12	1
9.	Z. Baumgartner	26.193	12	1
10.	F. Alonso	26.392	13	1
11.	J. Button	27.977	14	1
12.	J. Villeneuve	26.167	14	1
13.	R. Schumacher	26.992	15	1
14.	M. Webber	26.816	15	1
15.	T. Glock	27.176	15	1
16.	J.P. Montoya	27.646	16	1
17.	N. Heidfeld	26.400	17	1
18.	T. Sato	26.953	18	1
19.	M. Schumacher	26.436	20	1
20.	O. Panis	23.868	23	2
21.	Z. Baumgartner	25.898	23	2
22.	R. Zonta	24.065	25	2
23.	F. Massa	25.687	26	2
24.	G. Bruni	26.035	25	2
25.	K. Räikkönen	23.555	27	2
26.	G. Fisichella	25.379	27	2
27.	D. Coulthard	24.207	28	2
28.	R. Barrichello	23.665	29	2
29.	F. Alonso	27.367	33	2
30.	T. Glock	28.730	33	2
31.	R. Schumacher	28.189	34	2
32.	J. Villeneuve	26.871	34	2
33.	J. Button	28.313	35	2
34.	M. Webber	27.558	35	2
35.	M. Schumacher	27.561	35	2
36.	K. Räikkönen	26.787	36	3
37.	N. Heidfeld	27.909	36	2
38.	T. Sato	26.337	38	2
39.	J.P. Montoya	27.286	38	2
40.	D. Coulthard	27.640	38	3
41.	O. Panis	24.627	39	3
42.	Z. Baumgartner	33.020	38	3
43.	R. Barrichello	23.667	42	3
44.	G. Fisichella	25.048	42	3
45.	F. Massa	24.752	44	3
46.	M. Schumacher	24.593	47	3

Race leaders

Driver	Laps in the lead	Nber of Laps
R. Barrichello	1 > 12	12
J. Button	13 > 14	2
R. Schumacher	15	1
R. Barrichello	16 > 29	14
J. Button	30 > 35	6
R. Barrichello	36 > 56	21

Driver	Nber of Laps	Kilometers
R. Barrichello	47	256,007 km
J. Button	8	43,608 km
R. Schumacher	1	5,451 km

Gaps on the leader board

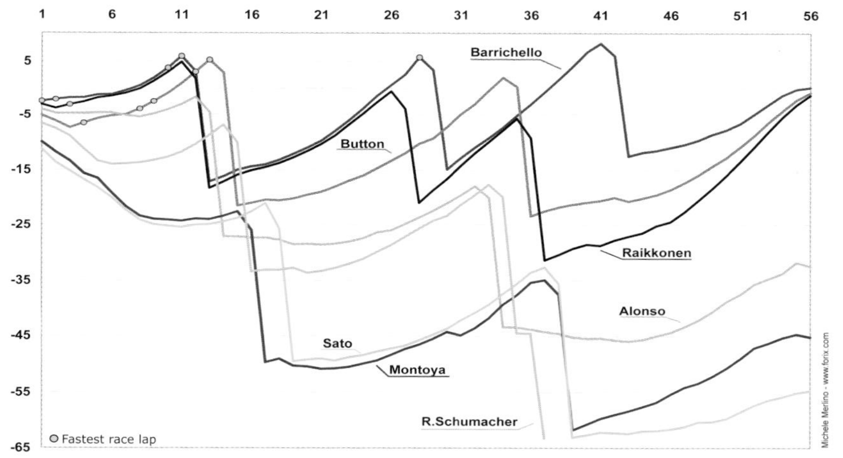

Lap Chart

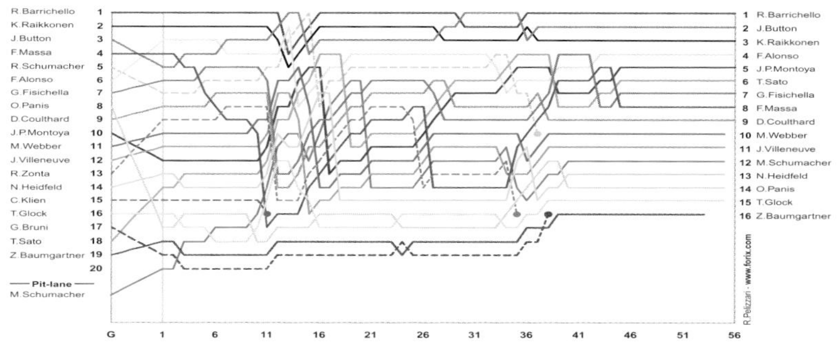

Championship after sixteen rounds

Drivers

1. **M. Schumacher** ....(12 wins) 136
2. R. Barrichello ....(2 wins) 108
3. J. Button 79
4. F. Alonso 50
5. J. Trulli ....(1 win) 46
6. J.P. Montoya 46
7. K. Räikkönen ....(1 win) 34
8. T. Sato 26
9. D. Coulthard 24
10. G. Fisichella 21
11. R. Schumacher 12
12. F. Massa 11
13. M. Webber 7
14. O. Panis 6
15. A. Pizzonia 6
16. C. Klien 3
17. C. Da Matta 3
18. N. Heidfeld 3
19. T. Glock 2
20. Z. Baumgartner 1
21. R. Zonta 0
22. M. Gené 0
23. J. Villeneuve 0
24. G. Pantano 0
25. G. Bruni 0

Constructors

1. **Scuderia Ferrari Marlboro** .(14 wins) 244
2. Lucky Strike B.A.R Honda 105
3. Mild Seven Renault F1 Team ..(1 win) 96
4. BMW WilliamsF1 Team...............................64
5. West McLaren Mercedes ....(1 win) 58
6. Sauber Petronas 32
7. Jaguar Racing 10
8. Panasonic Toyota Racing 9
9. Jordan Ford 5
10. Minardi Cosworth 1

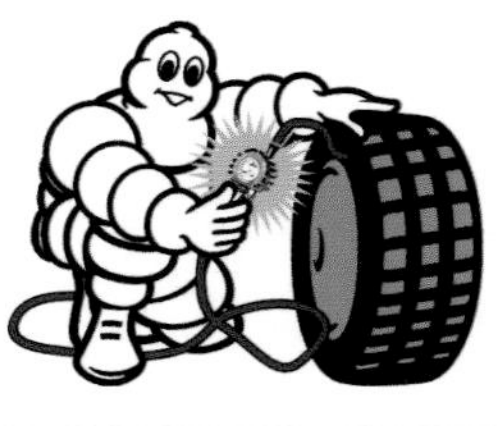

The circuit

Name	Shanghai International Circuit
Length	5451 meter
Distance	56 laps, 305,066 km
Date	September 26, 2004
Weather	Sunny, 27-29°c
Track temperature	36-40°c

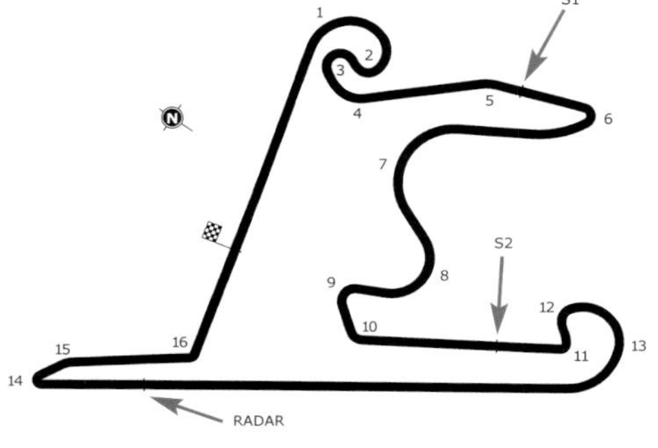

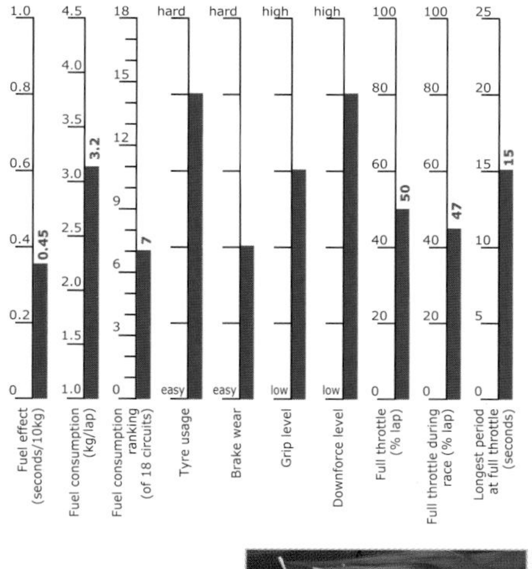

All results : © 2004 Formula One Administration Ltd,
6 Princes Gate, London, SW7 1QJ, England

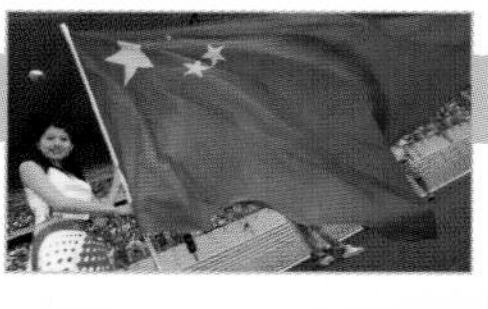

TAKUMA PACKS 'EM IN

Since Takuma Sato has shown just how good he is at the wheel of his BAR-Honda the Japanese fans' enthusiasm for F1 has been rekindled. At Suzuka all the seats were sold in advance and the spectators were not disappointed as their favourite son finished fourth.

The grand prix also marked the come back of Michael Schumacher who had not scored a victory for two months. At Suzuka the reigning world champion resumed his winning ways on what was a very busy day. For the first time in F1 qualifying took place less than four hours before the race because a typhoon had led to the cancellation of Saturday's practice sessions.

> Water, water everywhere !
On Friday showers drenched the circuit and few drivers went out. Olivier Panis covered only one lap in what was his last grand prix.

Typhoon hits Suzuka: Saturday's practice cancelled

The Chinese Grand Prix weekend had been an exciting one and it looked like the same thing was also going to happen in Japan but for different reasons. The imminent arrival of Typhoon no.22 led to the cancellation pure and simple of Saturday's practice. According to the Tsu weathermen (a small town bordering the circuit) it was going to be the most devastating typhoon to hit the country for ten years. The eye of the typhoon was supposed to pass over the centre of Suzuka around midday. In the following two hours a half metre of water per square centimetre was expected to fall. People were asked to stay barricaded at home as falling objects made any outing a perilous undertaking.

It would have left the circuit in a sorry state. On Friday evening the mechanics worked late into the night to protect their equipment from the tempest. The tents were taken down and their contents stored in the lorries and the iron curtains were lowered in front of the pits. The weekend's timing was completely rescheduled. Qualifying practice was to start on Sunday morning at 10h00 and the race was to start at 14h30.

All the supporting events were cancelled. It was a pity for the spectators who had spent all of Friday getting soaked to the skin and the number of times they saw a car could be counted on the fingers of one hand. They had to stay in their hotels on Saturday and maybe they did not even know about the cancellation as the decision had been taken on Friday evening.

In fact, on Saturday it was a storm in a teacup! If a lot of rain fell on the Suzuka circuit there was no wind and the sun came out in the early afternoon. So all the team members who had decided to spend a quiet day at their hotel went back to the track to reinstall the equipment dismantled the day before. *"It's ridiculous,"* thundered Jean-Pierre Reymond, the Renault logistics manager. *"The organisers will have to reimburse the tickets sold. In this era people overreact to the slightest hint of trouble."*

In brief

> With only two grands prix to go to the end of the season, there was no rest for some teams. Jaguar brought along a new chassis even if the team was supposed to vanish after Brazil. The BAR-Honda had a new evolution of its V10 and a new gearbox. The Anglo-Japanese outfit was battling to keep its second place in the Constructors' Championship. "This isn't the right moment to rest," said David Richards, the team boss. "We tested at Jerez last week and we'll do some more private testing before Brazil."

> Peter Sauber confirmed his intention to hire Jacques Villeneuve in 2005 even though the Canadian had not really shone in China. "It's got nothing to do with Shanghai. Taking on Jacques is the right decision for us both."

> Ralf Schumacher finished second in qualifying just behind his brother on a track that was drying out bit by bit.

> Zsolt Baumgartner did not take part in qualifying after spinning off in the Degner corner. Felipe Massa did not manage to complete a qualifying lap either.

> Michael Schumacher in practice on Friday. On Sunday morning the German qualified on pole, the 63rd of his career.

Starting grid

* Z. BAUMGARTNER
Penalty for an engine change and he start from his box

Front								
F. MASSA 19	T. GLOCK 17 1:43.533	R. BARRICHELLO 15 1:38.637	J.P. MONTOYA 13 1:37.653	F. ALONSO 11 1:36.663	J. VILLENEUVE 9 1:36.274	G. FISICHELLA 7 1:36.136	J. BUTTON 5 1:35.157	M. WEBBER 3 1:34.571	M. SCHUMACHER 1 1:33.542 (223,484 km/h)

Z. BAUMGARTNER* 20 1:48.069	G. BRUNI 18	N. HEIDFELD 16 1:41.953	C. KLIEN 14 1:38.258	K. RÄIKKÖNEN 12 1:36.820	O. PANIS 10 1:36.420	D. COULTHARD 8 1:36.156	J. TRULLI 6 1:35.213	T. SATO 4 1:34.897	R. SCHUMACHER 2 1:34.032

No.13 lucky for Michael

It was Michael's day. Overall it was a pretty full one what with qualifying on Sunday morning due to the typhoon expected on Saturday. So within a few hours the drivers did prequalifying, qualifying, the parade for the public and the race. "It was bizarre," stated Michael. "We did our qualifying laps without any preparation so there was no room for errors. It put a lot of pressure on the mechanics. It was fun for once but I prefer the usual system; it's better for everybody."

Michael had the advantage of going out last and set pole on a drying track. So it looked like it was going to be a good race for the world champion. He was never really under pressure and never lost first place even when refuelling. "In fact, the outcome of the race was decided during qualifying," he grinned after the event. "It was clear that we had a good race rhythm and if I made a good start victory looked on the cards. Ralf was not far behind early on and I was not able to open up as big a gap as I'd have liked. He refuelled before me and that decided the outcome."

In the closing laps the world champion let Felipe Massa unlap himself but did it not mean he was in trouble? "Of course not. Felipe was in front of me and we came up on Jacques and both allowed me to lap them. But afterwards Felipe wanted to go a bit quicker so I let him past. My race was very simple. No problems!"

Rubens Barrichello did not have the same luck. The Brazilian started from fifteenth spot on the grid and he had to fight his way back up through the field before being eliminated after a collision with David Coulthard. Ralf finished second behind his brother. "The car went well today," he stated after the race. "The team did a perfect job calculating the refuelling strategy, and that's the result. Last year we were quick on this circuit so we were expecting to be well placed here."

As the results of the drivers' and constructors' titles were already known the focal point of interest was the battle between BAR-Honda and Renault for

second place in the constructors' one. At Suzuka BAR scored eleven points for the third time running while Renault with only one car in the points was now sixteen behind its English rival. "It's been a really great season for us,' smiled Jenson Button. "It's my tenth time on the rostrum this year but we're not yet at the same level as Ferrari or Williams."

Two weeks later in Brazil Michael Schumacher would be on Barrichello's territory and his team-mate was really determined to score that elusive win in front of his public. "I know he wants it, every driver wants to win his home race. But, I'm very sorry for Rubens because I still want to win another grand prix this year. Anyway, he wouldn't like it if I helped".

Mark in the hot seat!

Mark Webber qualified third but had to retire rather than being roasted alive!. The Jaguar he drove had a new chassis and a cooling duct problem ended up by getting the better of the Australian. "On lap 7 I started to notice that it was getting a bit hot, especially on the right. I pitted, the mechanics cooled me down and I went back out. Then the heat became absolutely unbearable and I had to stop. You have to be 100% concentrated to drive these things and the heat destroyed my concentration to such an extent that I had to give up."

Jarno proves a point!

Jarno Trulli was absent from the Chinese Grand Prix after being fired by Renault. He was back in the cockpit at Suzuka and qualified his Toyota in sixth place, the best by the Japanese car in 2004. Good job Jarno!

"I'm exhausted. The car was virtually undriveable," said Jacques Villeneuve about his Renault R24. The Canadian finished tenth after a nightmarish race. Fernando Alonso came home fifth scoring four points; not nearly enough to worry BAR in the Constructors' classification.

A new Russian team in Formula 1

Portraits of Alex Shnaider's smiling face were everywhere in the press room. The Canadian of Russian origin announced his intention to launch a new F1 team in 2006. *"I don't understand why people don't realise that owning an F1 outfit is like sponsoring an NBA team in the USA, but with a world wide audience. We're counting on around 100 million dollars per year to run the team."*

Dallara in Italy will build the chassis but nothing has been decided yet concerning the engine.
This new arrival created a stir in the present difficult economic climate. Jaguar is destined to disappear and both Jordan and Minardi are in deep trouble. During the past few months the team owners have complained that they receive only a small percentage (23%) of the advertising and TV revenue generated by Formula 1. The rest goes to Bernie Ecclestone's company that holds the commercial rights.

The FIA president Max Mosley summed up these difficulties. *"I know the teams complain that they don't receive enough money,"* he commented. *"I've no sympathy for them. In 1998, they all signed a contract with Bernie Ecclestone in which the distribution was clearly laid out. They knew what they were getting into."*

Ford withdrawal via Jaguar did not surprise him. *"I knew such a decision was in the air. F1 is too expensive. The major manufacturers invest over 200 million euros per year just for engines. That can only be justified if you win all the races. And only one team's doing that at the moment. I know that another major manufacturer will probably leave F1 at the end of next year. I do everything I can to reduce costs but I can't do anything spectacular until the end of the present contracts in 2008. "*

Today the teams complain that the season is too long and don't want more than the seventeen grands prix laid down in their contract. Thus, Bernie has to shorten the calendar unless he pays the teams for the extra effort. Managing an F1 team in the present climate is a perilous financial exercise. Alex Shnaider will have all the time in the world to find out!

There was a huge crowd at Suzuka which came to cheer on Takuma Sato (on the right).

End of the road for David Coulthard?

David Coulthard's career is having a fairly chaotic ending. In China two weeks earlier he collided with Ralf Schumacher on lap 36. At Suzuka on lap 38 he hit Rubens Barrichello leading to the retirement of both cars with damaged suspension. The two drivers had it out in the paddock after the race. "I surprised David on the inside, he didn't see me. That's all. It was a racing incident," declared Barrichello. I don't think anyone was to blame," said David. "It's the type of thing that happens when you try to defend your place."

Practice

All the time trials

N°	Driver	N° Chassis - Engine	Practice 1 Friday	Pos.	Practice 2 Friday	Pos.	Practice 3 Saturday	Pos.	Practice 4 Saturday	Pos.	Pre-qual. Sunday	Pos.	Qualif. Sunday	Pos.
1.	Michael Schumacher	Ferrari F2004 239	1:47.906	1	1:45.388	1					1:38.397	2	1:33.542	1
2.	Rubens Barrichello	Ferrari F2004 240	1:49.846	3	1:46.874	4	Circuit being on the way of the				1:41.001	8	1:38.637	15
3.	Juan Pablo Montoya	Williams FW26 05 - BMW	1:53.517	8	1:50.060	13	Ma-On typhoon, the practice day				1:44.370	18	1:37.653	13
4.	Ralf Schumacher	Williams FW26 07 - BMW	1:55.632	12	1:49.736	12	was cancelled for security				1:38.864	3	1:34.032	2
5.	David Coulthard	McLaren MP4-19B 03 - Mercedes		23	1:48.033	5	reasons.				1:41.126	9	1:36.156	8
6.	Kimi Räikkönen	McLaren MP4-19B 01 - Mercedes	1:51.530	6	1:46.749	3					1:41.517	11	1:36.820	12
7.	Jacques Villeneuve	Renault R24-08	1:57.547	13	1:49.672	10					1:41.857	13	1:36.274	9
8.	Fernando Alonso	Renault R24-07	1:54.012	10	1:49.712	11					1.42.056	15	1.36.663	11
9.	Jenson Button	B.A.R 006-05 - Honda	1:49.937	4	1:53.482	20					1:41.423	10	1:35.157	5
10.	Takuma Sato	B.A.R 006-06 - Honda		22	1:49.370	8					1:40.135	6	1:34.897	4
11.	Giancarlo Fisichella	Sauber C23-04 - Petronas	1:48.362	2	1:46.102	2					1:40.151	7	1:36.136	7
12.	Felipe Massa	Sauber C23-03 - Petronas		19		22					1:41.707	12		19
14.	Mark Webber	Jaguar R5-05		20	1:50.666	15					1:39.170	4	1:34.571	3
15.	Christian Klien	Jaguar R5-01		21	1:52.232	17					1:42.054	14	1:38.258	14
16.	Jarno Trulli	Toyota TF104/10B	1:58.351	14	1:50.386	14					1:37.716	1	1:35.213	6
17.	Olivier Panis	Toyota TF104/09B		18		23					1:40.029	5	1:36.420	10
18.	Nick Heidfeld	Jordan EJ14/03 - Ford	1:51.438	5	1:49.286	7					1:42.434	16	1:41.953	16
19.	Timo Glock	Jordan EJ14/02 - Ford	1:52.602	7	1:49.277	6					1:43.682	17	1:43.533	17
20.	Gianmaria Bruni	Minardi PS04B/02 - Cosworth	2:02.825	16	1:53.194	19					1:45.415	19	1:48.069	18
21.	Zsolt Baumgartner	Minardi PS04B/04 - Cosworth	2:03.955	17	1:54.703	21						20		20
35.	Anthony Davidson	B.A.R 006-04 - Honda	2:00.712	15	1:49.598	9								
37.	Björn Wirdheim	Jaguar R5-06												
38.	Ryan Briscoe	Toyota TF104/11B												
39.	Robert Doornbos	Jordan EJ14/01 - Ford	1:53.603	9	1:51.007	16								
40.	Bas Leinders	Minardi PS04B/03 - Cosworth	1:55.455	11	1:52.942	18								

Maximum speed

N°	Driver	P1 Qualifs	Pos.	P1 Race	Pos.	P2 Qualifs	Pos.	P2 Race	Pos.	Finish Qualifs	Pos.	Finish Race	Pos.	Radar Qualifs	Pos.	Radar Race	Pos.
1.	M. Schumacher	290,9	1	294,5	5	311,8	6	313,2	9	290,0	1	292,1	7	289,0	1	312,1	4
2.	R. Barrichello	288,4	8	295,4	1	313,6	2	218,9	3	285,1	8	295,8	2	284,3	7	313,3	3
3.	J.P. Montoya	288,7	7	295,0	3	313,1	4	316,0	5	287,5	3	296,2	1	273,9	13	314,3	2
4.	R. Schumacher	289,7	3	294,9	4	312,5	5	314,3	7	289,0	2	292,2	6	289,0	2	309,3	6
5.	D. Coulthard	286,1	11	291,5	9	309,6	7	315,6	6	286,4	5	295,4	3	286,6	4	307,3	7
6.	K. Räikkönen	284,7	13	293,0	7	308,1	9	313,5	8	283,8	12	290,7	8	277,7	10	306,6	9
7.	J. Villeneuve	289,0	5	288,8	15	306,9	14	308,3	16	285,1	7	288,9	12	272,7	14	306,5	10
8.	F. Alonso	284,5	14	291,4	10	307,2	12	312,0	10	285,1	6	290,4	10	281,2	8	307,0	8
9.	J. Button	287,0	9	292,0	8	308,6	8	307,7	18	282,7	16	288,4	14	286,3	5	305,6	11
10.	T. Sato	289,5	4	291,1	12	307,9	11	309,6	14	283,3	14	287,0	17	277,3	11	304,1	12
11.	G. Fisichella	288,8	6	293,9	6	313,6	3	318,0	4	286,8	4	294,5	4	287,9	3	310,9	5
12.	F. Massa	286,5	10	295,2	2	315,9	1	320,6	1	283,4	13	292,6	5	259,4	18	314,6	1
14.	M. Webber	289,8	2	291,1	11	308,0	10	311,9	11	285,1	9	290,6	9	285,1	6	299,7	13
15.	C. Klien	281,6	16	285,5	18	307,2	13	319,0	2	283,3	15	289,5	11	267,3	17	293,7	18
16.	J. Trulli	282,6	15	289,3	13	305,5	16	307,1	19	284,5	10	287,0	16	279,1	9	298,4	15
17.	O. Panis	285,7	12	288,5	16	306,7	15	310,6	13	283,9	11	288,8	13	268,2	15	297,1	17
18.	N. Heidfeld	273,6	18	289,2	14	298,5	18	311,0	12	276,7	19	287,6	15	267,7	16	298,0	16
19.	T. Glock	275,9	17	287,6	17	297,0	19	308,9	15	279,5	17	286,7	18	275,2	12	299,2	14
20.	G. Bruni	266,1	19	282,2	20	299,5	17	306,0	20	276,8	18	282,9	20	255,3	19	285,9	19
21.	Z. Baumgartner			283,7	19			308,0	17			285,1	19			285,2	20

Race

Classification & Retirements

Pos.	Driver	Team	Lap	Time	Average
1.	M. Schumacher	Ferrari	53	1:24:26.985	218,524 km/h
2.	R. Schumacher	Williams BMW	53	+ 14.098	217,918 km/h
3.	J. Button	B.A.R Honda	53	+ 19.662	217,680 km/h
4.	T. Sato	B.A.R Honda	53	+ 31.781	217,162 km/h
5.	F. Alonso	Renault	53	+ 37.767	216,908 km/h
6.	K. Räikkönen	McLaren Mercedes	53	+ 39.362	216,840 km/h
7.	J.P. Montoya	Williams BMW	53	+ 55.347	216,163 km/h
8.	G. Fisichella	Sauber Petronas	53	+ 56.276	216,124 km/h
9.	F. Massa	Sauber Petronas	53	+ 1:29.656	214,725 km/h
10.	J. Villeneuve	Renault	52	1 lap	214,315 km/h
11.	J. Trulli	Toyota	52	1 lap	214,039 km/h
12.	C. Klien	Jaguar	52	1 lap	212,968 km/h
13.	N. Heidfeld	Jordan Ford	52	1 lap	212,612 km/h
14.	O. Panis	Toyota	51	2 laps	210,107 km/h
15.	T. Glock	Jordan Ford	51	2 laps	208,548 km/h
16.	G. Bruni	Minardi Cosworth	50	3 laps	203,977 km/h

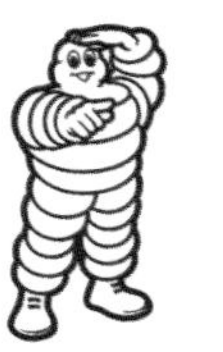

Driver	Team		Reason
Z. Baumgartner	Minardi Cosworth	42	Off
D. Coulthard	McLaren Mercedes	39	Right front suspension broken after collision with Barrichello
R. Barrichello	Ferrari	39	Right left suspension broken after collision with Coulthard
M. Webber	Jaguar	21	Unusual rise of temperature in the cockpit

Fastest laps

	Driver	Time	Lap	Average
1.	R. Barrichello	1:32.730	30	225,441 km/h
2.	M. Schumacher	1:32.796	41	225,281 km/h
3.	R. Schumacher	1:33.467	23	223,663 km/h
4.	F. Massa	1:33.614	40	223,312 km/h
5.	T. Sato	1:33.742	28	223,007 km/h
6.	J.P. Montoya	1:33.779	30	222,919 km/h
7.	J. Button	1:33.819	33	222,824 km/h
8.	G. Fisichella	1:33.850	44	222,751 km/h
9.	D. Coulthard	1:33.917	14	222,592 km/h
10.	K. Räikkönen	1:33.920	35	222,585 km/h
11.	M. Webber	1:34.229	13	221,855 km/h
12.	F. Alonso	1:34.279	29	221,737 km/h
13.	O. Panis	1:34.438	11	221,364 km/h
14.	J. Trulli	1:34.626	52	220,924 km/h
15.	C. Klien	1:35.261	32	219,451 km/h
16.	J. Villeneuve	1:35.290	28	219,385 km/h
17.	N. Heidfeld	1:35.524	25	218,847 km/h
18.	T. Glock	1:36.667	14	216,259 km/h
19.	G. Bruni	1:39.352	27	210,415 km/h
20.	Z. Baumgartner	1:39.434	26	210,241 km/h

Pit stops

	Driver	Time	Lap	Stop n°
1.	R. Schumacher	22.176	9	1
2.	O. Panis	21.173	9	1
3.	M. Webber	24.489	11	1
4.	J.P. Montoya	21.093	11	1
5.	F. Massa	21.930	11	1
6.	T. Glock	23.733	11	1
7.	G. Bruni	23.055	11	1
8.	T. Sato	21.730	12	1
9.	J. Trulli	21.394	12	1
10.	G. Fisichella	22.266	12	1
11.	R. Barrichello	21.865	12	1
12.	N. Heidfeld	22.311	12	1
13.	M. Schumacher	21.649	13	1
14.	F. Alonso	23.299	14	1
15.	K. Räikkönen	25.033	14	1
16.	J. Button	23.595	15	1
17.	D. Coulthard	22.275	15	1
18.	J. Villeneuve	23.891	15	1
19.	Z. Baumgartner	22.850	15	1
20.	C. Klien	23.909	16	1
21.	M. Webber	38.215	18	2
22.	O. Panis	21.610	20	2
23.	R. Schumacher	21.546	24	2
24.	T. Glock	26.490	24	2
25.	J. Trulli	21.018	25	2
26.	M. Schumacher	21.782	26	2
27.	T. Sato	21.956	26	2
28.	F. Massa	23.004	26	2
29.	N. Heidfeld	21.730	26	2
30.	G. Bruni	24.210	25	2
31.	G. Fisichella	22.243	27	2
32.	R. Barrichello	21.475	28	2
33.	J.P. Montoya	20.816	28	2
34.	Z. Baumgartner	28.295	27	2
35.	D. Coulthard	24.192	32	2
36.	F. Alonso	23.737	33	3
37.	C. Klien	23.989	33	2
38.	J. Villeneuve	23.008	34	2
39.	J. Button	23.374	35	2
40.	O. Panis	21.727	35	3
41.	K. Räikkönen	22.915	36	2
42.	F. Massa	21.470	38	3
43.	M. Schumacher	22.233	39	3
44.	J. Trulli	21.825	38	3
45.	R. Schumacher	21.553	39	3
46.	T. Glock	22.758	38	3
47.	N. Heidfeld	27.588	39	3
48.	G. Bruni	22.180	38	3
49.	T. Sato	21.496	41	3
50.	J.P. Montoya	22.248	41	3
51.	G. Fisichella	21.594	41	3
52.	Z. Baumgartner	22.084	40	3

Race Leader

Driver	Laps in the lead	Nber of laps
M. Schumacher	1 > 53	53

Driver	Nber of laps	Kilometers
M. Schumacher	53	307,573 km

Lap Chart

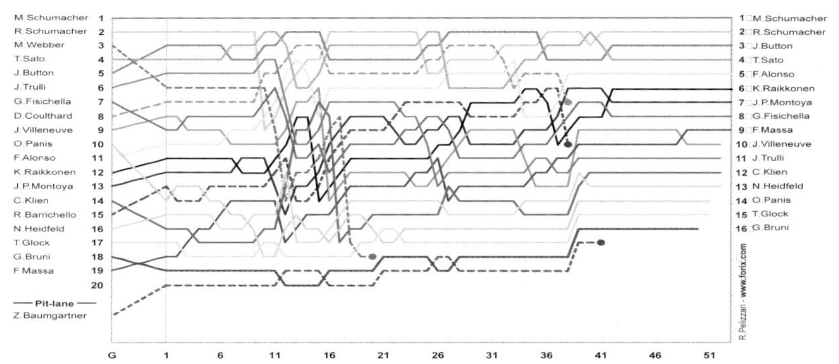

Gaps on the leader board

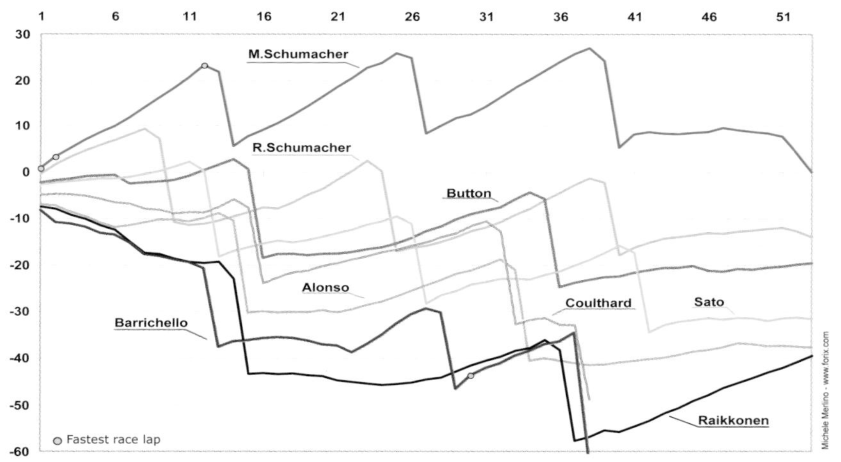

Championship after seventeen rounds

Drivers

1. **M. Schumacher** ....(13 wins) 146
2. R. Barrichello ....(2 wins) 108
3. J. Button 85
4. F. Alonso 54
5. J.P. Montoya 48
6. J. Trulli.....................(1 win) 46
7. K. Räikkönen ....(1 win) 37
8. T. Sato...31
9. D. Coulthard 24
10. G. Fisichella...22
11. R. Schumacher 20
12. F. Massa...11
13. M. Webber 7
14. O. Panis...6
15. A. Pizzonia 6
16. C. Klien 3
17. C. Da Matta...3
18. N. Heidfeld...3
19. T. Glock 2
20. Z. Baumgartner 1
21. R. Zonta 0
22. J. Villeneuve...0
23. M. Gené...0
24. G. Pantano..0
25. G. Bruni...0

Constructors

1. **Scuderia Ferrari Marlboro** .(15 wins).......254
2. Lucky Strike B.A.R Honda 116
3. Mild Seven Renault F1 Team ..(1 win) 100
4. BMW WilliamsF1 Team...................................74
5. West McLaren Mercedes........(1 win) 61
6. Sauber Petronas...33
7. Jaguar Racing 10
8. Panasonic Toyota Racing 9
9. Jordan Ford 5
10. Minardi Cosworth 1

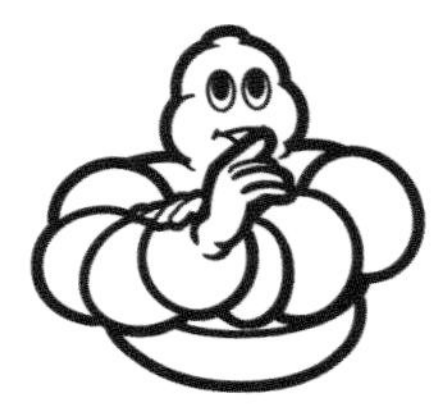

The circuit

Name	Suzuka Circuit
Length	5807 meters
Distance	53 laps, 307.573 km
Date	October 10, 2004
Weather	sunny, 28-29°c
Track temperature	32-34°c

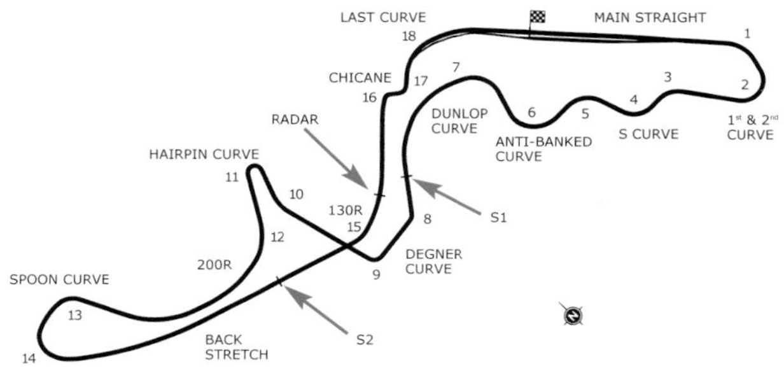

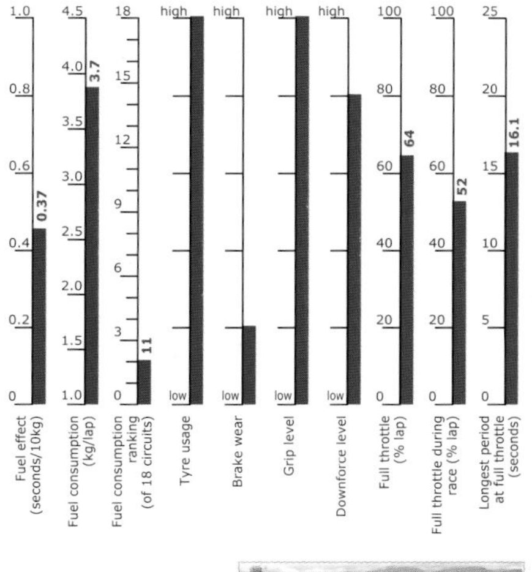

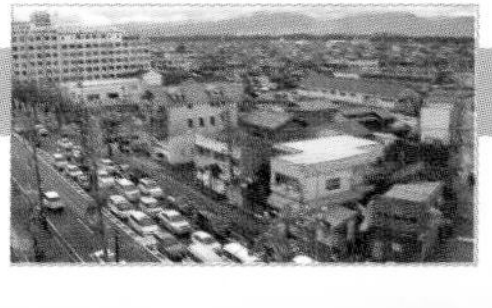

LAST ROUND
TO JUAN PABLO

Juan Pablo Montoya scored his first
victory of the year on the Interlagos
circuit in the final grand prix. It was
a very exciting race due a wet track
at the start which the dried out and
the fact that the circuit goes in anti-
clockwise direction.

Rubinho up against his jinx

Rubinho with his wife Sylvana who came to the circuit with the rest of the Barrichello family to cheer her husband on.

"Bar – ri – chel – lo, Bar – ri – chel – lo!" roared the crowd at 13h44 when they learned that the local boy had set pole for his home grand prix on the Sao Paolo circuit 2/10s ahead of his closest rival. The mass of spectators exploded with joy and began to chant the name of their hero to the rhythm of the samba. Barrichello raised a clenched fist in the cockpit of his Ferrari and savoured his lap of honour. He knew that this time he was in with a real chance of winning the Brazilian Grand Prix. The closest he has come to it was in 1999 when he led for twenty-three laps in his Stewart-Ford. "*After crossing the line I felt my legs give way,*" he said on Saturday. "*I gave my all during that lap. I knew that if I made a mistake the crowd would come after me right into the pits!*"
In 2003, he set pole before seeing his hopes dashed when his car ran out of fuel. "*Last year I should have won, I was ready,*" he confided. "*This time it's the same. I'm concentrated, the energy is positive; I'm going to give my very best. I've got a good car and I'm relaxed. I don't feel pressure any more. Tonight I'm going home to my parents and I'll sleep in my bed. For me it's just another day.*"
For Rubens winning his home race is a childhood dream. "*I lived here behind the circuit for twenty years. Today when I went out I felt the same emotions as when I did karting.*"

Up to now a jinx has always prevented him from scoring a victory in his grand prix. This time, though, everything seemed just right. He was on pole and his main rival, Michael Schumacher, was at the back of the grid. Would Lady Luck wear a samba costume this time? The first half of the morning practice was interrupted by a couple of dogs, which ran onto the track right in the middle of the session. The marshals chased them but it took a good twenty minutes before they were brought back on leads. So the session was reduced to twenty-five minutes and not forty-five. It got a laugh from the Ferrari team and Michael Schumacher but not Ron Dennis whose McLarens had done few laps so as to spare their engines.

Michael's big accident

Michael Schumacher surveys the damage to his car. The Ferrari hit the barriers very hard, then caught fire and was partially destroyed. The German was unhurt.

Michael Schumacher was the victim of his most serious accident of the season on the entry to the Ferradura corner at the end of Saturday's morning session. On Saturday evening he still did not know the reason for his crash as the Ferrari had got away from him without any warning. It hit the tyre barrier very hard and then caught fire before he managed to get out. Thus, he was obliged to qualify in the spare, which is considered as an engine change. He finished in eighteenth place on the grid as he qualified in a modest eighth place overall and was put back ten due to the regulation. His relatively poor time could be explained by the fact that his car was heavily loaded with petrol as his race strategy was based on his grid position.

Jordan does not know what the future holds. Eddie Jordan, though, will probably pull another rabbit out of his seemingly bottomless hat!

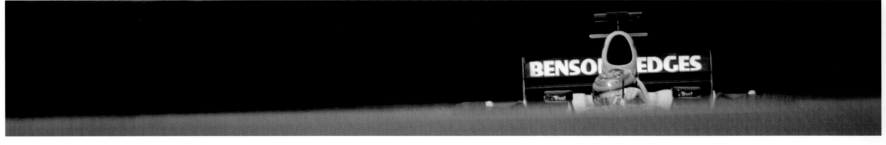

Starting grid

| 1 R. BARRICHELLO 1:10.646 (219,579 km/h) | 3 K. RÄIKKÖNEN 1:10.892 | 5 J. BUTTON 1:11.092 | 7 R. SCHUMACHER 1:11.131 | 9 J. TRULLI 1:11.483 | 11 M. WEBBER 1:11.665 | 13 J. VILLENEUVE 1:11.836 | 15 C. KLIEN 1:12.211 | 17 T. GLOCK 1:13.502 | 19 G. BRUNI* - | * M. SCHUMACHER, G. BRUNI et Z. BAUMGARTNER Penalty for an engine change |
| 2 J.P. MONTOYA 1:10.850 | 4 F. MASSA 1:10.922 | 6 T. SATO 1:11.120 | 8 F. ALONSO 1:11.454 | 10 G. FISICHELLA 1:11.571 | 12 D. COULTHARD 1:11.750 | 14 R. ZONTA 1:11.974 | 16 N. HEIDFELD 1:12.829 | 18 M. SCHUMACHER* 1:11.386 | 20 Z. BAUMGARTNER* 1:13.550 | Z. BAUMGARTNER Starts from pit lane / G. BRUNI Starts from his box |

Juan Pablo wins, Rubens loses. A great final

^
Nice atmosphere on the podium despite Rubens' disappointement.

Just at the moment that the cars were taking up their grid positions it began to rain. It was not that heavy but it transformed the circuit into a skating rink due to the accumulation of rubber and oil laid down since Friday.
In such conditions tyre choice was a dilemma, wet or dry? Out of the twenty drivers only Fernando Alonso, Jacques Villeneuve and David Coulthard opted for dry rubber. "*As I was starting from the front row I couldn't risk dry tyres,*» said Juan Pablo Montoya. "*I'd have been passed by everybody very quickly. My strategy was to take the lead straight away and I had no choice.*"
The Colombian made a cautious start and was fifth at the end of lap 1. On the next lap he passed Felipe Massa and Jenson Button. After putting on dry tyres his following victim was Rubens Barrichello. The turning point of

the race came on lap 5. Kimi Raïkkönen had just led for three laps and he came in to change to slicks at the same time as Montoya. The two drivers went back out side by side in the pit lane. The Colombian had to give way to the Finn but as soon as they were out on the rack he pulled out and passed him under braking for the "Descida do Lago" corner.
"*That where the outcome was decided*, said Juan Pablo."
"*He was better than me under braking,*" declared Raïkkönen. "*When we were leaving the pits I didn't see him in my mirrors and then under braking, wham, there he was beside me.*"
Although the race was far from over the Colombian began to open up a gap over the McLaren driver and took the lead when Alonso came in to refuel. From then on all he

had to do was maintain the gap. And so he duly won his fourth grand prix just ahead of Kimi Raïkkönen who will be his team-mate next year at McLaren. "*I'm very happy to work with Kimi,*" he grinned." *I think we're going to form a very efficient pair next year.*"
The unfortunate Brarrichello will have to wait another year to win his home grand prix. This time he finished third after spending most of the race in fifth place. "*The elements were against me,*" he pleaded. "*We're the best in the wet and in the dry but damp conditions are our weak point. And we had them today. We still have a lot of work to do in this area as our tyres are not as good as our rivals'.*"
So the Barrichello clan was not exactly in a rejoicing mood; that will have to wait for another year.

Juan Pablo in form

The last grand and his first 2004 victory; it was a big relief for Juan Pablo. "*It was an unbelievable race,*" he cried. "*It's great to have finished my four years at Williams with this win. I'd like to thank the team for giving me a fantastic car today. They were great especially when we had to change to dry tyres. They called me in at exactly the right moment.*"
The race was not that easy: "*the start was very tricky. I had problems bringing my tyres up to the right temperature on the first lap and I lost a few places. Then it seemed to me that I had more grip than the others. And when it started to rain again, I backed off so as not to take any risks. At the end my neck was hurting like hell. It was horrible. This circuit turns in an anti-clockwise direction and I was in agony.*"
The Colombian was never under threat apart from Kimi Raïkkönen who got very close at the end of the race. "*I wasn't afraid. I had enough power under my right foot and I could've upped the pace if necessary. Everything was OK.*"

<
The two Saubers finished together with only a second separating them during the final part of the race. Felipe Massa came home eighth scoring one point after leading his own grand prix on lap 7 when his rivals pitted. "*Leading the race was a fantastic sensation*", he gushed. "*I'll remember that seventh lap all my life. The car was very quick at the start in the wet and I could pass everybody. It was a lot tougher when we changed to dry tyres. I had problems finding the right rhythm.*"

A sad end for Jaguar

The Cat's last outing ended on a sad note. Both cars collided with each other on lap 24 and while Christian Klien finished fourteenth Mark Webber retired on the spot.

> Jacques Villeneuve finished in tenth spot in his third and last race with Renault. "*Things were against Jacques*," said Pat Symonds, the technical director. "*We didn't really get to know him well enough.*"

Jenson Button obliged to stay with BAR. A seat up for grabs.

The many drivers who have not yet found a drive for 2005 will be beating a path to Frank William's door as the FW 26 prove itself to be one of the most competitive cars in the field. The man responsible for this situation is Jenson Button, the BAR-Honda team driver who signed two contracts for 2005. The first was with BAR for three years until the end of 2005. At the start of the summer the British driver signed another contract with Williams for 2005 assuming that his contract with his first employer was null and void because of the non-renewal of the partnership between the team and Honda within the fixed deadline. Other sources claim that it was because of the non-payment of bonuses due to the British driver. This year Jenson Button revealed himself as one of the best drivers in F1 finishing third in the Drivers' Championship behind the Ferrari duo so both teams were desperate to have him.

The affair was put before the CRB (Contract Recognitions Board), the organism that deals with contract recognition whose decisions are accepted by everybody in F1 and on the Wednesday before Brazil it found in BAR's favour. This means that Jenson is obliged to spend another season with his present employer unless Williams offers a lot of money to buy out his contract, which, knowing how careful Frank is with cash seems highly unlikely.

So for the first time a driver has to collaborate with a team that he has rejected. It is an unhealthy situation, which BAR and Button seem to be able to put up with.

So who is going to drive the second Williams alongside Mark Webber? In the Sao Paolo paddock the names of Antonio Pizzonia, the current no1 Williams test driver and Anthony Davidson who fulfils the same role at BAR were being bandied around. Frank could also choose David Coulthard who is out of a job but he really has no future and not that much talent.

The Scot made the following proposal to Frank Williams: to drive for nothing except money for the points scored. "*Money isn't my principal aim,*" said the Scot. "*I know that my talent could be useful to Frank Williams.*"

David Coulthard has already driven for the Englishman as it with the Williams team that he made his F1 debut after Ayrton Senna's death in 1994.

The other alternative would be Jacques Villeneuve under contract to Sauber. The Canadian would probably be very happy to go back to the team with which he won the F1 World Championship for Drivers in 1997, his second year in F1. There too Williams would have to spend a small fortune to buy out Villeneuve's contract. Frank's choice is not all that easy.

> The drivers lined up for the end of season snapshot except for Michael Schumacher who was late. However, the photographers found a stand-in for the German champion!

Michael Schumacher messes up his race

Michael Schumacher made another mistake. When he does not start from the head of the field and tries to fight his way up through the pack, he often attempts to go beyond the limits of his car. At Säo Paolo he spun on lap 3 when having a go at Christian Klien's Jaguar. "*When I saw the rain, I thought it was a good opportunity for me,*" he said, "*but it wasn't heavy enough for us. This being said I think we can be proud of what we've accomplished this season. I still feel great and I could race in several more grands prix but I'll have to relax before next year.*"

Sauber against Ferrari

On Saturday evening a communiqué signed by all the teams except Ferrari was surreptitiously handed out in the Interlagos paddock. It was entitled "*An initiative from the teams to reduce costs in Formula One is a substantial and tangible manner.*" The main gist of the text was the reduction of private testing between the grands prix to cope with the extra expenses caused by extending the season to 19 grands prix. Reading between the lines it was obvious that there was a desire to impose a single tyre manufacturer again aimed at limiting tyre testing.

Naturally Ferrari was against such a proposal. "*We've invested in circuits for private testing (Mugello and Fiorano) as we feel it's the best tool for developing our cars,*" counter-attacked Luca Colajanni, porte-parole of Jean Todt, the Scuderia's manager.

The nine teams cannot get their initiative passed without unanimity, thus Ferrari can block it. In this context Peter Sauber found himself in a dilemma. However, his close links with Ferrari (which supplies him with the engine and gearbox) did not prevent him from signing the communiqué, which was basically anti-Scuderia. On Saturday, the man from Zurich published a communiqué explaining, "*how difficult it was for him to sign the cost reduction initiative. This signature does not constitute an action against Ferrari,*" clarified Peter Sauber. "*The reduction in costs is vital for the future of F1.*"

Practice

All the time trials

N°	Driver	N° Chassis - Engine	Practice 1 Friday	Pos.	Practice 2 Friday	Pos.	Practice 3 Saturday	Pos.	Practice 4 Saturday	Pos.	Pre-qual. Saturday	Pos.	Qualif. Saturday	Pos.
1.	Michael Schumacher	Ferrari F2004 239	1:14.042	11	1:11.334	2	1:11.740	6	1:10.352	2	1:10.192	4	1:11.386	8
2.	Rubens Barrichello	Ferrari F2004 240	1:13.855	9	1:11.166	1	1:11.641	4	1:10.229	1	1:09.822	1	1:10.646	1
3.	Juan Pablo Montoya	Williams FW26 05 - BMW	1:12.547	1	1:12.280	11	1:12.208	10	1:11.157	11	1:09.862	2	1:10.850	2
4.	Ralf Schumacher	Williams FW26 07 - BMW	1:12.873	3	1:12.235	10	1:11.714	5	1:10.997	7	1:10.258	5	1:11.131	7
5.	David Coulthard	McLaren MP4-19B 03 - Mercedes	1:13.277	6	1:12.430	15	1:12.085	9	1:10.413	4	1:10.418	7	1.11.750	13
6.	Kimi Räikkönen	McLaren MP4-19B 01 - Mercedes	1:13.150	4	1:11.526	3	1:11.591	3	1:10.385	3	1:10.440	8	1:10.892	3
7.	Jacques Villeneuve	Renault R24-08	1:14.585	17	1:12.316	12			1:11.321	12	1:10.708	13	1:11.836	14
8.	Fernando Alonso	Renault R24-07	1:13.990	10	1:12.005	7	1:12.563	13	1:10.683	6	1.10.637	12	1:11.454	9
9.	Jenson Button	B.A.R 006-05 - Honda	1:14.187	14	1:11.731	4	1:11.466	1	1:10.480	5	1:10.607	11	1:11.092	5
10.	Takuma Sato	B.A.R 006-06 - Honda	1:13.839	8	1:11.988	6	1:11.580	2	1:11.127	8	1:10.373	6	1:11.120	6
11.	Giancarlo Fisichella	Sauber C23-04 - Petronas	1:14.118	12	1:12.631	17	1:11.985	7	1:11.425	13	1:10.467	9	1:11.571	11
12.	Felipe Massa	Sauber C23-01 - Petronas	1:14.479	16	1:12.183	8	1:12.064	8	1:11.142	10	1:09.930	3	1:10.922	4
14.	Mark Webber	Jaguar R5-05	1:14.147	13	1:12.816	18	1:12.356	12	1:11.130	9	1:11.230	14	1:11.665	12
15.	Christian Klien	Jaguar R5-06	1:15.476	21	1:13.509	21	1:12.612	14	1:12.248	16	1:11.912	17	1:12.211	16
16.	Jarno Trulli	Toyota TF104/10B	1:13.512	7	1:12.545	16	1:12.263	11	1:11.711	15	1:10.478	10	1:11.483	10
17.	Ricardo Zonta	Toyota TF104/09B	1:14.207	15	1:12.347	14	1:13.025	15	1:11.688	14	1:11.315	15	1:11.974	15
18.	Nick Heidfeld	Jordan EJ14/03 - Ford	1:15.414	20	1:13.114	19	1:13.327	16	1:12.299	17	1:11.394	16	1:12.829	17
19.	Timo Glock	Jordan EJ14/02 - Ford	1:15.647	23	1:13.966	22	1:14.805	19	1:13.818	14	1:12.242	18	1:13.502	18
20.	Gianmaria Bruni	Minardi PS04B/02 - Cosworth	1:16.406	24	1:13.467	20	1:14.336	18	1:14.411	20	1:12.916	19		20
21.	Zsolt Baumgartner	Minardi PS04B/04 - Cosworth	1:15.490	22	1:13.979	23	1:14.284	17	1:12.990	18	1:13.032	20	1:13.550	19
35.	Anthony Davidson	B.A.R 006-04 - Honda	1:13.232	5	1:11.920	5								
37.	Björn Wirdheim	Jaguar R5-01	1:15.065	19	1:14.303	24								
38.	Ryan Briscoe	Toyota TF104/11B	1:12.614	2	1:12.209	9								
39.	Robert Doornbos	Jordan EJ14/01 - Ford	1:14.966	18	1:12.345	13								
40.	Bas Leinders	Minardi PS04B/03 - Cosworth			1:14.754	25								

Maximum speed

N°	Driver	P1 Qualifs	Pos.	P1 Race	Pos.	P2 Qualifs	Pos.	P2 Race	Pos.	Finish Qualifs	Pos.	Finish Race	Pos.	Radar Qualifs	Pos.	Radar Race	Pos.
1.	M. Schumacher	311,3	3	327,0	1	259,5	14	267,6	3	320,2	2	330,6	1	324,3	1	326,8	2
2.	R. Barrichello	313,6	1	321,1	2	265,8	3	265,0	6	320,4	1	327,5	4	321,3	5	323,4	8
3.	J.P. Montoya	310,6	4	319,7	3	266,3	1	267,9	1	316,1	10	325,3	6	315,3	15	320,3	12
4.	R. Schumacher	307,1	10	319,4	5	265,2	4	267,7	2	317,2	9	323,4	10	317,7	14	323,8	5
5.	D. Coulthard	308,4	7	315,4	11	266,2	2	263,4	10	318,0	7	324,8	7	319,3	8	319,7	13
6.	K. Räikkönen	309,0	6	319,5	4	265,0	5	266,2	5	317,7	8	322,0	11	319,3	7	323,8	6
7.	J. Villeneuve	307,5	9	317,0	9	261,1	10	262,1	11	319,7	3	323,6	8	319,3	6	322,0	10
8.	F. Alonso	307,0	11	317,2	8	262,3	7	264,1	8	319,3	5	323,4	9	322,5	3	324,5	4
9.	J. Button	306,2	12	304,9	20	262,9	6	228,2	20	315,0	13	308,3	20	318,4	10	270,8	20
10.	T. Sato	304,7	15	316,8	10	262,3	8	266,7	4	315,4	11	327,8	2	318,3	12	322,3	9
11.	G. Fisichella	309,4	5	318,5	6	261,4	9	264,1	7	318,4	6	325,7	5	322,2	4	325,9	3
12.	F. Massa	311,7	2	317,6	7	260,8	11	263,8	9	319,7	4	327,8	3	324,1	2	326,8	1
14.	M. Webber	303,7	17	312,9	14	255,1	17	259,9	13	313,1	16	321,4	12	314,4	17	323,5	7
15.	C. Klien	302,6	19	315,2	12	258,9	15	260,6	12	310,7	18	319,1	15	312,0	19	317,4	16
16.	J. Trulli	305,1	14	311,1	15	260,0	13	259,2	14	313,4	15	319,5	14	318,4	11	318,8	14
17.	R. Zonta	305,8	13	313,7	13	260,4	12	259,2	15	315,0	12	320,0	13	319,0	9	320,9	11
18.	N. Heidfeld	303,5	18	306,5	18	249,0	19	245,6	19	311,5	17	313,6	19	315,0	16	303,7	19
19.	T. Glock	304,3	16	310,3	17	253,2	18	255,1	16	309,8	19	314,0	17	313,9	18	316,7	17
20.	G. Bruni			306,4	19			252,4	18			313,9	18			314,9	18
21.	Z. Baumgartner	308,0	8	310,8	16	255,2	16	254,5	17	261,3	18	316,7	16	318,1	13	318,7	15

Race

Classification & Retirements

Pos.	Driver	Team	Lap	Time	Average
1.	J.P. Montoya	Williams BMW	71	1:28:01.451	208,516 km/h
2.	K. Räikkönen	McLaren Mercedes	71	+ 1.022	208,476 km/h
3.	R. Barrichello	Ferrari	71	+ 24.099	207,569 km/h
4.	F. Alonso	Renault	71	+ 48.908	206,603 km/h
5.	R. Schumacher	Williams BMW	71	+ 49.740	206,571 km/h
6.	T. Sato	B.A.R Honda	71	+ 50.248	206,551 km/h
7.	M. Schumacher	Ferrari	71	+ 50.626	206,537 km/h
8.	F. Massa	Sauber Petronas	71	+ 1:02.310	206,085 km/h
9.	G. Fisichella	Sauber Petronas	71	+ 1:03.842	206,026 km/h
10.	J. Villeneuve	Renault	70	1 lap	205,452 km/h
11.	D. Coulthard	McLaren Mercedes	70	1 lap	204,902 km/h
12.	J. Trulli	Toyota	70	1 lap	204,389 km/h
13.	R. Zonta	Toyota	70	1 lap	203,467 km/h
14.	C. Klien	Jaguar	69	2 laps	202,233 km/h
15.	T. Glock	Jordan Ford	69	2 laps	200,288 km/h
16.	Z. Baumgartner	Minardi Cosworth	67	4 laps	196,743 km/h
17.	G. Bruni	Minardi Cosworth	67	4 laps	196,134 km/h

Driver	Team		Reason
M. Webber	Jaguar	24	Collision with Klien
N. Heidfeld	Jordan Ford	16	Clutch problem
J. Button	B.A.R Honda	4	Engine broken

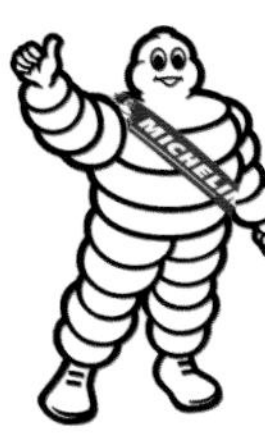

Fastest laps

	Driver	Time	Lap	Average
1.	J.P. Montoya	1:11.473	49	217,038 km/h
2.	K. Räikkönen	1:11.562	52	216,768 km/h
3.	R. Barrichello	1:11.672	22	216,435 km/h
4.	M. Schumacher	1:11.763	49	216,161 km/h
5.	R. Schumacher	1:11.764	23	216,158 km/h
6.	G. Fisichella	1:11.877	69	215,818 km/h
7.	T. Sato	1:11.941	51	215,626 km/h
8.	F. Massa	1:12.066	68	215,252 km/h
9.	F. Alonso	1:12.118	42	215,097 km/h
10.	J. Villeneuve	1:12.210	68	214,823 km/h
11.	J. Trulli	1:12.435	65	214,156 km/h
12.	D. Coulthard	1:12.522	40	213,899 km/h
13.	C. Klien	1:12.891	49	212,816 km/h
14.	R. Zonta	1:12.961	69	212,612 km/h
15.	M. Webber	1:13.197	20	211,926 km/h
16.	T. Glock	1:13.905	68	209,896 km/h
17.	Z. Baumgartner	1:14.743	45	207,543 km/h
18.	G. Bruni	1:14.756	50	207,507 km/h
19.	N. Heidfeld	1:15.855	11	204,500 km/h
20.	J. Button	1:24.440	2	183,709 km/h

Pit stops

	Driver	Time	Lap	Stop n°
1.	R. Schumacher	25.234	4	1
2.	K. Räikkönen	24.378	5	1
3.	J.P. Montoya	24.115	5	1
4.	T. Sato	23.712	5	1
5.	J. Trulli	24.767	5	1
6.	M. Schumacher	23.943	5	1
7.	R. Barrichello	23.354	6	1
8.	C. Klien	26.627	6	1
9.	M. Webber	35.387	6	1
10.	R. Zonta	24.222	6	1
11.	T. Glock	26.044	6	1
12.	Z. Baumgartner	30.820	6	1
13.	F. Massa	25.664	7	1
14.	N. Heidfeld	25.059	8	1
15.	G. Fisichella	24.155	8	1
16.	G. Bruni	25.338	8	1
17.	D. Coulthard	25.927	14	1
18.	F. Alonso	26.452	18	1
19.	J. Villeneuve	26.289	20	1
20.	R. Zonta	24.424	23	2
21.	C. Klien	34.720	24	2
22.	Z. Baumgartner	27.032	24	2
23.	R. Schumacher	25.245	26	2
24.	T. Sato	25.971	27	2
25.	R. Barrichello	24.073	27	2
26.	J.P. Montoya	25.002	28	2
27.	M. Schumacher	24.355	28	2
28.	J. Trulli	24.079	28	2
29.	K. Räikkönen	25.616	29	2
30.	G. Bruni	25.149	31	2
31.	F. Massa	26.065	33	2
32.	T. Glock	25.632	33	2
33.	G. Fisichella	24.630	34	2
34.	D. Coulthard	27.039	41	2
35.	J. Trulli	24.108	45	3
36.	J. Villeneuve	25.130	46	2
37.	F. Alonso	25.888	47	2
38.	R. Schumacher	26.287	48	3
39.	Z. Baumgartner	36.145	46	3
40.	R. Barrichello	24.261	49	3
41.	J.P. Montoya	25.048	50	3
42.	R. Zonta	25.059	49	3
43.	M. Schumacher	24.077	50	3
44.	G. Bruni	33.306	48	3
45.	C. Klien	24.708	51	3
46.	F. Massa	24.125	53	3
47.	T. Sato	24.137	54	3
48.	G. Fisichella	23.801	54	3
49.	K. Räikkönen	23.939	55	3
50.	T. Glock	25.843	54	3

Race leaders

Driver	Laps in the lead	Nber of Laps
K. Räikkönen	1 > 3	3
R. Barrichello	4 > 5	2
F. Massa	6 > 7	2
F. Alonso	8 > 18	11
J.P. Montoya	19 > 28	10
K. Räikkönen	29	1
J.P. Montoya	30 > 50	21
K. Räikkönen	51 > 55	5
J.P. Montoya	56 > 71	21

Driver	Nber of Laps	Kilometers
J.P. Montoya	47	202,523 km
F. Alonso	11	47,399 km
K. Räikkönen	9	38,571 km
R. Barrichello	2	8,618 km
F. Massa	2	8,618 km

Lap chart

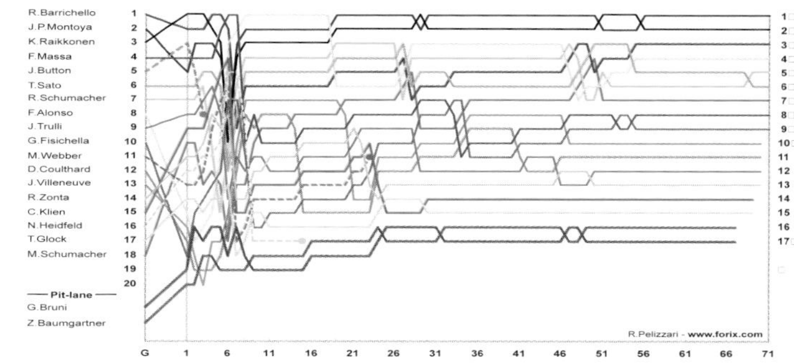

Gaps on the leader board

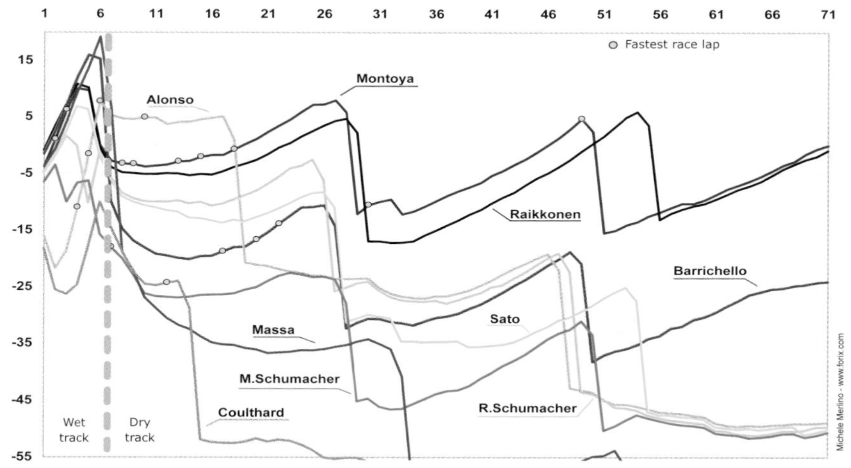

Championship after eighteen rounds

Drivers

1. **M. Schumacher** ....(13 wins) 148
2. R. Barrichello ....(2 wins) 114
3. J. Button 85
4. F. Alonso 59
5. J.P. Montoya.............(1 win) 58
6. J. Trulli ....(1 win) 46
7. K. Räikkönen ....(1 win) 45
8. T. Sato 34
9. R. Schumacher 24
10. D. Coulthard 24
11. G. Fisichella 22
12. F. Massa 12
13. M. Webber 7
14. O. Panis 6
15. A. Pizzonia 6
16. C. Klien 3
17. C. Da Matta 3
18. N. Heidfeld 3
19. T. Glock 2
20. Z. Baumgartner 1
21. J. Villeneuve 0
22. R. Zonta 0
23. M. Gené 0
24. G. Pantano 0
25. G. Bruni 0

Constructors

1. **Scuderia Ferrari Marlboro** .(15 wins) 262
2. Lucky Strike B.A.R Honda 119
3. Mild Seven Renault F1 Team ..(1 win) 105
4. BMW WilliamsF1 Team ....(1 win) 88
5. West McLaren Mercedes ....(1 win) 69
6. Sauber Petronas 34
7. Jaguar Racing 10
8. Panasonic Toyota Racing 9
9. Jordan Ford 5
10. Minardi Cosworth 1

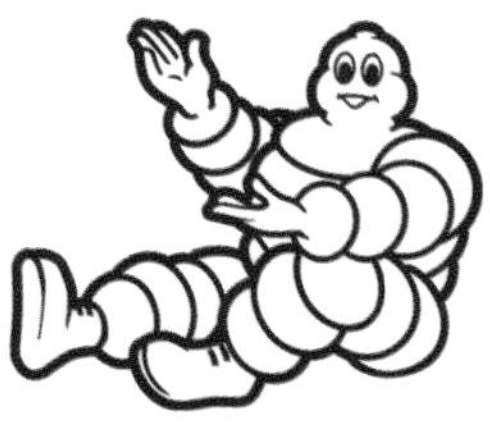

The circuit

Name	Autodromo José Carlos Pace, Interlagos, Sao Paulo
Length	4309 meters
Distance	71 laps, 305.909 km
Date	October 24, 2004
Weather	overcast, start on wet track, some drizzle later on, 25-24°c
Track temperature	28-26°c

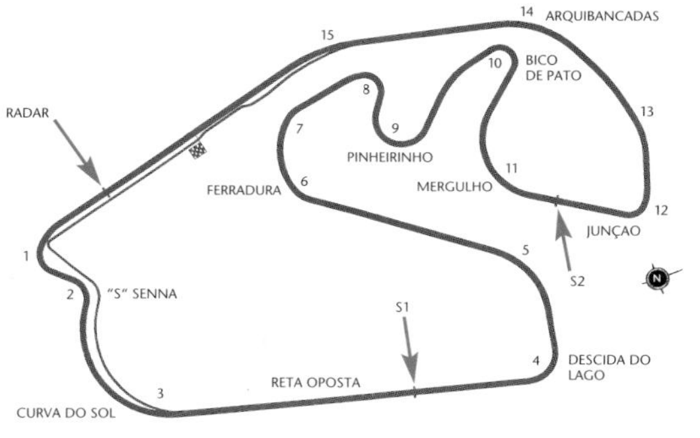

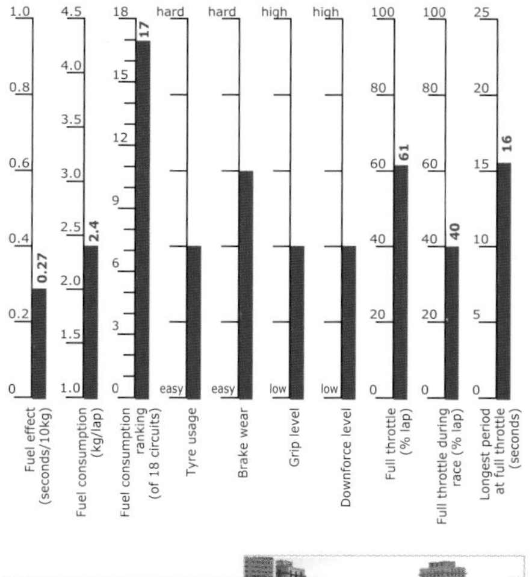

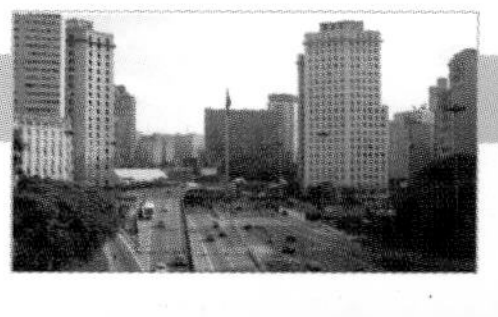

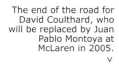

You have just finished reading all about the 2004 Formula 1 season, so now it's time to look at what 2005 has to offer. Too soon? Premature? Not at all, because, like a shark, the world of grand prix racing never sleeps. As a colleague said to me with a weary sigh, as he packed away his computer on Sunday night in Interlagos, *"see you in Melbourne in nineteen weeks!"*

Writing this in mid-November, the teams are already well on the road to designing and building next year's cars and by the end of the month, testing will resume, as teams try out their new drivers, experiment with different liveries representing new sponsors and bolt 2005 components onto 2004 chassis.

And the one thing you can be sure of is that, come the first day of practice in Australia, all the engineers will complain they did not have enough time to get their new cars fully ready and tested. For once, they will not be emulating the boy who cried wolf, because the technical and sporting regulations for 2005 have yet to be finalised and that poses a genuine problem for the men at the CAD/CAM computer screens. However, they only have themselves to blame.

At the beginning of July, FIA President Max Mosley asked the teams to come up with a set of rules aimed at achieving three prime objectives: reduce costs, reduce speeds and improve the show. Given that it would be easier to get a room full of monkeys with typewriters to produce the complete works of Shakespeare than to expect ten team principals to agree on anything, the first two deadlines for the new Utopia came and went. Therefore, in Brazil, the FIA put out a set of rules that are due to apply from the start of next season.

In essence, cars will have smaller wings plus other changes to reduce downforce by 20%, use only one set of tyres per driver for qualifying and the race and an engine must last for two complete race weekends instead of the current one event. This last rule is quite frankly ridiculous.

How does one expect the casual spectator or TV viewer to understand that the driver who sets the pole time will actually start halfway down the grid, because his engine blew up in the previous race? It might also prove difficult to comprehend why an 8 year old in an amateur kart race can use more tyres than the best drivers in the world!

However, rest assured that when the cars take to the track for qualifying next year, they will soon approach 2004 lap times, because the combined and very sharp brains

of the teams' technical geniuses will always outwit the FIA.

A more interesting question than how quickly the cars will qualify is when they will qualify, because the race weekend timetable and qualifying format is yet to be decided. In Brazil, having dropped their rules bombshell on Friday, a day later the FIA issued another statement outlining the qualifying rules. Instead of having pre-qualifying immediately followed by qualifying on Saturday afternoon, a first qualifying session, run with drivers going out in reverse order to the previous race result, so that the winner would go out last, instead of first, as in 2004, would take place on Saturday. The quickest man in this session would then go out last on Sunday morning and, here's the catch, the time of both sessions will be aggregated.

Unless my ears deceived me, I heard several team owners, Max Mosley and Bernie Ecclestone all say they did not want to see more than 17 races on the calendar

---

The idea of holding final qualifying on race morning was a knee jerk reaction to what happened in Japan this year. The typhoon threat had wiped out all of Saturday's programme and twenty four hours later, the race day crowd were treated to the fantastic spectacle of having the entire qualifying and race programme crammed into the one day: great value for money! As one anonymous chief mechanic said to me on Sunday in Suzuka: "it suits us, because to be honest under the old format, I had to make the mechanics look busy in the garage, so that the boss didn't realise they had nothing to do!" However, it now seems that the TV companies are unhappy with the new idea as it makes Saturday's qualifying a meaningless spectacle for their viewers. Back to the drawing board.

Further complicating matters comes the fact that, in Brazil, nine of the ten team owners - we will come to the missing one in a moment - waited until the day after FIA had

issued the new rules to come up with their own proposals. Why they could not do this before the regulations were issued is something I would question, but for the fact I have spent most of my working life in F1 and have therefore been immunised against absurdity! In brief, they wanted to restrict private testing during the season to only ten days, reduce the GP weekend to just Saturday and Sunday, with Friday an "anything goes" free test session.

To we English, General de Gaulle is best remembered as the man who always said "Non!" Step forward, his fellow countryman and natural successor, Jean Todt, who said "Non" to these proposals and would not sign the document. He was painted as Public Enemy No 1 by his opposite numbers and the media, but what else could he do? While some team owners built new technical palaces that might only serve as a mausoleum to their over-reaching self importance, others built swanky nightclubs, re-upholstered their private jets or bought ever bigger penis-substitute yachts, Ferrari invested in two test tracks at Fiorano and Maranello. No testing? You must be joking! Would McLaren's Ron Dennis have signed up to the testing ban if his plans of a few years ago to buy the Lydden Hill circuit near Dover had come to fruition?

So, if we are not sure what the rules will be in 2005, surely we can discuss the race calendar. Actually, no we cannot, because that won't be decided until 10th December at the earliest, after "The Formula 1 Yearbook" is flying off the shelves in the shops. With 18 grands prix, 2004 was the longest season in the history of Formula 1. Now, we have a draft calendar with 19 dates

on it - all the 2004 events, plus a new one in Turkey. At some point this year, unless my ears deceived me, I heard several team owners, Max Mosley and Bernie Ecclestone all say they did not want to see more than 17 races on the calendar. We will probably have all nineteen, even if Bernie is playing his usual cat and mouse games, this time with the French and British Grands Prix. All F1's ringmaster had to do was dangle the dollar carrot in front of the donkey team bosses.

There is an argument which says that too many grands prix will devalue the sport on the basis that if you eat caviar every day, then you get bored with it. It has to be said

however, that we could get rid of the Hungarian circuit where the grand prix always tastes more like stinky herring eggs than those of the magnificent sturgeon. If the calendar continues expanding at its current rate then teams will have to run two squads of mechanics to avoid fatigue. The big danger is that we will lose the classic European circuits, which would be a disaster for the sport. Venues like Malaysia and Bahrain might offer magnificent facilities, but the tracks themselves are as dull as an airfield (unlike good old Silverstone, which actually was an airfield, but always produces a good race.) More importantly, the inhabitants of Bahrain and Malaysia have absolutely no interest in racing and the crowd size will always be disappointing. But of course, we have to go there to allow the cigarette companies to display their logos on the cars. It's a shortsighted policy given the ever increasing global ban on tobacco advertising. Shanghai on the other hand turned out to be a magnificent track for racing, although the paddock was so unnecessarily big, I asked an FIA official if there were plans to run 20 F1 teams in the future.

By the time we got to China, it actually looked as though there would only be seven teams next season, with news that Jaguar and Cosworth were shutting down and Jordan and Minardi begging for money out of the back of their garages. Come November and it seems that we will still have ten teams on the grid. Jaguar has been bought, lock stock and barrel by energy drinks giant Red Bull, Jordan has done a deal to run Toyota engines and Minardi now know they can still have Cosworth power as the engine firm has also found new owners.

If the optimistic view is therefore that everything is rosy for 2005, trouble is looming further ahead in 2006 and this time, it could be some of the top players dropping out of the sport. BMW, Honda and Mercedes have all threatened to take FIA to court over the governing body's decision that, from 2006, engines must be 90 degree V8s with a capacity of 2400cc and a minimum weight of 95 kilos.

This muscle flexing from the manufacturers brings us to another subject that might eat up plenty of column inches in 2005, namely the GPWC. The Grand Prix World

∧
How long will the honeymoon between Frank Williams and Mario Theissen last?

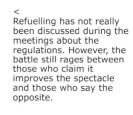

<
Refuelling has not really been discussed during the meetings about the regulations. However, the battle still rages between those who claim it improves the spectacle and those who say the opposite.

Championship, an organisation made up of the car companies involved in F1, moves around the paddock like the wind in the desert, changing the shape of the landscape, but never seen.

No one has ever taken seriously the GPWC threat to run its own rival F1 series when the current Concorde Agreement expires at the end of 2007. It is simply trying to push Ecclestone, the F1 Commercial Rights Holder, into cutting the teams a better financial deal. Now, Ecclestone is in trouble, because the three banks who own 75% of his Formula One Holdings company have won the legal right to go to court in their efforts to gain total control of this company. If they succeed, then they will no doubt put the management of the sport into the hands of the GPWC and Bernie Ecclestone will therefore be left out in the cold. When, as happened at Monza this year, even Ferrari president Luca di Montezemolo, attacked what he called Ecclestone's "one man show," then we can assume the GPWC threat is a real one.

It would be wrong to think that Ecclestone is losing his grip just yet. Late in the season, Mr. E's pet dog was splashed across pages of all the English newspapers for attacking other dogs in the exclusive gardens attached to his palatial London residence! And just like a cornered dog under pressure, this is when the old ringmaster is at his most dangerous. Politically therefore, 2005 could see some fireworks in the courtroom and the paddock.

But Grand Prix racing is not Communism

While a more powerful GPWC might see a fairer division of the F1 cash cake, it will do little to level the playing field on the technical front. If we assume that, come Sunday afternoon, F1 is a sport, not a business, then there will always be some teams that are better than others, which is after all the basis of all sporting contests. Paul Stoddart (Minardi) and Eddie Jordan, who led the team

owners revolt in Brazil seem to have an idealised view that they should be challenging the likes of Ferrari and other top teams on equal terms. But grand prix racing is not Communism and to paraphrase the famous line from George Orwell's novel, "Animal Farm: "All teams are equal, but some teams are more equal than others."

Whatever the rules, there will be no radical change to the pecking order in the paddock. Regulation changes tend to favour the bigger teams who have the resources to evaluate a larger number of possible solutions. There is no reason to think Ferrari will not be the dominant force once again. Michael Schumacher will be the oldest man on the grid, but he is not exactly at pensionable age and more importantly he still loves winning and hates losing. There are signs that his rivals could get closer to the seven times world champion and the most tantalising aspect of 2005 will be to see if BAR-Honda will be able to maintain the momentum that took them to second place in the 2004 championship. Its driver, Jenson Button, really came of age and

with no more contractual wranglings to distract him, he could be a force to be reckoned with.

If life was fair, which it's not, then Kimi Raikkonen, the biggest untapped talent on the grid, would be winning races on a regular basis, but a power struggle within Mercedes-Benz and the fact that Ron Dennis is considering retirement, forced or otherwise, adds to the uncertainty surrounding McLaren's hopes for the coming season. When Dennis and Frank Williams were making their way up the F1 ladder, they were pretty much the same age as their drivers, but now they are old enough to be their parents, if not quite their grandparents. In 2004, these two great teams seemed tired and careworn and that aspect of their packages will not improve in

2005. However, in the shape of Mark Webber, Williams finally have a driver that fits their mould and that should give them a boost. They will not be sad to see the back of Ralf Schumacher and Juan Pablo Montoya, both of whom I expect to struggle in their respective new homes at Toyota and McLaren.

As for the middle order on the grid, it is hard to predict how it will shake out. The most interesting point to watch among the Second Division teams will be Sauber's switch to Michelin, after a similar move worked wonders for BAR in 2004. However, with Massa and Villeneuve, the Swiss team has its weakest driver line-up for several years.

Now the more observant among you may have spotted the one glaring error with this long

and rambling conclusion: namely that I have drawn no conclusions! What did you expect? I work in Formula 1, where sitting on the fence is the house speciality. The real reason skirting round the issue of what we can expect on the race tracks of the world over the next few months is also the reason that you are reading this book and why Formula 1 has enduring appeal: namely that, like every year, no one really knows what we can expect from this fascinating sport. It is a popular pastime to talk of crisis in F1, but no one would mention the "c" word if Ferrari had not crushed the opposition. Now we must put our hope in the other teams to end the Prancing Horse's reign, or at least to make them work harder. There's not much point in having a 19 race series, if the title trophies are returned to Maranello halfway through the year.

<
In 2005, Toyota will supply engines to the Jordan team ensuring the survival of the Silverstone based outfit.

Recap of the 2004 season

Position in the Championship	Driver	Team	1. Australia	2. Malaysia	3. Bahraïn	4. San Marino	5. Spain	6. Monaco	7. Europe	8. Canada	9. United States of America	10. France	11. Great Britain	12. Germany	13. Hungary	14. Belgium	15. Italy	16. China	17. Japan	18. Brazil	Number of pole positions	Number of wins	Number of fastest laps	Number of podiums	Number of laps in the lead	Number of GP in the lead	Number of kilometers in the lead	Number of points
1	Michael SCHUMACHER	Ferrari	**1**	**1**	**1**	**1**	**1**	A	**1**	**1**	**1**	**1**	**1**	**1**	**1**	2	2	12	**1**	7	8	13	10	15	683	16	3356,446	148
2	Rubens BARRICHELLO	Ferrari	2	4	2	6	2	3	2	2	2	3	3	12	2	3	**1**	**1**	A	3	4	2	4	14	102	8	535,683	114
3	Jenson BUTTON	B.A.R Honda	6	3	3	2	8	2	3	3	A	5	4	2	5	A	3	2	3	A	1	-	-	10	52	5	277,598	85
4	Fernando ALONSO	Renault	3	7	6	4	4	A	5	A	A	2	10	3	3	A	A	4	5	4	1	-	-	4	60	8	276,505	59
5	Juan Pablo MONTOYA	Williams BMW	5	2	13	3	A	4	8	A	A	8	5	5	4	A	5	5	7	**1**	-	1	2	3	51	3	226,128	58
6	Jarno TRULLI	Renault / Toyota	7	5	4	5	3	**1**	4	A	4	4	A	11	A	9	10		11	12	2	1	-	2	89	3	340,137	46
7	Kimi RÄIKKÖNEN	McLaren Mercedes	A	A	A	8	11	A	A	5	6	7	2	A	A	1	A	3	6	2	1	1	2	4	50	4	302,075	45
8	Takuma SATO	B.A.R Honda	7	15	5	16	5	A	A	A	3	A	11	8	6	A	4	6	4	6	-	-	-	1	2	1	10,296	34
9	Ralf SCHUMACHER	Williams BMW	4	A	7	7	6	10	A	A	A							A	2	5	1	-	-	1	30	2	131,920	24
10	David COULTHARD	McLaren Mercedes	8	6	A	12	10	A	A	6	7	6	7	4	9	7	6	9	A	11	-	-	-	-	-	-	-	24
11	Giancarlo FISICHELLA	Sauber Petronas	10	11	11	9	7	A	6	4	9	12	6	9	8	5	8	7	8	9	-	-	-	-	-	-	-	22
12	Felipe MASSA	Sauber Petronas	A	8	12	10	9	5	9	A	A	13	9	13	A	4	12	8	9	8	-	-	-	-	2	1	8,618	12
13	Mark WEBBER	Jaguar	A	A	8	13	12	A	7	A	A	9	8	6	10	A	9	10	A	A	-	-	-	-	-	-	-	7
14	Olivier PANIS	Toyota	13	12	9	11	A	8	11	A	5	15	A	14	11	8	A	14	14		-	-	-	-	-	-	-	6
15	Antonio PIZZONIA	Williams BMW												7	7	A	7				-	-	-	-	1	1	6,976	6
16	Christian KLIEN	Jaguar	11	10	14	14	A	A	12	9	A	11	14	10	13	6	13	A	12	14	-	-	-	-	-	-	-	3
17	Cristiano DA MATTA	Toyota	12	9	10	A	13	6	A	A	A	14	13	A							-	-	-	-	-	-	-	3
18	Nick HEIDFELD	Jordan Ford	A	A	15	A	A	7	10	8	A	16	15	A	12	11	14	13	13	A	-	-	-	-	-	-	-	3
19	Timo GLOCK	Jordan Ford								7								15	15	15	-	-	-	-	-	-	-	2
20	Zsolt BAUMGARTNER	Minardi Cosworth	A	16	A	15	A	9	15	10	8	A	A	16	15	A	15	16	A	16	-	-	-	-	-	-	-	1
21	Jacques VILLENEUVE	Renault																11	10	10	-	-	-	-	-	-	-	0
22	Ricardo ZONTA	Toyota													A	10	11	A		13	-	-	-	-	-	-	-	0
23	Marc GENÉ	Williams BMW										10	12								-	-	-	-	-	-	-	0
24	Giorgio PANTANO	Jordan Ford	14	13	16	A	A	A	13		A	17	A	15	A	A	A				-	-	-	-	-	-	-	0
25	Gianmaria BRUNI	Minardi Cosworth	A	14	17	A	A	A	14	A	A	18	16	17	14	A	A	A	16	17	-	-	-	-	-	-	-	0

Number of laps and kms completed in 2004

Driver	Maximum 1122 laps	Maximum 5472.382 kms	GP finished / GP contested
1. Barrichello	1107	5385.277	17/18
2. M. Schumacher	1089	5360.051	17/18
3. Montoya	1076	5250.033	15/18
4. Fisichella	1032	5153.997	16/18
5. Button	991	4873.079	15/18
6. Coulthard	983	4884.572	14/18
7. Massa	969	4798.781	14/18
8. Alonso	949	4660.759	13/18
9. Trulli	943	4611.617	14/17
10. Heidfeld	910	4478.651	11/18
11. Panis	904	4399.988	14/17
12. Sato	901	4448.030	11/18
13. Klien	886	4469.275	14/18
14. Baumgartner	874	4225.326	11/18
15. Webber	787	3851.437	10/18
16. Räikkönen	752	3681.477	10/18
17. Bruni	736	3629.705	9/18
18. Da Matta	592	2770.401	8/12
19. R. Schumacher	579	2765.060	7/12
20. Pantano	549	2718.713	6/14
21. Glock	243	1189.413	4/4
22. Zonta	230	1220.718	2/5
23. Pizzonia	219	1127.125	3/4
24. Villeneuve	177	902.981	3/3
25. Gené	130	616.941	2/2

Number of wins

M. Schumacher	83	J. Herbert	3
A. Prost	51	P. Hill	3
A. Senna	41	M. Hawthorn	3
N. Mansell	31	D. Pironi	3
J. Stewart	27	E. De Angelis	2
J. Clark	25	P. Depailler	2
N. Lauda	25	J-F Gonzales	2
J.M. Fangio	24	J-P. Jabouille	2
N. Piquet	23	P. Revson	2
D. Hill	22	P. Rodriguez	2
M. Häkkinen	20	J. Siffert	2
S. Moss	16	P. Tambay	2
J. Brabham	14	M. Trintignant	2
E. Fittipaldi	14	W. Von Trips	2
G. Hill	14	B. Vukovich	2
A. Ascari	13	J. Alesi	1
D. Coulthard	13	F. Alonso	1
Ma. Andretti	12	G. Baghetti	1
A. Jones	12	L. Bandini	1
C. Reutemann	12	J-P. Beltoise	1
J. Villeneuve	11	J. Bonnier	1
G. Berger	10	V. Brambilla	1
J. Hunt	10	J. Bryan	1
R. Peterson	10	F. Cevert	1
J. Scheckter	10	L. Fagioli	1
R. Barrichello	9	G. Fisichella	1
D. Hulme	8	P. Flaherty	1
J. Ickx	8	P. Gethin	1
R. Arnoux	7	R. Ginther	1
T. Brooks	6	S. Hanks	1
J. Laffite	6	I. Ireland	1
R. Patrese	6	J. Mass	1
J. Rindt	6	L. Musso	1
R. Schumacher	6	A. Nannini	1
J. Surtees	6	G. Nilson	1
G. Villeneuve	6	C. Pace	1
M. Alboreto	5	O. Panis	1
G. Farina	5	J. Parsons	1
C. Regazzoni	5	K. Räikkönen	1
K. Rosberg	5	L. Scarfiotti	1
J. Watson	5	B. Sweikert	1
D. Gurney	4	J. Rathman	1
E. Irvine	4	T. Ruttman	1
B. McLaren	4	P. Taruffi	1
J.P. Montoya	4	J. Trulli	1
T. Boutsen	3	L. Wallard	1
P. Collins	3	R. Ward	1
H-H. Frentzen	3		

Total number of points scored

M. Schumacher	1186	E. De Angelis	122
A. Prost	798.5	J. Trulli	117
A. Senna	614	G. Fisichella	116
N. Piquet	485.5	F. Alonso	114
N. Mansell	482	J. Rindt	109
D. Coulthard	475	R. Ginther	107
R. Barrichello	451	G. Villeneuve	107
N. Lauda	420.5	P. Tambay	103
M. Häkkinen	420	D. Pironi	101
G. Berger	385	M. Brundle	98
J. Stewart	360	J. Herbert	98
D. Hill	360	P. Hill	98
C. Reutemann	310	F. Cevert	89
G. Hill	289	S. Johanson	88
E. Fittipaldi	281	C. Amon	83
R. Patrese	281	J-F Gonzales	77.64
J.M. Fangio	277.5	J-P. Beltoise	77
J. Clark	274	O. Panis	76
J. Brabham	261	T. Brooks	75
R. Schumacher	259	M. Trintignant	72.33
J. Scheckter	255	P. Rodriguez	71
D. Hulme	248	J. Mass	71
J. Alesi	241	D. Warwick	71
J. Laffite	228	E. Cheever	70
J.P. Montoya	221	J. Siffert	68
J. Villeneuve	219	A. Nannini	65
C. Regazzoni	212	P. Revson	61
A. Jones	206	A. De Cesaris	59
R. Peterson	206	L. Bandini	58
B. McLaren	196.5	C. Pace	58
E. Irvine	191	W. Von Trips	56
M. Alboreto	186.6	J. Behra	51.14
S. Moss	186.5	L. Villoresi	49
R. Arnoux	181	P. Collins	47
J. Ickx	181	I. Ireland	47
Ma. Andretti	180	L. Musso	44
J. Surtees	180	P. Taruffi	41
J. Hunt	179	J. Bonnier	39
H-H. Frentzen	174	T. Sato	39
K. Räikkönen	169	M. Salo	33
J. Watson	169		
K. Rosberg	159.5	**Then**	
P. Depailler	141	N. Heidfeld	28
A. Ascari	140	M. Webber	26
D. Gurney	133	F. Massa	16
T. Boutsen	132	C. Da Matta	10
J. Button	130	A. Pizzonia	6
M. Hawthorn	127.5	M. Gené	4
N. Farina	127.3	C. Klien	3
		R. Zonta	3
		T. Glock	2
		Z. Baumgartner	1

Number of Grands Prix contested (707 drivers)

Riccardo Patrese	256	Bruce McLaren	100	Fernando Alonso	50	Mike Beuttler	28
Michael Schumacher	211	Jackie Stewart	99	Mark Webber	50	Enrique Bernoldi	28
Gerhard Berger	210	Pedro Diniz	98	Mike Hailwood	49	Cristiano da Matta	28
Andrea de Cesaris	208	Jo Siffert	96	Jean Pierre Jabouille	49	Wolfgang von Trips	27
Nelson Piquet	204	Chris Amon	96	Derek Daly	49	Trevor Taylor	27
Jean Alesi	201	Patrick Depailler	95	Nicola Larini	49	Piers Courage	27
Alain Prost	199	Ukyo Katayama	94	Phil Hill	48	Jose Froilan Gonzalez	26
Rubens Barrichello	195	Ivan Capelli	93	Jackie Oliver	48	Luis Perez-Sala	26
Michele Alboreto	194	James Hunt	92	Luca Badoer	48	Ricardo Rosset	26
Nigel Mansell	187	Dan Gurney	86	Roy Salvadori	47	Tony Maggs	25
Graham Hill	176	Jean Pierre Beltoise	84	Manfred Winkelhock	47	Bob Anderson	25
Jacques Laffite	176	Jenson Button	84	Bertrand Gachot	47	Rupert Keegan	25
David Coulthard	175	Nick Heidfeld	84	François Cevert	46	Huub Rothengatter	25
Niki Lauda	171	Maurice Trintignant	82	Mike Hawthorn	45	Jan Magnussen	25
Thierry Boutsen	163	Marc Surer	82	Eric Bernard	45	Luigi Musso	24
Ayrton Senna	161	Jonathan Palmer	82	Lorenzo Bandini	42	Eliseo Salazar	24
Mika Häkkinen	161	Stefan Johansson	79	Tom Pryce	42	Yannick Dalmas	24
Johnny Herbert	160	Alessandro Nannini	76	Hector Rebaque	41	David Brabham	24
Martin Brundle	158	Hans Joachim Stuck	74	Olivier Grouillard	41	Tarso Marques	24
Olivier Panis	157	Vittorio Brambilla	74	Roberto Moreno	41	Johnny Claes	23
Heinz-Harald Frentzen	156	Piercarlo Ghinzani	74	Karl Wendlinger	41	Raul Boesel	23
John Watson	152	Satoru Nakajima	74	Alessandro Zanardi	41	Jan Lammers	23
René Arnoux	149	Mauricio Gugelmin	74	Christian Fittipaldi	40	Toulo de Graffenried	22
Carlos Reutemann	146	Jim Clark	72	Louis Rosier	38	Reine Wisell	22
Derek Warwick	146	Carlos Pace	71	Tony Brooks	38	Giancarlo Baghetti	21
Eddie Irvine	146	Didier Pironi	70	Masten Gregory	38	Roberto Guerrero	21
Emerson Fittipaldi	144	Stefano Modena	70	Gabriele Tarquini	38	Gaston Mazzacane	21
Giancarlo Fisichella	141	Bruno Giacomelli	69	Emanuele Pirro	37	Stefan Bellof	20
Jean Pierre Jarier	134	Juan Pablo Montoya	68	Mike Spence	36	Zsolt Baumgartner	20
Jacques Villeneuve	133	Gilles Villeneuve	67	Mauro Baldi	36	Prince Bira	19
Clay Regazzoni	132	Gianni Morbidelli	67	Marc Gené	36	Harald Ertl	19
Eddie Cheever	132	Kimi Räikkönen	67	Takuma Sato	36	Brian Henton	19
Mario Andretti	128	Stirling Moss	66	Ricardo Zonta	36	Francois Hesnault	19
Jarno Trulli	128	Teo Fabi	64	Howden Ganley	35	Andrea Montermini	19
Ralf Schumacher	127	Aguri Suzuki	64	Wilson Fittipaldi	35	Piero Taruffi	18
Jack Brabham	126	J J Lehto	62	Christian Danner	35	Ian Scheckter	18
Ronnie Peterson	123	Pedro de la Rosa	62	Tim Schenken	34	Chico Serra	18
Pierluigi Martini	119	Mark Blundell	61	Brett Lunger	34	Johnny Cecotto	18
Alan Jones	116	Jochen Rindt	60	Felipe Massa	34	Taki Inoue	18
Damon Hill	115	Erik Comas	59	Nino Farina	33	Christian Klien	18
Jacky Ickx	114	Arturo Merzario	57	Shinji Nakano	33	Gianmaria Bruni	18
Keke Rosberg	114	Harry Schell	56	Alberto Ascari	32	Roberto Mieres	17
Patrick Tambay	114	Henri Pescarolo	56	Peter Collins	32	Hans Herrmann	17
Denny Hulme	112	Alex Caffi	56	Pedro Lamy	32	Lucien Bianchi	17
John Surtees	111	Pedro Rodriguez	54	Toranosuke Takagi	32	Nanni Galli	17
Jody Scheckter	111	Rolf Stommelen	53	Luigi Villoresi	31	Cliff Allison	16
Philippe Alliot	109	Philippe Streiff	53	Gunnar Nilsson	31		
Mika Salo	109	Jean Behra	52	Peter Revson	30		
Elio de Angelis	108	Richie Ginther	52	Peter Gethin	30	**Then**	
Jos Verstappen	106	Alexander Wurz	52	Andrea de Adamich	29	Antonio Pizzonia	15
Jo Bonnier	104	Juan Manuel Fangio	51	Robert Manzon	28	Giorgio Pantano	14
Jochen Mass	104	Innes Ireland	50	Carel Godin de Beaufort	28	Timo Glock	4

Number of pole positions

A. Senna	65	J. Laffite	7
M. Schumacher	63	E. Fittipaldi	6
J. Clark	33	P. Hill	6
A. Prost	33	J.P. Jabouille	6
N. Mansell	32	A. Jones	6
J.M. Fangio	29	C. Reutemann	6
M. Häkkinen	26	C. Amon	5
N. Lauda	24	G. Farina	5
N. Piquet	24	C. Regazzoni	5
D. Hill	20	K. Rosberg	5
Ma. Andretti	18	R. Schumacher	5
R. Arnoux	18	P. Tambay	5
J. Stewart	17	M. Hawthorn	4
S. Moss	16	D. Pironi	4
A. Ascari	14	F. Alonso	3
J. Hunt	14	T. Brooks	3
R. Peterson	14	E. De Angelis	3
R. Barrichello	13	T. Fabi	3
J. Brabham	13	J-F. Gonzales	3
G. Hill	13	D. Gurney	3
J. Ickx	13	J-P. Jarier	3
J. Villeneuve	13	K. Räikkönen	3
G. Berger	12	J. Scheckter	3
D. Coulthard	12		
J.P. Montoya	11	**Then**	
J. Rindt	10	J. Trulli	2
J. Surtees	8	J. Button	1
R. Patrese	8	G. Fisichella	1

Number of fastest laps

M. Schumacher	66	R. Peterson	9
A. Prost	41	J. Villeneuve	9
N. Mansell	30	J. Hunt	8
J. Clark	28	G. Villeneuve	8
M. Häkkinen	25	R. Schumacher	7
N. Lauda	24	E. Fittipaldi	6
J.M. Fangio	23	H-H. Frentzen	6
N. Piquet	23	J-F. Gonzalez	6
G. Berger	21	D. Gurney	6
D. Hill	19	M. Hawthorn	6
S. Moss	19	P. Hill	6
A. Senna	19	J. Laffite	6
D. Coulthard	18	K. Räikkönen	6
R. Barrichello	15	C. Reutemann	6
C. Regazzoni	15	M. Alboreto	5
J. Stewart	15	G. Farina	5
J. Ickx	14	C. Pace	5
A. Jones	13	D. Pironi	5
R. Patrese	13	J. Scheckter	5
R. Arnoux	12	J. Watson	5
J. Brabham	12	J. Alesi	4
A. Ascari	11	J.P. Beltoise	4
J.P. Montoya	11	P. Depailler	4
Ma. Andretti	10	J. Siffert	4
G. Hill	10	**Then**	
J. Surtees	10	F. Alonso	1
D. Hulme	9	G. Fisichella	1

Number of laps in the lead

M. Schumacher	4'657	B. Vukovich	485
A. Senna	2'986	E. Fittipaldi	478
A. Prost	2'684	D. Hulme	449
N. Mansell	2'089	J. Rindt	387
J. Clark	1'943	R. Schumacher	387
J. Stewart	1'921	J.P. Montoya	382
N. Piquet	1'600	C. Regazzoni	360
N. Lauda	1'592	N. Farina	338
M. Häkkinen	1'488	J. Surtees	312
D. Hill	1'358	D. Pironi	295
J.M. Fangio	1'348	J. Laffite	283
S. Moss	1'181	J. Watson	282
G. Hill	1'102	J-F. Gonzalez	272
A. Ascari	926	J. Alesi	265
D. Coulthard	893	M. Hawthorn	225
J. Brabham	825	M. Alboreto	218
Ma. Andretti	798	J. Bryan	216
R. Peterson	707	K. Räikkönen	209
R. Barrichello	699	D. Gurney	200
G. Berger	692	P. Tambay	195
J. Scheckter	675	**Then**	
J. Hunt	666	F. Alonso	157
C. Reutemann	649	J. Trulli	141
J. Villeneuve	633	G. Fisichella	36
A. Jones	589	J. Button	70
R. Patrese	567	C. Da Matta	17
G. Villeneuve	534	O. Panis	16
J. Ickx	529	F. Massa	2
K. Rosberg	517	T. Sato	2
R. Arnoux	506	M. Webber	2

Number of kilometers in the lead

M. Schumacher	21'954	K. Rosberg	2'165
A. Senna	13'672	J. Surtees	2'117
A. Prost	12'481	D. Hulme	1'971
J. Clark	10'125	J. Rindt	1'898
N. Mansell	9'642	C. Regazzoni	1'851
J.M. Fangio	9'322	R. Schumacher	1'722
J. Stewart	9'191	M. Hawthorn	1'635
N. Piquet	7'611	D. Gurney	1'612
M. Häkkinen	7'189	J.P. Montoya	1'565
N. Lauda	7'064	P. Hill	1'528
S. Moss	6'372	J.F. Gonzalez	1'525
D. Hill	6'309	J. Laffite	1'519
G. Hill	4'767	J. Alesi	1'285
J. Brabham	4'540	T. Brooks	1'268
D. Coulthard	4'190	D. Pironi	1'240
G. Berger	3'718	J. Watson	1'218
Ma. Andretti	3'577	K. Räikkönen	1'071
J. Hunt	3'363	P. Tambay	962
R. Peterson	3'262	J.P. Jabouille	948
C. Reutemann	3'255	P. Collins	946
J. Ickx	3'119	**Then**	
J. Villeneuve	2'970	F. Alonso	718
J. Scheckter	2'851	J. Trulli	574
A. Jones	2'847	J. Button	358
G. Farina	2'651	G. Fisichella	176
R. Arnoux	2'571	C. Da Matta	87
R. Patrese	2'553	O. Panis	53
R. Barrichello	2'853	T. Sato	10
G. Villeneuve	2'251	F. Massa	9
E. Fittipaldi	2'235	M. Webber	8

The 55 World Champions

Year	Driver	Country	Team	Number of GP	Number of poles	Number of wins	Number of fastest laps
1950	Giuseppe Farina	ITA	Alfa Romeo	7	2	3	3
1951	Juan Manuel Fangio	ARG	Alfa Romeo	8	4	3	5
1952	Alberto Ascari	ITA	Ferrari	8	5	6	5
1953	Alberto Ascari	ITA	Ferrari	9	6	5	4
1954	Juan Manuel Fangio	ARG	Mercedes/Maserati	9	5	6	3
1955	Juan Manuel Fangio	ARG	Mercedes	7	3	4	3
1956	Juan Manuel Fangio	ARG	Lancia/Ferrari	8	5	3	3
1957	Juan Manuel Fangio	ARG	Maserati	8	4	4	2
1958	Mike Hawthorn	GB	Ferrari	11	4	1	5
1959	Jack Brabham	AUS	Cooper Climax	9	1	2	1
1960	Jack Brabham	AUS	Cooper Climax	10	3	5	3
1961	Phil Hill	USA	Ferrari	8	5	2	2
1962	Graham Hill	GB	BRM	9	1	4	3
1963	Jim Clark	GB	Lotus Climax	10	7	7	6
1964	John Surtees	GB	Ferrari	10	2	2	2
1965	Jim Clark	GB	Lotus Climax	10	6	6	6
1966	Jack Brabham	AUS	Brabham Repco	9	3	4	1
1967	Denny Hulme	NZ	Brabham Repco	11	0	2	2
1968	Graham Hill	GB	Lotus Ford	12	2	3	0
1969	Jackie Stewart	GB	Matra Ford	11	2	6	5
1970	Jochen Rindt	AUT	Lotus Ford	13	3	5	1
1971	Jackie Stewart	GB	Tyrrell Ford	11	6	6	3
1972	Emerson Fittipaldi	BRE	Lotus Ford	12	3	5	0
1973	Jackie Stewart	GB	Tyrrell Ford	15	3	5	1
1974	Emerson Fittipaldi	BRE	McLaren Ford	15	2	3	0
1975	Niki Lauda	AUT	Ferrari	14	9	5	2
1976	James Hunt	GB	McLaren Ford	16	8	6	2
1977	Niki Lauda	AUT	Ferrari	17	2	3	3
1978	Mario Andretti	USA	Lotus Ford	16	8	6	3
1979	Jody Scheckter	SA	Ferrari	15	1	3	1
1980	Alan Jones	AUS	Williams Ford	14	3	5	5
1981	Nelson Piquet	BRE	Brabham Ford	15	4	3	1
1982	Keke Rosberg	FIN	Williams Ford	16	1	1	0
1983	Nelson Piquet	BRE	Brabham BMW Turbo	15	1	3	4
1984	Niki Lauda	AUT	McLaren TAG Porsche Turbo	16	0	5	5
1985	Alain Prost	FRA	McLaren TAG Porsche Turbo	16	2	5	5
1986	Alain Prost	FRA	McLaren TAG Porsche Turbo	16	1	4	2
1987	Nelson Piquet	BRE	Williams Honda Turbo	16	4	3	4
1988	Ayrton Senna	BRE	McLaren Honda Turbo	16	13	8	3
1989	Alain Prost	FRA	McLaren Honda	16	2	4	5
1990	Ayrton Senna	BRE	McLaren Honda	16	10	6	2
1991	Ayrton Senna	BRE	McLaren Honda	16	8	7	2
1992	Nigel Mansell	GB	Williams Renault	16	14	9	8
1993	Alain Prost	FRA	Williams Renault	16	13	7	6
1994	Michael Schumacher	GER	Benetton Ford	14	6	8	9
1995	Michael Schumacher	GER	Benetton Renault	17	4	9	7
1996	Damon Hill	GB	Williams Renault	16	9	8	5
1997	Jacques Villeneuve	CAN	Williams Renault	17	10	7	3
1998	Mika Häkkinen	FIN	McLaren Mercedes	16	9	8	6
1999	Mika Häkkinen	FIN	McLaren Mercedes	16	11	5	6
2000	Michael Schumacher	GER	Ferrari	17	9	9	2
2001	Michael Schumacher	GER	Ferrari	17	11	9	3
2002	Michael Schumacher	GER	Ferrari	17	7	11	7
2003	Michael Schumacher	GER	Ferrari	16	5	6	5
2004	Michael Schumacher	GER	Ferrari	18	8	13	10

Constructors Championship 2004

Position	Team	Number of points	Number of pole positions	Number of wins	Number of laps in the lead	Number of laps in the lead	Number of kms in the lead
1.	Ferrari	262	12	15	14	785	3892,129
2.	B.A.R Honda	119	1	-	-	54	287,894
3.	Renault	105	3	1	-	149	616,642
4.	Williams BMW	88	1	1	2	82	365,024
5.	McLaren Mercedes	69	1	1	2	50	302,075
6.	Sauber Petronas	34	-	-	-	2	8,618
7.	Jaguar	10	-	-	-	-	-
8.	Toyota	9	-	-	-	-	-
9.	Jordan Ford	5	-	-	-	-	-
10.	Minardi Cosworth	1	-	-	-	-	-

Number of Constructors Championship (since 1958)

14: Ferrari 1961 - 64 - 75 - 76 - 77 - 79 - 82 - 83 - 99 - 2000 - 01 - 02 - 03 - 04

9: Williams 1980 - 81 - 86 - 87 -92 93 - 94 - 96 - 97

8: McLaren 1974 - 84 - 85 - 88 - 89 - 90 - 91 - 98

7: Lotus 1963 - 65 - 68 - 70 -72 73 - 78

2: Cooper 1959 - 60 / Brabham 1966 - 67

1: Vanwall 1958 / BRM 1962 / Matra 1969 / Tyrrell 1971 / Benetton 1995

Number of pole positions per make

Ferrari	178
Williams	124
McLaren	115
Lotus	107
Brabham	39
Renault	36
Benetton	15
Tyrrell	14
Alfa Romeo	12
Cooper	11
BRM	11
Maserati	10
Ligier	9
Mercedes	8
Vanwall	7
Kurtis Kraft	6
March	5
Matra	4
Shadow	3
Lancia	2
Watson	2
Jordan	2
Stevens	1
Lesovsky	1
Ewing	1
Lola	1
Porsche	1
Honda	1
Wolf	1
Arrows	1
Toleman	1
Stewart	1
B.A.R	1

Number of wins per make

Ferrari	182
McLaren	138
Williams	113
Lotus	79
Brabham	35
Benetton	27
Tyrrell	23
BRM	17
Renault	17
Cooper	16
Alfa Romeo	10
Mercedes	9
Maserati	9
Vanwall	9
Matra	9
Ligier	9
Kurtis Kraft	5
Jordan	4
Watson	3
March	3
Wolf	3
Salih	2
Honda	2
Kuzma	1
Porsche	1
Eagle	1
Hesketh	1
Penske	1
Shadow	1
Stewart	1

Number of fastest laps per make

Ferrari	181
Williams	128
McLaren	113
Lotus	71
Brabham	41
Benetton	36
Tyrrell	20
Renault	19
Maserati	15
BRM	15
Cooper	14
Alfa Romeo	14
Matra	12
Mercedes	9
Ligier	9
Kurtis Kraft	7
March	7
Vanwall	6
Surtees	3
Epperly	2
Eagle	2
Honda	2
Shadow	2
Wolf	2
Toleman	2
Jordan	2
Gordini	1
Lancia	1
Lesovsky	1
Watson	1
Hesketh	1
Parnelli	1
Kojima	1
Ensign	1

Number of Grand Prix per make

Ferrari	704
McLaren	577
Williams	496
Lotus	491
Tyrrell	430
Brabham	394
Ligier	326
Minardi	321
Arrows	291
Benetton	260
Jordan	231
BRM	197
March	197
Sauber	197
Renault	174
Lola	148
Osella	132
Cooper	129
Surtees	117
Alfa Romeo	112
Shadow	104
Fittipaldi	103
B.A.R	101
Ensign	99
Footwork	91
ATS	89
Jaguar	85
Prost	83
Dallara	78
Maserati	70
Matra	60
Toleman	57
Zakspeed	53
Hesketh	52
Toyota	51

Family picture of the 2004 World Championship. From left to right, back row: Jarno Trulli, Fernando Alonso, Jenson Button, Takuma Sato, Olivier Panis and Cristiano Da Matta. Second row: Ralf Schumacher, Juan Pablo Montoya, Giancarlo Fisichella, Felipe Massa, Nick Heidfeld, Giorgio Pantano, Kimi Räikkönen and David Coulthard. Front row: Mark Webber, Christian Klien, Michael Schumacher, Rubens Barrichello, Zsolt Baumgartner and Gianmaria Bruni.

Sporting regulations

The FIA will organise the FIA Formula One World Championship (the Championship) which is the property ofthe FIA and comprises two titles of World Champion, one for drivers and one for constructors. It consists of theFormula One Grand Prix races which are included in the Formula One calendar and in respect of which the ASNs and organisers have signed the organisation agreement provided for in the 1998 Concorde Agreement (Events). All the participating parties (FIA, ASNs, organisers, competitors and circuits) undertake to apply as well as observe the rules governing the Championship and must hold FIA Super Licences which are issued to drivers, competitors, officials, organisers and circuits.

REGULATIONS

1. The final text of these Sporting Regulations shall be the English version which will be used should any dispute arise as to their interpretation. Headings in this document are for ease of reference only and do not form part of these Sporting Regulations.
2. These Sporting Regulations were published on 30 October 2002 and come into force on 1 January 2003 and replace all previous FIA Formula One World Championship Sporting Regulations.

LICENCES

10. All drivers, competitors and officials participating in the Championship must hold a FIA Super Licence. Applications for Super Licences must be made to the FIA through the applicant's ASN. The driver's name will remain on the list for Super Licences for one year.

CHAMPIONSHIP EVENTS

11. Events are reserved for Formula One cars as defined in the Technical Regulations.
12. Each Event will have the status of an international restricted competition.
13. The distance of all races, from the start signal referred to in Article 151 to the chequered flag, shall be equal to the least number of complete laps which exceed a distance of 305 km. However, should two hours elapse before the scheduled race distance is completed, the leader will be shown the chequered flag when he crosses the control line (the Line) at the end of the lap during which the two hour period ended. The Line is a single line which crosses both the track and the pit lane.
14. The maximum number of Events in the Championship is 17, the minimum is 8.
15. The final list of Events is published by the FIA before 1st January each year.
16. An Event which is cancelled with less than three months written notice to the FIA will not be considered for inclusion in the following year's Championship unless the FIA judges the cancellation to have been due to force majeure.
17. An Event may be cancelled if fewer than 12 cars are available for it.

WORLD CHAMPIONSHIP

18. The Formula One World Championship driver's title will be awarded to the driver who has scored the highest number of points, taking into consideration all the results obtained during the Events which have actually taken place.
19. The title of Formula One World Champion Constructor will be awarded to the make which has scored the highest number of points, results from both cars being taken into account.
20. The constructor of an engine or rolling chassis is the person (including any corporate or unincorporated body) which owns the intellectual property rights to such engine or chassis. The make of an engine or chassis is the name attributed to it by its constructor. If the make of the chassis is not the same as that of the engine, the title will be awarded to the former which shall always precede the latter in the name of the car.
21. Points for both titles will be awarded at each Event according to the following scale: 1st: 10 points,
2nd: 8 points, 3rd: 6 points, 4th: 5 points, 5th: 4 points, 6th: 3 points, 7th: 2 points, 8th: 1 point
22. If a race is stopped under Articles 165 and 166, and cannot be restarted, no points will be awarded in case A, half points will be awarded in case B and full points will be awarded in case C.
23. The drivers finishing first, second and third in the Championship must be present at the annual FIA Prize Giving ceremony.

DEAD HEAT

24. Prizes and points awarded for all the positions of competitors who tie, will be added together and shared equally.
25. If two or more constructors or drivers finish the season with the same number of points, the higher place in the Championship (in either case) shall be awarded to:
a) the holder of the greatest number of first places,
b) if the number of first places is the same, the holder of the greatest number of second places,
c) if the number of second places is the same, the holder of the greatest number of third places and so on until a winner emerges.
d) if this procedure fails to produce a result, the FIA will nominate the winner according to such criteria as it thinks fit.

COMPETITORS APPLICATIONS

41. Applications to compete in the Championship may be submitted to the FIA at any time between 1 March two years prior to the Championship in which the applicant wishes to compete and 15 November immediately preceding such Championship, on an entry form as set out in Appendix 2 hereto accompanied by the entry fee provided for in the Agreement, together with the deposit provided for in Article 44 where applicable. Applications from Teams not already competing in the Championship will only be considered where a place is available, taking into account all the Teams who are entitled to compete under the Agreement. Entry forms will be made available by FIA who will notify the applicant of the result of the application within thirty days of its receipt. Successful applicants are automatically entered in all Events of the Championship and will be the only competitors at Events.
42. Applications shall include:
a) confirmation that the applicant has read and understood the Agreement (including its schedules), the Code, the Technical Regulations and the Sporting Regulations and agrees, on its own behalf and on behalf of everyone associated with its participation in the Championship, to observe them,
b) the name of the team (which must include the name of the chassis),
c) the make of the competing car,
d) the make of the engine,
e) the names of the drivers. A driver may be nominated subsequent to the application upon payment of a fee fixed by the FIA,
f) an undertaking by the applicant to participate in every Event with the number of cars and drivers entered.
g) an undertaking that the car does not make use of any component, system, software or device which has been (or might reasonably be suspected to have been) designed, supplied or constructed by or with the help of anyone who has been involved on behalf of the FIA with checking Formula One electronic systems during the 24 months immediately preceding the application.
43. A competitor may change the make and/or type of engine at any time during the Championship. All points scored with an engine of different make to that which was first entered in the Championship will count (and will be aggregated) for the assessment of Benefits, however such points will not count towards (nor be aggregated for) the FIA Formula One Constructors Championship.
44. With the exception of those whose cars have scored points in the Championship of the previous year, applicants must supply information about the size of their company, their financial position and their ability to meet their prescribed obligations. Any applicant which did not take part in the Championship for the previous year must also deposit US$48,000,000 (forty-eight million United States dollars) with the FIA when submitting its application. This sum will be returned to it forthwith if its application is refused or in twelve equal monthly instalments (including interest) commencing immediately after the first Event in which it competes, provided it has met and continues to meet all the requirements of the Agreement and its schedules. If the applicant fails to appear for the Championship for which it has entered, its deposit will be forfeit save only that the applicant may delay its participation by one year, in which case US$12,000,000 (twelve million United States dollars) will be forfeit and the balance repaid as set out above.
45. All applications will be studied by the FIA which will publish the list of cars and drivers accepted together with their race numbers on 1 December (or the following Monday if 1 December falls on a week-end), having first notified unsuccessful applicants as set out in Article 41.
46. No more than 24 cars will be admitted to the Championship, two being entered by each competitor.
47. If in the opinion of the Formula One Commission a competitor fails to operate his team in a manner compatible with the standards of the Championship or in any way brings the Championship into disrepute, the FIA may exclude such competitor from the Championship forthwith.

INCIDENTS

52. Incident means any occurrence or series of occurrences involving one or more drivers, or any action by any driver, which is reported to the stewards by the race director (or noted by the stewards and referred to the race director for investigation) which:
- necessitated the stopping of a race under Article 165;
- constituted a breach of these Sporting Regulations or the Code;
- caused a false start by one or more cars;
- caused a collision;
- forced a driver off the track;
- illegitimately prevented a legitimate overtaking manoeuvre by a driver;
- illegitimately impeded another driver during overtaking.

53. (a) It shall be at the discretion of the stewards to decide, upon a report or a request by the race director, if
a) driver or drivers involved in an incident shall be penalised.
b) If an incident is under investigation by the stewards, a message informing all Teams of this will be displayed on the timing monitors.
Provided that such a message is displayed no later than five minutes after the race has finished the driver or drivers concerned may not leave the circuit without the consent of the stewards.
54. The stewards may impose any one of three penalties on any driver involved in an Incident:
a) A drive-through penalty. The driver must enter the pit lane and re-join the race without stopping at his pit;
b) A ten second time penalty. The driver must enter the pit lane, stop at his pit for at least ten seconds and then re-join the race.
c) a drop of ten grid positions at the driver's next Event. However, should either of the penalties under a) and b) above be imposed during the last five laps, or after the end of a race, Article 55 b) below will not apply and 25 seconds will be added to the elapsed race time of the driver concerned.
55. Should the stewards decide to impose either of the penalties under Article 54a) or b), the following procedure will be followed:
a) The stewards will give written notification of the penalty which has been imposed to an official of the team concerned and will ensure that this information is also displayed on the timing monitors.
b) From the time the stewards' decision is notified on the timing monitors the relevant driver may cover no more than three complete laps before entering the pit lane and, in the case of a penalty under Article 54b), proceeding to his garage where he shall remain for the period of the time penalty.
Whilst a car is stationary in the pit lane as a result of incurring a time penalty it may not be worked on. However, if the engine stops it may be started after the time penalty period has elapsed.
c) When the time penalty period has elapsed the driver may rejoin the race.
d) Any breach or failure to comply with Articles 55 b) or 55 c) may result in the car being excluded.

PROTESTS

56. Protests shall be made in accordance with the Code and accompanied by a fee of 2000 US Dollars.

SANCTIONS

57. The stewards may inflict the penalties specifically set out in these Sporting Regulations in addition to or instead of any other penalties available to them under the Code.

CHANGES OF DRIVER

58. a) During a season, each team will be permitted to use four drivers (excluding any third driver taking part in either of the free practice sessions on the first day of practice). Changes may be made at any time before the start of the qualifying practice session provided any change proposed after 16.00 on the day of scrutineering receives the consent of the stewards.
Additional changes for reasons of force majeure will be considered separately.
Any new driver may score points in the Championship.
b) In addition to the above all teams, other than those who finished in the top four positions of the previous year's World Chmapionship for Constructors, will be permitted to run a third driver during both free sessions on the first day of practice provided:
- he is not one of the team's nominated drivers for the Event in question;
- he is in possession of a Super Licence;
- he has not been a nominated driver for a Formula One team in more than six World Championship Events during the two previous World Championships.

If one of the team's nominated drivers is unable to drive at some stage after the end of initial scrutineering, and the stewards consent to a change of driver, the third driver may take part in the remainder of the Event. Under such circumstances the driver concerned must use the engine and tyres which were allocated to the original driver (see Articles 75 and 86).

DRIVING

59. The driver must drive the car alone and unaided.

TESTING

63. (a) No testing is permitted at sites which are not currently approved for use by Formula 1 cars. In order to ensure that venue licence conditions are respected at all times during testing, Competitors are required to inform the FIA of their test schedule in order that an observer may be appointed if deemed necessary.
b) During all Formula One testing :
- red flag procedures must be respected ;
- no other type of vehicle is permitted on the track ;
- every reasonable effort should be made to ensure that the recommendations concerning emergency services detailed in Article 16 of Appendix H to the Code are followed.

PIT LANE

64. (a) For the avoidance of doubt and for description purposes, the pit lane shall be divided into two lanes. The lane closest to the pit wall is designated the "fast lane", and the lane closest to the garages is designated the "inner lane". Other than when cars are at the end of the pit lane under Articles 148 or 169, the inner lane is the only area where any work can be carried out on a car.
b) Unless a car is pushed from the grid at any time during the start procedure, cars may only be driven from the team's designated garage area to the end of the pit lane.
c) Any driver intending to start the race from the pit lane may not drive his car from his team's designated garage area until the 15 minute signal has been given and must stop in a line in the fast lane.
Under these circumstances working in the fast lane will be permitted but any such work is restricted to :
- starting the engine and any directly associated preparation ;
- the fitting or removal of cooling and heating devices ;
- changing wheels when a change of climatic conditions has been confirmed (see Article 130) ;
- changing wheels if a spare car is used.

When cars are permitted to leave the pit lane they must do so in the order they arrived at the end of the pit lane unless another car is unduly delayed. At all times drivers must follow the directions of the marshals.
d) Other than tyre rubber left when cars leave their pit stop position, Competitors may not attempt to enhance the grip of the surface in the pit lane unless a problem has been clearly identified and a solution agreed by the FIA safety delegate.
e) Competitors must not paint lines on any part of the pit lane.
f) Other than under c) above no equipment may be left in the fast lane.
g) Team personnel are only allowed in the pit lane immediately before they are required to work on a car and must withdraw as soon as the work is complete.
h) It is the responsibility of the Competitor to release his car after a pit stop only when it is safe to do so.

SPORTING CHECKS

65. At the first Event of each Championship, the FIA will check all licences.

SCRUTINEERING

66. Between 10.00 and 16.00 on the day before first practice initial scrutineering of all cars will take place in the garage assigned to each team.
67. Unless a waiver is granted by the stewards, competitors who do not keep to these time limits will not be allowed to take part in the Event.
68. No car may take part in the Event until it has been passed by the scrutineers.
69. The scrutineers may:
a) check the eligibility of a car or of a competitor at any time during an Event,
b) require a car to be dismantled by the competitor to make sure that the conditions of eligibility or conformity are fully satisfied,
c) require a competitor to pay the reasonable expenses which exercise of the powers mentioned in this Article may entail,
d) require a competitor to supply them with such parts or samples as they may deem necessary.
70. Any car which, after being passed by the scrutineers, is dismantled or modified in a way which might affect its safety or call into question its eligibility, or which is involved in an accident with similar consequences, must be re-presented for scrutineering approval.
71. The race director or the clerk of the course may require that any car involved in an accident be stopped and checked.
72. Checks and scrutineering shall be carried out by duly appointed officials who shall also be responsible for the operation of the parc fermé and who alone are authorised to give instructions to the competitors.
73. The stewards will publish the findings of the scrutineers each time cars are checked during the Event. These results will not include any specific figure except when a car is found to be in breach of the Technical Regulations.

SUPPLY OF TYRES IN THE CHAMPIONSHIP AND TYRE LIMITATION DURING THE EVENT

74. Supply of tyres:
a) Any tyre company wishing to supply tyres to Formula One Teams must notify the FIA of its intention to do so no later than 1 January preceding the year during which such tyres will be supplied.
Any tyre company wishing to cease the supply of tyres to Formula One Teams must notify the FIA of its intention to do so no later than 1 January of the year preceding that in which such tyres were to be supplied.
b) No tyre may be used in the Championship unless the company supplying such tyre accepts and adheres to the following conditions:
- one tyre supplier present in the Championship: this company must equip 100% of the entered teams on ordinary commercial terms;
- two tyre suppliers present: each of them must, if called upon to do so, be prepared to equip up to 60% of the entered teams on ordinary commercial terms;
- three or more tyre suppliers present: each of them must, if called upon to do so, be prepared to equip up to 40% of the entered teams on ordinary commercial terms;
- each tyre supplier must undertake to provide no more than two specifications of dry-weather tyre to each team at each Event, each of which must be of one homogenous compound. Any modification or treatment, other than heating, carried out to a tyre or tyres will be considered a change of specification ;
- each tyre supplier must undertake to provide no more than one specification of wet-weather tyre at each Event which must be of one homogenous compound;
- if, in the interests of maintaining current levels of circuit safety, the FIA deems it necessary to reduce tyre grip, it shall introduce such rules as the tyre suppliers may advise or, in the absence of advice which achieves the FIA's objectives, specify the maximum permissible contact areas for front and rear tyres.

75. Quantity and type of tyres:
a) During the Event no driver may use more than forty dry-weather tyres and twenty eight wet-weather tyres. (twenty front and twenty rear) and twenty eight wet-weather tyres (fourteen front and fourteen rear).
If a driver change is made during an Event the tyres allocated to the original driver must be used by the new driver.
From the forty dry-weather tyres each driver will be allocated twelve (six front and six rear) for use on the first day of practice, these tyres may not be used at any other time during the Event. No more than eight (four front and four rear) of the twelve tyres allocated for the first day of practice may be of one specification.
Before 09.00 (or 08.00 during Events taking place in North America) on the second day of practice each driver must nominate which specification of tyre he will use for the remainder of the Event. However, if both free practice sessions on the first day of practice are declared wet this decision may be deferred until 13.00 (or 12.00 during Events taking place in North America).
b) All dry-weather tyres must incorporate circumferential grooves square to the wheel axis and around the entire circumference of the contact surface of each tyre.
c) Each front dry-weather tyre, when new, must incorporate 4 grooves which are:
- arranged symmetrically about the centre of the tyre tread;
- at least 14mm wide at the contact surface and which taper uniformly to a minimum of 10mm at the lower surface;
- at least 2.5mm deep across the whole lower surface;
- 50mm (+/- 1.0mm) between centres.

Furthermore, the tread width of the front tyres must not exceed 270mm.
d) Each rear dry-weather tyre, when new, must incorporate 4 grooves which are:
- arranged symmetrically about the centre of the tyre tread;
- at least 14mm wide at the contact surface and which taper uniformly to a minimum of 10mm at the lower surface;
- at least 2.5mm deep across the whole lower surface;
- 50mm (+/- 1.0mm) between centres.

The measurements referred to in c) and d) above will be taken when the tyre is fitted to a wheel and inflated to 1.4 bar.
e) A wet-weather tyre is one which has been designed for use on a wet or damp track. All wet-weather tyres must, when new, have a contact area which does not exceed 280cm² when fitted to the front of the car and 440cm² when fitted to the rear. Contact areas will be measured over any square section of the tyre which is normal to and symmetrical about the tyre centre line and which measures 200mm x 200mm when fitted to the front of the car and 250mm x 250mm when fitted to the rear. For the purposes of establishing conformity, only void areas which are greater than 2.5mm in depth will be considered.
Prior to use at an Event, each tyre manufacturer must provide the technical delegate with a full scale drawing of each type of wet-weather tyre intended for use.
Prior to the start of the qualifying practice session, and subject to the requirements of Articles 127-135, wet-weather tyres may only be used after the track has been declared wet by the race director, following which wet or dry-weather tyres may be used for the remainder of the relevant session.
f) Tyre specifications will be determined by the FIA no later than 1 September of the previous season. Once determined in this way, the specification of the tyres will not be changed during the Championship season without the agreement of the Formula One Commission.
76. Control of tyres:
a) The outer sidewall of all tyres which are to be used at an Event must be marked with a unique identification.
b) Other than in cases of force majeure (accepted as such by the stewards of the meeting),all tyres intended for use at an Event must be presented to the FIA technical delegate for allocation prior to the end of initial scrutineering.
c) From among the forty (twenty front and twenty rear) dry-weather tyres available to each driver, the FIA technical delegate will choose at random sixteen tyres (eight front and eight rear) which are the only dry-weather tyres which such driver may use in the qualifying practice session.
d) At any time during an Event, and at his absolute discretion, the FIA technical delegate may select alternative dry-weather tyres to be used by any team or driver from among the relevant stock of tyres which such team's designated supplier has present at the Event.
e) A competitor wishing to replace one unused tyre by another unused one must present both tyres to the FIA technical delegate.
f) The use of tyres without appropriate identification may result in deletion of the relevant driver's qualifying times or exclusion from the race.
g) The only permitted type of tyre heating devices are blankets which use resistive heating elements.
77. Wear of tyres:
The Championship will be contested on grooved tyres. The FIA reserve the right to introduce at any time a method of measuring remaining groove depth if performance appears to be enhanced by high wear or by the use of tyres which are worn so that the grooves are no longer visible.

WEIGHING

78. (a) During each qualifying practice session cars will be weighed as follows:
1) the FIA will install weighing equipment in the first pit garage (the FIA garage) which will be used for the weighing procedure;
2) all cars which complete a flying lap will undergo the weighing procedure. The FIA technical delegate will inform the driver by means of a red light at the beginning of the pit lane ;
3) the driver will proceed directly to the FIA garage and stop his engine ;
4) the car will then be weighed with driver (and without driver if necessary) and the result given to the driver in writing ;
5) if the car is unable to reach the FIA garage under its own power it will be placed under the exclusive control of the marshals who will take the car to be weighed;
6) a car or driver may not leave the FIA garage without the consent of the FIA technical delegate;
7) if a car stops on the circuit and the driver leaves the car, he must go to the FIA garage immediately on his return to the pit lane in order for his weight to be established.
b) After the race each car crossing the Line will be weighed. If a driver wishes to leave his car before it is weighed he must ask the technical delegate to weigh him in order that this weight may be added to that of the car.
c) The relevant car may be excluded should its weight be less than that specified in Article 4.1 of the Technical Regulations when weighed under a) or b) above, save where the deficiency in weight results from the accidental loss of a component of the car.
d) No solid, liquid, gas or other substance or matter of whatsoever nature may be added to, placed on, or removed from a car after it has been selected for weighing or has finished the race or during the weighing procedure. (Except by a scrutineer when acting in his official capacity).
e) No oneother than scrutineers and officials may enter or remain in the FIA garage without the the specific permission of the FIA technical delegate.
79. Any breach of these provisions for the weighing of cars may result in the delegation of the relevant driver's qualifying times or exclusion from the race.

SPARE CARS AND ENGINES

83. Subject to the requirements of Article 86, a competitor may use several cars for practice and the race provided that:
a) he has no more than four cars available for use at any one time;
b) he uses no more than two cars for each of the free practice sessions held under Article 118a) and b) (other than when a third driver is used under Article 58) ;
c) he uses no more than three cars during each part of the qualifying practice session. Prior to the start of the second part of the qualifying practice session he must nominate which two cars he intends to use for that part. If a driver wants to change to a spare car after the start of the second part that car must carry the same fuel load as his original car and, to ensure that this is the case, the original car will be weighed at the end of the session for comparison purposes.
d) they are all of the same make and were entered in the Championship by the same competitor,
e) they have been scrutineered in accordance with these Sporting Regulations,
f) each car carries its driver's race number.
With reference to b) and c) above, a car will be deemed to have been used once the timing transponder has shown that it has left the pit lane.
84. Any driver who decides to use another race car or a spare car following the qualifying practice session, and before the end of the pit lane is closed for the start of the race, must start the race from the pit lane following the procedures detailed in Article 148. Under these circumstances no restrictions on fuel load will be applied and tyres may be changed.
85. No change of car is permitted after the start of the race, any driver wishing to change car, must have got out of his original car and left the grid before the 15 second signal which immediately precedes the start.
A change of car will be deemed to have taken place once a driver is seated in his new car and such changes may only take place in the pit lane or the team's designated garage area.
86. Only one engine may be used by each driver during all practice sessions and the race. Should it become necessary for a driver to use another engine he will drop ten places on the starting grid each time one is used. However, should an engine change be carried out after the qualifying practice session, any drivers concerned will be required to start the race from the back of the starting grid in accordance with Article 131.
After consultation with the relevant engine supplier the FIA will attach seals to each engine in order to ensure that no significant moving parts can be rebuilt or replaced.
Other than the straightforward replacement of one engine unit with another, a change will also be deemed to have taken place if any of the FIA seals are damaged or removed from the original engine after it has been used for the first time in any practice session held under Articles 118 and 119.

GENERAL SAFETY

87. Official instructions will be given to drivers by means of the signals laid out in the Code. Competitors must not use flags similar in any way whatsoever to these.
88. Drivers are strictly forbidden to drive their car in the opposite direction to the race unless this is absolutely necessary in order to move the car from a dangerous position.
89. Any driver intending to leave the track should signal his intention to do so in good time making sure that he can do this without danger.
90. (a) During practice and the race, drivers may use only the track and must at all times observe the provisions of the Code relating to driving behaviour on circuits.
(b) Other than by driving on the track, Competitors are not permitted to attempt to alter the grip of any part of the track surface.
91. A driver who abandons a car must leave it in neutral or with the clutch disengaged and with the steering wheel in place.
92. The organiser must make at least two fire extinguishers of 5kg capacity available to each competitor and ensure that they work properly.
93. a) Refuelling is allowed only in the pit lane at the team's designated garage area.
b) With the exception of cars forced to abort their qualifying run due to red flags being displayed on the circuit which may then be refuelled before a new qualifying attempt, or any adjustment to the fuel level when a spare car is needed during the second part of the qualifying practice session, fuel may not be added to nor removed from a car between the start of the second part of the qualifying practice session and the start of the race.
c) Other than a fuel breather and an external fuel pressurising device for starting the engine (in which case only fuel on board the car may be used for running the engine), no connection may be made to the fuel system of the car between the start of the second part of the qualifying practice sessions and the start of the race.
94. The driver may remain in his car throughout refuelling but, unless an FIA approved race refuelling system is used, the engine must be stopped.
With the exception of the first part of the qualifying practice session and until the start of the second part, race refuelling systems may not be used during, or immediately after, any practice session.
Whilst being used during the qualifying practice session and the race, any refuelling carried out with the race system must take place in the pit lane and all team personnel working on the car must wear clothing which will protect all parts of their body from fire. Each competitor must ensure that an assistant equipped with a suitable fire extinguisher of adequate capacity is beside the car throughout all refuelling operations.
95. Save as specifically authorised by the Code or these Sporting Regulations, no one except the driver may touch a stopped car unless it is in the paddock, the team's designated garage area, the pit lane or on the starting grid.
96. At no time may a car be reversed in the pit lane under its own power.
97. During the period commencing 15 minutes prior to and ending 5 minutes after every practice session and the period between the commencement of the formation lap which immediately precedes the race and the time when the last car enters the parc fermé, no one is allowed on the track, the pit entry or the pit exit with the exception of :
a) marshals or other authorised personnel in the execution of their duty ;
b) drivers when driving or on foot, having first received permission to do so from a marshal ;
c) team personnel clearing equipment from the grid after all cars have left the grid on the formation lap;
d) mechanics under Article 150 only.
98. During a race, the engine may only be started with the starter except :
a) in the pit lane or the team's designated garage area where the use of an external starting device is allowed, or ;
b) under Article 155c) or d).
99. Drivers taking part in practice and the race must always wear the clothes, helmets and head and neck supports specified in the Code.
100. A speed limit of 60km/h will be imposed in the pit lane during all free practice sessions, this will be raised to 100km/h for the remainder of the Event. Under exceptional circumstances the Permanent Bureau of the Formula One Commission may amend these limits.
Except in the race, any driver who exceeds the limit will be fined US$250 for each km/h above the limit (this may be increased in the case of a second offence in the same Championship season).
During the race, the stewards may impose either of the penalties under Article 54a) or b) on any driver who exceeds the limit.
101. If a driver has serious mechanical difficulties during practice or the race he must leave the track as soon as it is safe to do so.
102. The car's rear light must be illuminated at all times when it is running on wet-weather tyres. It shall be at the discretion of the race director to decide if a driver should be stopped because his rear light is not working. Should a car be stopped in this way it may re-join when the fault has been remedied.
103. Only six team members per participating car (all of whom shall have been issued with and wearing special identification) are allowed in the signalling area during practice and the race. People under 16 years of age are not allowed in the pit lane.
104. Animals, except those which may have been expressly authorised by the FIA for use by security services, are forbidden on the track, in the pit lane, in the paddock or in any spectator area.
105. The race director, the clerk of the course or the FIA medical delegate can require a driver to have a medical examination at any time during an Event.
106. Failure to comply with the general safety requirements of the Code or these Sporting Regulations may result in the exclusion of the car and driver concerned from the Event.

FREE AND QUALIFYING PRACTICE SESSIONS

107. Save where these Sporting Regulations require otherwise, pit lane and track discipline and safety measures will be the same for all practice sessions as for the race.
108. No driver may start in the race without taking part in a qualifying practice session.
109. During all practices there will be a green and a red light at the pit exit. Cars may only leave the pit lane when the green light is on. Additionally, a blue flag and/or a flashing blue light will be shown at the pit exit to warn drivers leaving the pits if cars are approaching on the track.
110. Unless written permission has been given by the FIA to do otherwise, the circuit may only be used for purposes other than the Event after the last practice session on each day of practice and on the day of the race no less than one hour before the pit lane is opened to allow cars to cover a reconnaissance lap.
111. The interval between the fourth free practice session and the qualifying practice session may never be less than one hour.
112. If a car stops during practice it must be removed from the track as quickly as possible so that its presence does not constitute a danger or hinder other competitors. If the driver is unable to drive the car from a dangerous position, it shall be the duty of the marshals to assist him.
113. In the event of a driving infringement during practice the Stewards may delete the relevant driver's time from the second part of qualifying. In this case, a team will not be able to appeal against the steward's decision.
114. The clerk of the course may interrupt practice as often and for as long as he thinks necessary to clear the track or to allow the recovery of a car. In the case of free practice only, the clerk of the course with the agreement of the stewards may decline to prolong the practice period after an interruption of this kind.
Furthermore if, in the opinion of the stewards, a stoppage is caused deliberately, the driver concerned may have his times from that session cancelled and may not be permitted to take part in any other practice session that day.
115. On the second day of practice, all cars abandoned on the circuit during the first free practice session will be brought back to the pit lane or the team's designated garage area prior to the start of the second session.
116. Should one or more sessions be thus interrupted, no protest can be accepted as to the possible effects of the interruption on the qualification of drivers admitted to start.
117. Each driver's lap completed on the track during the second part of qualifying practice session will be timed to determine the driver's position at the start of the race.
118. Free practice sessions will take place :
a) The day after initial scrutineering from 11.00 to 12.00 and from 14.00 to 15.00.
b) The day before the race from 10.00 to 10.45 and from 11.15 to 12.00 (from 09.00 to 09.45 and from 10.15 to 11.00 during Events taking place in North America).
119. The qualifying practice session will take place the day before the race commencing at 14.00 (at 13.00 during Events taking place in North America). This session, which will comprise of two parts separated by two minutes, will be run as follows :
- During the first part each driver will carry out a single timed lap starting in the order they were classified in at the end of the previous race. Any drivers who were not classified will be arranged according to the number of laps they completed during the previous race, the one with the highest number going first. At the first race of the year the order of the last race of the previous year's World Championship will be used and, in all cases, any new drivers will be arranged in numerical order.
- The first part will be deemed to have finished when the last car in sequence enters the pit lane. If the last car fails to leave the pit lane, stops on the circuit or comes back to the pits before completing three laps, the second part will start five minutes later.
- The running order for the second part will be determined by the times achieved in the first part with the slowest driver going first.
- If more than one car fails to record a time during the first part of the session they will start the second part in first part order reversed.
- If two or more drivers set identical times during the first part priority will be given to the one who set it first.
- If a car stops on the track in the first part it may not be used during the second part, if the car is brought back to the pits before the end of the session it must remain in parc fermé until the end of the session.
- If more than one car fails to record a time during the second part they will start the race in second part order reversed.

120. The following procedure will be used during both parts of the qualifying practice session :
- Each driver will be given one minute to join the track, this will be signalled by the light at the end of the pit lane turning green. The first green light will be shown at 14.00 (at 13.00 during Events held in North America).
- As each driver crosses the Line to start his flying lap, other than those 5th, 10th and 15th in sequence, the light at the end of the pit lane will be turned green for one minute for the following driver.

- The light for the 6th, 11th and 16th cars in sequence will be turned green for one minute two minutes after the previous driver crosses the Line to complete his flying lap.
Any driver failing to leave the pit lane in the allotted minute will not be permitted to take any further part in that part of the qualifying practice session. Under these circumstances the green light for the next car, other than one which is 6th, 11th and 16th in sequence, will be turned on two minutes later. If any car 5th, 10th or 15th in sequence fails to leave the pit lane during the allotted minute the green light for the following car will be turned on two minutes after the previous car enters the pit lane.

121. If a car stops on the circuit during the qualifying practice session red flags will normally be shown and the driver concerned will not be permitted to take any further part in that part of the session. Unless a longer stoppage is deemed necessary (in which case at least two minutes warning will be given) the light at the end of the pit lane will be turned green five minutes after the signal to stop was given. Any car obliged to return to the pit lane under these circumstances, having not completed a flying lap, may be refuelled and the tyres may be changed, the driver will then be permitted a further attempt to qualify.
However, if the stopped car is in a safe position, or can be removed quickly without hindering another driver attempting to qualify, the session will continue. Under these circumstances :
- if any car stops on its out lap, other than one which is 5th, 10th or 15th in sequence, the green light for the following car will be shown two minutes later ;
- if any car 5th, 10th or 15th in sequence stops on its out lap the green light for the following car will be turned on two minutes after the previous car enters the pit lane ;
- if any car 5th, 10th or 15th in sequence stops on its flying lap or in lap the green light for the following car will be shown two minutes later.

122. If a car returns to the pit lane before completing three laps during the qualifying practice session:
- if any car enters the pit lane at the end of its out lap, other than one which is 5th, 10th or 15th in sequence, the green light for the following car will be shown 30 seconds later ;
- if any car 5th, 10th or 15th in sequence enters the pit lane at the end of its out lap the green light for the following car will be shown two minutes after the previous car enters the pit lane ;
- if any car 5th, 10th or 15th in sequence enters the pit lane at the end of its flying lap the green light for the following car will be shown two minutes later.

123. Other than any car required to enter the pit lane if the qualifying practice session is stopped, any car returning to the pit lane without completing three laps will not be permitted to join the track again until its next scheduled run, if applicable.

124. If, in the opinion of the stewards, a driver deliberately stops on the circuit or impedes another driver in any way during the qualifying practice session his time from the relevant part of the session will be cancelled.

POST QUALIFYING PARC FERMÉ

125. After weighing during the first part of the qualifying practice session, and any further random checks deemed necessary by the FIA technical delegate have been carried out, cars will be returned to the relevant team.

126. After weighing during the second part of the qualifying practice session (see Article 78), cars will then be moved to the parc fermé, the procedures thereafter are laid out in Articles 127-136.

127. Every car which took part in the second part of the qualifying practice session, or was intended for use during that part of the session (in the event of a driver failing to leave the pit lane), will be required in parc fermé. Any car which failed to leave the pit lane during the second part of the session must be taken by the team to the parc fermé immediately. If a car is damaged during the second part of the session the FIA technical delegate may make alternative arrangements according to the level of damage and any other circumstances he deems relevant.
Each car will be deemed to be in parc fermé from the time at which the light at the end of the pit lane turns green for the start of its qualifying run in the second part of the session until the green lights are illuminated at the start of the formation lap which immediately precedes the first start of the race.
Between these times, other than when cars are returned to the parc fermé overnight, the following work may be carried out :
- cooling devices may be fitted ;
- changes to improve the drivers comfort. In this context anything other than addition or removal of padding (or similar material) and adjustment of mirrors and pedals may only be carried out with the specific permission of the FIA technical delegate ;
- a fuel breather may be fitted ;
- bodywork (excluding radiators) may be removed and / or cleaned ;
- cosmetic changes may be made to the bodywork ;
- any part of the car may be cleaned ;
- any parts which are removed from the car in order to carry out any work specifically permitted below must remain close to it and, at all times, be visible to the scrutineer assigned to the relevant car ;
- fluids used for replenishment must conform to the same specification as the original fluid ;
- on board cameras, timing transponders and any associated equipment may be removed, refitted or checked.

128. After weighing during the second part of the qualifying practice session all cars will be detained in the parc fermé for further checks. Whilst the cars are being detained there three appropriate members from each team will be permitted in the parc fermé at any one time for the purpose of:
- checking tyre pressures ;
- connecting a jump battery under the supervision of the FIA ;
- downloading data by physical connection to the car under the supervision of the FIA ;
- fitting water heaters ;
- engine oil may be drained ;
- changing tyres before the car is pushed back to the team's garage. These, or any other tyres, may be used when the car is returned to the parc fermé the same evening and back to the team's garage on Sunday morning. The wheels and tyres used for qualifying will be marked and / or sealed by the scrutineers before being released to the team ;
- carrying out any work required by the FIA technical delegate. Once any such work has been carried out the team personnel must leave the parc fermé immediately.
No other work of any kind will be permitted at this time unless deemed absolutely necessary by the FIA technical delegate.

129. Once the qualifying practice session has finished, and all preliminary checks have been carried out by the FIA, the cars held in the parc fermé will be released simultaneously and teams will be permitted to push them back to their garages. Cars will remain under parc fermé conditions throughout. From this point, and until 18.30 (17.30 during Events taking place in North America), teams will be permitted to carry out the following work under supervision of the scrutineers :
- wheels may be removed ;
- removal of any parts genuinely necessary to carry out essential safety checks ;
- removal of spark plugs to carry out an internal engine inspection and cylinder compression checks ;
- engines may be started (an external fuel pressurising system may be used if necessary but only fuel on board the car may be used for running the engine) ;
- with the exception of fuel, fluids with a specific gravity less than 1.1 may be drained and/or replenished ;
- draining and / or addition of compressed gases ;
- heating devices may be fitted ;
- on board electrical units may be freely accessed via a physical connection to the car ;
- repair bona fide accident damage ;
No other work will be permitted during this time unless the FIA technical delegate is satisfied that it is absolutely necessary and has specifically authorised it.
At some time before 18.30 (17.30 during Events taking place in North America) all cars used during the second part of the qualifying practice session (or which were intended for use but failed to leave the pit lane) must be taken back to the parc fermé, with all parts used for qualifying re-fitted (other than wheels and tyres, which if they are not fitted to the car, must be taken separately), where they will remain secure until the following day. Whilst cars are in the parc fermé they may be covered and fitted with devices to keep them warm, no team personnel will be permitted there unless specifically authorised by the FIA technical delegate.

130. At 08.30 (at 07.30 during Events taking place in North America) on the day of the race, or at other times if the relevant Event timetable makes this necessary, teams will be permitted to take their cars back to their garages where, again, they will remain under parc fermé conditions until the green lights are illuminated at the start of the formation lap which immediately precedes the first start of the race. Only the following work on the cars will be permitted during this time :
- repair bona fide accident damage ;
- wheels and tyres may be removed, rebalanced, tyre pressures adjusted and tyre heating devices fitted ;
- other than when a change of climatic conditions has been confirmed, during all reconnaissance laps every car must be fitted with the same wheels and tyres as the driver used for his qualifying lap, the race must also be started with these same wheels and tyres. If one or more tyres are damaged, and are deemed unusable by the FIA technical delegate, they may be replaced by other tyres which have been used for a greater number of laps than the damaged ones ;
- with the exception of fuel, fluids with a specific gravity less than 1.1 may be drained and / or replenished, however, no replenishment may take place less than one hour and 30 minutes before the start of the formation lap unless specific approval has been given by the FIA. In order to ensure that fluids are not being used as ballast, and that the car is therefore being raced as it was qualified, the FIA reserves the right to weigh cars at random during the one hour period commencing one hour and 30 minutes before the start of the formation lap. When a car is weighed in this way its weight must be within 3kg of its weight at the completion of its qualifying lap, if not, fluids other than fuel may be replenished or drained under FIA supervision ;
- draining and / or addition of compressed gases ;
- the aerodynamic set up of the front wing may be adjusted using the existing parts. No parts may be added, removed or replaced ;
- on board electrical units may be freely accessed via a physical connection to the car ;
- removal of spark plugs to carry out an internal engine inspection and cylinder compression checks ;
- engines may be started (an external fuel pressurising system may be used if necessary but only fuel on board the car may be used for running the engine) ;
- the main electrical battery and radio batteries may be changed and a jump battery connected ;
- the brake system may be bled ;
- tape may be applied to bodywork joints and fasteners ;
- if the FIA technical delegate is satisfied that changes in climatic conditions necessitate alterations to the specification of a car tyres may be changed and changes may be made to the brake cooling ducts and radiator exit ducts. The changes listed above may be made at any time after the message "CHANGE IN CLIMATIC CONDITIONS" is shown on the timing monitors, from this point the choice of tyres, brake cooling ducts and radiator exit ducts is free.
Any work not listed above may only be undertaken with the approval of the FIA technical delegate following a written request from the team concerned. It must be clear that any replacement part a team wishes to fit is similar in mass, inertia and function to the original. After the work has been carried out the car must be submitted for re-scrutineering. Any parts removed will be retained by the FIA.

131. If a competitor wishes to change an engine whilst the car is being held under parc fermé conditions the relevant driver must start the race from the back of the starting grid. If more than one car is involved they will line up at the back of the grid in qualifying order.

132. If a competitor wishes to modify any part on the car or to make changes to the set up of the suspension whilst the car is being held under parc fermé conditions the relevant driver must start the race from the pit lane and follow the procedures laid out in Article 148.

133. One scrutineer will be allocated to each car for the purpose of ensuring that no unauthorised work is carried out whilst cars are being held under parc fermé conditions. If any such unauthorised work is carried out a report will be made to the stewards of the meeting.

134. A list of parts replaced with the specific agreement of the FIA technical delegate whilst cars are being held under parc fermé conditions will be published and distributed to all teams prior to the race.

135. In order that the scrutineers may be completely satisfied that no alterations have been made to the suspension systems or aerodynamic configuration of the car (with the exception of the front wing) whilst in post-qualifying parc fermé, it must be clear from physical inspection that changes cannot be made without the use of tools.

STOPPING THE PRACTICE

136. Should it become necessary to stop the practice because the circuit is blocked by an accident or because weather or other conditions make it dangerous to continue, the clerk of the course shall order a red flag and the abort lights to be shown at the Line. Simultaneously, red flags will be shown at all marshal posts.
When the signal is given to stop, all cars shall immediately reduce speed and proceed slowly back to their respective pits, and all cars abandoned on the track will be removed to a safe place.
At the end of each practice session all drivers may cross the Line only once.

PRESS CONFERENCES AND DRIVERS PARADE

137. The FIA press delegate will choose a maximum of five drivers who must attend a press conference in the media centre for a period of one hour at 15.00 on the day before first practice. At Events taking place in North or South America this press conference will take place at 11.00. These drivers' Teams will be notified no less than 48 hours before the conference. In addition, a maximum of two team personalities may be chosen by the FIA press delegate to attend this press conference.
On the first day of practice, a minimum of three and a maximum of six drivers and/or team personalities, (other than those who attended the press conference on the previous day and subject to the consent of the team principal) will be chosen by ballot or rota by the FIA press delegate during the Event and must make themselves available to the media for a press conference in the media centre for a period of one hour at 16.00.
No driver may enter into a contract which restricts his right to talk to any representative of the media during an Event. It shall be the duty of each Team to ensure that their drivers do not unreasonably refuse to speak to any representative of the media during the Event.

138. Immediately after the qualifying practice session the first three drivers in qualifying will be required to make themselves available for television interviews in the unilateral room and then attend a press conference in the media centre for a maximum period of 30 minutes.

139. Two hours and forty five minutes before the race all drivers must attend a drivers parade, Competitors will be given details of the parade by the Press Delegate.

THE GRID

140. At the end of the second qualifying practice session the fastest time achieved by each driver during the second part of the session will be officially published.

141. The grid will be drawn up in the order of the fastest time achieved by each driver in the second part of the qualifying practice session. Should two or more drivers have set identical times, priority will be given to the one who set the fastest time in the first part of the qualifying precice session.

142. The fastest driver will start the race from the position on the grid which was the pole position in the previous year or, on a new circuit, has been designated as such by the FIA safety delegate.

143. The starting grid will be published four hours before the race. Any competitor whose car(s) is (are) unable to start for any reason whatsoever (or who has good reason to believe that their car(s) will not be ready to start) must inform the clerk of the course accordingly at the earliest opportunity and, in any event, no later than 45 minutes before the start of the race. If one or more cars are withdrawn the grid will be closed up accordingly. The final starting grid will be published 45 minutes before the start of the race.

144. The grid will be in a staggered 1 x 1 formation and the rows on the grid will be separated by 16 metres.

MEETINGS

145. Meetings, chaired by the race director, will take place at 16.00 on the day before first practice and 18.00 on the first day of practice. The first must be attended by all team managers and the second by all drivers.
Should the race director consider another meeting necessary it will take place three hours before the race, Competitors will be informed no later than three hours after the end of the second qualifying practice. All drivers and team managers must attend.

STARTING PROCEDURE

146. 30 minutes before the start of the formation lap the cars will leave the pit lane to cover a reconnaissance lap. At the end of this lap they will stop on the grid in starting order with their engines stopped.
Should they wish to cover more than one reconnaissance lap, this must be done by driving down the pit lane at greatly reduced speed between each of the laps.

147. Any car which has not taken up its position on the grid by the time the five minute signal is shown will not be permitted to do so and must start from the pit lane in accordance with Article 148.

148. 17 minutes before the start of the formation lap, a warning signal will be given indicating that the end of the pit lane will be closed in two minutes.
15 minutes before the start of the formation lap the end of the pit lane will be closed and a second warning signal will be given. Any car which is still in the pit lane can start from the end of the pit lane provided it got there under its own power. If more than one car is affected they must line up in the order in which they reached the end of the pit lane. These cars may then join the race once the whole field has passed the end of the pit lane for the first time after the start.

149. The approach of the start will be announced by signals shown ten minutes, five minutes, three minutes, one minute and fifteen seconds before the start of the formation lap, each of which will be accompanied by an audible warning.
When the ten minute signal is shown, everybody except drivers, officials and team technical staff must leave the grid.
When the five minute signal is shown all cars must have their wheels fitted. After this signal wheels may only be removed in the pit lane. Any car which does not have all its wheels fully fitted at the five minute signal must start the race from the back of the grid or the pit lane.
When the one minute signal is shown, engines should be started and all team personnel must leave the grid by the time the 15 second signal is given. If any driver needs assistance after the 15 second signal he must raise his arm and, when the remainder of the cars able to do so have left the grid, his team may attempt to rectify the problem. In this case, marshals with yellow flags will stand beside any car (or cars) concerned to warn drivers behind.
When the green lights are illuminated, the cars will begin the formation lap with the pole position driver leading.
When leaving the grid, all drivers must proceed at a greatly reduced speed until clear of any team personnel standing beside the track. Marshals will be instructed to push any car (or cars) which remain on the grid into the pit lane by the fastest route immediately after cars able to do so have left the grid. If the driver is able to re-start the car whilst it is being pushed he may rejoin the formation lap.
During the formation lap practice starts are forbidden and the formation must be kept as tight as possible.
Overtaking during the formation lap is only permitted if a car is delayed when leaving its grid position and cars behind cannot avoid passing it without unduly delaying the remainder of the field. In this case, drivers may only overtake to re-establish the original starting order.
Any driver who is delayed leaving the grid may not overtake another moving car if he was stationary after the remainder of the cars had crossed the Line, and must start the race from the back of the grid. If more than one driver is affected, they must form up at the back of the grid in the order they left to complete the formation lap.
If the Line is not situated in front of pole position, and for the purposes of this Article as well as 150 and 164(o), it will be deemed to be a white line one metre in front of pole position.
Either of the penalties under Article 54a) or b) will be imposed on any driver who, in the opinion of the Stewards, unnecessarily overtook another car during the formation lap.

150. Any driver who is unable to start the formation lap must raise his arm and, after the remainder of the cars have crossed the Line, of the cars have crossed the Line, the car will be pushed into the pit lane by the fastest route.

151. When the cars come back to the grid at the end of the formation lap, they will stop on their respective grid positions, keeping their engines running.
There will be a standing start, the signal being given by means of lights activated by the permanent starter.
Once all the cars have come to a halt the five second light will appear followed by the four, three, two and one second lights. At any time after the one second light appears, the race will be started by extinguishing all red lights.

152. Unless specifically authorised by the FIA, during the start of a race the pit wall must be kept free of all persons with the exception of officials and fire marshals.

153. Any car which is unable to maintain starting order during the entire formation lap or is moving when the one second light comes on must enter the pit lane and start from the end of the pit lane as specified in Article 149.
This will not apply to any car which is temporarily delayed during the lap and which is able to regain its position, without endangering itself or any other car, before the leading car has taken up its position on the grid.

154. If, after returning to the starting grid at the end of the formation lap, a car develops a problem that could endanger the start, the driver must immediately raise his hands above his head and the marshal responsible for that row must immediately wave a yellow flag.
If the start is delayed as a result, a marshal with a yellow flag will stand in front of the car concerned to prevent it from moving until the whole field has left the grid on the new formation lap. The driver concerned may then start the race from the back of the grid and any vacant positions will not be filled.
Should there be more than one car involved, their new positions at the back of the grid will be determined in accordance with their respective final grid positions.
If a problem cannot be rectified before the commencement of the new formation lap the car must be pushed into the pit lane by the shortest route. The team may then attempt to rectify the problem and, if successful, the car may then start from the pit lane. Should there be more than one car involved their starting order from the pit lane will be determined by the order in which they reached the end of the pit lane under their own power.

155. If a problem arises when the cars reach the starting grid at the end of the formation lap the following procedure shall apply:
a) If the race has not been started, the abort lights will be switched on, all engines will be stopped and the new formation lap will start 5 minutes later with the race distance reduced by one lap. The next signal will be the three minute signal.
b) If the race has been started the marshals alongside the grid will wave their yellow flags to inform the drivers that a car is stationary on the grid.
c) If, after the start, a car is immobilised on the starting grid, it shall be the duty of the marshals to push it into the pit lane by the fastest route. If the driver is able to re-start the car whilst it is being pushed he may rejoin the race.
d) If the driver is unable to start the car whilst it is being pushed his mechanics may attempt to start it in the pit lane. If the car then starts it may rejoin the race. The driver and mechanics must follow the instructions of the track marshals at all times during such a procedure.

156. Should Article 154 apply, the race will nevertheless count for the Championship no matter how often the procedure is repeated, or how much the race is shortened as a result.

157. Either of the penalties under Article 54a) or b) will be imposed for a false start judged using an FIA supplied transponder which must be fitted to the car as specified.

158. Only in the following cases will any variation in the start procedure be allowed:
a) If it starts to rain after the five minute signal but before the race is started and, in the opinion of the race director teams should be given the opportunity to change tyres, the abort lights will be shown on the Line and the starting procedure will begin again at the 15 minute point. If necessary the procedure set out in Article 154 will be followed.
b) If the start of the race is imminent and, in the opinion of the race director, the volume of water on the track is such that it cannot be negotiated safely even on wet-weather tyres, the abort lights will be shown on the Line simultaneously with a "10" board with a red background.
This "10" board with a red background will mean that there is to be a delay of ten minutes before the starting procedure can be resumed. If weather conditions have improved at the end of that ten minute period, a "10" board with a green background will be shown. The "10" board with a green background will mean that the green light will be shown in ten minutes.
Five minutes after the "10" board with the green background is shown, the starting procedure will begin and the normal starting procedure signals (i.e. 5, 3, 1 min., 15 second) will be shown.
If however, the weather conditions have not improved within ten minutes after the "10" board with the red background was shown, the abort lights will be shown on the Line and the "10" board with the red background will be shown again which will mean a further delay of ten minutes before the starting procedure can be resumed.
This procedure may be repeated several times.
At any time when a "10" board (with either a red or green background) is shown, it will be accompanied by an audible warning.
c) If the race is started behind the safety car, Article 164(o) will apply.

159. The stewards may use any video or electronic means to assist them in reaching a decision. The stewards may overrule judges of fact. A breach of the provisions of the Code or these Sporting Regulations relating to starting procedure, may result in the exclusion of the car and driver concerned from the Event.

THE RACE

160. Team orders which interfere with a race result are prohibited.

161. A race will not be stopped in the event of rain unless the circuit is blocked or it is dangerous to continue (see Article 165).

162. If a car stops during the race it must be removed as quickly as possible so that its presence does not constitute a danger or hinder other competitors. If the driver is unable to drive the car from a dangerous position, it shall be the duty of the marshals to assist him.

163. During the race, drivers leaving the pit lane may only do so when the light at the end of the pit lane is green and on their own responsibility, a marshal with a blue flag, or a flashing blue light, will also warn the driver if cars are approaching on the track.

SAFETY CAR

164. (a) The FIA safety car will be driven by an experienced circuit driver. It will carry an FIA observer capable of recognising all the competing cars, who is in permanent radio contact with race control.
b) 30 minutes before the race start time the safety car will take up position at the front of the grid and remain there until the five minute signal is given. At this point (except under o) below) it will cover a whole lap of the circuit and enter the pit lane.
c) The safety car may be brought into operation to neutralise a race upon the decision of the clerk of the course.
It will be used only if competitors or officials are in immediate physical danger but the circumstances are not such as to necessitate stopping the race.
d) When the order is given to deploy the safety car, all observer's posts will display waved yellow flags and a board "SC" which shall be maintained until the intervention is over.
e) During the race, the safety car with its orange lights on, will start from the pit lane and will join the track regardless of where the race leader is.
f) All the competing cars will form up in line behind the safety car no more than 5 car lengths apart. All overtaking on the track is forbidden (except under o) below), unless a car is signalled to do so from the safety car.
g) When ordered to do so by the clerk of the course the observer in the car will use a green light to signal to any cars between it and the race leader that they should pass. These cars will continue at reduced speed and without overtaking until they reach the line of cars behind the safety car.
h) The safety car shall be used at least until the leader is behind it and all remaining cars are lined up behind him.
Once behind the safety car, the race leader must keep within 5 car lengths of it (except under j) below) and all remaining cars must keep the formation as tight as possible.
i) While the safety car is in operation, competing cars may enter the pit lane, but may only rejoin the track when the green light at the end of the pit lane is on. It will be on at all times except when the safety car and the line of cars following it are about to pass or are passing the pit exit. A car rejoining the track must proceed at reduced speed until it reaches the end of the line of cars behind the safety car.
j) When the clerk of the course calls in the safety car, it must extinguish its orange lights, this will be the signal to the drivers that it will be entering the pit lane at the end of that lap.
At this point the first car in line behind the safety car may dictate the pace and, if necessary, fall more than five car lengths behind it.
As the safety car is approaching the pit entry the yellow flags and SC boards at the observer's posts will be withdrawn and waved green flags will be displayed for no more than one lap.
k) Green flags and lights will be shown when the safety car has pulled off the circuit but overtaking remains forbidden until the cars cross the Line. However, any car which slows with an obvious problem may be overtaken.
l) Each lap completed while the safety car is deployed will be counted as a race lap.
m) If the race is stopped under Article 166 Case C, the safety car will take the chequered flag and all cars able to do so must follow it into the pit lane and into the parc fermé.
n) If the race ends whilst the safety car is deployed it will enter the pit lane at the end of the last lap and the cars will take the chequered flag as normal without overtaking.
o) In exceptional circumstances the race may be started behind the safety car. In this case, at any time before the one minute signal its orange lights will be turned on. This is the signal to the drivers that the race will be started behind the safety car. When the green lights are illuminated the safety car will leave the grid with all cars following in grid order no more than 5 car lengths apart. There will be no formation lap and race will start when the green lights are illuminated.
Overtaking, during the first lap only, is permitted if a car is delayed when leaving its grid position and cars behind cannot avoid passing it without unduly delaying the remainder of the field. In this case, drivers may only overtake to re-establish the original starting order.
Any driver who is delayed leaving the grid may not overtake another moving car if he was stationary after the remainder of the cars had crossed the Line, and must form up at the back of the line of cars behind the safety car. If more than one driver is affected, they must form up at the back of the field in the order they left the grid.
Either of the penalties under Article 54a) or b) will be imposed on any driver who, in the opinion of the Stewards, unnecessarily overtook another car during the first lap.

STOPPING A RACE

165. Should it become necessary to stop the race because the circuit is blocked by an accident or because weather or other conditions make it dangerous to continue, the clerk of the course shall order a red flag and the abort lights to be shown at the Line. Simultaneously, red flags will be shown at all marshal posts. When the signal is given to stop all cars shall immediately reduce speed in the knowledge that:
- the race classification will be that at the end of the penultimate lap before the lap during which the signal to stop the race was given,
- race and service vehicles may be on the track,
- the circuit may be totally blocked because of an accident,
- weather conditions may have made the circuit undriveable at racing speed,
- the pit lane will be open.

166. The procedure to be followed varies according to the number of laps completed by the race leader before the signal to stop the race was given:
Case A. Less than two full laps. If the race can be restarted, Article 167 will apply.
Case B. Two or more full laps but less than 75% of the original race distance (rounded up to the nearest whole number of laps and calculated cumulatively if more than one stoppage occurs). If the race can be restarted, Article 168 will apply.
Case C. 75% or more of the race distance (rounded up to the nearest whole number of laps and calculated cumulatively if more than one stoppage occurs). The cars will be sent directly to the parc fermé and the race will be deemed to have finished when the leading car crossed the Line for the penultimate time before the race was stopped.

RESTARTING A RACE

167. Case A.
a) The original start shall be deemed null and void.
b) The length of the restarted race will be the full original race distance.
c) The drivers who are eligible to take part in the race shall be eligible for the restart either in their original car or in a spare car.
d) Any driver who was forced to start from the back of the grid or the pit lane during the original start may start from his original grid position;
e) After the signal to stop the race has been given, all cars able to do so will proceed directly but slowly to either:
- the pit lane or;
- if the grid is clear, to their original grid position or;
- if the grid is not clear, to a position behind the last grid position as directed by the marshals.
f) Cars may be worked on in the pit lane the team's designated garage area or on the grid. If work is carried out on the grid this must be done in the car's correct grid position and must in no way impede the re-start.
g) Refuelling will only be allowed in the pits at the team's designated garage area.

168. Case B.
a) Other than the race order at the end of the penultimate lap before the lap during which the signal to stop was given, the number of classified laps completed by each driver and the time taken by the leader to complete his classified laps, the original race will be deemed null and void.
b) The length of the re-started race will be three laps less than the original race distance less the number of classified laps completed by the leader before the signal to stop was given.
c) The grid for the re-started race will be arranged in the race order at the end of the lap two laps prior to that during which the signal to stop was given.
d) Only cars which took part in the original start will be eligible for the re-start and then only if they returned under their own power by an authorised route to either:
- the pit lane or;
- to a position behind the last grid position as directed by the marshals.
e) No spare car will be eligible.
f) Cars may be worked on in the pit lane, the team's designated garage area or on the grid. If work is carried out on the grid, this must be done in the car's correct grid position and must in no way impede the re-start.
g) Refuelling is only permitted in the pit lane. If a car is refuelled it must take the re-start from the back of the grid and, if more than one car is involved, their positions will be determined by their race order at the end of the penultimate lap before the lap during which the signal to stop was given. In this case their original grid positions will be left vacant.

169. In both Case A and Case B:
a) 10 minutes after the stop signal, the pit lane will be closed.
b) 15 minutes after the stop signal, the five minute signal will be shown, the grid will close and the normal start procedure will recommence.
c) Any car which is unable to take up its position on the grid before the five minute signal will be directed to the pit lane. It may then start from the pits as specified in Article 148.
The Organiser must have sufficient personnel and equipment available to enable the foregoing timetable to be adhered to even in the most difficult circumstances.

FINISH

170. The end-of-race signal will be given at the Line as soon as the leading car has covered the full race distance in accordance with Article 13. Should two hours elapse before the full distance has been covered, the end-of-race signal will be given to the leading car the first time it crosses the Line after such time has elapsed.

171. Should for any reason (other than under Article 167) the end-of-race signal be given before the leading car completes the scheduled number of laps, or the prescribed time has been completed, the race will be deemed to have finished when the leading car last crossed the Line before the signal was given. Should the end-of- race signal be delayed for any reason, the race will be deemed to have finished when it should have finished.

172. After receiving the end-of-race signal all cars must proceed on the circuit directly to the race parc fermé without stopping, without receiving any object whatsoever and without any assistance (except that of the marshals if necessary).
Any classified car which cannot reach the post race parc fermé under its own power will be placed under the exclusive control of the marshals who will take the car to the parc fermé.

POST RACE PARC FERME

173. Only those officials charged with supervision may enter the post race parc fermé. No intervention of any kind is allowed there unless authorised by such officials.

174. When the parc fermé is in use, parc fermé regulations will apply in the area between the Line and the parc fermé entrance.

175. The parc fermé shall be secured such that no unauthorised persons can gain access to it.

CLASSIFICATION

176. The car placed first will be the one having covered the scheduled distance in the shortest time, or, where appropriate, passed the Line in the lead at the end of two hours. All cars will be classified taking into account the number of complete laps they have covered, and for those which have completed the same number of laps, the order in which they crossed the Line.

177. If a car takes more than twice the time of the winner's fastest lap to cover its last lap this last lap will not be taken into account when calculating the total distance covered by such car.

178. Cars having covered less than 90% of the number of laps covered by the winner (rounded down to the nearest whole number of laps), will not be classified.

179. The official classification will be published after the race. It will be the only valid result subject to any amendments which may be made under the Code and these Sporting Regulations.

PODIUM CEREMONY

180. The drivers finishing the race in 1st, 2nd and 3rd positions and a representative of the winning constructor must attend the prize-giving ceremony on the podium and abide by the podium procedure set out in Appendix 3 (except Monaco); and immediately thereafter make themselves available for a period of one hour and 30 minutes for the purpose of television unilateral interviews and the press conference in the media centre.

Meaning of the flags

- White flag: service vehicle on track
- Blue flag: (immobile): a car is close behind you
  (waving): a car is about to overtake you
- Yellow flag: (immobile): overtaking is prohibited, danger
  (waving) immediate danger, slow down
- Red flag: (by marshals and the Clerk of the race): stopping of the race on the Line
- Green flag: end of danger, free track
- Yellow with red stripes flag: danger, slippery surface
- Black flag: (with car number): stop on the next lap
- Black with yellow circle flag: your car is in danger
- Black and white flag: non-sporting behaviour, warning
- Chequered flag: end of the race or of the practice

SHARE THE DETERMINATION

Michelin celebrates the determination of our partner teams and our people this season. Their passion for competition drives us ahead in the race for performance tyre perfection. For the track or for you, every Michelin tyre shares this strength.

www.michelinsport.com